Structural Reforms

Jakob de Haan • Jante Parlevliet
Editors

Structural Reforms

Moving the Economy Forward

Springer

Editors
Jakob de Haan
De Nederlandsche Bank
Amsterdam, The Netherlands

University of Groningen
Groningen, The Netherlands

Jante Parlevliet
De Nederlandsche Bank
Amsterdam, The Netherlands

ISBN 978-3-030-08981-8 ISBN 978-3-319-74400-1 (eBook)
https://doi.org/10.1007/978-3-319-74400-1

Printed on acid-free paper

This Springer imprint is published by the registered company Springer International Publishing AG part of Springer Nature.
The registered company address is: Gewerbestrasse 11, 6330 Cham, Switzerland

Foreword

The case for structural reforms in the euro zone has been amply made—let me reiterate the two main reasons.[1] First, euro area countries can greatly benefit from higher structural growth, provided they take measures that boost participation and productivity. Importantly, the benefits may not be confined to individual economies but may well spill over to the wider euro area through trade and investment linkages. Second, the crisis has made painfully clear that the capacity of individual countries to adjust to shocks is poor. This, consequently, raises the costs of a monetary union.[2] Improving countries' resilience is hence another key—and shared—concern.

At the same time, the discussion on reforms in the euro zone gets complicated when getting into details: What reforms are needed most? What can we realistically expect in terms of their macroeconomic impact? When is the best time to implement reforms? What supporting policies can strengthen the political acceptance of reforms?

The aim of this book is to move this important debate forward, on both methodological and material counts. Overall, the chapters in this volume confirm the large fruits euro area economies can reap from structural measures to boost participation and, perhaps more notably, productivity growth. Furthermore, several contributions draw attention to the role macroeconomic policies can play to strengthen the benefits of reforms also in the short run. Finally, the book also contributes to our understanding of the political economy of reforms and draws attention to the role of fiscal councils in advocating reforms and the role fiscal policies can play to compensate potential losers.

In order to make such broad messages more concrete, I would like to reflect on what reforms have meant for the Netherlands in recent decades. I will discuss three

[1] For an assessment of the importance of structural reforms to the euro area, see Draghi (2015) and Thimann (2015).

[2] For this reason, various papers have investigated whether or not EMU would spur reforms. See e.g. Saint-Paul and Bentolila (2000), Duval and Elmeskov (2005) and Bednarek-Sekunda et al. (2010).

phases[3]: first, the economic difficulties in the 1970s and 1980s; second, the "Dutch miracle" in the 1990s; and third, the crisis, which had a more severe impact than in neighbouring countries, not least due to neglected reform prior to the crisis.

In the late 1970s and early 1980s, the Dutch economy was in a dire state, more so than other economies suffering from the oil price shocks. By 1983, unemployment had risen to over 14%, relative to 8% in the OECD.[4] Several factors were at play. First, there were widespread concerns over the "Dutch disease". After the discovery of gas reserves in 1959, gas exports started to flourish. Meanwhile, the non-gas exporting sector was growing less and less competitive. This dismal performance was attributed to the gas windfalls, driving up the real exchange rate and eroding competitiveness.[5]

Second, wage bargaining was in a deadlock. Since the late 1960s, automatic price compensation was common practice. With inflation even crossing the 10% threshold in 1975, this spurred a wage-price spiral. At several instances, the Minister decided to intervene by topping wage increases. Likewise, the government—which at the time was in charge of exchange rate matters—tried to offer temporary relief through devaluations.

Third, the growth of the welfare state was reaching its limits. On top of the 14% unemployment rate came a large and increasing share of inactive workers. The disability scheme played an important role in this. Incentives for reintegration were virtually absent, and the scheme was widely used to lay off less productive workers. In the late 1970s, there were more than half a million persons in the disability scheme (with a workforce of less than 6 million).

During the late 1980s and 1990s, economic performance in the Netherlands vastly improved. By 1990, unemployment had dropped to just over 7% and would continue to fall to even 2.5% in 2001 (against an OECD average of 6.5%). Labour force participation increased from 57% in 1980 to 70% in 1995 and rose further to almost 80% today. In the meantime, GDP grew steadily, and between 1982 and 1999, GDP per capita rose by 50% in real terms. This development did not go unnoticed abroad. Indeed, in the late 1990s the Dutch economy was widely celebrated as an economic miracle.[6] What factors had contributed to this?

First, an abrupt change of course was initiated in November 1982 when, unexpectedly, the leaders of the main employers' and workers' federations agreed on a package of job sharing and wage moderation. As the text of the agreement was short and vague, it was not clear a priori that things would change. But as it turned out, trade unions lowered their wage claims, firms' profitability was restored and

[3]For the first two phases, we draw on Van Ark et al. (1996) and Visser and Hemereijck (1998).

[4]This figure (and those mentioned below) refers to the unemployment rate for those aged 15–65 (source: OECD LFS).

[5]Empirical evidence, however, does not consistently suggest that the guilder was highly overvalued; see e.g. Van Ark et al. (1996).

[6]See e.g. chapter 1 of Visser and Hemereijck (1998).

job growth revived. Furthermore, the agreement heralded a strong tradition of social dialogue that persists today.

Second, efforts to reduce rampant social spending were intensified. This was not easy, despite growing consensus that some welfare programmes were being misused. But as the need for reform gradually became engrained in the mind of the political elite and the wider public, the late 1980s and 1990s saw an extended series of measures to strengthen incentives to rejoin the workforce.

Last, the Dutch miracle would not have been possible without the steady entry of Dutch women into the labour market. Up until the late 1970s only around a third of all females participated in the labour market, much lower than the OECD average. This share started to increase to 40% in the mid-1980s and 50% in the mid-1990s. Currently, participation of women is 65%—well above the OECD average—with three-quarters of them working part-time.

Let me now turn to the recent crisis. Although not comparable to the unemployment levels witnessed in countries like Spain, in 2014 unemployment in the Netherlands was at its highest level since the early 1980s and with 6.9% very close to the OECD average of 7.5%. Being an open economy, the Netherlands of course immediately felt the effect of the fall in world trade. But the double dip our economy experienced was also due to internal imbalances. Until recently, Dutch households were offered virtually unlimited tax relief on their mortgage payments. It was commonplace to acquire a loan of over 110% of the collateral value. In the meantime, amortisation was kept to a minimum. This scheme was clearly not sustainable. Given that housing supply in our densely populated country is highly inelastic, tax subsidies have merely inflated house prices. As a central bank, DNB has often warned about the risks of these fiscal subsidies and so did the CPB Netherlands Bureau of Economic Policy Analysis and international organisations like the IMF and the OECD. As with the disability scheme of the 1990s, however, the reform was unpopular and politicians continued to delay it. It was only in 2012, in the midst of the crisis, that the government finally decided to reform the system.[7] It is tempting to think that had we managed to bend the system a decade earlier, the crisis might have been less severe.

What can we learn from the Dutch experience? When it comes to measuring the impact of reforms, the Dutch experience makes clear that this is a tedious exercise. First, reforms have happened in tandem. But then, what was the main recipe of the Dutch miracle: the strategy of wage moderation, the increased trust between social partners, activation measures in social security or, rather, the entry of women into the labour market? For policymakers, it is important to disentangle the impact of different factors, something that is also highly relevant when it comes to the recent strong employment growth in e.g. Germany.

[7]To be precise, the maximum tax relief on mortgage interest payments is slowly being reduced. For new mortgages, tax relief is only granted in the case of mortgages with full amortisation. Furthermore, the maximum loan-to-value ratio of mortgages is gradually reduced to 100% in 2018. See Verbruggen et al. (2015).

Second, reforms have often been taken in the midst of a severe crisis.[8] Hence, they cannot be treated as exogenous events, and we should take due care when modelling them. Furthermore, supportive fiscal policies or accompanying reforms can soften the effect. For instance, the wage moderation initiated in the Wassenaar agreement was accompanied by generous tax relief. Furthermore, it can be argued that the prolonged strategy of wage moderation was only feasible because household income was boosted by the increased female labour force participation.

The Dutch experience also offers some lessons on the prospect of reforms in the euro area. First, whichever their precise quantitative impact, it is clear that reforms were at the basis of the Dutch employment and income growth. Likewise, economic reforms will also be at the basis of future long-run growth in the euro zone. This makes them a common concern, and stronger benchmarking is needed to facilitate their adoption.

Second, the Netherlands has experienced both "diseases" and "miracles". The same has been the case in Germany, which was considered "a sick man" not so long ago and has recently been applauded as an economic miracle.[9] There are countries in the euro zone where employment is in even more dire shape than in Netherlands in the 1980s and Germany in the 1990s. It is by no means an automatism, but I am confident that some time from now, there will be new employment miracles in the euro zone.

Last, I believe the Dutch experience shows that institutions can foster a culture of reform-mindedness. After the Wassenaar agreement, social partners realised compromises that could be mutually beneficial facilitated future reforms in a vast domain of issues. Worth mentioning is the CPB Netherlands Bureau for Economic Policy Analysis, which plays an important role in public discussions on reforms. I believe that there is scope in other euro area countries for fiscal councils to play a more prominent role in the fostering of reforms.

De Nederlandsche Bank
Amsterdam
The Netherlands
December 2017

Klaas Knot

[8]Several empirical papers have confirmed that for more countries, reforms are more likely to occur in crisis times. See e.g. Pitlik and Wirth (2003), Duval and Elmeskov (2005) and Agnello et al. (2015).

[9]See e.g. Dustmann et al. (2014), Krebs and Scheffel (2013) and Rinne and Zimmermann (2013).

References

Agnello L, Castro, V, Tovar Jalles J, Sousa R (2015) What determines the likelihood of structural reforms? Eur J Polit Econ 37:129–145

Bednarek-Sekunda E, Jong-A-Pin R, de Haan J (2010) The European Economic and Monetary Union and labour market reform. Eur Union Polit 11(1):3–27

Draghi M (2015) Structural reforms, inflation and monetary policy. Introductory speech by Mario Draghi, President of the ECB, ECB Forum on Central Banking Sintra, 22 May 2015

Dustmann C, Fitzenberger B, Schönberg U, Spitz-Oener A (2014) From sick man of Europe to economic superstar: Germany's resurgent economy. J Econ Perspect 28(1):167–188

Duval R, Elmeskov J (2005) The effects of EMU on structural reforms in labour and product markets. OECD working paper

Krebs T, Scheffel M (2013) Macroeconomic evaluation of labor market reform in Germany. IMF Econ Rev 61(4):664–701

Pitlik H, Wirth S (2003) Do crises promote the extent of economic liberalization? An empirical test. Eur J Polit Econ 19(3):565–581

Rinne U, Zimmermann KF (2013) Is Germany the North star of labor market policy? IMF Econ Rev 61(4):702–729

Saint-Paul G, Bentolila S (2000) Will EMU increase eurosclerosis? CEPR discussion paper 2423

Thimann C (2015) The microeconomic dimensions of the Eurozone crisis and why European politics cannot solve them. J Econ Perspect 29(3):141–164

Van Ark B, de Haan J, de Jong H (1996) Characteristics of economic growth in the Netherlands during the postwar period. In: Crafts N, Toniolo G (eds) Economic growth in Europe since 1945. Cambridge University Press, Cambridge

Verbruggen J, van der Molen R, Jonk S, Kakes J, Heeringa W (2015) Effects of further reductions in the LTV limit. DNB Occasional Study 2

Visser J, Hemereijck A (1998) Een Nederlands Mirakel; published in 1999 as A Dutch Miracle: job growth, welfare reform and corporatism in the Netherlands. Amsterdam University Press, Amsterdam

References

Contents

About the Authors

Henk-Wim de Boer is economist at CPB Netherlands Bureau for Policy Analysis.

Anna Rose Bordon is economist at the European Department of the International Monetary Fund.

Andrea Colciago is economist at the Research Department of De Nederlandsche Bank and associate professor at the Department of Economics of the University of Milano Bicocca.

Christian Ebeke is the deputy resident representative to the European Union for the International Monetary Fund.

Balázs Égert is economist at the Economics Department of the OECD and is at EconomiX at the University of Paris X-Nanterre and research fellow of CESifo.

Pascal Jacquinot is senior economist at the European Central Bank.

Egbert Jongen is economist at CPB Netherlands Bureau for Policy Analysis and associate professor at Leiden University.

Peter Gal is economist at the Economics Department of the OECD.

Laura van Geest is director of CPB Netherlands Bureau for Policy Analysis.

Jakob de Haan is head of Research of De Nederlandsche Bank and professor of political economy at the University of Groningen and research fellow of CESifo.

Alexander Hijzen is senior economist at the Directorate for Employment, Labour and Social Affairs of the OECD.

Andreas Kappeler is economist at the Economics Department of the European Investment Bank.

Klaas Knot is president of De Nederlandsche Bank, member of the Governing Council of the European Central Bank, as well as governor of the International Monetary Fund. Furthermore, he is professor of economics of central banking at the University of Groningen and professor of monetary stability at the University of Amsterdam.

Mauro Mastrogiacomo is senior economist at the Economic Policy Department of De Nederlandsche Bank and associate professor of economics at VU University of Amsterdam.

Mathilde Pak is economist at the Economics Department of the OECD; she is also at Université Paris-Dauphine (Paris IX) and at INSEE.

Jante Parlevliet is head of the Economic Policy Department of De Nederlandsche Bank.

Beatrice Pierluigi is head of section at the Directorate General Economics Department of the European Central Bank.

Werner Roeger is head of the Unit Models and Databases at the Directorate General for Economics and Finance at the European Commission in Brussels.

Oke Röhe is economist at the Directorate General for Economics of the Deutsche Bundesbank.

Simon Savsek is economist at the European Investment Bank. His contributions were written while he was at the European Central Bank.

Cyrille Schwellnus is senior economist at the Economics Department of the OECD.

Kazuko Shirono is economist at the European Department of the International Monetary Fund.

Nikolai Stähler is economist at the Directorate General for Economics of the Deutsche Bundesbank.

Máté Tóth is senior economist at the European Central Bank.

Janos Varga is economist at the Directorate General for Economics and Finance at the European Commission in Brussels.

Jan in't Veld is head of the Sector Model-based Economic Analysis at the Directorate General for Economics and Finance at the European Commission in Brussels.

Igor Vetlov is senior economist at the European Central Bank.

Daniël van Vuuren is head of the Public Finance Department at CPB Netherlands Bureau for Policy Analysis and professor at Tilburg University.

Chapter 1
Structural Reforms: An Introduction

Jakob de Haan and Jante Parlevliet

1.1 The Need for Structural Reform

> In every press conference since I became ECB President, I have ended the introductory statement with a call to accelerate structural reforms in Europe. The same message was also conveyed repeatedly by my predecessors, in three quarters of all press conferences since the introduction of the euro. The term "structural reforms" is actually mentioned in approximately one third of all speeches by various members of the ECB Executive Board. By comparison, it features in only about 2% of speeches by governors of the Federal Reserve (Draghi 2015).

This quote of Mario Draghi illustrates the importance European monetary authorities attach to structural reforms. And rightly so. According to many indicators, structural rigidities in most euro area (EA) countries are higher than those in the best-performing countries (the global frontier). Figure 1.1 demonstrates this for the World Bank Doing Business indicator, a composite index that measures business regulations in a broad set of policy areas such as starting a business, access to credit, the efficiency of the fiscal system and hiring and firing practices. It shows that many EA countries are rather far-off from the average of the three best-performing countries and the United States. Furthermore, the figure shows a large variation

---

The views expressed in this chapter are those of the authors and should not be attributed to De Nederlandsche Bank.

J. de Haan (✉)
De Nederlandsche Bank, Amsterdam, The Netherlands

University of Groningen, Groningen, The Netherlands
e-mail: jakob.de.haan@rug.nl

J. Parlevliet
De Nederlandsche Bank, Amsterdam, The Netherlands
e-mail: j.parlevliet@dnb.nl

J. de Haan, J. Parlevliet (eds.), *Structural Reforms*,
https://doi.org/10.1007/978-3-319-74400-1_1

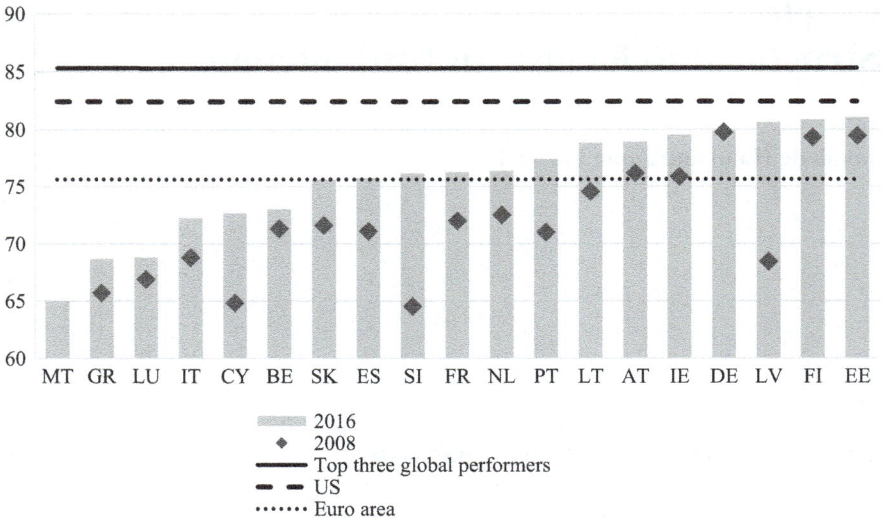

Fig. 1.1 Doing business indicator: euro area, US, and global frontier. Notes: The higher the value, the closer the country is to the best possible score (100). No value is available for MT for 2008. Source: World Bank, Doing Business

across EA countries. Finally, and on a more positive note, it becomes clear that since the global crisis hit in 2008, EA member states have made quite some progress in improving their overall business climate. While in many countries these reforms have been home grown, in some of them reforms have also been carried out under European adjustment programs.

Structural reforms are believed to have many potential benefits. First of all, *structural reforms may have substantial positive effects on output (growth).* The channels for this may be explained by decomposing GDP per capita into its three main ingredients: the number of people working as share of the population (employment rate), the number of hours worked per worker, and productivity per hour worked. The triangles (and lines) on the left of Fig. 1.2 compare GDP per capita of the EA (and the range within EA countries) to that of the United States for the years 1999 (start of the Economic and Monetary Union, EMU), 2007 (just before the crisis) and 2016. Several conclusions can be drawn. First, with a ratio of 0.71 in 2016, GDP per capita in the euro area is lagging behind that in the United States with more than a quarter. Second, this ratio has fallen since 1999. In other words, there has been no convergence to US living standards since the start of EMU. Third, the dispersion across EA countries is large, although there is some catching up by poorer member states (notably the Baltic states).

The other triangles and lines in Fig. 1.2 tell us something about the causes of this poor performance. In the first place, while in 1999 labour utilisation (on the extensive margin) was only 0.89 of that in the United States, in 2016 this gap had become much smaller (0.95). This increase reflects the many reforms introduced in recent years to boost participation. The downside is, of course, that in many EA

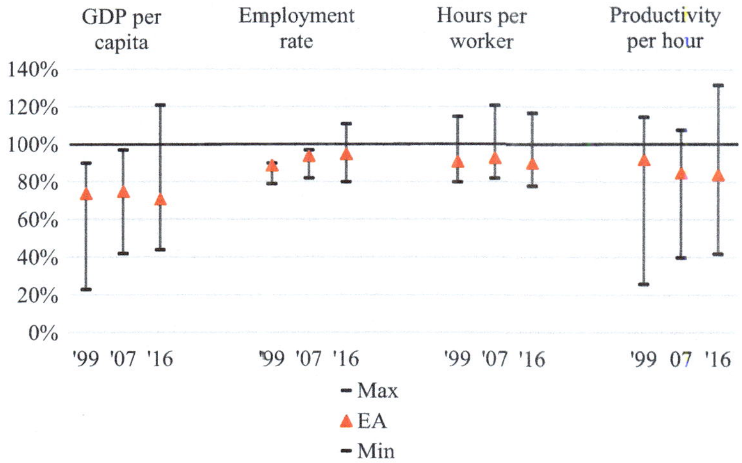

Fig. 1.2 GDP per capita and its ingredients in the Euro Area, relative to the United States. Notes: the figure shows the level of GDP per capita and its three components as % of the US level. The triangle represents the EA19 average, the upper and lower levels of the line represent the minimum and maximum of the 16 EA economies in the OECD; Luxembourg is not included given its specific economic features and missing values were disregarded. Source: OECD, calculations by authors

countries the potential for future growth increases due to employment growth has decreased. Still, for the time being, there is some scope to further improve labour utilisation in several EA countries.

In the second place, average hours worked per person are lower than in the United States. A popular view is that these differences are explained by long-standing cultural differences. However, Europeans worked more than Americans as late as the 1960s. According to Alesina et al. (2006), European labour market regulations explain the bulk of the difference in hours worked per person between the U.S. and Europe.

Last, there is a substantial gap in terms of productivity per hour worked with the United States (84% in 2016)[1] and the dispersion across EA countries is particularly large here. On an optimistic note, this means that many EA countries in principle have a high potential to catch-up. However, for several other EA economies catch-up growth is not an option since they are already at the frontier when it comes to productivity per hour. Furthermore, it has to be noted that *productivity growth at the frontier* has recently been subdued. The global slowdown in multi-factor productivity growth began before the Great Recession and is therefore at best only partly related to the economic downturn (Andrews et al. 2016).

Regulation is widely believed to play a role in explaining these productivity differences, as regulation limits the competitive pressures that challenge firms to

[1]Since the early 1990s the rate of growth of productivity in the euro area has been lower than that in the United States (Van Ark 2014).

thrive (Nicoletti and Scarpetta 2003; Aghion and Griffith 2005; Cette et al. 2016). A first channel through which reform may enhance productivity growth is firm dynamics, i.e., the process of entry, thrive, and exit from the market. Firm entry and exit (business churning) is often regarded as key to economic growth, as this mechanism (Schumpeterian creative destruction) facilitates the resource shifts from less productive firms to more productive ones, fostering innovation and adoption of new technology (ECB 2018). Business churning is affected by country-specific conditions influencing the incentives for firms to invest in new technology or adapt existing technologies to maintain their competitive edge. But competitive pressure may also spur productivity growth through other channels. For instance, the entry of new competitors may directly encourage productivity growth in incumbent firms (Aghion et al. 2004), while more competition in the markets for intermediate goods allows firms to boost productivity through cheaper inputs (Bourlès et al. 2013).

Second, *structural reforms may improve the resilience of economies in the face of adverse shocks*. In Chap. 8, Alexander Hijzen, Andreas Kappeler, Mathilde Pak and Cyrille Schwellnus define resilience in terms of the social and economic costs of economic downturns, i.e. the capacity of an economy to limit persistent deviations in output and labour market outcomes from pre-crisis trends in the aftermath of adverse aggregate shocks. This definition encompasses the avoidance of excessive fluctuations in output and labour market outcomes as well as the swiftness of the rebound.

More flexible labour and product markets tend to limit the negative impact of adverse shocks on output and employment. For instance, the results of Duval and Vogel (2008) indicate that rigid labour and product markets lengthen the time it takes for output to return to potential following a shock and increase the cumulative output loss incurred over the period.

Nominal rigidities cause output to react more than prices to a negative shock, with the latter effect being more protracted, as it takes longer for prices to fall and restore the previous level of activity. In the event of adverse supply shocks, declines in output and employment will therefore be higher the higher the degree of frictions in the economy. The results of Hijzen et al. (Chap. 8) suggest that in the OECD as a whole, labour markets have recovered more strongly from the Great Recession of 2008–2009 than output. Overall, around half of the cross-country variation in unemployment resilience is explained by output developments. Furthermore, these authors find that employment protection of regular workers and the centralisation/co-ordination of collective wage bargaining are significantly related with labour market resilience. Paradoxically, stricter employment protection legislation makes the unemployment rate more sensitive to a given shock by promoting the use of temporary contracts (which are more cyclical) and reducing the number of people hired on regular contracts in the subsequent recovery. A better co-ordination of collective bargaining arrangements across sectors or firms can help to reduce the impact of an adverse shock on unemployment in the short term by facilitating adjustments in wages and working time, so that layoffs can be avoided. The importance of collective bargaining per se, as measured by the share of workers covered in the total economy, is not associated with resilience. Finally, illustrating the importance of taking other policies into account (see Sect. 1.4 below), they find that fiscal support during economic downturns—both through automatic fiscal stabilisers (i.e. increases in government spending and declines in tax revenues that occur directly as a result of a downturn in economic activity) and additional discretionary measures—promotes labour market resilience by stabilising aggregate demand. Despite the importance of fiscal policy for labour market resilience, the authors' empirical evidence suggests that differences among countries' fiscal policies can only explain a small part of cross-country differences in labour market resilience, which are largely explained by differences in the size and nature of the economic shock in each country and the design of each country's structural policies and institutions.

Finally, and underlying the plea of Draghi in his numerous press conferences, *structural reforms may enhance the effectiveness of monetary policy in the EMU*. In the first place, price and wage flexibility is particularly important in a currency union, as countries can no longer adjust to asymmetric shocks through exchange rate changes and the common monetary policy cannot take country-specific developments into account. This implies that a high degree of national economic flexibility is indispensable notably so if the frequency of asymmetric shocks is high and countries' business cycles are not synchronized (and labour mobility and international risk sharing are low).[2]

Furthermore, the effectiveness of the common monetary policy rests, inter alia, on price and wage flexibility. The higher the degree of nominal rigidities, the more aggressive monetary policy needs to respond to inflation shocks to restore price stability.[3] This is often phrased in terms of the Phillips-curve, which characterizes the relationship between (wage) inflation and a measure of economic slack. A flatter Phillips curve implies a lower responsiveness of wages and prices to slack (and vice versa). There is an extensive literature about the changing steepness of the Phillips curve. Ball and Muzumber (2011) argue that models of costly price adjustment suggest that the slope of the Phillips curve should be time varying. If nominal price adjustment is costly, firms will choose to adjust more frequently when the level and variance of inflation are higher. So when a credible central bank commitment to price stability leads to lower and more stable inflation, the Phillips curve will flatten. Several studies suggest that the Phillips curve has become flatter. According

[2]Bayoumi and Eichengreen (1993) show that before the start of the euro area there was a core of countries where shocks were highly synchronized, and a periphery where synchronization was significantly lower. However, in their update of the Bayoumi-Eichengreen study, Campos and Macchiarelli (2016) conclude that the core-periphery pattern has weakened. Likewise, some studies suggest that business cycles have become more synchronized within the euro area due to, inter alia, increasing trade relationships following monetary integration (see de Haan et al. 2008 for a discussion).

[3]However, Galí and Monacelli (2016) question the importance of wage flexibility in a monetary union by arguing that lower interest rates via country-specific monetary policy are a key mechanism behind positive growth impacts of lower wage growth (or wage cuts), while such a monetary policy response is not possible for individual countries in a monetary union.

to Blanchard (2016), the flattening of the Phillips curve in the U.S. goes back to the 1980s and has not changed since the financial crisis. However, there is also evidence suggesting that the Phillips curve has become steeper. For instance, Skarica and Nobile (2016) report that in Spain and Italy the responsiveness of inflation to slack has increased since the crisis. These authors argue that this might reflect the effectiveness of the structural reforms undertaken in both countries. These reforms tend to make prices more flexible and more sensitive to changes in the amount of slack in the economy. Likewise, the results of Oinonen and Paloviita (2014) suggest that the slope of the euro area Phillips curve has become steeper since 2012.

Although structural reforms may enhance the monetary union, a common monetary policy and tighter constraints on fiscal policy within EMU may also limit the possibility to accommodate structural reforms at the country level by expansionary macroeconomic policy in order to reduce short-term costs for households and firms. This constraint on the compensation of short-term costs may make reforms politically more difficult (see Vogel 2017 and Sect. 1.5).

1.2 What Type of Reform?

1.2.1 Labour and Product Market Reform

Reform is often used as a catchall term. Most chapters in this book attach a central role to labour market and product market reforms for two reasons. First, while euro area countries might score well on issues such as governance (Kaufmann et al. 2010) and educational outcomes (OECD 2015), they tend to score less well when it comes to the regulation of their product and labour markets. Second, given the centrality of labour and product markets to the functioning of the economy, it is not surprising that the output effects of reforms in these fields are typically very large (ECB 2018).

In Chap. 2, Jante Parlevliet, Simon Savsek and Máté Tóth review the literature on some of the channels through which such reforms impact on employment and output, and how such reforms are operationalized in empirical and theoretical research.

In Chap. 3, Balázs Égert and Peter Gal discuss a new simulation framework of the OECD that quantifies the impact of labour and product market reforms on per capita income through the components of the production function. The overall medium to long-term supply side impact is derived through: multi-factor productivity (MFP), capital intensity and the employment rate. The framework is based on relationships estimated over a period including the immediate post-crisis years (1985–2011). In line with studies mentioned above, the authors report a strong negative relationship between product market regulations and MFP. Within the framework, three labour market regulation indicators are used: employment protection legislation (EPL), spending on active labour market policies (ALMP) and the unemployment benefit replacement ratio. Only ALMP is statistically significantly related to MFP. Product market regulation has a fairly robust negative relationship with the capital stock. Also the EPL indicator has a strong and quantitatively important negative link with the capital stock. Finally, lower unemployment benefit replacement rates, increased spending on active labour market policies, and lower labour tax wedges tend to boost employment. Also product market regulation is negatively correlated with aggregate employment.

Using typical past reforms as a basis for simulation, the new framework provides a number of results for the main policy variables. First, 5 years after the reforms, product market regulation has the largest overall single policy impact. This is because this type of reform influences per capita income through all three supply-side channels (productivity, capital deepening and the employment rate). However, the combined impact of all labour market policies is considerably larger than that of product market regulation and the remaining policies combined (corporate taxes and R&D spending). But adding up the effect of all labour market policies implies that reforms are carried out simultaneously in all quantifiable policy areas, which seems rather challenging in practice.

Second, policy can have different impacts at different horizons. For some policies, the overall long-term effects on GDP per capita can be considerably larger than the 5- to 10-year impacts. This is particularly the case of policies that influence GDP per capita through capital deepening (product market regulation, employment protection legislation and spending on active labour market policies). The long-term impact of other policies, mostly labour market policies transiting only via the employment rate channel, materialises at shorter horizon.

Finally, there is no robust relationship between employment protection legislation reform and aggregate employment, although it does have a heterogeneous impact across various segments of the population. This is in line with the findings of other studies (Kahn 2007).

1.2.2 Other Types of Reform

Of course, besides labour market and product market reforms, many other policy fields are relevant and have been extensively examined in the literature. For instance, there is a large literature on *financial liberalization*, i.e. policies that focus on deregulating credit as well as interest rate controls, removing entry barriers for foreign financial institutions, privatizing financial institutions, and/or removing restrictions on foreign financial transactions (Abiad and Mody 2005). It is widely believed that financial liberalization raises the efficiency with which the financial sector can transform saving into investment, ultimately improving the growth performance of a country. At the same time, however, financial liberalization policies have been criticized for their potential role in triggering financial and economic crises. Furthermore, there is evidence that financial liberalization leads to higher income inequality (de Haan and Sturm 2017), which in turn may reduce economic growth (Berg and Ostry 2011). The question, therefore, is whether or not these policies lead to higher economic growth. Bumann et al. (2013) perform a meta-analysis of the relationship between financial liberalization and economic growth based on 60 different empirical studies. Their analysis suggests that, on average, there is a positive albeit weak effect of financial liberalization on growth. Their results also show that studies that take into account a measure of the level of financial development report lower significance of the relationship between liberalization and growth.[4]

Likewise, *educational reforms* have received some attention in the literature (see, for instance, Fabella 2017 and references cited therein) as better education may stimulate growth through the provision of additional and/or more productive human capital, which brings the economy closer to the production frontier. For instance, Ciccone and Papaioannou (2009) show that countries with high-quality education experienced faster value-added and employment growth in schooling-intensive industries in the 1980s and 1990s. Furthermore, as pointed out by ECB (2018), better education may increase international convergence, as the social and private returns of education are higher in countries with lower per capita income (Psacharopoulos 1994).

Also *tax reforms* are often discussed (and are sometimes considered under the heading of labour market reforms). It is widely believed that removing the distortionary effects of tax systems may increase output and employment. For instance, by reducing the tax wedge labour supply may increase, thereby reducing unemployment and increasing growth.[5]

In Chap. 4, Jan in 't Veld, Janos Varga and Werner Roeger include, inter alia, educational and tax reforms in their quantitative assessment of the potential macroeconomic impact of reforms. Besides various labour market reforms to boost participation of e.g. the elderly and several product market reforms (services sector mark-ups, entry barriers), they also include skill structure (share of high and low skilled, expenditure on high and medium skilled education), tax structure (labour to consumption tax ratio), and R&D tax credits. The potential for reform is defined as a 50% reduction of the gap in these indicators vis-à-vis the three best-performing countries in the EU. Model simulations based on a semi-endogenous growth model specifically adapted for the analysis of structural reforms suggest that even such modest reforms can have significant macroeconomic effects. The long-run gains of reforms in individual countries are largest for Greece: its GDP is 17.5% higher

---

[4]Financial liberalization may also spur financial development. Although there is substantive evidence that financial development may enhance growth, recent research suggests a non-linear relationship between financial development and economic growth for several reasons. At high levels of financial development, the further deepening of financial markets may be associated with financial services that have a lower growth potential, such as mortgage finance. Financial development may also be associated with a higher frequency of financial crises. Furthermore, the financial sector may attract human capital away from the real economy. Finally, financial development may lead to more income inequality.

[5]This could be especially effective in a currency union. Farhi et al. (2014) demonstrate how such changes in taxes can act as a devaluation.

after 20 years (9.2% after 10 years), even when only half of the gap is closed. Italy, Malta and Romania show similar large gains of between 17 and 15% after 20 years. As expected, countries closest to the best performance frontier have the smallest output gains, although even there benefits from further reforms can be significant. For Sweden, GDP is 2.6% higher after 20 years, for Denmark, Estonia, and the UK between 5 and 7%. Other countries lie between these two extremes, with their output gains roughly proportional to the identified structural gaps. The authors also consider the effects of reforms when all countries introduce them simultaneously. Demand spillovers of simultaneous reforms can boost exports in other countries and raise GDP, but competitiveness-improving reforms can have a negative impact. The authors find that the long-run output effects of simultaneous reforms are only slightly larger: after 20 years GDP is 11% higher in the EU (vs. 10.0 in the 'acting alone' case).

Finally, several studies focus on *institutional reforms*. While the direction of causality is generally difficult to prove there is broad agreement in the literature that high-quality institutions are positively related to long-term growth. Although there is little debate about the importance of some institutions, such as secure property rights and absence of corruption, there is less of a consensus about other institutions, like democratic accountability. Using a number of historical episodes, Acemoglu et al. (2004) argue that institutions shape long-term economic outcomes. These authors define institutions as the set of rules and policies able to deliver a level playing field for all economic actors and ensure that sound economic incentives are in place for encouraging people to invest, innovate, save and solve problems of collective action, and for ensuring the efficient provision of public goods. The study by Masuch et al. (2016) provides support for the view that the quality of institutions is an important determinant of long-term growth also in European countries.

Also some chapters in this book examine institutional reform, in conjunction with other types of reform. For instance, in Chap. 5, Beatrice Pierluigi and Igor Vetlov analyse the consequences of broad reform packages in Italy and Germany, using simulations of the Euro Area and Global Economy (EAGLE) model—a global extension of the New Area-Wide Model with tradable and non-tradable sectors and a monetary union. Besides labour and product market reforms, the package for Italy includes: the reduction of licencing procedures and improved functioning of the judicial system and a set of competition and investment-enhancing policies (including the effective implementation of the new competition law and strengthening of insolvency procedures). The package for Germany includes a reduction of bottlenecks in administrative capacity and a more efficient use of public procurement rules.

The model-based simulation results show that implementation of a policy package consistent with policy recommendations recently brought about by international institutions in case of Italy and Germany can lead to a significantly higher growth in both countries. Assuming that the implementation of the reforms starts in 2017, the first year impact on the level of GDP is 0.7% in both countries. This relatively large impact is due to the fact that all reforms are assumed to start to be implemented simultaneously, which, in countries with problems of administrative capacity, could be a rather optimistic assumption. Five years after the start of the reform package, the GDP level is 2.5% higher in Germany and 3.8% higher in Italy. The overall higher impact in Italy is due to the bigger gap with the best performers. In both countries higher MFP and investment efficiency accounts for the largest part of the GDP gains.

1.3 Methodological Issues

While theory often predicts positive gains from reforms in the long run, evaluating real-life reforms has proven particularly challenging. Chapter 2 by Parlevliet et al. provides a detailed overview of the most important challenges and methods used to overcome these.

One of most troubling challenges in empirical research is the issue of *endogeneity*. Reforms do not occur at random. For instance, several studies suggest that economic and financial crises facilitate the adoption of reforms (cf. Pitlik and Wirth 2003; Dias Da Silva et al. 2017). Likewise, the effects of structural reforms may be endogenous to the economic environment in which reforms are conducted. For instance, the business cycle or macroeconomic policies pursued could affect the magnitude of the impact of structural reforms (see Sect. 1.4 for a further discussion).

As pointed out in Chap. 2, several approaches have been proposed to deal with this endogeneity issue. In micro-econometric studies, the state of the art is to use or imitate a natural experiment for identification, or exploit arbitrary discontinuity in policies in a regression discontinuity design. Likewise, when regulations do not affect all sectors, regions or countries to the same extent a differences-in-difference approach may be used. Moreover, when a variable can be found that correlates with the reform but not with the observed outcomes under study, an instrumental variable estimation is possible.

In Chap. 7, Anna Rose Bordon, Christian Ebeke, and Kazuko Shirono investigate the impact of structural reforms on employment, controlling for endogeneity using the local projection approach. Local projections allow for estimating the dynamic effects of structural reform by computing the cumulative impact of a reform shock on the change of employment over a 5-year horizon. To address endogeneity, the authors adopt the augmented inverse probability weighting (AIPW) method which estimates the treatment effects of reforms while controlling for potential selection bias. Their empirical results suggest that structural reforms have a lagged but positive impact on employment. This positive effect tends to be larger once the endogeneity of the decision to reform is taken into account.

Another methodological question in empirical research is *how to estimate elasticities* of key behavioural variables such as labour supply. While many studies use variation over countries and time, micro-data can be used to estimate labour supply elasticities for subgroups in the population. In Chap. 11, Henk-Wim de Boer, Egbert Jongen and Mauro Mastrogiacomo use a large administrative dataset to estimate structural models for labour supply on the Dutch labour market. The overall estimates are quite a bit lower than previous estimates for the Netherlands, and of those used to analyse fiscal policy in Chap. 4 by In't Veld et al. Furthermore, the results suggest substantial heterogeneity across subgroups and decision margins in the behavioural responses. Singles and men in couples are rather unresponsive to changes in financial incentives. On the other hand, single parents and women in couples with young children are relatively responsive. The authors use their estimation results in a micro-simulation model for tax-benefit reforms. The authors find that most of the response is in the participation rate (the extensive margin), the response in hours worked per week per employed (the intensive margin) is much smaller. The simulations also suggest that reducing tax bracket rates is not very effective in stimulating labour supply. More effective are policies explicitly targeted at the extensive margin, such as increasing in-work tax credits. The most effective in terms of labour supply are tax credits and (child care) subsidies for single parents and secondary earners with young children, as they are the most responsive to changes in financial incentives.

Turning beyond empirical research, a large part of academic research—including several chapters in this book—employs (calibrated) DSGE models to analyse the consequences of reform. The most widely used DSGE models typically feature a degree of monopolistic competition stemming from imperfect substitutability across types of goods and workers resulting in price and wage mark-ups. Structural reforms are typically modelled as permanent negative shocks to mark-ups, representing more competition in product and labour markets. As such, the issue of endogeneity is less of a concern in simulations of calibrated DSGE models. However, DSGE models face other challenges. When it comes to evaluating real-life reforms, the key challenge is how to translate often-multifaceted reforms to parameters that feature in the theoretical model. For traditional DSGE models, the choice is often only between wage or price mark-ups, while recent models have introduced more complex rigidities that offer more choice of channels. Chapter 5 provides an example of how various reforms in Italy and Germany can be incorporated in the EAGLE model.

1.4 The Role of the Effective Lower Bound, the Business Cycle and Fiscal Policy

1.4.1 Effective Lower Bound

Evaluating or estimating the impact of reforms in the recent crisis was greatly complicated by the fact that the monetary environment was not neutral. Several recent papers have examined the impact of short-term impact of reforms against the backdrop of constrained monetary policy. Fernández-Villaverde et al. (2011) use a two-period new Keynesian model in which monetary policy would normally increase interest rates in response to higher present consumption, which is not the case under the effective lower bound (ELB) constraint. Overall they find that anticipated future increases in productivity boost demand in the present and thus can, to some extent, substitute demand side policies when the latter are constrained.

Eggertson et al. (2014) challenge the view that product and labour market reforms can support adjustment of countries during crises. They argue that downward adjustments in prices and wages to restore competitiveness may aggravate, rather than attenuate, output and employment losses in the short term. As nominal interest rates become constrained by their effective lower bound, reforms that lead to lower price pressures in the short run imply that monetary policy becomes more contractionary and fuels expectations of prolonged deflation, which in turn raises real interest rates and further depresses aggregate demand.[6] So reforms become contractionary over the short run. This short-term negative effect on output is increasing with the magnitude of the reforms and becomes particularly large when reforms are not fully credible (i.e. if there is a chance of policy reversal at a later stage).

In discussing this paper, Fernández-Villaverde (2014) argues that the timing of the reforms is important. Product and labour market reforms as currently under discussion in Europe are likely to be implemented with some lag, possibly beyond the period over which the ELB is binding. In this case, reforms implemented in the future can well be expansionary even in the short run. Fernández-Villaverde also criticises that the model of Eggertson et al. (2014) excludes capital, thereby neglecting effects of reforms that reduce mark-ups on capital accumulation.[7] Furthermore, if output increases in the long run due to reforms, worries about debt sustainability may be reduced, thereby lowering risk premia and increasing confidence, which can boost short-run growth. Likewise, the wealth effect triggered by higher future productivity induces an increase in consumption today and a decrease in the desire to save. The resulting higher aggregate demand today translates into higher output in the short run (ECB 2018).

In Chap. 6, Pascal Jacquinot, Simon Savsek, Máté Tóth and Igor Vetlov study the macroeconomic effects of service sector liberalisation and reform combinations and different sequencing of product and labour reforms. Special emphasis is put on the role of the ELB constraining monetary policy. To this end, the authors employ model-based simulations obtained using the Eurosystem's EAGLE model (see Gomes et al. 2012 and Vogel 2017 for the same exercise with the QUEST model). It has been calibrated for a large euro area economy, the rest of the euro area, the US

[6]This implies that the authors ignore the effectiveness of unconventional monetary policy instruments in alleviating the effective lower bound.

[7]The response of investments to credible structural reforms is also key in Gerali et al. (2015) who examine the effects of reform of the service sector in a small economy within a monetary union. They find that even in the context of the ELB such a reform increases GDP over the short-to-medium run and this effect critically hinges upon the response of investments. Likewise, Gomes (2014) finds that permanent structural reforms can help to alleviate the impact of the recession driving nominal interest rates towards the ELB, but reform coordination across member countries is necessary to reduce the time spent at the ELB.

and the rest of world. The key contribution of this chapter is to provide insight into the design of reform measures such as sequencing, packaging and coordination. It follows from the simulations that starting with labour market reform and delaying product market deregulation produces somewhat more favourable outcomes, in particular on the inflation dynamics. As a matter of fact, cutting services mark-up influences prices more directly. Moreover, the simulations introduce shocks mimicking the impact of the ECB's non-standard monetary policy measures to provide insight into the complementarity or substitutability of structural and monetary policy measures. The simulations show that any type of easing that reduces the stringency of the effective lower bound constraint can be beneficial for reform implementation.

1.4.2 Business Cycle

The effects of structural reforms may also depend on the business cycle. For example, the resources freed up by structural reforms may not be absorbed in more efficient sectors because excess capacity exists and aggregate demand is low. In addition, reforms launched during recessions could increase (policy) uncertainty Under those circumstances, structural reforms may not achieve the desired improvements, having small or even negative effects in depressed economies.[8] For instance, using simulations of the IMF's Global Integrated Monetary and Fiscal model, Anderson et al. (2014) find that weak demand conditions could dampen the short-run impact of structural reform. Likewise, Bouis et al. (2012) find that the state of the economy matters, especially for the impact of unemployment benefit reform and employment protection of regular workers. They report evidence that some labour market reforms pay off more quickly in good times than in bad times, and can even entail short-term losses in severely depressed economies.

Based on analysis of a new database of major policy changes for 26 advanced economies over the past four decades, Duval and Furceri (2016) find that product market reforms raise productivity and output. Labour market reforms primarily affect employment, but their impact depends on overall business cycle conditions—unlike that of product market reforms. The authors also find that lowering labour tax wedges and higher spending on ALM policies have larger effects during periods of slack, while reforming employment protection arrangements and unemployment benefit systems can become contractionary in periods of slack.

In Chap. 7, Bordon et al. present estimates of the impact of actual structural reforms on employment while controlling for the business cycle. The impact of labour and product market reforms on employment is positive and statistically significant when these reforms are launched when there is limited slack in the

[8]Furthermore, the business cycle may not only affect the likelihood of a reform or shape the reform's impact on macroeconomic outcomes, but also prompt a macroeconomic policy response which could affect the estimated impact of the reform (see below).

economy. However, in case of higher slack the effect differs depending on the type of reforms. More specifically, the effect of labour market reforms (here a significant decline in the employment protection of regular workers) launched during bad times is negative and statistically significant, and these effects are felt almost immediately after the reform has been implemented. These results are in line with the view that a reduction in the protection of regular workers during periods of slack in the economy leads to more job destruction. In contrast, product market reforms launched during bad times do not necessarily lead to negative and significant employment losses—a somewhat surprising result as it is often thought that the additional supply capacity created by structural reforms will not be absorbed when aggregate demand is weak, leading to deflationary pressures.

1.4.3 The Role of Fiscal Policies

Do structural reforms deliver better results if implemented in periods of supportive fiscal policies? This is an important question, as several countries had to implement reforms in conjunction with fiscal consolidations.

Greece provides a well-known example of reforms being implemented simultaneously with fiscal consolidations. Papageorgiou and Vourvachaki (2017) analyse the impact of product and labour market structural reforms and the effects of their joint implementation with alternative debt consolidation strategies using a dynamic general equilibrium model calibrated for the Greek economy. Their findings suggest strong positive long-run GDP gains from implementing these structural reforms. These gains materialize earlier in case of swift implementation. Their results also suggest that it matters how the fiscal consolidation is implemented in conjunction with the reforms. Labour market reforms amplify the costs of fiscal tightening only when simultaneously implemented with a labour tax-based debt consolidation.

In Chap. 7, Bordon et al. consider how fiscal (and monetary) policy may interact with structural reforms. Their estimates suggest that the impact of product market reforms on employment when initiated with non-restrictive fiscal policy is positive and significant in the medium term. The employment rate has increased by more than 1% point 5 years after the reform. On the other hand, when the fiscal policy stance is restrictive, the impact of product market reforms on the employment rate is negative and statistically significant 5 years after the reform has been launched. The results for the interaction of labour and product market reforms and supportive monetary policy are similar in nature. The employment rate rises significantly for reforms occurring along with non-restrictive monetary policy, after the reform. In the case of non-accommodative monetary policies, the positive effect of reforms fully disappears.

1.5 Redistribution and the Political Economy of Reform

Reforms can have substantial redistributional effects.[9] Some recent papers have stressed that especially reforms that deregulate labour markets can increase inequality. For instance, Jaumotte and Osorio Buitron (2015) find evidence that the deregulation of labour markets is associated with the rise of income inequality in advanced economies, notably at the top of the income distribution. Importantly, the decline in unionization is related to the rise of top income shares and less redistribution, while they also find that the downward pressure on minimum wages is correlated with considerable increases in overall inequality. Likewise, the evidence of Dustmann et al. (2014) suggests that the effective decentralisation of bargaining in Germany contributed to a reduction in wage growth and to an increase in inequality.

The (perceived) redistributional effects of reforms are an important explanation for the unpopularity of reforms. Although structural reforms may have a positive impact for the large majority of citizens (winners), they may also affect some groups negatively (losers). The distribution of the costs and benefits of reform may affect the likelihood that reforms will be implemented. First, resistance to reform can be broad-based when it is not yet clear how large the gains will be, and to whom they are attributed. Poor understanding of how reforms work may be at the basis of this. For instance, in a survey for Germany and Italy, Boeri et al. (2002) find that the perception of a pension crisis is lower among those who are poorly informed about how the pension system works, making them less likely to support reform measures. In that case, people may tend to favour the status quo, as they are particularly wary of being worse off relative to the status quo (Fernandez and Rodrik 1991). So even though social welfare is expected to increase for most citizens, the ex-ante uncertainty about their distributional consequences may hamper reforms. Public awareness of the precise benefits that structural reforms could bring may be crucial in building support for such reforms (Parlevliet 2017).

Second, particular groups in society affected by reforms may have an incentive to delay the reform. By not giving in, they may try to shift the burden of reform to other groups in society ('war of attrition'). As long as the costs of delaying the reform are less than the gains from shifting its potential costs to others, they will block reform (Alesina and Drazen 1991).[10] The more successfully the group of those unwilling to reform is represented by interest groups (like labour unions) and the more complex

[9]The redistributional consequences of structural reform have received limited attention in the literature. A clear exception is the impact of financial liberalization, which has been extensively researched; the results of the various studies are very mixed as de Haan and Sturm (2017) show in their review of the literature.

[10]Also several other political-economy factors have been researched in the literature. For instance, Da Silva et al. (2017) examine for a sample of 40 OECD countries the driving forces of four main areas of reform: labour market, product market, framework conditions and FDI restrictions, taking some political-economy factors into account. Their results suggest that having one party with majority in all houses increases the likelihood of reform implementation, while the proximity

the link between the reform and the benefits for the majority, the more difficult the implementation of reforms becomes.

From the latter perspective, the effect on the distribution of income between capital and labour may be relevant. As pointed out by the IMF (2017), the labour share of income—i.e. the share of national income paid in wages, including benefits, to workers—has been on a downward trend in many countries. Although the decline differs somewhat across countries, in most advanced economies labour income shares began trending down in the 1980s, reaching their lowest level prior to the financial crisis, and have not recovered since. Furthermore, the decline in the labour share has been concomitant with increases in income inequality for two reasons (IMF 2017). First, lower-skilled workers have borne the brunt of the fall in labour share. Second, that capital ownership is typically concentrated among the top of the income distribution and hence an increase in the share of income accruing to capital tends to raise income inequality.

While the literature mainly attributes declining labour shares to technological change and labour market reforms, in Chap. 9, Andrea Colciago shows that also the type of product market competition might play a role. To be precise, he studies the effects of structural reforms in goods and labour market on the labour share using a DSGE model. As the competiveness of markets matters, the author distinguishes between monopolistic and oligopolistic competition in the goods market. Two specific structural reforms are considered. The first one is a reduction in sunk-entry costs for new firms due to deregulation. The second one is a reduction in the unemployment benefits for unemployed workers. Lower entry costs boost competition in the final good market. Under oligopolistic competition this leads, via strategic interactions, to lower price mark-ups. A lower price mark-up implies that a larger fraction of the marginal product of labour is distributed to workers in the form of wages. As a result, the labour share of income increases in the long run, while the profit share decreases. On the contrary, under monopolistic competition, where the price mark-up is a constant, the labour share of income permanently decreases. This suggests that the form of competition in the goods market affects the evolution of the distribution of income between capital and labour in the aftermath of reforms. In the model, lower unemployment benefits bring about a reduction in the taxes required to finance them. The result is a positive income effect which implies that the reform has no short-run costs attached to the transition period. A reduction in unemployment benefits leads to a permanent reduction in the real wage. This results in a permanently lower labour share of income and a mirror increase in the profit share.

Two solutions may overcome political economy obstacles to reforms discussed above. First, by offering the losers of reforms compensation the distributional effects may be softened and hence opposition towards reform may be reduced. Chapter 10 offers an analysis of compensation using the German Harz reform as a case in point,

---

to national elections or the political orientation of the government does not appear to influence reform implementation. See de Haan et al. (2006) for a discussion of older studies.

while Chap. 11 employs Dutch micro data. Second, if an independent institution can provide objective information about the objectives and consequences of reform, the debate about these reforms can be sanitized. Chapter 12 illustrates this for the case of the CPB Netherlands Bureau for Economic Policy Analysis.

In Chap. 10, Oke Röhe and Nikolai Stähler analyse labour market reforms in Germany, commonly known as the Hartz reforms. The authors evaluate the impact of the reforms using an extended version of the medium-scale open economy DSGE model FiMod. In this model, an exogenously given percentage of households does not participate in asset markets but consumes all of its income in each period ('rule of thumb' consumers). The simulations suggest that the reform had a positive impact on GDP, consumption and employment. However, the reform also increased consumption inequality and negatively affected liquidity-constrained households by reducing their steady-state consumption level. This reflects that 'rule of thumb' consumers cannot benefit from the improved labour market efficiency and the lower unit labour costs for German firms, because they do not receive dividends or capital income (in contrast to optimising households). These unintended redistributional effects of the reform can be mitigated by tax policies (which were part of the German reform agenda between 1999 and 2008). The simulations show that a budget-neutral compensation of 'rule of thumb' consumers in the form of lower labour income and higher consumption tax rates, Hartz-type of reforms do not entail any consumption losses for both types of households. The gain in net income resulting from a reduction in the labour income tax rate overcompensates the increased consumption costs stemming from higher consumption taxes. Since the measure is fiscally budget-neutral, no adverse effects from higher financing costs occur. Furthermore, the reduction in gross wages as a result of workers' lower outside option due to the decreased generosity of the unemployment insurance system as well as lower labour income taxes (augmenting the net income directly) additionally fosters relative factor productivity, international competitiveness and exports.

In Chap. 11, de Boer et al. also consider how participation-enhancing reforms can affect the income distribution. Among other things, they find that overall changes to tax bracket rates have large effects on the income distribution, but have hardly any effect on labour supply. Furthermore, while reductions in income support for low-income households are effective in boosting labour supply, they come at the cost of large increases in inequality. On the other hand, increasing in-work benefits is effective in increasing labour supply, and would reduce inequality rather than increase it.

From a political-economy perspective, the presence of an independent and qualified institution that is able to provide policy analyses may also be helpful. In Chap. 12, Laura van Geest and Daniel van Vuuren discuss the experience of CPB Netherlands Bureau for Economic Policy Analysis, which has an independent position and has built a reputation for providing solid policy analyses. CPB produces policy relevant economic research which frequently focuses on policy reform. Based on the Dutch experience, the authors come up with several lessons. First, they advise a division of labour between those producing the facts and analyses and those who decide on policy. It enhances a level-headed debate on policy goals and options.

Likewise, mixing positive and normative analysis increases the risk that politicians ignore the facts, arguing that they are just personal opinions. Second, it took CPB time to establish a reputation as a dependable source of economic forecasts and analyses. Its portfolio of activities has been expanded gradually. The institute started modestly and built on its successes. Third, competitiveness is a multi-faceted and ever changing concept. This argues against fixating on a simple score board and favours a broad mandate so that research on the economy and relevant policies can change over time. Finally, never waste a good crisis. Under situations of economic distress, the desire for evidence-based policy to solve issues effectively and efficiently may be strongest. The finding in the literature that some reforms may be contractionary in periods of slack, should therefore not be an argument for delay, but rather for a well-designed policy package.

References

Abiad A, Mody A (2005) Financial reform: what shakes it? what shapes it? Am Econ Rev 95(1):66–88

Acemoglu D, Johnson S, Robinson J (2004) Institutions as the fundamental cause of long-term growth. NBER Working Paper 10481

Aghion P, Griffith R (2005) Competition and growth: reconciling theory and evidence. MIT Press, Cambridge

Aghion P, Blundell R, Griffith R, Howitt P, Prantl S (2004) Entry and productivity growth: evidence from micro-level panel data. J Eur Econ Assoc 2(2–3):265–276

Alesina A, Drazen A (1991) Why are stabilizations delayed? Am Econ Rev 81(5):1170–1188

Alesina A, Glaeser E, Sacerdote B (2006) Work and leisure in the US and Europe. Why so different? NBER Macroecon Annu 2005(20):1–100

Anderson D, Barkbu B, Lusinyan L, Muir D (2014) Macroeconomic impact of structural reforms in the Euro Area. In: Jobs and growth: supporting the European recovery. IMF, Washington

Andrews D, Criscuolo C, Gal P (2016) The best versus the rest: the global productivity slowdown, divergence across firms and the role of public policy. OECD Productivity Working Paper 05

Ball L, Mazumder S (2011) Inflation dynamics and the Great Recession. Brook Pap Econ Act 42(1):337–405

Bayoumi T, Eichengreen B (1993) Shocking aspects of European monetary integration. In: Torres F, Giavazzi F (eds) Adjustment and growth in the European Monetary Union. Cambridge University Press, Cambridge

Berg A, Ostry J D (2011) Inequality. and unsustainable growth: two sides of the same coin? IMF Staff Discussion Note 11/08

Blanchard O (2016) The Phillips curve: back to the '60s? Am Econ Rev Pap Proc 106(5):31–34

Boeri T, Börsch-Supan A, Tabellini G (2002) Pension reforms and the opinions of European citizens. Am Econ Rev Pap Proc 92(2):396–401

Bouis R, Causa O, Demmou L, Duval R, Zdzienicka A (2012) The short-term effects of structural reforms: an empirical analysis. OECD Economics Department Working Paper 949

Bourlès R, Cette G, Lopez J, Mairesse J, Nicoletti G (2013) Do product market regulations in upstream sectors curb productivity growth? Panel data evidence for OECD countries. Rev Econ Stat 95(5):1750–1768

Bumann S, Hermes N, Lensink R (2013) Financial liberalization and economic growth: a meta-analysis. J Int Money Financ 33:255–281

Campos NF, Macchiarelli C (2016) Core and periphery in the European Monetary Union: Bayoumi and Eichengreen 25 years later. Econ Lett 147:127–130
Cette G, Lopez J, Mairesse J (2016) Market regulations, prices, and productivity. Am Econ Rev Pap Proc 106(5):104–108
Ciccone A, Papaioannou E (2009) Human capital, the structure of production and growth. Rev Econ Stat 91(1):66–82
de Haan J, Sturm J-E (2017) Finance and income inequality: a review and new evidence. Eur J Polit Econ 50:171–195
de Haan J, Sturm J-E, Lundstrom S (2006) Market-oriented institutions and policies and economic growth: a critical survey. J Econ Surv 20(2):157–191
de Haan J, Inklaar R, Jong-A-Pin RM (2008) Will business cycles in the euro area converge? a critical survey of empirical research. J Econ Surv 22:234–273
Dias da Silva A, Givone A, Sondermann D (2017) What drives structural reform implementation? ECB Working Paper 2078
Draghi M (2015) Structural reforms, inflation and monetary policy. Introductory speech by Mario Draghi, President of the ECB, ECB Forum on Central Banking Sintra, 22 May 2015
Dustmann C, Fitzenberger B, Schönberg U, Spitz-Oener A (2014) From sick man of Europe to economic superstar: Germany's resurgent economy. J Econ Perspect 28(1):167–188
Duval R, Furceri D (2016) The effects of labor and product market reforms: the role of macroeconomic conditions and policies. IMF/Mimeo, New York
Duval R, Vogel L (2008) Economic resilience to shocks. The role of structural policies. OECD J Econ Stud 44(1):201–238
Eggertson G, Ferrero A, Raffo A (2014) Can structural reforms help Europe? J Monet Econ 61(C):2–22
European Central Bank (2018) Structural reforms in Europe, forthcoming
Fabella VM (2017) Political-economic determinants of education reform: evidence on interest groups and student outcomes. Eur J Polit Econ 48:144–161
Farhi E, Gopinath G, Itskhoki O (2014) Fiscal devaluations. Rev Econ Stud 81:725–760
Fernandez R, Rodrik D (1991) Resistance to reform: status quo bias in the presence of individual specific uncertainty. *Am Econ Rev* 81:1146–1155.
Fernández-Villaverde J (2014) Discussion of "Can structural reforms help Europe?" by G. Eggertsson, A. Ferrero, and A. Raffo. J Monet Econ 61(C):23–31
Fernández-Villaverde J, Guerrón-Quintana P, Rubio-Ramírez J (2011) Supply-side policies and the zero lower bound. NBER Working Paper 17543
Galí J, Monacelli T (2016) Understanding the gains from wage flexibility: the exchange rate connection. Am Econ Rev 106(12):3829–3868
Gerali A, Notarpietro A, Pisani M (2015) Structural reforms and zero lower bound in a monetary union. Bank of Italy Working Paper 1002
Gomes S (2014) Euro area structural reforms in times of a global crisis. Banco de Portugal Working Paper 8
Gomes S, Jacquinot P, Pisani M (2012) The EAGLE. A model for policy analysis of macroeconomic interdependence in the Euro area. Econ Model 29(5):1686–1714
IMF (2017) World economic outlook. Washington, IMF
Jaumotte F, Osorio Buitron C (2015) Inequality and labor market institutions. IMF Staff Discussion Note 15/14
Kahn L (2007) The impact of employment protection mandates on demographic temporary employment patterns: international microeconomic evidence. Econ J 117(521):F333–F356
Kaufmann D, Kraay A, Mastruzzi M (2010) The worldwide governance indicators: methodology and analytical issues. World Bank Policy Research Working Paper 5430.
Masuch K, Moshammer E, Pierluigi B (2016) Institutions, public debt and growth. ECB working Paper 1963
Nicoletti G, Scarpetta S (2003) Regulation, productivity and growth: OECD evidence. Econ Policy 36:11–72
OECD (2015) PISA 2015 results. http://www.oecd.org/pisa/

Oinonen S, Paloviita M (2014) Updating the euro area Phillips curve: the slope has increased. Bank of Finland Research Discussion Paper 31/2014

Papageorgiou D, Vourvachaki E (2017) Macroeconomic effects of structural reforms and fiscal consolidations: trade-offs and complementarities. Eur J Polit Econ 48:54–73

Parlevliet J (2017) What drives public acceptance of reforms? Longitudinal evidence from a Dutch pension reform. Public Choice 173(1–2):1–23

Pitlik H, Wirth S (2003) Do crises promote the extent of economic liberalization? An empirical test. Eur J Polit Econ 19(3):565–581

Psacharopoulos G (1994) Returns to investment in education: a global update. World Dev 22(9):1325–1343

Skarica B, Nobile N (2016) Revisiting the Eurozone Phillips curve. Oxford Econ Econ Outlook 40:28–36

Van Ark, B (2014) Total factor productivity: lessons from the past and directions for the future. BNB Working Paper 271

Vogel L (2017) Structural reforms at the zero bound. Eur J Polit Econ 48:74–90

Chapter 2
The Impact of Structural Reforms: A Review of the Literature

Jante Parlevliet, Simon Savsek, and Máté Tóth

2.1 Introduction

The slowdown in trend growth rates following the global recession and the European sovereign debt crisis, and the constraints surrounding demand side policies have spurred interest in structural reforms. Structural reforms are typically defined as pro-competitive changes to the rules and institutions governing labour and product markets (but sometimes broader). While the leeway for demand side policies was considered limited, in recent years policymakers have often called for the introduction of deep-seated changes in the functioning of product and labour markets. According to some estimates, such reforms could boost the collective GDP of G20 countries by 2% in 5 years' time (OECD and IMF 2014). Similarly, as noted in Chap. 1, ECB President Mario Draghi frequently ended his introductory statements at press conferences following the ECB's Governing Council meetings with a call for structural reforms to boost growth and resilience of Eurozone economies (Draghi 2015).

The views expressed in this chapter are those of the authors and should not be attributed to De Nederlandsche Bank, the European Central Bank or the European Investment Bank.

J. Parlevliet (✉)
Department of Economic Policy, De Nederlandsche Bank, Amsterdam, The Netherlands
e-mail: j.parlevliet@dnb.nl

S. Savsek
European Investment Bank, Luxembourg, Luxembourg
e-mail: s.savsek@eib.org

M. Tóth
European Central Bank, Frankfurt, Germany
e-mail: mate.toth@ecb.europa.eu

J. de Haan, J. Parlevliet (eds.), *Structural Reforms*,
https://doi.org/10.1007/978-3-319-74400-1_2

These high expectations from structural reforms raise various critical questions, including:

- How can we properly measure reforms?
- What can we realistically expect from reforms in the long run?
- How can we identify in practice what gains can be attributed to reforms?
- Do structural reforms lead to immediate gains, or can they imply short-run transitional costs?

The goal of this chapter is to give a broad overview of the relevant literature on the impact of reforms, focusing on labour and product markets (hence excluding issues like education, the quality of government spending, etc.). To this end it provides a selective survey of a large literature from various disciplines, including empirical labour economics and macroeconomics. In doing so, it will also discuss different approaches that have been used to assess the impact of reforms, both empirical and theoretical. Several dimensions of structural reforms are not discussed in greater detail in this literature review.[1]

This chapter is set-up as follows. The next section provides an overview of approaches used to measure the impact of reforms, including a discussion of how empirical studies have dealt with the issue of endogeneity. Section 2.3 then discusses the results of empirical approaches to measure the impact of reforms, distinguishing between micro-based studies that tend to concentrate on a single reform and cross-country studies that often look at a series of reforms. Section 2.4 discusses the outcomes of theoretical approaches (mainly DSGE models). Section 2.5 briefly discusses the political economy of reforms. Finally, Sect. 2.6 concludes.

2.2 Approaches to Measuring the Impact of Reforms

A large literature has related labour and product market reforms to macroeconomic outcomes such as employment, productivity growth and GDP growth. We first discuss empirical approaches to estimating the impact of structural reforms, including ways to correct for endogeneity of reforms. We then continue with theoretical approaches, with a focus on DSGE models.

2.2.1 Empirical Studies and the Issue of Endogeneity

There is a vast empirical literature linking institutions or reforms to macroeconomic outcomes, both at the country level and across jurisdictions. Country studies

[1] For example, studies using changes in measures of economic freedom as a proxy for reform are neglected to large extent (see de Haan et al. 2006 for a discussion).

typically look at the impact of a single institution or reform, such as the retirement age, the duration of unemployment benefits and the ease of entry in product markets. Cross-country studies often look at series of reforms jointly, often using indices developed by the OECD.

Empirical studies aiming to identify the causal effects of reforms have to overcome several methodological issues. Of these, the endogeneity of reforms is perhaps the most serious. A large body of literature has established that institutions, such as labour laws, are not exogenous (or randomly assigned across countries) but are the result of historical specificities and social preferences. For instance, the legal origins of a country have an important influence on the regulation of employment contracts (Campos and Nugent 2012). Endogeneity is also an issue when the focus is on measuring the impact of *changes* to institutions over time, or reforms. Structural reforms are typically preceded by adverse economic conditions that create a political-economy environment where the introduction of reforms is more likely. For instance, a large body of literature has found that economic and financial crises facilitate the adoption of reforms (see Sect. 2.5).

Various approaches have been proposed to deal with this endogeneity issue. In micro-econometric studies, the state of the art is to use or attempting to imitate a natural experiment for identification. For instance, researchers have exploited arbitrary discontinuity in policies ("regression discontinuity design") (see e.g. Lalive 2007). Furthermore, when regulations are not binding to the same extent for all sectors, a difference-in-difference specification allows deriving the effect of reform policies on the basis of variation between sectors (see e.g. Bassanini et al. 2009; Bourlès et al. 2013). Moreover, when a variable can be found that correlates with the reform but not with the observed outcomes under study, an instrumental variable estimation is possible. For instance, Griffith et al. (2010) instrument the EU Single Market reforms with its ex ante estimated impact. An alternative route can be a treatment-effect approach involving a two-stage estimation procedure. For instance, Bordon et al. (Chap. 7) first estimate the probability of implementing structural reform with a probit model and then use these treatment effects of reforms in a second stage regression to correct for selection bias and more precisely evaluate the economic effects of labour and product market reforms.[2]

There are also some other challenges to estimate the impact of reforms. First of all, there can be non-linearities or threshold effects in the relationship between institutions and outcomes. For instance, very long duration of unemployment benefits has been found to diminish job search and increase unemployment duration (Lalive 2007). At the same time, very short unemployment benefits may lower

[2]Researchers have also used several other econometric techniques to deal with endogeneity. Bassanini and Duval (2006) estimate their model using a GMM specification in which policies/institutions are instrumented with their lags. Furthermore, thresholds can be imposed to lower the risk of endogeneity. For instance, Bouis et al. (2012) model a structural reform as a change in the institutional variable by at least two standard deviations of the average annual change. Focusing solely on these large "reform episodes" can limit endogeneity issues.

the efficiency of the subsequent job match and as such productivity (Caliendo et al. 2013). Similarly, it has been proposed that some employment protection can raise economic growth up to a certain level, but deterring economic growth when it becomes very rigid (Belot et al. 2007). Country studies can, in principle, deal more accurately with such threshold effects than aggregate studies.

Secondly, the impact of certain policies may depend on the wider institutional context. For instance, Bassanini and Duval (2006, 2009) find that active labour market policies can reduce the negative employment effect of generous unemployment insurance while Murtin et al. (2014) find that a high tax wedge is especially detrimental to employment in the presence of collective bargaining coverage extensions. Cross-country studies can to some extent control for the wider institutional context by including a series of institutions and institutional interaction terms. Unfortunately, there is not usually enough variation in the cross-country data to test for all possible policy interactions (Bassanini and Duval 2009).

Finally, proper measurement of reforms can be a challenge. Cross-country studies typically rely on OECD indicators to measure changes in structural policies as, for example, in the study by Égert and Gal (Chap. 3). One important advantage of this approach is that reform indicators are standardized across countries and can be therefore widely used in empirical cross-country applications. However, as these indicators typically quantify legislation as opposed to implementation they inevitably contain some measurement error. For instance, for institutions such as the minimum wage and employment protection the gap between *de jure* and *de facto* practices can be rather large (see e.g. Boeri and Jimeno 2005; Venn 2009). To address this issue, the narrative approach is sometimes used in empirical studies instead. For example, this approach is used in Duval et al. (2018), who identify the precise date of reform implementation and construct a broader cross-country and time-series coverage. However, the narrative approach incorporates at least some degree of subjectivity when deciding, for instance, on the significance of the reform measure.[3] And while employment and unemployment can be measured adequately, this is not the case for all metrics of labour market outcomes. For example, Bils (1985) and Solon et al. (1994) have argued that cyclical changes in the composition of employment may explain the apparently a-cyclical evolution of real wages. Properly controlling for such composition effects requires detailed micro-data (see e.g. Carneiro et al. 2012). Furthermore, in aggregate data it is sometimes difficult to recognize and differentiate between the impact of policies that may have observationally equivalent effects in the short run. For example, during the recent crisis, several euro area countries implemented substantial reform measures, but at the same time were also pursuing fiscal consolidation which makes it difficult to disentangle the impact of reforms.

[3] As an alternative, Wiese (2014) suggests using structural break filters in conjunction with a careful analysis of policy documents to identify structural reforms.

2.2.2 Structural Model Based Approaches

Structural model based—or theoretical—approaches to investigate the impact of structural reforms are an important complement to the empirical approaches. In these approaches the causal link between reforms and outcomes is not measured but assumed, thus—to the extent the underlying models are good enough approximations of the economies in question—endogeneity and confounding factors are less of an issue. While these approaches are not necessarily well suited to measure the exact quantitative impact of reforms, they can shed light on key propagation mechanisms and policy interactions at play.

Nowadays, the vast majority of the theoretical literature adopts DSGE models. The most widely used DSGE models typically feature Stiglitz-Dixit type monopolistic competition in both the goods and the labour markets. As a result, goods are priced with a mark-up over marginal costs and wages are characterized by a mark-up over the marginal rate of substitution between consumption and hours worked. In these models, structural reforms are typically captured as permanent negative shocks to mark-ups, representing more competition in product and labour markets resulting in higher output/employment and a lower price/wage level. Such an approach towards modelling the impact of structural reforms is, for example, employed in in't Veld et al. (Chap. 4), Pierluigi and Vetlov (Chap. 5) and Jacquinot et al. (Chap. 6). Thus, in DSGE frameworks reforms can be seen as measures aiming at reducing the distance to the frictionless first best allocation.

While shocking price and wage mark-ups may be a crude way of capturing complex product and labour market reforms, it can be thought of as a first approximation which captures a key element of most structural reforms: enhancing competition. However, product and labour markets often feature a complex web of interacting institutions, thus a model featuring price and wage mark-ups as the only imperfections targeted by structural reforms may provide limited insight into real world policy challenges.

By introducing more complex underlying rigidities and propagation mechanisms the impact of more specific structural reforms and more complex interactions can also be analysed. In this spirit, instead of relying on price and wage mark-ups, Cacciatore et al. (2016) consider a DSGE model with labour market search. In their framework the number of producers is endogenized through fixed entry costs. Mark-ups depend endogenously on the number of firms in the markets through a demand-side mechanism. In this case, the effect of a reform aimed at improving competition is simulated assuming a reduction in entry costs which boosts entry and reduces mark-ups. Thus, with respect to earlier studies, the reduction in mark-up has a deeper economic meaning and more grounded micro-foundations. Likewise, Colciago (Chap. 9) endogenizes both the number of producers and the unemployment rate. Price mark-ups are endogenously determined through a supply side mechanism, namely by introducing oligopolistic competition between (the endogenous number of) producers. Furthermore, Jimeno and Thomas (2013) capture collective bargaining mechanisms via sector level wage fixing in a context where firm-worker pairs are subject to idiosyncratic productivity shocks. Of course, it is not only complexity that matters; in order to provide valid results, the frictions introduced in the model need to be relevant to the structural problem at hand.

It is worth noting that there are strong complementarities between theoretical and empirical approaches. In particular, the empirical literature on the impact of structural reforms can provide a first point of reference for calibrating theoretical models, in terms of coefficients, shock sizes and impulse responses. For example, disaggregated data can be used to estimate the impact of product market regulation on service sector mark-ups (see e.g. Thum-Thysen and Canton 2015), which in turn can help the calibration of the size of a non-tradable sector mark-up shock in response to an assumed regulatory change in a DSGE model. Empirical results are also crucial for creating a mapping between real-word reform measures and the shocks DSGE models can interpret.

2.3 An overview of Results from Empirical Studies

2.3.1 Micro-level Evidence

A large body of micro-econometric studies has analysed the impact of institutions and reforms on unemployment and productivity. It is beyond the scope of this chapter to review this literature in detail (see Jaumotte 2011; Boeri and Van Ours 2013; Blanchard et al. 2014; Boeri et al. 2015 for recent reviews). Rather, in this section, we highlight some main conclusions.

Overall, the micro-econometric literature has corroborated the following findings. First, product market deregulation—such as easier entry—tends to facilitate aggregate productivity growth. For instance, on the basis of UK firm-level data, Aghion et al. (2004) find that increased competition spurs productivity growth of incumbent firms. Furthermore, on the basis of firm-level data of OECD countries, Arnold et al. (2008) show that anti-competitive service regulations hamper productivity growth in ICT-using sectors, especially in a very productive segment. Additionally, Arnold et al. (2011) find that product market regulations that curb competitive pressures tend to reduce the productivity performance of firms. Furthermore, Bourlès et al. (2013), who look at the effect of product market regulation in sectors producing intermediary inputs on multifactor productivity in downstream sectors, find that regulation has significantly hampered productivity growth. In line with predictions from neo-Schumpeterian growth theory, this effect is particularly strong the closer firms are to the productivity frontier. Building on this framework, Cette et al. (2014) disentangle the effects of product market regulation (higher rents) and employment regulation (higher rent sharing of workers) on productivity growth. For most countries, the gains from product market deregulation outweigh those of employment protection deregulation.

Second, generous unemployment benefits (in both duration and its conditions) have been found to increase employment duration and unemployment (Tatsiramos and Van Ours 2014). At the same time, evidence for Germany indicates that very short benefits may hurt the quality of the subsequent job match (Caliendo et al. 2013). Using Austrian data, Lalive (2007) does not find an effect on job quality although short benefits may reduce the odds of transition into regular jobs.

Furthermore, evaluating European policies that reduced the retirement age with the aim of alleviating youth unemployment, Gruber and Wise (2010) do not find that the earlier exit of older workers has supported the employment prospects of the young. In turn, raising the retirement age has been found to boost employment, also in the short run (Cribb et al. 2014).

Fourth, high tax wedges reduce labour demand and supply and can as such reduce employment rates. On the demand side, high taxes increase cost for firms. On the supply side, they reduce take-home pay, negatively impacting labour supply. These distortions are also effected by the progressivity and different schemes of household income taxation (Eissa 1995; Disney 2000; Jongen et al. 2015).

In addition, a high minimum wage can reduce employment prospects especially for the young and lower skilled. At the same time, if employers have strong bargaining power vis-à-vis low-skilled workers, a minimum wage can improve earnings without compromising employment (see Boeri and Van Ours 2013; Boeri et al. 2015).

Probably most controversial is the role of employment protection legislation and collective wage bargaining. As to the first, stringent employment protection legislation (EPL) can be expected to dampen both job separations and hiring rates. In line with this, cross-country studies initially found ambiguous effects on employment and unemployment (e.g. OECD 2004). More recently however, micro-based work—which in principle can more accurately identify causal effects—found some employment effects. For instance, exploiting a difference-in-difference setting for American states Autor et al. (2006) report a negative effect from wrongful discharge law on employment rates. Yet, micro-based results for other countries indicate no robust effects on employment or employment flows (see e.g. Bauer et al. 2007 for Germany and Von Below and Thoursie 2010 for Sweden and Martins 2009 for Portugal). Hijzen et al. (Chap. 8) find that stricter EPL makes the unemployment rate more sensitive to shocks directly by promoting the use of temporary contracts, thereby reducing labour market resilience.

Furthermore, there is evidence that EPL deters firm growth. Exploiting a 1990 reform in Italy that increased EPL for smaller firms, Schivardi and Torrini (2008) find that small firms were more likely to remain small. For the same reform, Cingano et al. (2016) show that higher EPL resulted in an increase in the capital-labour ratio and a decline in total factor productivity in small firms relative to larger firms. Furthermore, several studies have confirmed that EPL influences the composition of employment, favouring permanent employment for prime age males and temporary jobs for other employees such as women, lower-skilled workers and immigrants (see e.g. Kugler et al. 2005 and Kahn 2007). This latter finding is corroborated by Égert and Gal (Chap. 3).

The literature has also investigated the effects of EPL on productivity growth. In theory, EPL can support productivity growth by facilitating investments in firm-specific skills but harm it by deterring radical innovations and reducing job effort. Most empirical studies have found that strict EPL hampers productivity growth. Using sector-level data of a set of OECD countries and a difference-in-difference framework, Bassanini et al. (2009) report that TFP growth is lower in industries where employment protection is binding, where their design suggests a causal effect. As a possible channel between EPL and productivity growth, Gautier et al. (2016) propose that higher employment protection discourages taking risky but on average higher rewarding investments. Furthermore, using harmonized firm-level data for 21 OECD countries, Andrews and Cingano (2014) find that stricter employment protection legislation makes the reallocation of resources across heterogeneous firms less efficiency enhancing.

The literature has also studied dimensions of collective bargaining. Several studies have investigated the impact of union membership on individual earnings. In general, older studies typically found significant premiums of union membership sometimes in the two-digit range. These studies, however, could not account for selection effects. On the basis of a regression discontinuity design, DiNardo and Lee (2004) find no wage effect of unionised firms in the United States. On the other hand, Breda (2015) looks at the wage difference between unionised and unionised firms in France and finds that workers in unionised firms enjoy a 2–3% wage premium.

At the macroeconomic level, wage growth that outpaces productivity developments can lead to competitiveness losses and translate into higher unemployment, unless mechanisms exist to internalise such costs. A well-known hypothesis is that such internalising mechanisms are strongest in case of decentralised bargaining—where union members are directly exposed to the consequences of excessively high wage claims—and fully centralised schemes—where the bargaining process is more likely to take macroeconomic externalities into account due to political economy considerations (Calmfors and Driffill 1988). Empirically, the impact of the degree of wage bargaining centralisation on employment is not straightforward. On the one hand, studies have found that firm-level bargaining supports employment growth. For instance, Dustmann et al. (2014) show that possibilities to opt out of sector-level agreements in Germany have facilitated employment growth. Furthermore, the widespread use of extensions of sector agreements in Portugal has been found to negatively affect employment (Martins 2014). In addition, Marotzke et al. (2016) show that collective pay agreements reduce the probability of downward wage adjustment in Europe, thereby also confirming previous studies on wage rigidities in Europe. Anderton et al. (2017) show that such wage rigidities seem to be particularly binding in downturns. On the other hand, macroeconomic outcomes seem to differ substantially within the group of countries where sector-level wage bargaining is dominant, probably because of large differences in the rules of the game (Blanchard et al. 2014; IMF 2016). The analysis of Hijzen et al. (Chap. 8) points to the potential beneficial effects of centralised or co-ordinated collective bargaining systems for labour market resilience.

Another feature of collective bargaining is the duration of contracts in the context of large economic shocks. Especially when contracts are bargained just before a shock, and do not contain clauses to deviate in case of hardship, they can endanger employment. This was also relevant in the recent crisis, where long contracts were found to exacerbate employment losses in Spain (Díez-Catalán and Villanueva 2015).

2.3.2 Cross-Country and Cross-Reform Studies

Using country-level data, Bassanini and Duval (2006) provide a comprehensive account of the impact of a series of structural policies and institutions (and interactions) on employment outcomes (similar results are presented in Bassanini and Duval 2009). They find that high and long-lasting unemployment benefits, high marginal tax wedges and high product market regulation (all captured by OECD indicators) increase structural unemployment. On the other hand, highly centralized or coordinated wage bargaining is associated with lower unemployment. Active labour market policies (ALMPs) do not significantly impact on unemployment, at least for the overall indicator, nor does employment protection or union density. These authors also investigate the impact of institutions on employment. An important aggregate finding is that high unemployment benefits and high tax wedges decrease employment. Similarly, they test whether institutions interact with shocks. Relatively robust findings are that high unemployment benefits amplify the adverse unemployment effect of a shock, while on the other hand high corporatism decreases this impact. As mentioned above, they also find some evidence of interaction effects. For instance, ALMPs can reduce the negative employment effect of unemployment benefits. Regarding the impact of a number of reform measures by aggregating over the effects on physical capital, employment and productivity through a production function, Égert and Gal (Chap. 3) show that product market deregulation has the largest overall single policy impact 5 years after the reforms. At the same time, a package of various labour market policies under study can have a considerably larger impact.

The empirical literature also studied the interaction between shocks and institutions. In a panel of 20 OECD countries, Blanchard and Wolfers (2000) find that this interaction is crucial to explain the rise in unemployment since the 1960s as well as the increased heterogeneity between countries. This notion follows also from the recent paper by Hantzsche et al. (2018), which investigates propagation of financial shocks in a country-sector panel of euro area countries. Authors report that responses to a financial shock are asymmetric depending on the sign of the shock, different in magnitude depending on the sectoral composition, and sensitive to labour market institutions, such as EPL and union density.

Bouis et al. (2012) present a systematic empirical assessment of the short-run impact of various structural reforms. They look at the effects of reform shocks on variables such as employment, unemployment, participation and GDP growth over a 1–5 year horizon. They find no evidence of large short-run employment and growth costs of reforms. An exception is the reduction of employment protection of temporary workers; the authors find that in the short run this is associated with lower employment, participation and growth. At the same time, various reforms can yield significant short-run benefits. This is particularly true for unemployment benefit reform, which yields positive employment effects relatively quickly. By some indicators, there can be benefits in year 1–2 already, albeit small. These findings are in contrast with Cacciatore and Fiori (2016), who use panel VAR estimation for 20 OECD countries over the period 1981–2005 and provide evidence that labour and product markets deregulation involves potential short-run costs materialized by higher unemployment and lower output.

Bouis et al. (2012) furthermore find that the state of the economy matters, especially for the impact of unemployment benefit reform and employment protection of regular workers. While in the baseline scenario there are short-run employment gains (for reform of unemployment benefits) or at least no losses (for reform of employment protection), in a depressed economy reforms are associated with employment losses.

This underscores the potential role of other macroeconomic policies. For instance, the analysis of Bordon et al. (Chap. 7) points out that some structural reforms are best initiated in conjunction with supportive fiscal or monetary policy. This is also what Hijzen et al. find in their study of labour market resilience in the recent global financial crisis (Chap. 8).

Following the theoretical work of Blanchard and Giavazzi (2003), who demonstrated a degree of substitutability between product and labour market regulations in a general equilibrium setting, several studies have also empirically investigated this relationship. Estevão (2005), for example, finds that if product market regulation is low, the impact of lower labour costs on GDP is larger. It seems that ALMPs complements some other labour market institutions in facilitating employment (Estevão 2007). Berger and Danninger (2006) also report sizable interaction effects from both regulations. Positive interactions are also found in a case study by Annett (2007). Furthermore, Nicoletti and Scarpetta (2005), Bassanini and Duval (2006, 2009) and Bassanini et al. (2009) report that significant gains can be obtained by deregulating product and labour markets, suggesting complementarity between those types of regulations. However, not all empirical findings support this conclusion. For instance, Bouis et al. (2012) report that product market reforms might reduce employment and increase unemployment when employment protection is weak, suggesting some degree of substitutability between product and labour market regulations.

This relationship is still debated in the theoretical (structural model based) literature, which we present in the next section.

2.4 An Overview of Results from Structural Model Based Exercises

Structural models typically find large long-run gains from labour and product market reforms to output, consumption, investment and employment. For instance, based on simulations with the European Commission's QUEST model, in't Veld et al. find considerable long-run gains from moving structural policies in Italy, France, Spain and Portugal in line with the top performers in the EU (Chap. 4). This also goes for simulations of Pierluigi and Vetlov and Jacquinot et al. with the ESCB's EAGLE model reported in Chaps. 5 and 6.

However, there is more disagreement regarding the short-term dynamics. For example, Blanchard and Giavazzi (2003) point out that increasing competition in labour and product markets causes incumbent firms to disappear or decline, leading to a temporary decrease in employment and real wages. Kilponen and Ripatti (2006) underline that factors causing short-run costs are the wealth effects induced by a temporary reduction in profits triggered by the increase in competition, as well as the temporary increase in the real interest rate caused by the slowdown of expected domestic inflation induced by higher competition. Cacciatore and Fiori (2016) claim that product market deregulation increases unemployment due to a time-consuming reallocation of workers between shrinking and expanding firms. Moreover, product market deregulation requires new investments as new firms are entering the market and these needs to be financed by reducing consumption. On the other hand, labour market deregulation affects the hiring and firing incentives of existing firms, regardless of the number of firms in the market. While hiring new staff takes more time, immediate layoff of workers operated by incumbent firms temporarily raises unemployment and reduces GDP. For example, Jacquinot et al. (Chap. 6) show mutually reinforcing impacts from a combination of labour and product market reforms at the effective lower bound. However, Cacciatore et al. (2016) confirm complementarity between these regulations only in the short run, while substitutability between regulations seems to be present in the longer run. Therefore, this relationship seems to still be unclear from a theoretical perspective.

Some theoretical papers put the above results into perspective by showing that the short-run effects of structural reforms are uncertain and depend on the type of reform adopted (Cacciatore and Fiori 2016; Cacciatore et al. 2016) or even provide evidence of benefits in terms of GDP from reforms already in the short run. On the other hand, proper implementation seems to eliminate or significantly reduce possible short-term negative effects in some macroeconomic aggregates. As a matter of fact, Jacquinot et al. (Chap. 6) show that even though structural reforms may entail transitory output costs, those can be reduced or eliminated by an appropriate sequencing, cross-country coordination and supportive fiscal policy or monetary policy.

Cross-country spillovers induced by reforms to the rest of the world have also been investigated. These are typically found positive but small or insignificant. For example, in't Veld et al. (Chap. 4) show that compared to the 'acting alone' scenario, jointly implementing reforms yields only minor additional benefits in terms of GDP. However, some studies reach different conclusions. For instance, Gomes et al. (2013) suggest that reform coordination across countries turns out to be very important, as it would work to the direction of eliminating macroeconomic heterogeneity across countries. This argument also follows from the analysis of Pierluigi and Vetlov (Chap. 5), which shows that spillovers from a euro-area wide implementation of a reform package can be very substantial. Due to their general equilibrium setup, DSGE models are particularly well suited to examine the interaction of different policy areas.

The short-to-medium term impacts of structural reforms do not only depend on the type and size of the reform shock, but also on the response of fiscal and monetary policy which in normal times react endogenously to the shocks hitting the economy. Thus, constraints on demand side policies can also influence the impact of structural policies.

DSGE frameworks have been used recently to examine the interaction of structural reforms and monetary policy, with the latter being constrained to react to the short-term effects of reforms. The constraint can come from a binding effective lower bound (ELB) on nominal interest rates or membership in a monetary union, where common monetary policy reacts to country-level developments only to a limited extent. While the long-run effects of reforms typically remain unaffected, constrained monetary policy can have a bearing on their short-term impact. For example, if monetary policy is not able to react to short-run deflationary effects of some reforms, the real interest rate will increase, which dampens the response of consumption and investment. In most models, the net short-run impact of reform shocks in the context of constrained monetary policy depends on the relative strength of the intertemporal substitution and permanent income or wealth effects. For a more detailed discussion see Chap. 6 of this book.

2.5 The Political Economy of Reforms[4]

Political economy considerations are important to understand what determines and hinders structural reforms. On the one hand, the uncertainty associated with the unequal distribution of gains and losses of reforms turns out to be the most significant hindrance of efficiency-enhancing reforms. On the other hand, there is evidence suggesting that policymakers should never waste a good crisis, especially because it tends to provide an accommodating environment for progress. Also, compensating the losers of reforms is important, but rather through bundling reforms than by means of direct monetary transfers.

One of the most pronounced obstacles for (structural) reforms is the uncertainty about the distribution of gains and losses of reforms. As a consequence, people

[4]We thank Patrick Kosterink for his input in writing this section.

tend to favour the *status quo*, implying that they are particularly wary of being worse off relative to the situation as is (Fernandez and Rodrik 1991). An interesting example thereof is workers opposing privatization, even though they know most will benefit in the end, because they do not know whether their individual skills will be demanded after the reform (de Haan et al. 2006). As such, uncertainty about the distributional pattern of reforms *ex ante* may hamper their occurrence, even while social welfare is expected to increase *ex post*.

Additionally, an unequal distribution of the costs of reforms amongst a polarized political landscape, make that structural change is less likely to happen. The argument is that socioeconomic groups, unevenly affected by the reform, have an incentive to delay the reform, in particular because by doing so they may shift a disproportionate share of its burden to other interest groups. So they effectively engage in a 'war of attrition', whereby they make a trade-off between the costs of delaying the reform against the gain from averting its potential costs. So, even though all parties may agree that reform is required, the disagreement about how the burden is to be shared may cause serious delays (Alesina and Drazen 1991).

Given these large obstacles to reforms, it is perhaps not surprising that several authors have found that crises make reforms more likely (Pitlik and Wirth 2003; Duval and Elmeskov, 2005; Agnello et al. 2015; Dias Da Silva et al. 2017). In times of economic distress, policymakers have to fight tooth to nail in order to keep the economy afloat. The economic situation as such may, in that regard, actually be helpful to bring about structural changes to support the recovery. That is to say, it will strengthen the insight of politicians that something needs to be done. Furthermore, crises tend to diminish the strength of interest groups which were formerly able to hinder the progression of reforms. And, finally, 'wars of attrition' may be shortened considerably in particular because dire economic circumstances alter the balance of pay-offs of the game, i.e. in general the costs of delaying reforms rise significantly (Pitlik and Wirth 2003).

A final insight from the political-economy literature is that compensating the losers of reform is important, but policymakers should rather do this by bundling reforms instead of through direct monetary transfers (Haggard and Webb 1994). In a world where there might be considerable uncertainty about the distributional consequences of reform, even direct compensation schemes may prove to be ineffective to incentivize economic agents to favour structural reforms. This is the case because direct compensation schemes are arguably time-inconsistent, in particular because the *ex post* majority in favour of the reforms may have an incentive to renege on the compensation arrangement agreed upon *ex ante* (Fernandez and Rodrik 1991). In fact, the identification of losers and winners *ex ante* remains an issue in practice. Bundling reforms such that potential losers from one reform would benefit from the prospective gains of other reform could overcome at least partly this problem. Furthermore, supportive fiscal policies may be used to soften possible costs, as was done in Germany at the time of the Hartz reforms (see Chap. 10).

2.6 Conclusion

The impact of structural reforms has been studied extensively in recent years and this literature review only provides a snap shot of the on-going directions and outstanding issues. Our tentative conclusions are the following.

First, with the development of new databases and modelling approaches, researchers and policy makers have become increasingly more confident about the impact of structural measures. However, in empirical work it is still hard to identify and disentangle the causal effects of reform measures due to selection bias and a wide range of confounding factors. Researchers have to make critical assumptions about the timing, channels or use imperfect indicators to eliminate the impacts of reforms. On the other hand, results from structural model based approaches depend crucially on modelling choices concerning *inter alia* the nature of structural rigidities, calibration of parameters and policy interactions. Yet, in both empirical and theoretical work there is broad consensus on long-run aggregate gains in terms of output and/or employment in response to most product market- and labour market reform measures.

Second, short-term effects of reforms are potentially more difficult to measure in the first place, while reforms are made to affect the long-run steady state of the economy. Therefore, interpreting their short-term impact should be done more cautiously. The literature review shows that proper implementation and timing play a key role in determining successfulness of reforms. Supportive demand side policies, where available, can to a large extent dampen possible short-term costs. In this context, it is rather unfortunate that reforms are typically introduced in crisis periods—when demand side policies can become constrained, while there are not many reforms implemented in good times.

Finally, the question on how to build institutions that will help bring about a sense of reform urgency also in normal times is probably the most difficult to answer. The literature reviewed here suggests that the bundling of reforms and accommodating fiscal policies may facilitate the adoption of reforms. Apart from this, we see a further need for academia and policy institutions to investigate the supply side issues. As an example, Chaps. 11 and 12 describe how analytical tools and the institutional role of the Netherlands Bureau for Economic Policy Analysis (CPB) helped advocating various labour market reforms in the Netherlands.

References

Aghion P, Blundell R, Griffith R, Howitt P, Prantl S (2004) Entry and productivity growth: evidence from micro-level panel data. J Eur Econ Assoc 2(2–3):265–276

Agnello L, Castro V, Jalles J, Sousa R (2015) What determines the likelihood of structural reforms? Eur J Polit Econ 37:129–145

Alesina A, Drazen A (1991) Why are stabilizations delayed? Am Econ Rev 81(5):1170–1188

Anderton R, Hantzsche A, Savsek S, Tóth M (2017) Sectoral wage rigidities and labour and product market institutions in the Euro Area. Open Econ Rev 28(5):923–965

Andrews D, Cingano F (2014) Public policy and resource allocation: evidence from firms in OECD countries. Econ Policy 29(78):253–296

Annett A (2007) Lessons from successful labor market reformers in Europe. IMF policy discussion paper 07/1

Arnold J, Nicoletti G, Scarpetta S (2008) Regulation, allocative efficiency and productivity in OECD countries. OECD economics department working paper 616

Arnold J, Nicoletti G, Scarpetta S (2011) Does anti-competitive regulation matter for productivity? Evidence from European firms. IZA discussion paper 5511

Autor D, Donohue J, Schwab S (2006) The costs of wrongful discharge laws. Rev Econ Stat 88(2):211–231

Bassanini A, Duval R (2006) Employment patterns in OECD countries: reassessing the role of policies and institutions. OECD economics department working paper 486

Bassanini A, Duval R (2009) Unemployment, institutions, and reform complementarities: re-assessing the aggregate evidence for OECD countries. Oxf Rev Econ Policy 25(1):40–59

Bassanini A, Nunziata L, Venn D (2009) Job protection legislation and productivity growth in OECD countries. Econ Policy 24(58):349–402

Bauer T, Bender S, Bonin H (2007) Dismissal protection and worker flows in small establishments. Economica 74(296):804–821

Belot M, Boone J, van Ours J (2007) Welfare-improving employment protection. Economica 74(295):381–396

Berger H, Danninger S (2006) The employment effects of labor and product markets deregulation and their implications for structural reform. CESifo working paper 1709

Bils M (1985) Real wages over the business cycle: evidence from panel data. J Polit Econ 93(4):666–689

Blanchard O, Giavazzi F (2003) Macroeconomic effects of regulation and deregulation in goods and labor markets. Q J Econ 118(3):879–907

Blanchard O, Wolfers J (2000) The role of shocks and institutions in the rise of European unemployment: the aggregate evidence. Econ J 110(462):1–33

Blanchard O, Jaumotte F, Loungani P (2014) Labor market policies and IMF advice in advanced economies during the great recession. IZA J Labor Policy 3(2):1–23

Boeri T, Jimeno J (2005) The effects of employment protection: Learning from variable enforcement. Eur Econ Rev 49(8):2057–2077

Boeri T, van Ours J (2013) The economics of imperfect labor markets, 2nd edn. Princeton University Press, Princeton, NJ

Boeri T, Cahuc P, Zylberberg A (2015) The costs of flexibility-enhancing structural reforms. A literature review. OECD economics department working paper 1264

Bouis R, Causa O, Demmou L, Duval R, Zdzienicka A (2012) The short-term effects of structural reforms: an empirical analysis. OECD economics department working paper 949

Bourlès R, Cette G, Lopez J, Mairesse J, Nicoletti G (2013) Do product market regulations in upstream sectors curb productivity growth? Panel data evidence for OECD countries. Rev Econ Stat 95(5):1750–1768

Breda T (2015) Firms' rents, workers' bargaining power and the union wage premium. Econ J 125(589):1616–1652

Cacciatore M, Fiori G (2016) The macroeconomic effects of goods and labor market deregulation. Rev Econ Dyn 20:1–24

Cacciatore M, Duval R, Fiori G, Ghironi F (2016) Short-term pain for long-term gain? Market deregulation and monetary policy in small open economies. J Int Money Financ 68:358–385

Caliendo M, Tatsiramos K, Uhlendorff A (2013) Benefit duration, unemployment duration and job match quality: a regression-discontinuity approach. J Appl Econom 28(4):604–627

Calmfors L, Driffill J (1988) Bargaining structure, corporatism and macroeconomic performance. Econ Policy 3(6):13–61

Campos NF, Nugent J (2012) The dynamics of the regulation of labor in developing and developed countries since 1960. IZA discussion paper 6881
Carneiro A, Guimarães P, Portugal P (2012) Real wages and the business cycle: accounting for worker, firm, and job title heterogeneity. Am Econ J Macroecon 4(2):133–152
Cette G, Lopez J, Mairesse J (2014) Product and labor market regulations, production prices, wages and productivity. NBER working paper 20563
Cingano F, Leonardi M, Messina J, Pica G (2016) Employment protection legislation, capital investment and access to credit: evidence from Italy. Econ J 126(595):1798–1822
Cribb J, Emmerson C, Tetlow G (2014) Labour supply effects of increasing the female state pension age in the UK from age 60 to 62. IFS working paper 14/19
de Haan J, Sturm J-E, Lundstrom S (2006) Market-oriented institutions and policies and economic growth: a critical survey. J Econ Surv 20(2):157–191
Dias Da Silva A, Givone A, Sondermann D (2017) When do countries implement reforms? ECB working paper 2078
Díez-Catalán L, Villanueva E (2015) Contract staggering and unemployment during the great recession: evidence from Spain. Banco de España working paper 1431
DiNardo J, Lee D (2004) Economic impacts of unionization on private sector employers: 1984–2001. NBER working paper 10598
Disney R, (2000) The impact of tax and welfare policies on employment and unemployment in OECD countries. IMF working paper 164
Draghi M, (2015) Structural reforms, inflation and monetary policy. Introductory speech by Mario Draghi, President of the ECB, ECB Forum on Central Banking Sintra, 22 May 2015
Dustmann C, Fitzenberger B, Schönberg U, Spitz-Oener A (2014) From sick man of Europe to economic superstar: Germany's resurgent economy. J Econ Perspect 28(1):167–188
Duval R, Elmeskov J (2005) The effects of EMU on structural reforms in labour and product markets. OECD Economics Department working paper 438
Duval R, Furceri D, Hu B, Jalles J, Nguyen H (2018) A narrative database of major labor and product market reforms in advanced economies. IMF working paper 18/19
Eissa N (1995) Taxation and labour supply of married women: the tax reform act of 1986 as a natural experiment. NBER working paper 5023
Estevão M (2005) Product market regulation and the benefits of wage moderation. IMF working paper 05/191
Estevão M (2007) Labor policies to raise employment. IMF Staff Pap 54(1):113–138
Fernandez R, Rodrik D (1991) Resistance to reform: status quo bias in the presence of individual-specific uncertainty. Am Econ Rev 81(5):1146–1155
Gautier PA, Bartelsman EJ, de Wind J (2016) Employment protection, technology choice, and worker allocation. Int Econ Rev 57(3):787–826
Gomes S, Jacquinot P, Mohr M, Pisani M (2013) Structural reforms and macroeconomic performance in the Euro area countries: a model-based assessment. Int Financ 16(1):23–44
Griffith R, Harrison R, Simpson H (2010) Product market reform and innovation in the EU. Scand J Econ 112(2):389–415
Gruber J, Wise DA (2010) Social security programs and retirement around the world: the relationship to youth employment. NBER working paper 14647
Haggard S, Webb SB (eds) (1994) Voting for reform: democracy, political liberalization, and economic adjustment. World Bank, Washington
Hantzsche A, Savsek S, Weber S (2018) Labour market adjustments to financing conditions under sectoral rigidities in the euro area. Forthcoming in Open Econ Rev
IMF (2016) Time for a supply-side boost? Macroeconomic effects of labor and product market reforms in advanced economies. Chapter 3 in World economic outlook, April 2016
Jaumotte F (2011) The Spanish labor market in a cross-country perspective. IMF working paper 11/11
Jimeno JF, Thomas C (2013) Collective bargaining, firm heterogeneity and unemployment. Eur Econ Rev 59:63–79

Jongen E, de Boer H, Dekker P (2015) De effectiviteit van fiscaal participatiebeleid. CPB policy brief 2015-02, CPB Netherlands bureau for economic policy analysis, The Hague

Kahn L (2007) The impact of employment protection mandates on demographic temporary employment patterns: international microeconomic evidence. Econ J 117(521):F333–F356

Kilponen J, Ripatti A (2006) Labour and product market competition in a small open economy – simulation results using a DGE model of the Finnish economy. Bank of Finland research discussion paper 5/2006

Kugler A, Jimeno JF, Hernanz V (2005) Employment consequences of restrictive permanent contracts: evidence from Spanish labor market re-forms. Mimeo, University of Houston. Available at www.uh.edu/~adkugler/Kugler_SR.pdf

Lalive R (2007) Unemployment benefits, unemployment duration, and post-unemployment jobs: a regression discontinuity approach. Am Econ Rev 97(2):108–112

Marotzke P, Anderton R, Bairrao A, Berson C, Tóth P (2016) Wage adjustment and employment in Europe. University of Nottingham discussion papers 19, GEP

Martins P (2009) Dismissals for cause: the difference that just eight paragraphs can make. J Labor Econ 27(2):257–279

Martins P (2014) 30,000 minimum wages: the economic effects of collective bargaining extensions. IZA discussion paper 8540

Murtin F, de Serres A, Hijzen A (2014) Unemployment and the coverage extension of collective wage agreements. European Economic Review 71:52–66

Nicoletti G, Scarpetta S (2005) Product market reforms and employment in OECD countries. OECD economics department working paper 472

OECD (2004) Employment protection regulation and labour market performance. Chapter 2 in OECD employment outlook 2004. Paris, OECD

OECD and IMF (2014) Quantifying the impact of G-20 members' growth strategies. Note prepared for meetings of G-20 finance ministers and central bank governors, Cairns, Australia, Sept 2014

Pitlik H, Wirth S (2003) Do crises promote the extent of economic liberalization? An empirical test. Eur J Polit Econ 19(3):565–581

Schivardi F, Torrini R (2008) Identifying the effects of firing restrictions through size-contingent differences in regulation. Labour Econ 15(3):482–511

Solon G, Barsky R, Parker J (1994) Measuring the cyclicality of real wages: how important is composition bias? Q J Econ 109:1–25

Tatsiramos K, van Ours J (2014) Labor market effects of unemployment insurance design. J Econ Surv 28(2):284–311

Thum-Thysen A, Canton E (2015) Estimation of service sector mark-ups determined by structural reform indicators. European economy economic papers 547

Venn D (2009) Legislation, collective bargaining and enforcement: updating the OECD employment protection indicators. OECD social, employment and migration working paper 89

Von Below D, Thoursie PS (2010) Last-in first-out? Estimating the effect of seniority rules in Sweden. Labour Econ 17:987–997

Wiese R (2014) What triggers reforms in OECD countries? Improved reform measurement and evidence from the healthcare sector. Eur J Polit Econ 34:332–352

Chapter 3
The Quantification of the Effects of Structural Reforms in OECD Countries

Balázs Égert and Peter Gal

3.1 Introduction

This chapter describes and discusses a new simulation framework that quantifies the impact of structural reforms on per capita income. The overall medium- to long-term supply side impact is derived through components of the production function: multi-factor productivity, capital intensity and the employment rate. It builds on and extends the previous frameworks developed in the OECD's Economics Department, which include Bouis and Duval (2011) and Barnes et al. (2013) and the long-term scenario model elaborated in Johansson et al. (2013). In what follows, this will be referred to as the old framework.

The chapter benefitted from useful comments and suggestions from Andrea Bassanini, Gilbert Cette, Alain de Serres, Sean Dougherty, Falilou Fall, Andrea Garnero, Alexander Hijzen, Catherine L. Mann, Fabrice Murtin and Jean-Luc Schneider. A short version was published in OECD Economic Studies 2016(1), 91–108 and a longer version appeared as OECD Economics Department working paper No. 1354. The views expressed in the paper are those of the author and do not necessarily reflect the opinions of the OECD or any other institution the authors are affiliated with. The underlying work to this chapter has also been published in the OECD Economic Journal, 4(1), 91–108, 2016, under the title "The quantification of structural reforms in OECD countries: A new framework".

B. Égert (✉)
University of Paris, Paris, France

Economics Department, OECD, Paris, France

CESifo, Munich, Germany
e-mail: Balazs.Egert@oecd.org

P. Gal (✉)
Economics Department, OECD, Paris, France
e-mail: Peter.Gal@oecd.org

J. de Haan, J. Parlevliet (eds.), *Structural Reforms*,
https://doi.org/10.1007/978-3-319-74400-1_3

In developing a new empirical framework for the quantification of the medium- to long-term impact of reforms, a number of objectives have been established at the outset (OECD 2015a). First, to extend the set of policy channels included in the framework to significantly broaden the range of quantifiable reforms. Second, to update the framework to cover the post-crisis period. Third, to improve the framework's internal consistency with respect to the country and time coverage, the empirical specification and econometric method used to estimate policy impacts. Fourth, country-specific policy effects should be better taken into account. And finally: a better integration of emerging market economies.

This chapter is a first step towards addressing the first three objectives. First, relative to the old framework, the number of policy variables and channels through which they influence GDP per capita is increased. Second, the new framework is based on relationships estimated over a period including the immediate post-crisis years (1985–2011), although it ends in 2011 due to the availability of some policy indicators. Third, internal consistency is increased by a considerable extent: new estimates for the three supply-side channels are based on a similar sample of countries and time span. The sample size is almost identical for the individual supply-side channels.[1] The estimates are also based on a unified estimation framework (dynamic OLS in a panel setting).

The results presented in this chapter are based on *average* policy effects obtained on an OECD sample. Country-specific effects can be identified in a panel setting by conditioning the impact of individual policies on the stance of other policies or via policy interactions. This will allow for the incorporation of a potentially large set of additional policy areas including institutions and policy areas with limited time-series availability (e.g. subcomponents of the PMR indicator, housing market regulations or the rule of law indicator). Work on integrating EMEs into the quantification framework will also be completed in the next phase.

This chapter is structured as follows. Section 3.2 compares the main features of the old and the new frameworks. In particular, it discusses how the new framework improves on the old framework by (i) incorporating more policy channels, (ii) enhancing the internal consistency of the policy impacts, and (iii) using updated estimates for them. Section 3.3 presents in detail how these new coefficient estimates are obtained. Section 3.4 sets out the new simulation framework and shows the impact of policy changes on per capita income and its supply-side components. It differs from typical OECD studies analysing *specific* policy impacts in a number of ways. First, the simulation framework considers the impact of a large number

[1]For instance, policy effects on labour market outcomes are analysed for specific policies (independently of other possibly relevant policies) on substantially different country samples. The effects of unemployment benefits, tax wedge and active labour market policies are taken from Bassanini and Duval (2006). The effect of childcare spending reported in Jaumotte (2003) is used. The first study covers 20 countries and the period 1982–2003, and uses OLS and SUR for estimation purposes. The second paper looks at 17 countries and 1985–1999. It employs 2-stage least squares to estimate policy effects. For a more detailed comparison, see Tables A1.1 and A1.2. in Égert and Gal (2016).

of policies by controlling for a wide range of other policies (including them in the regressions at the same time). Second, most projects typically look at the isolated relationship between policies on the one hand productivity, investment or labour market outcomes on the other hand. The framework is used to aggregate these effects into an overall impact on per capita income. Finally, Sect. 3.5 concludes.

3.2 A Consistent Framework to Quantify the Impact of Structural Reforms

We follow previous OECD papers by assessing the impact of structural reforms on per capita income based on a production function approach (Barnes et al. 2013; Bouis and Duval 2011; Johansson et al. 2013). In this chapter, the influence of policies on GDP is assessed through their influence on its supply side components multi-factor productivity (MFP), capital intensity and employment. Within this framework, the relationship between policies and these components is obtained from a range of cross-country reduced-form panel regressions. The overall impact on GDP per capita is obtained by aggregating the policy effects of the various channels.[2]

The framework presented in this chapter seeks to improve on a number of dimensions compared to previous OECD studies. First, a considerably larger number of policy determinants are analysed for MFP and employment and policy determinants of capital deepening are introduced. Second, internal consistency is improved in three ways. To start with, supply-side channels are used in a consistent manner: different levels of disaggregation of the supply side components are not mixed across policy areas (e.g. employment for some policies, the labour force participation and unemployment rate for others). In addition, econometric estimates are obtained using the very same up-dated dataset (SPIDER dataset) for as many countries as possible (25 for the employment rate and above 30 for MFP and capital deepening) and estimation technique. Finally, changes in policy measures and the horizons at which their impact is measured are standardised. The last major improvement relates to the updating of the coefficient estimates. We make use of econometric estimates covering the post-crisis period (mostly until 2011–2013) for all three supply-side channels (MFP, capital deepening and the employment rate).

[2]Appendix 1 in Égert and Gal (2016) provides a detailed comparison of the old and new frameworks.

3.3 Empirical Estimates Used in the Simulation Framework

The baseline estimates used in the simulation framework are taken from Égert (2017a, b) and Gal and Theising (2015). They are summarised hereafter.[3]

3.3.1 Multi-factor Productivity

We calculate aggregate MFP as the residual of output once capital and labour are accounted for. Human capital is included in our measure of MFP: MFP series, which exclude human capital (output minus human and physical capital and labour) are implausible: a decline over decades in countries close to the frontier, and the USA being far from the frontier (see details in Égert 2017a).

The policy determinants of MFP are taken from Égert (2017a) and the main results are summarised in Table 3.1 (columns 1 to 3). These results suggest that a strong negative relationship can be identified between product market regulations, captured by the overall Energy, Transport and Communication Regulation (ETCR) indicator (and its subcomponents measuring the degree of barriers to entry and the extent of public ownership in the energy, transport and communication sectors), and MFP if only country but no year fixed effects are used.[4] If both country and time fixed effects are included in the regressions, only the coefficient estimate on public ownership is found to be statistically significant, overall ETCR and barriers to entry have large standard errors for the full sample. When using a subsample, given by data available on general spending on basic research (rather than business spending on R&D funded by industry used for the large sample), the overall ETCR indicator and its subcomponents become again negative and statistically significant.

Three labour market regulation indicators are used: employment protection legislation (EPL) for permanent contracts, spending on active labour market policies

[3]Several sensitivity checks are carried out in Égert (2017a, b) and Gal and Theising (2015). They confirm that the results summarised hereafter are fairly robust to alternative specifications regarding time and country coverage, different controls and estimation methods.

[4]The MFP and ETCR series have common trends captured by year fixed effects. These trends are strongly correlated with each other. The correlation between the time fixed effects of MFP and the demeaned overall ETCR series is 0.72 (the series are also demeaned in the regressions including country fixed effects). When we compare the time fixed effects in the MFP and ETCR series, the correlation is 0.77. This is not surprising as time fixed effects explain about 89% of the variation of the demeaned overall ETCR series. When decomposing the overall ETCR indicator into (i) barriers to entry and (ii) public ownership, public ownership survives the inclusion of year fixed effects. This variable could potentially be used for the purpose of quantification (at the expense of covering fewer policy areas).

Table 3.1 MFP and investment: long-term coefficient estimates used in the simulations

	Dependent variable				
	Multi-factor productivity			log(capital stock/output)	
Explanatory variables	(1)	(2)	(3)	(4)	(5)
Product market regulation					
ETCR aggregate	−0.037**		−0.047**	−0.035**	−0.025**
ETCR public ownership		−0.027**			
Labour market policies					
log ALMP			0.029**		
EPL					−0.152**
Intermediate outcomes					
trade openness (size adjusted)	0.007**	0.008**	0.006**		
business exp. On R&D by industry	0.071**	0.059**	0.047**		
Elements of the user cost of capita					
log relative investment prices				−0.377**	−0.608**
long–term real interest rate				0.002	0.004*
corporate taxes/GDP				−0.024**	−0.026**
error correction term	−0.033**	−0.043**	−0.052**	−0.026**	−0.022**
Adjusted R-squared	0.952	0.959	0.964	0.919	0.947
Country/year fixed effects	Yes/No	Yes/Yes	Yes/No	Yes/Yes	Yes/Yes
No. of observations/countries	755/34	755/34	570/32	705/32	600/31
Years	1985–2011	1985–2012	1985–2013	1985–2013	1985–2013

Notes: Estimates based on using the dynamic OLS (DOLS) estimator with one lag and one lead. The MFP regressions include human capital and output gap and the capital deepening regression output gap as control variables. Standard errors are heteroscedasticity robust. ** and * denote significance at the 5% and 10% level, respectively

(ALMP) and the unemployment benefit replacement ratio. None of these labour market regulation indicators is statistically significantly related to MFP when added one by one to the baseline regression.[5] But ALMP becomes statistically significant if used in logs. The positive sign on ALMP may indicate that more

[5]The finding that EPL is statistically not significant stands somewhat in contrast with the literature using sector- and firm-level data relying on difference-in-difference approaches. For instance Bassanini et al. (2009) finds for a set of 16 OECD countries from 1982 to 2003 that country-level EPL is associated with lower MFP growth in sectors with higher layoff rates. Rincon-Aznar and Siebert (2012) show the negative relation to hold for manufacturing sectors but not for the services sectors. Using firm-level data for the USA, Autor et al. (2007) report mixed evidence on the negative relation between employment protection and the level of MFP: the coefficient estimates are negative but only one coefficient in two is precisely estimated. Dougherty et al.

spending on ALMP helps labour reallocation towards more productive uses by reducing skill mismatches (Adalet-McGowan and Andrews 2015). Adding year fixed effects to the regressions switches off the innovation intensity variable. In the simulations, estimates obtained using country fixed effects only will be used.

3.3.2 Capital Deepening

The policy determinants of capital deepening are taken from Égert (2017b). The results are summarised in Table 3.1 (columns 4 and 5). In the baseline specification, K/Y is regressed on the user cost of capital (decomposed into relative investment prices, the real interest rate (proxied by long-term government bond yields deflated by the inflation rate) and corporate taxes (measured as the corporate income tax-to-GDP ratio) and product market regulation. Labour market policies are added to the regressions in a later stage. The results show that the corporate taxes-to-GDP ratio and the relative investment price variable bear the expected negative sign and are statistically significant. But the real interest rate is found to be only weakly related to the capital stock. To be fully consistent with theory, we keep all three components of the user cost of capital in the specifications augmented by structural policy indicators.

Product market regulation, measured by the ETCR indicator, shows a fairly robust negative relationship with the capital stock series. It is robust to alternative (smaller) country samples and time coverage (excluding the crisis). Finally, the results do not change ostensibly if the regressions are carried out on a reduced common sample covering all labour market policy indicators as well (Table 3.1).

The employment protection legislation (EPL) indicator has a strong and quantitatively important negative relationship to the capital stock. Its coefficient estimate is precisely estimated for both the level and log-linear specifications. The estimated elasticities indicate that a one-step increase in EPL is associated with a decline of about 0.2% in the capital stock-to-output ratio.[6] It should be noted that the negative

(2011) show that state-level employment regulation lowers MFP levels in Indian firms operating in more-labour intensive industries.

[6]This negative relationship is robust to alternative country coverages (for narrower samples composed of more developed OECD countries) and to the definition of the capital stock (real capital stock, capital stock/output, capital stock/workers). This result needs qualification. The effect of EPL on investment is not clear-cut in the existing body of research. The literature reports no evidence that labour market regulation has any impact of investment at the macroeconomic level and for several OECD countries (Kerdrain et al. 2010). There is mixed evidence on the relation between capital stock and labour market regulation at the firm level. There is evidence for European firms that more stringent EPL reduces investment per worker and capital per worker (Cingano et al. 2010). By contrast, for US firms, research suggests higher firing costs (wrongful discharge exceptions) are linked to higher capital stock and capital-to-labour ratios. But the effect becomes negative when state-specific trends are used. A rise in capital may be related to a correction of an

relation between the ETCR indicator and the capital stock remains statistically significant and of the same magnitude (Table 3.1).

3.3.3 Employment Rate

Policy determinants of the employment rate are taken from Gal and Theising (2015), who build on previous work from the OECD Reassessed Jobs Strategy (Bassanini and Duval 2006). The impact of policies on the aggregate employment rate is derived from estimation results obtained for four demographic groups (youth, prime age women and man; and the elderly). Such a breakdown makes it possible to capture more types of policy than regressions focusing on the overall employment rate or a breakdown by skill levels. Estimation results, summarised in Table 3.2, show that lower unemployment benefit replacement rates, increased spending on active labour market policies, and lower labour tax wedges tend to boost employment. These findings broadly confirm existing results but are based on an updated dataset and on a somewhat different methodology.[7] Regarding wage-setting institutions, the excess coverage of wage agreements—i.e. the difference between the percentage of employees to whom the results of wage negotiations apply and those that are members of labour unions—its interaction with the tax wedge and the minimum-wage level tend to affect employment rates negatively. Product market regulation captured by the ETCR indicator correlates negatively with the aggregate employment rate. Finally, while the EPL indicator has no robust relationship with the aggregate employment rate (Égert and Gal 2016), it does have a heterogeneous impact across various segments of the population. This makes aggregate effects potentially dependent on the composition of the working age population by skills and demographic groups.

Indeed, some of the other policy effects also show significant and intuitive heterogeneity across segments of the population:

- Higher unemployment benefit replacement rates have the strongest negative effect on employment of the elderly and the low educated;
- ALMP spending has positive effects for each segments of the population, mostly so for the youth;

earlier downturn and that the introduction of more stringent firing regulations followed a rise of the capital-to-labour ratio (Autor et al. 2007). For Italian firms, estimation results show that the introduction of unjust-dismissal costs raises the capital-to-labour ratio in firms with less than 15 employees, compared to larger firms (Cingano et al. 2015).

[7]These results are robust to various sensitivity checks, including different estimation methodologies, control variables and a time period covering only the pre-financial crisis period (Gal and Theising 2015). Nevertheless, jack-knifing the sample, i.e. dropping one country at a time from the sample, shows some sensitivity to the country coverage.

Table 3.2 Employment rate: long-term coefficient estimates

	Dependent variable: employment rate			
	Youth	Prime age women	Prime age men	Elderly
Explanatory variables	(1)	(2)	(3)	(4)
Tax-benefit and activation policies				
UE benefit replacement rate	−0.183**	−0.204**	−0.147**	−0.343**
ALMP spending on unemployed, as % of GDP/capita (HP-trend)	0.147**	0.092**	0.047**	0.063**
Tax wedge (single, no ch.)	−0.866**			
Tax wedge (couple, 2 ch.)		0.004	−0.274**	−0.260**
Wage setting institutions				
Excess coverage	0.072	−0.171**	0.025	0.105
Excess coverage * tax wedge (single, no ch.)	−3.627**			
Excess coverage * tax wedge (couple, 2 ch.)		−0.938**	0.079	0.623*
Minimum wage (%median)	−0.311**	−0.421**	0.043	−0.093
Labour and product market regulations				
EPL regular contracts	1.599	−2.746*	−0.569	1.710
ETC regulation	1.032	−1.533**	0.232	0.630
Policies primarily affecting women				
Family benefits in cash (% of GDP)		−0.967		
Family benefits in kind (% of GDP)		4.698**		
Number of weeks of maternity leave		0.265**		
Pension system—primarily affecting the elderly				
Legal age for pensions (total)				0.851**
Error correction term	−0.303**	−0.145**	−0.294**	−0.160**
Adjusted R-squared	0.978	0.960	0.907	0.977
Country/year fixed effects	Yes/Yes	Yes/Yes	Yes/Yes	Yes/Yes
No. of observations/countries	422/25	420/25	420/25	422/25
Years	1987–2010	1987–2010	1987–2010	1987–2010

Notes: Estimates based on using the dynamic OLS (DOLS) estimator with one lag and one lead. Heteroskedasticity and autocorrelation robust (Newey-West) standard errors are shown in parentheses. The regressions also include the output gap, government employment, the government budget balance, a measure of average educational attainment (adjusted mean years of schooling) and an indicator for the presence of minimum wages as further controls. For more details, see Gal and Theising (2015). ** and * denote significance at the 5% and 10% level, respectively

- The impact of minimum wages is stronger for the youth than for prime age men and the elderly.[8] Its impact is even stronger for prime wage women.[9]
- Stricter employment protection legislation tends to decrease female employment rates, although this result is not robust to the exclusion of family policies. The effects of EPL on men are ambiguous. It also has opposing effects on the low educated (lowering employment) and on the highly educated (increasing employment); see Égert and Gal (2016). The explanation can be that stricter EPL may hold back less the hiring of highly qualified workers (they are more likely to provide a better match for the firm) and may impact their firing less (which may be more costly). These opposing effects across groups of the population help to explain why it is difficult to find robust aggregate effects;
- Raising the legal retirement age increases labour force participation for the elderly;
- More spending on in-kind family benefits, such as childcare and longer maternity leaves, increase employment rates of the working-age female population.

3.4 The New Simulation Framework

This section illustrates the new quantification framework. Appendix describes how policy impact on the three supply-side channels can be aggregated to total per capita income effects.

3.4.1 Choosing the Size of Policy Changes for Illustrative Purposes

One needs to determine the magnitude of changes in the structural policy indicators to quantify the impact of structural policies on per capita income. Ideally, in each case, one should use details on planned policy changes and translate them into the policy indicators used for the estimations. In practice, this is not always possible. Details are not always sufficient and if they are, it is not always easy to map them

[8]The magnitude of the estimated impact (−0.3 for the youth) seems consistent with studies showing elasticities of −0.1 to −0.2 (see recent surveys by Neumark 2015 and OECD 2015b). This is because we use the Kaitz index (median to minimum wage), which in our sample averages at 50% (Gal and Theising 2015). Hence a 1% point increase in it translates into a 2% point increase, on average, for the minimum wage level. Therefore, coefficients obtained when using the level of the minimum wage should be multiplied by two to make them comparable with our coefficients.

[9]Our coefficient estimates for prime-age women are larger than those reported in the literature using similar datasets (Addison and Ozturk 2012). The differences may be due to different model specification and data coverage. Therefore, care should be taken when using these estimates for quantification.

into our policy indicators. For such cases and for illustrative purposes, we define a reform measure for each policy, which is based on policy changes observed in the past. More specifically, reforms are determined as the average improvements in the policy indicators over 2-year windows. Only those consecutive years are used when which policy indicators suggested reform in both years. It is important to stress that the impact of reforms is linear: if reform intensity (the change in the policy indicator) doubles, the impact on per capita income will also double.[10]

3.4.2 Obtaining Policy Effects Over Different Horizons

Policy effects identified by the coefficient estimates are the long-run effects (Tables 3.1 and 3.2). This implies full convergence, which can take a very long time, depending on the estimated speed of adjustment parameters. For MFP and capital deepening, the estimated error correction terms are estimated in the range of –0.03 to –0.05, and for employment, they are around –0.2 (Égert and Gal 2016). A speed of adjustment coefficient of $\rho = -0.05$ implies that 90% of the convergence occurs after about 45 years.[11] This long-term convergence can be speeded up if the short- term effect is large and points in the same direction. Such an initial "boost" is found for the ETCR impact on MFP, for instance (see Fig. 3.1). Policymakers are typically interested in policy impacts at shorter time horizons. Therefore, policy impacts are also calculated and presented for 5 and 10 years after the reforms took place.

The adjustment path is calculated using the estimated error correction term and the contemporaneous, short run policy effect from the error correction model. The adjustment path uses estimates of the short-run effects and the speed of adjustment terms from Égert and Gal (2016). The overall impact will therefore depend on the adjustment path to the long-run equilibrium and the number of years considered after the policy changes. To compute policy impacts over the desired horizon, the convergence path for each policy is evaluated for each supply-side channel. These effects are then aggregated across policies and supply side components, in accordance with Eq. (3.5) in Appendix.

The policy effects are linear with respect to changing *the size* of the reform measure, but they are non-linear depending on the *time horizon* over which they are evaluated. Put differently, the impact of reforms is twice as much if the reform shock is twice as large. However, the impact 5 years after reforms occurred can be different from half of the impact predicted for 10 years after the reforms were introduced.

[10] Appendix 5 in Égert and Gal (2016) discusses alternative reform scenarios.

[11] $ln(1-0.9)/\ ln\ (1-0.05) \approx 45$ years. The half-life, i.e. the time over which half of the convergence to the new long-run equilibrium happens, can be calculated as $ln(1-0.5)/\ ln\ (1-0.05) \approx 13.5$ years.

The impact of a unit ETCR-reform on MFP unit reform: -0.31 point
unit reform: 3.18 percentage points

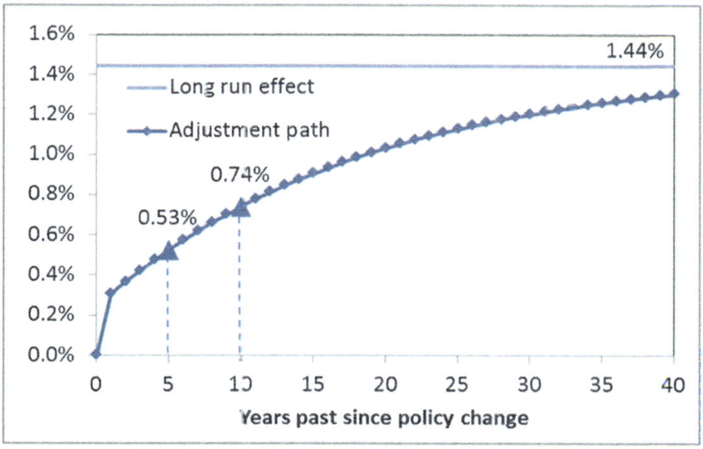

The impact of a unit ALMP reform on the employment rate (in percentage points)

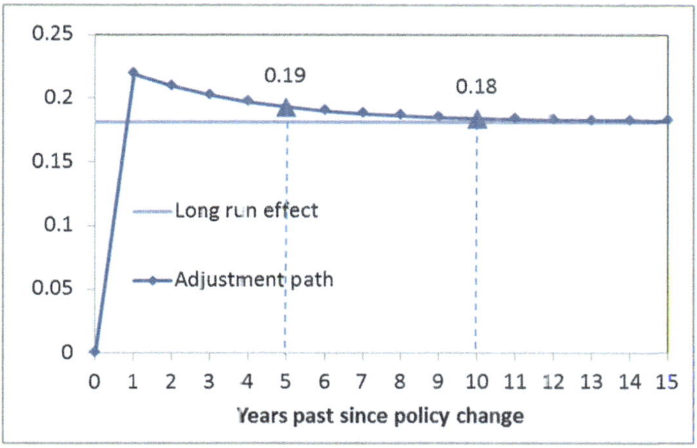

Fig. 3.1 Adjustment path towards the long-run impact: two examples. Notes: ETCR stands for Energy, Transport and Communication Regulation. The size of the reforms are measured by the average changes of the indicators to a more favourable direction, observed over two consecutive years, across all OECD countries in the sample and years (1985–2013). For each year t following the policy change, the adjustment path of the policy effect is $[1-(1+\rho)^{t-1}](\beta x-\gamma x)+\gamma x$, where ρ, β and γ are the estimates for the speed of adjustment, the long run and the short run impact of the policy, and x is the size of the reform shock

As described above, the shape of the adjustment path to the total long-term effect determines the short-run effect. Figure 3.1 shows these adjustment paths and the resulting non-linear impacts in terms of different horizons for two different policies. The adjustment path for a change in ETCR on MFP is slow and decelerating, while the adjustment of a change in ALMP on the employment rate is characterised by an initial overshooting and then a gradual return to the long-run equilibrium.

3.4.3 Simulation Results

This section presents the impact of policies on per capita income levels. The overall impact mostly reflects average effects across countries, as country-specific effects play a much smaller role in the new framework at the current stage.

3.4.3.1 Average Country Effects in the New Framework

Let's first zoom in on the *overall impact* on per capita income 5 years after the policy changes took place (Fig. 3.2 and Table 3.3. The results suggest that product market regulation, as measured by the ETCR indicator, has the largest overall direct policy impact: 0.7%. This is because ETCR influences per capita income through all three supply-side channels (productivity, capital deepening and the employment rate). The impact through MFP is 0.5. This is comparable with the impact of other policies. For instance, the impact of increased ALMP spending, a reduction in the tax wedge and in the minimum wage or in the number of maternity leave weeks, ranges from 0.36

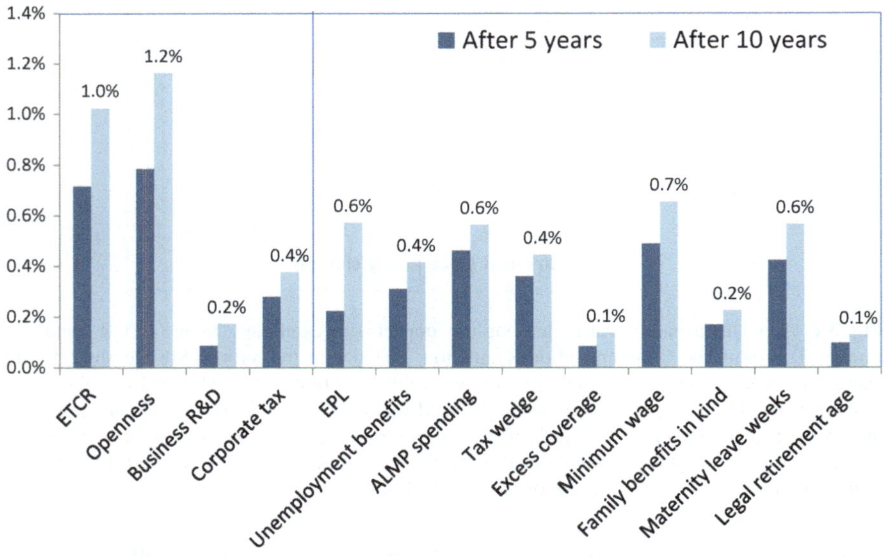

Fig. 3.2 The impact of reforms on GDP per capita 5 and 10 years after the reforms. Notes: Typically observed reforms are measured here by the average of all beneficial 2-year policy changes that were observed over two consecutive years in the sample

Table 3.3 The impact of reforms on GDP per capita and its supply side components 5 years after the reforms

Structural policy areas	Size of a typically observed	Total effect on GDP per capita	Impact on supply side components		
			MFP	K / Y	L / N
		in percent	in percent		in percentage points
Product market regulation		**0.72**			
ETCR (0-6, 6 is strictest)	−0.31	0.72	0.53	0.07	0.10
Intermediate policy channels mainly affecting		**0.87**			
Openness	4.01	0.79	0.79		
R&D (business exp.)	0.10	0.09	0.09		
Investment specific policies		**0.28**			
Corporate tax	−0.98	0.28		0.57	
Labour market policies		**2.88**			
Labour market regulations		**0.22**			
EPL (regular contr., 0-6, 6 is strictest)	−0.30	0.22		0.24	0.07
Tax-benefit and activation policies		**1.39**			
Unemployment benefits	−1.42	0.31			0.21
ALMP spending	3.18	0.46	0.09		0.25
Tax wedge	−2.28	0.36			0.24
Tax wedge (single)	−1.39	0.25			0.17
Wage setting institutions		**0.58**			
Excess coverage	−1.89	0.09			0.06
Minimum wage	−2.48	0.49			0.32
Labour market policies for	**0.69**				
Family benefits in kind	0.11	0.17			0.11
Maternity leave weeks	4.83	0.42			0.28
Legal retirement age	0.57	0.10			0.06

Notes: Typically observed reforms are measured here by the average of all beneficial 2-year policy changes that were observed over two consecutive years in the sample. The total GDP/capita effect uses the employment effects from the aggregation across demographic groups, and it uses the formula in Eq. (3.5) to aggregate across supply side components to 0.49% (see column (2) in Table 3.3). The influence of trade openness is similar in magnitude to that of ETCR. However, it requires further empirical work to pin down through which channels openness impacts MFP and thus per capita income.

Some policies have only a minor impact on per capita income levels. For instance, raising the legal retirement age, increasing business spending R&D funded by industry and cutting excess coverage add about 0.1% to per capita income when using past positive policy changes over two consecutive years (column (2) in Table 3.4). The small impact of R&D may seem puzzling. There is some evidence that less developed OECD countries may benefit more from technology diffusion and adoption through the trade channel, and that innovation intensity (more spending on R&D) may be more important for more advanced OECD countries (Égert 2017a).

The overall impact of all labour market policies is considerably larger than the overall effect of ETCR and the remaining policies (corporate taxes and R&D spending). Nevertheless, adding up the effect of all labour market policies implies that reforms are carried out simultaneously in all quantifiable policy areas, which is rather implausible in practice.

Table 3.3 can provide precious help for policy makers for the elaboration of comprehensive structural reform packages. Depending on the ease with which reforms can be implemented, policies could be picked to reach policy objectives in terms of overall impact on per capita income.

When we compare the impact of policies across *different horizons*, i.e. 5 and 10 years after policy changes and the long-run effect (Table 3.4), the following results stand out. First, for some policies, the overall long-term effects on GDP per capita can be considerably larger than the 5- to 10-year impacts. These policies include ETCR, EPL and ALMP spending. Furthermore, the total impact of other policies, mostly labour market policies transiting only via the employment rate channel, materialises at a shorter horizon. Hence, the impact at different horizons (reported in Table 3.4) is similar in magnitude.

As to the impact of policies on the separate *supply-side channels* (Fig. 3.3),[12] some results are worth highlighting. To start with, the results suggest that different policies have different impacts on the separate supply-side channels. For instance, corporate taxes have a much larger impact on investment compared to product market regulations (ETCR). The impact of legal retirement age on the employment rate is roughly 5 times smaller than those found for minimum wages, maternity leave weeks or ALMP spending (Fig. 3.4).

The impact of EPL reform on the employment rate is subject to large uncertainties. The effect is very small and negative if estimates from aggregate employment equations are used, reflecting the mechanism that in the short run, less strict EPL can induce more firings. However, when the overall impact is obtained by aggregating the impacts across separate segments of the population—either by educational

[12]In addition to the baseline results based on demographic groups, the predicted impacts for the employment rate and the core set of policies are shown for two alternative approaches: (i) results obtained for the overall employment rate; and (ii) results obtained for skill groups.

Table 3.4 The impact of reforms on GDP per capita at different horizons

Structural policy areas	Size of a typically observed reform	Total effect on GDP per capita		
		After 5 years	After 10 years	After full convergence (long run)
Product market regulation		**0.72**	**1.02**	**2.09**
ETCR (0-6, 6 is strictest)	−0.31	0.72	1.02	2.09
Intermediate policy channels mainly affecting productivity		**0.87**	**1.34**	**2.86**
Openness (perc. of GDP)	4.01	0.79	1.17	2.40
R&D (business exp.) (perc. of GDP)	0.10	0.09	0.17	0.46
Investment specific policies		**0.28**	**0.38**	**1.25**
Corporate tax (as perc. of GDP)	−0.98	0.28	0.38	1.25
Labour market policies		**2.88**	**4.03**	**5.78**
Labour market regulations		**0.22**	**0.57**	**1.83**
EPL (regular contr., 0-6, 6 is strictest)	−0.30	0.22	0.57	1.83
Tax-benefit and activation policies		**1.39**	**1.74**	**2.10**
Unemployment benefits (perc. of earnings)	−1.42	0.31	0.42	0.45
ALMP spending (per unemployed, as perc. of GDP/capita)	3.18	0.46	0.57	0.85
Tax wedge (perc.points)	−2.28	0.36	0.45	0.47
Tax wedge (single) (perc.points)	−1.39	0.25	0.31	0.32
Wage setting institutions		**0.58**	**0.79**	**0.86**
Excess coverage (perc.points)	−1.89	0.09	0.14	0.15
Minimum wage (perc. of median)	−2.48	0.49	0.66	0.70
Labour market policies for		**0.69**	**0.92**	**0.99**
Family benefits in kind (perc. of GDP)	0.11	0.17	0.23	0.24
Maternity leave weeks	4.83	0.42	0.57	0.61
Legal retirement age	0.57	0.10	0.13	0.14

Notes: Typically observed reforms are measured here by the average of all beneficial 2-year policy changes that were observed over two consecutive years in the sample. The total GDP/capita effect uses the employment effects from the aggregation across demographic groups, and it uses the formula in Eq. (3.5) to aggregate across supply side components

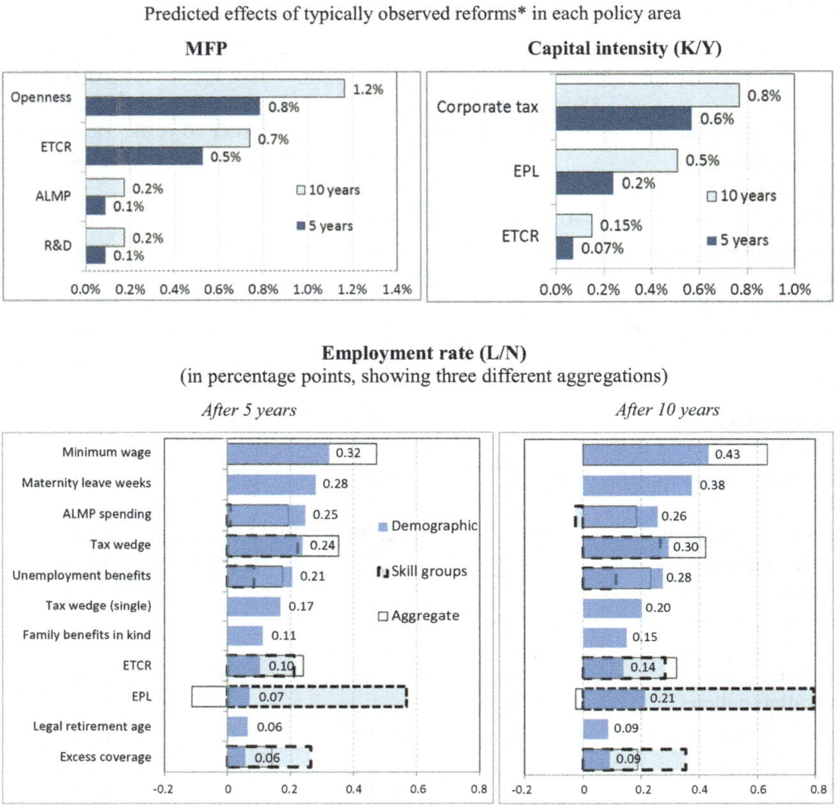

Fig. 3.3 Effects of improving structural policy areas: details by supply side components after 5 and 10 years. Notes: *Typically observed reforms are measured as the average improvements in the policy indicators over all 2 year windows that show improvements in both periods (see Table 3.4, column 2). The employment rate effects use all three aggregation approaches, and the size of the effects is indicated by numbers for the aggregation using demographic groups

attainment levels or by demographic groups—positive effects can be identified, up to half a percentage point. Uncertainties about the average employment impact of EPL have also been emphasised in earlier findings in the literature (Boeri et al. 2015).

3.4.3.2 Country-Specific Effects in the New Framework

The new simulation framework allows for country heterogeneity in three different ways. First, heterogeneous effects may results from different reform intensity. Second, heterogeneous effects may occur through the interaction of wage setting institutions. The effect of the labour tax wedge is found to depend on the level of excess coverage of wage bargaining (Gal and Theising 2015; de Serres et al. 2014).

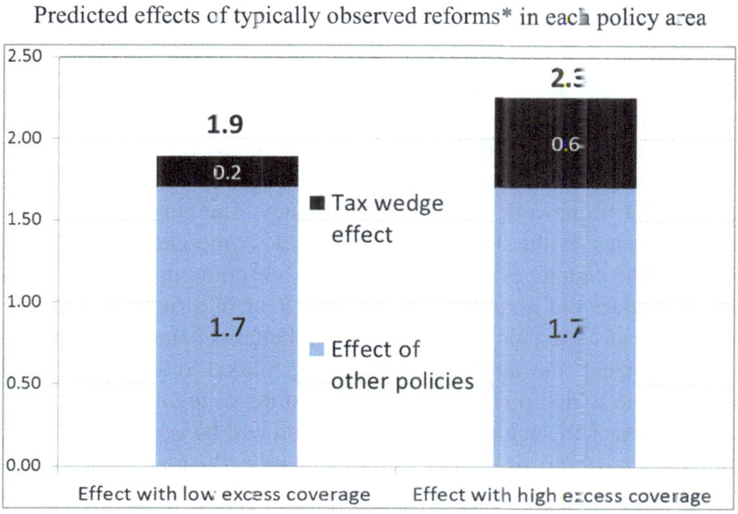

Fig. 3.4 Employment effects of tax wedge reforms in a low vs. high excess coverage country. Notes: *Typically observed reforms are measured as the average improvements in the policy indicators over all 2 year windows that show improvements in both years. The low and high excess coverage country corresponds to the 25th and 75th percentile of the excess coverage distribution in 2011 (Poland and Greece, respectively)

The payoffs from lowering the average labour tax wedge can be substantially higher for countries with higher excess coverage. The gains in the employment rate from a cut in the labour tax wedge (a reduction corresponding to the average observed over two consecutive years) are by 0.4 percentage point larger for a country with a high excess coverage than for one where it is low (Fig. 3.4).

Finally, heterogeneous effects may result from differences in the age, gender and skill composition of the population. In principle, they can be another source of country-specificity in the framework, as the labour market results show heterogeneity across these groups. However, these effects are rather small in practice. For instance, using the lowest and the highest shares of the most responsive groups to policies (i.e. youth or low educated) makes only a marginal difference (0.1–0.2 percentage point) for the final impact on aggregate employment (these results are not reported here). Hence in practice, differences in the relative size of these demographic groups, as well as in the skill composition of countries have only limited effects on per capita income. This serves as one more motivation to expand the framework with more non-linear effects and interactions between policy areas.

3.5 Conclusion

This chapter describes and discusses a new simulation framework that quantifies the impact of structural reforms on per capita income. Compared to earlier attempts, the new framework developed in this chapter broadens the range of quantifiable reforms, updates the underlying empirical relationships, covers the post-crisis period and improves the framework's internal consistency. The chapter presents the new coefficient estimates on the three main supply-side components (MFP, capital and employment). The chapter is a step in a gradual, on-going process to continuously improve and update the quantification of the effect of structural reforms on per capita income levels. Further work is needed to better account for country-specific effects and to extend the analysis to emerging market economies. Last but not least, the extent to which the macroeconomic estimates are consistent with results obtained on the basis of sector- and firm-level data will be verified in future work.

Using typical past reforms as a basis for simulation, the new framework provides a number of results for the main policy variables. First, 5 years after the reforms, product market regulation has the largest overall single policy impact. However, the combined impact of all labour market policies is considerably larger than that of product market regulation and the remaining policies combined (corporate taxes and R&D spending). Some specific policies only have a minor impact on per capita income levels. They include the legal retirement age and business spending on R&D.

Second, policy impacts can differ at different horizons. For some policies, the overall long-term effects on GDP per capita can be considerably larger than the 5- to 10-year impacts. This is particularly the case of policies that influence GDP per capita through capital deepening (product market regulation, employment protection legislation and spending on active labour market policies). The long-term impact of other policies, mostly labour market policies transiting only via the employment rate channel, materialises at shorter horizon.

Third, the new framework shows the determinants of policies through the separate supply-side channels.

Fourth, different policies have different impacts on the separate supply-side channels. For instance, corporate taxes have a much larger impact on investment than product market regulations. The impact of legal retirement age on the employment rate is roughly 5 times smaller than that found for minimum wages, maternity leave weeks or ALMP spending.

Finally, there is no robust relationship between employment protection legislation reform and the aggregate employment rate. Some policy areas (family benefits, pension age) can be assessed and included in the framework only by demographic groups. Hence as a benchmark in future quantification exercises, the effects found when aggregating across demographic groups could be used.

Appendix: Calculating Total Policy Impacts on Per Capita Income

Theoretical Considerations

In the new framework, similarly to previous frameworks, structural policies affect per capita income through the supply side components. The appropriate aggregation across the components is straightforward in a standard neo-classical model with a Cobb-Douglas aggregate production of the following form:

$$Y = K^{\alpha}(hL)^{1-\alpha}, \quad 0 < \alpha < 1 \tag{3.1}$$

with h denoting labour-augmenting (Harrod-neutral) technological progress. Note that the empirical construction of the MFP measure that is used for the estimations relies on the formulation in Eq. (3.1).[13] However, under the assumption of constant returns to scale, Eq. (3.1) can be rewritten in the following way:

$$Y = MFP\left(K^{\alpha}L^{1-\alpha}\right) \tag{3.2}$$

where there is a very close link between multi-factor productivity (MFP) and h:$MFP = h^{1-\alpha}$. Introducing per capita measures and after\vadjust{\pagebreak} some rearrangements, per capita income can be expressed as a function of MFP, the capital-output ratio ($^{K}/_{Y}$) and the employment rate ($^{L}/_{N_{wa}}$):

$$\ln\left(\frac{Y}{N_{pop}}\right) = \frac{1}{1-\alpha}\ln(MFP) + \frac{\alpha}{1-\alpha}\ln\left(\frac{K}{Y}\right) + \ln\left(\frac{L}{N_{wa}}\right) + \ln\left(\frac{N_{wa}}{N_{pop}}\right) \tag{3.3}$$

where N_{pop} and N_{wa} stand for total population and working age population, respectively.

The advantage of this formulation is that in a standard setting, all components are separable and independent from each other. Specifically, the capital-output ratio does not depend on either productivity or employment, neither is the employment rate influenced by productivity or capital.[14]

---

[13]MFP used for the estimations is calculated as follows:

$$\ln(MFP_t) = \ln(Y_t)/(1-\alpha) - \ln(L_t) - \ln\left(CLF_t - \alpha/(1-\alpha)\ln(K)_t,\right.$$

where CLF adjusts labour input for people working but not living in the country or those working abroad for domestic companies $\alpha = 0.33$, the standard value in the literature and fixed across countries and over time for ensuring comparability in a simple manner.

[14]Considering capital intensity, when r is the real interest rate, the capital-output ratio in equilibrium is given by $\frac{K}{Y} = \frac{\alpha}{r}$. In a more elaborate setting, the real interest rate can be replaced by the user cost of capital, which includes the relative price of investment goods and corporate

For simulating the effects of changes in policies, the above equation will be used in growth rates:

$$\Delta\ln\left(\frac{Y}{N_{pop}}\right)=\frac{1}{1-\alpha}\Delta\ln(MFP)+\frac{\alpha}{1-\alpha}\Delta\ln\left(\frac{K}{Y}\right)+\Delta\ln\left(\frac{L}{N_{wa}}\right)+\Delta\ln\left(\frac{N_{wa}}{N_p}\right) \tag{3.4}$$

where Δ captures differences over time, which can be interpreted as percentage changes. As mentioned above, MFP in our empirical framework uses the Harrod-neutral specification. Hence Eq. (3.4) can be rewritten as follows:

$$\Delta\ln\left(\frac{Y}{N_{pop}}\right)=\Delta\ln(h)+\frac{\alpha}{1-\alpha}\Delta\ln\left(\frac{K}{Y}\right)+\Delta\ln\left(\frac{L}{N_{wa}}\right)+\Delta\ln\left(\frac{N_{wa}}{N_p}\right) \tag{3.5}$$

Similar to the calculation of MFP a standard value for capital elasticity is set in the simulations ($\alpha = 0.33$). The last term capturing the share of working age population will be assumed to be unchanged over the simulation horizon. Alternatively, demographic projections by the United Nations could be used over the projection horizon (long-term scenarios project of the OECD, see Johansson et al. 2013).

Practical Considerations

MFP and capital deepening are measured in logarithms, while the employment rate is measured in percentage points (between 0 and 100). The simulation framework requires that the reform impacts are expressed in log-points for each supply side component, Percentage point changes in the employment rate are thus transformed into log-points by dividing the changes in the employment rate by the latest observed employment rate for the working age population L/N_{wa} (which was 67% in 2013, averaged across all countries in the sample):

$$\Delta\ln\left(L/N_{wa}\right)=\frac{\Delta\left(L/N_{wa}\right)}{L/N_{wa}}$$

Another issue about aggregation is how to obtain the aggregate employment effect from the demographic and skill groups of the population. Policy effects for

taxes as further determinants. In addition, excessive regulation can introduce frictions that suppress capital accumulation—a mechanism that can be captured by product and labour market regulation indicators. As for the employment rate, both labour supply and labour demand determinants enter as policy channels in equilibrium (hence no need to include wages or productivity on top of them).

these groups are aggregated using the groups' weight in the working age population. For the illustrative simulations presented in this paper, the population structure of the average OECD country is used in the latest available year.

References

Adalet-McGowan M, Andrews D (2015) Labour market mismatch and labour productivity: evidence from PIAAC data. OECD Economics Department working paper 1209
Addison JT, Ozturk OD (2012) Minimum wages, labor market institutions and female employment: a cross-country analysis. Ind Labor Relat Rev 65(4):779–809
Autor DH, Kerr WR, Kugler AD (2007) Does employment protection reduce productivity? Evidence from US States. Econ J 117(521):189–217
Barnes S, Bouis R, Briard P, Dougherty S, Eris M (2013) The GDP impact of reform: a simple simulation framework. OECD Economics Department working paper 834
Bassanini A, Duval R (2006) Employment patterns in OECD countries: reassessing the role of policies and institutions. OECD Social, Employment and Migration working paper 35
Bassanini A, Nunziata L, Venn D (2009) Job protection legislation and productivity growth in OECD countries. Econ Policy 24(58):249–402
Boeri T, Cahuc P, Zylberberg A (2015) The costs of flexibility-enhancing structural reforms: a literature review. OECD Economics Department Working Papers, No. 1264. OECD Publishing, Paris. http://dx.doi.org/10.1787/5jrs558c5r5f-en
Bouis R, Duval R (2011) Raising potential growth after the crisis. OECD Economics Department working paper 835
Cingano F, Leonardi M, Messina J, Pica G (2010) The effect of employment protection legislation and financial market imperfections on investment: evidence from a firm-level panel of EU countries. Econ Policy 25(61):117–163
Cingano F, Leonardi M, Messina J, Pica G (2015) Employment protection legislation, capital investment and access to credit: evidence from Italy. Econ J 126(595):1798–1822
De Serres A, Hijzen A, Murtin F (2014) Unemployment and the coverage extension of collective wage agreements. Eur Econ Rev 71:52–66
Dougherty S, Frisancho Robles VC, Krishna K (2011) Employment protection legislation and plant-level productivity in India. NBER working paper 17693
Égert B (2017a) Regulation, institutions and productivity: new macroeconomic evidence from OECD countries. OECD Economics Department working paper 1393
Égert B, (2017b) Regulation, institutions and aggregate investment: new evidence from OECD countries. OECD Economics Department working paper 1392
Égert B, Gal P (2016) The quantification of structural reforms: introducing country-specific policy effects. OECD Economics Department working paper 1354
Gal P, Theising A (2015) The macroeconomic impact of policies on labor market outcomes in OECD countries: a reassessment. OECD Economics Department working paper 1271
Jaumotte F (2003) Labour force participation of women: empirical evidence on the role of policy and other determinants in OECD countries. OECD Econ Stud 37:51–108
Johansson A, Guillemette Y, Murtin F, Turner D, Nicoletti G, de la Maisonneuve C, Bagnoli P, Bousquet G, Spinelli F (2013) Long-term growth scenarios. OECD Economics Department working paper 1000
Neumark D (2015) The effects of minimum wages on employment. Federal Reserve Bank of San Francisco Economic Letter, 2015-37

OECD (2015a) Quantification of structural reforms. ECO/CPE/WP1/2015(5)

OECD (2015b) OECD employment outlook. OECD, Paris

Rincon-Aznar A, Siebert WS (2012) Employment production, productivity, wages and jobs in Europe. INDICSER discussion paper 36

Chapter 4
The Impact of Structural Reforms in the EU

Jan in't Veld, Janos Varga, and Werner Roeger

4.1 Introduction

The gradual decline in potential growth rates has provided an impetus for structural reforms with the aim to raise growth. Structural reforms can boost growth and employment and help reinvigorate growth in the EU.

This chapter provides a quantitative assessment of the potential macroeconomic impact of reforms using a semi-endogenous growth model specifically adapted for the analysis of structural reforms, and which includes an R&D production sector. The model follows the structure of Roeger et al. (2008) in a multi-country setting (Varga et al. 2014), and includes the EU Member States individually and the rest of the world as a single separate region, thus allowing an analysis of spillover effects in a context of simultaneous reforms. Previous exercises using this model have shown that structural reforms can have sizeable macroeconomic effects.[1] Similar conclusions have been reached in other studies which have quantified the potential gains from EU structural reforms through regression analysis and/or model simulations of exogenous productivity or aggregate mark-up shocks.[2]

The views expressed in this chapter are those of the authors and should not be attributed to the European Commission. The underlying work to this chapter has also been published in European Commission (2013a, 2016).

[1] See Roeger et al. (2008) and D'Auria et al. (2009) for the effect of standardized structural reforms across the European Union Member States. European Commission (2013a) and Varga et al. (2014) apply the same benchmarking methodology as this chapter but only for a selected number of euro area countries.

[2] See e.g. Bouis and Duval (2011) and Barkbu et al. (2012).

J. in't Veld (✉) · J. Varga · W. Roeger
European Commission, Brussels, Belgium
e-mail: Jan.Intveld@ec.europa.eu; Janos.Varga@ec.europa.eu; Werner.Roeger@ec.europa.eu

J. de Haan, J. Parlevliet (eds.), *Structural Reforms*,
https://doi.org/10.1007/978-3-319-74400-1_4

The model is then applied in a benchmarking exercise based on structural indicators of labour and product markets, using a distance-to-frontier approach to quantify the potential for reform by assuming a gradual and partial closure of the gap vis-à-vis the average of the three best EU performers. Crucially, to avoid setting unrealistic and/or unattainable targets, the scenarios involve only half of the gaps being gradually closed. Assuming the results are roughly linear, more ambitious reforms closing the full gap would double the effects, while reforms closing only part of the gap can be expected to have a proportionally lower impact. In a second application, results are shown of an impact assessment of actual reform measures in four Member States.

The chapter is structured as follows. The next section describes the model and calibration, Sect. 4.3 outlines our benchmarking methodology, and describes the reform areas and the corresponding transmission mechanism in the model. Section 4.4 then shows results from an impact assessment of selected reform measures in Italy, France, Spain and Portugal. The final section concludes.

4.2 The Model

In order to assess the impact of various structural reforms like greater competition in the final goods sector, reducing administrative entry barriers in the intermediate sector, skill-upgrading of the labour force and increasing R&D subsidies, we develop a semi-endogenous growth model based on Jones (2005). This model is a closed economy semi-endogenous model with only one type of households supplying labour services for final and R&D goods production. We extend this model by introducing mark-ups for the final goods sector and entry costs for the intermediate sector. We also add two types of households, liquidity and non-liquidity constrained, a feature which has become common in dynamic stochastic general equilibrium modelling. We consider three types of labour skills that allow us to conduct more detailed human capital reforms. The model also includes a fiscal and monetary authority with the appropriate decision rules. Importantly, our extended model is a multi-country model in which individual country blocks are interlinked with international trade and knowledge spill-over effects. Finally, while the models of Jones (1995, 2005) were theoretical and illustrative, we bring our model to the data and calibrate it on actual data of the countries of interest.

The model assumes that the economy consists of households, final and intermediate goods producing firms, a research industry, a monetary and a fiscal authority. In the final goods sector, firms produce differentiated goods which are imperfect substitutes for goods produced abroad. Final good producers use a composite of intermediate goods and three types of labour, i.e. low-, medium-, and high-skilled labour. Non-liquidity constrained households buy the patents of designs produced by the R&D sector and license them to the intermediate goods producing firms. The intermediate sector is composed of monopolistically competitive firms which produce intermediate products from rented capital input using the designs licensed from the household sector. The production of new designs takes place in research labs, employing high-skilled labour and making use of the commonly available domestic and foreign stock of knowledge. Technological change is modelled as increasing product variety in the tradition of Dixit and Stiglitz (1977). A detailed description of the model and its calibration can be found in the appendix to this chapter.

4.3 Benchmarking Exercise

In the first exercise we apply a benchmarking methodology. Reform shocks are based on a set of structural reform indicators covering a wide range of areas, including market competition and regulation, R&D expenditure, skill structure, tax structure, labour market participation, unemployment benefit 'generosity' and active labour market policies. We define the potential for reform as a closing by one-half of the gap in these indicators vis-à-vis the three best-performing countries in the EU. To allow for implementation lags, all reforms are phased-in gradually. Closing half the gap implies that for almost all Member States there is potential to introduce further reforms, without imposing 'unrealistic' changes for countries that fall far short of best performance.

It is important to note a number of caveats as to the scope of this exercise. First, the focus here is on the main macroeconomic variables, in particular GDP, employment, trade balance and government balances. However, reforms can have important distributional consequences, with some measures affecting certain household groups more than others (Causa et al. 2016; Roeger et al. 2017). If poorer households are supported by compensatory measures, the economic gains may be smaller than reported here.

Second, while this benchmarking approach shows the potential that reforms could deliver, it is not an assessment of measures that have actually been taken. This is done in Sect. 4.5. The indicators used in this exercise are based on the most recent available data (for sources see Fig. 4.1), but these may not always capture some recent changes due to reforms that have already been adopted. In particular, some Member States (particularly some of the most vulnerable) have recently launched ambitious reform processes, the benefits of which would be included in the simulations presented here.

Third, there could be considerable time lags before actual reforms have a measurable macroeconomic impact. Delays in implementing reform measures are likely and it also takes time before measures have a visible impact on structural indicators (e.g. there is a time lag between creating more childcare facilities and an actual rise in female participation rates). In this exercise, we assume that reforms are implemented gradually. 'Speed limits' are applied, i.e. changes in mark-ups can be at most one percentage point (pp) per year. Likewise, tax reforms are phased in over a 5-year period, while educational reforms lead to only very gradual changes in

		AT	BE	BG	CY	CZ	DE	DK	EE	EL	ES	FI	FR	HR	HU	IE	IT	LT	LU	LV	MT	NL	PL	PT	RO	SE	SI	SK	UK	Average 3 best EU performers
Market competition	Services sector markups (%)	15.3	15.9	11.9	13.4	17.0	15.0	12.7	16.4	19.7	14.9	17.3	15.7	n.a.	15.2	13.8	14.1	17.6	18.2	19.1	10.6	13.9	15.4	15.1	20.8	13.3	15.2	17.2	12.2	11.6
Market regulation	Entry costs (%)	11.7	6.3	5.9	14.3	12.6	9.1	1.8	3.3	23.8	12.3	4.9	2.7	9.2	9.5	2.6	18.0	6.2	4.8	6.5	20.3	6.4	22.1	3.2	5.3	5.0	1.6	5.4	3.9	2.0
Tax reform	Labour to consumption tax revenue ratio	2.4	3.0	0.7	1.1	1.7	2.5	1.9	1.3	1.7	2.6	2.0	2.8	1.0	1.4	1.6	3.0	1.4	1.9	1.4	1.2	2.6	1.5	1.3	1.0	1.9	1.7	1.7	1.5	0.9
Skill enhancing reforms	Share of high-skilled (%)	6.4	7.9	6.4	9.1	6.0	9.2	7.5	11.4	7.3	9.8	12.2	8.5	4.5	4.9	9.3	4.2	9.9	8.2	7.2	3.5	6.3	6.0	4.1	4.9	9.0	6.7	5.2	9.4	11.2
	Expenditure on high-skilled education (% GDP)	0.4	0.2	0.2	0.4	0.3	0.4	0.5	0.3	0.4	0.3	0.7	0.3	0.2	0.2	0.4	0.2	0.3	0.3	0.2	0.2	0.2	0.2	0.3	0.2	0.5	0.4	0.2	0.3	0.5
	Share of low-skilled (%)	16.9	27.2	18.2	21.5	7.2	13.7	21.7	9.4	32.8	44.5	14.1	24.9	18.7	17.5	23.3	41.8	6.6	19.5	10.6	59.4	24.2	9.9	60.2	23.7	16.8	14.6	8.1	21.6	7.3
	Expenditure on medium-skilled education (% GDP)	3.8	4.0	2.1	4.8	2.8	3.3	4.8	3.1	3.2	2.6	4.3	3.5	1.6	2.8	3.5	2.6	3.4	2.6	2.5	6.2	3.9	2.6	3.0	1.7	3.9	3.1	2.5	3.4	2.9
Labour market reforms	Female non-participation (%, 25-55ys):																													
	- low-skilled	30.1	44.4	47.1	28.8	34.1	38.2	32.0	34.3	39.9	27.8	38.4	33.2	47.3	43.6	54.4	50.2	36.5	27.1	36.3	59.1	34.7	46.9	22.4	46.5	31.8	29.2	39.8	40.5	25.8
	- medium-skilled	12.9	19.6	18.1	20.4	17.2	16.2	13.9	17.4	27.8	17.8	17.6	15.3	22.9	20.6	31.2	27.7	14.9	22.5	17.3	21.7	15.4	24.8	8.7	27.6	11.6	11.4	18.9	19.8	10.8
	- high-skilled	8.8	9.0	10.0	11.2	19.1	11.1	7.3	13.6	10.9	10.3	11.7	8.7	8.0	17.2	15.8	17.3	4.5	13.3	9.1	10.8	7.3	9.3	4.8	8.5	6.6	4.9	17.1	11.8	4.8
	Low-skilled male non-participation (%, 25-55ys)	17.1	19.6	33.2	12.3	20.2	16.5	20.2	19.2	7.9	10.4	21.1	13.6	25.4	27.8	20.6	15.0	28.4	8.0	17.6	7.7	14.9	28.0	10.6	22.1	13.9	18.7	24.7	18.0	7.9
	Elderly non-participation (%, 55-64ys):																													
	- low-skilled	22.9	25.0	19.9	19.5	29.5	13.2	16.0	14.4	20.5	15.0	23.6	22.4	28.7	25.6	17.9	20.0	18.3	19.5	16.4	22.6	17.6	32.1	14.5	19.6	12.6	31.4	28.2	14.5	13.4
	- medium-skilled	10.5	10.6	11.2	7.0	11.2	8.3	8.1	9.3	9.9	6.1	9.7	11.9	12.9	14.0	6.7	7.6	11.4	13.9	10.3	6.8	6.9	15.6	4.2	12.3	4.8	15.9	11.4	7.1	5.0
	- high-skilled	5.5	6.5	6.7	4.6	3.5	4.6	4.4	4.5	7.5	3.5	5.4	5.6	8.0	7.0	4.1	4.4	4.0	4.6	4.3	4.4	4.2	4.6	5.0	5.0	2.6	7.3	5.2	5.5	3.2
	ALMP (% of GDP over unemployment share)	25.2	18.9	3.8	7.5	4.4	12.3	36.7	3.9	3.9	6.5	22.7	15.2	2.4	12.7	10.3	7.7	2.3	19.8	2.4	1.8	22.9	7.3	5.7	1.0	24.0	4.3	2.8	2.0	28.6
	Benefit replacement rate* (%)	68.8	65.1	38.5	n.a.	57.4	60.9	73.1	42.8	10.8	46.9	71.7	57.8	n.a.	30.1	74.1	9.2	52.5	72.5	56.6	52.8	71.7	45.6	48.8	25.6	64.3	61.0	39.0	62.2	52.3
R&D measure	R&D tax-credit rates	0.12	0.15	n.a.	n.a.	0.18	-0.02	-0.01	n.a.	0.01	0.34	0.25	0.38	n.a.	0.25	0.26	0.12	n.a.	-0.01	n.a.	n.a.	0.23	0.00	0.49	n.a.	-0.01	0.16	-0.01	0.17	0.41

Fig. 4.1 Structural indicators and benchmarks. Notes: * for benefit replacement rate: EU average. Darker shades correspond to larger gap vis-à-vis the benchmark. Sources: Services mark-ups, 2013: based on Thum-Thysen and Canton (2015); entry costs: starting business costs in % of income per capita, 2014: Doing business database. www.doingbusiness.org; Tax revenues, 2012: European Commission, Taxation trends in the European Union, 2014 edition, Luxembourg, 2014; Skill-shares, non-participation rates, 2013 or latest available: EUROSTAT, low-skilled correspond to ISCED 0–2 categories, high-skilled correspond to scientists and engineers (in natural science, mathematics, computing, manufacturing or construction), the rest of the population is defined as medium-skilled; Education expenditures: 2011 or latest available: EUROSTAT, corrected with the share of high and medium skilled shares; ALMP: 2012 or latest available: EUROSTAT; benefit replacement rates, 2012: OECD, Benefits and Wages Statistics. www.oecd.org/els/benefitsandwagesstatistics.htm; average of net replacement rates over 60 months of unemployment, 2012; R&D tax-credit rates, EL and IT: 2008 data, average over large and small firms (Source: Warda 2009), AT, BE, CZ, DE, DK, EL, ES, FI, FR, HU, IE, LU, NL, PL, PT, SE, SI, SK, UK: 2013 data, average over large and small firms; Source: OECD (2013)

skill levels due to cohort effects. However, the overall results may still overestimate how quickly reforms can have an impact in the short term, in particular at the current juncture, with depressed demand and tight credit conditions due to public and private deleveraging.[3] We therefore focus our discussion mainly on effects over 5 and 10 years, rather than on the short-term impact.

Fourth, the improvement in public finances due to higher tax revenues, and lower unemployment transfers, is gradually recycled through lower taxes on labour. In the model the debt-to-GDP ratio is stabilised in the long run through a fiscal closure rule that gradually reduces labour taxes to target the initial debt-to-GDP ratio. This stabilisation is not instantaneously, but only in the medium to long run, and the assumption of no change in the steady state debt ratio permits us to focus on the direct effects of structural reforms excluding debt-consolidation effects.[4]

Another reason why the results could be considered as an upper limit is that some reforms may have considerable budgetary costs which could not always be taken into account, as they can be difficult to quantify. As regards improving childcare facilities and all-day schools, budgetary implications have been included that are based on gaps in public expenditure on pre-primary education, but in many other cases budgetary costs could not be accounted for. To the extent that reform measures have additional costs which would have to be financed through higher taxes their macroeconomic impact could be smaller than those presented here.

4.3.1 Market Competition and Regulation

We distinguish between service-sector reforms and manufacturing reforms. The stylised facts from mark-up estimates indicate that mark-ups in services are larger than in manufacturing and vary more across countries (see Thum-Thysen and Canton 2015; Christopoulou and Vermeulen 2012). This finding is explained by high international competition in manufacturing, which limits the ability of manufacturing firms to reap large economic rents. While mark-up estimates indicate that there is scope for reducing profit margins in services, there also remains

[3]Some authors have also claimed the impact of structural reforms on economic activity in the short term can be counter-productive when the effective bound (ELB) on monetary policy rates is temporarily binding, due to the downward pressure on prices and increase in real interest rates [e.g. mark-up reductions in Eggertsson et al. (2014)]. In a larger macroeconomic model like our model, the contractionary short term effects of deflationary supply-side reforms at the ELB are smaller due to various mitigating factors: the impact of reforms on the profitability of investment, the disposable income of liquidity-constrained households and the competitiveness effect in external trade. The adverse real interest rate effect also depends on the short-term deflationary impact of the reform (which can be smaller for other measures; see European Commission 2014).

[4]A lower debt-to-GDP ratio reduces debt financing costs and allows for more fiscal space, which could be used for higher productive investment or lower taxes, both of which have positive growth effects. A scenario in which the fiscal closure rule is turned off for 25 years shows large improvements in public balances, which are then subsequently recycled though lower labour taxes.

some room for reforms in manufacturing. In the simulations, we also consider administrative entry barriers in the form of the costs of setting up a business, for which country-specific indicators exist.

Negative Mark-Up Shocks in Services Reforms which increase competition force firms to reduce prices by lowering mark-ups. Depending on demand elasticity, this raises output and increases demand for all factors of production (tangible capital, intangible capital and labour) in the medium term. The combination of price declines and increased factor demand yields comprehensive benefits. In particular, wage income rises due to higher employment and real wages. Real wages also benefit from higher investment rates. Because of higher labour-supply elasticities for low-skilled workers, the positive employment effects will be greater for the low skilled. Mark-up reductions also reduce export prices. In the short to medium term, the trade balance improves, largely due to a decline of private consumption in the short term due to a fall in economic rents. In turn, workers' consumption rises more gradually. With higher consumption, the trade balance returns to baseline values. Since competition-enhancing reforms are likely to be difficult to implement and it may take time before potential competitors enter the market, speed limits are introduced in the simulations which restrict a reduction of mark-ups to 1 pp. per year until the target is reached.

Reducing Entry Barriers for Start-Ups in Manufacturing By lowering profit requirements to cover initial costs, reducing administrative entry barriers increases the entry of new firms in manufacturing and the search for new business ideas. This is captured in the model as increased demand for patents, which comes from high-skilled workers. It is important to note that a reduction of entry barriers lowers fixed costs for firms and does not translate into price declines and productivity improvements at the firm level, but to a wider variety of goods produced in the country in question (product innovation). Nevertheless, domestic firms can benefit indirectly from the use of more innovative intermediate and investment goods. The aggregate real wage increases, because there is a higher proportion of high-skilled workers, but their wage also rises due to short-to-medium-term high-skilled labour supply constraints. These wage increases partly offset the gains from wider variety, due to product innovation. In the short term, the effects on GDP can actually be slightly negative, since increased demand for R&D leads to a reallocation of workers from the production of goods and services into research. However, the innovation resulting from R&D activities (as measured by the number of patents) yields marketable benefits in the medium term. Because of persistent growth effects generated by reduced entry barriers and increased demand for labour resulting in higher wage income early on, this policy already increases important tax bases and generates beneficial budgetary effects in the short term.

4.3.2 Tax Reform

Shifting the burden of taxation from labour incomes to consumption in a budget-neutral way makes returns to labour income more attractive and hence boosts employment, particularly at the lower end of the wage scale. Labour supply (and therefore wages) depends on the total tax burden, but shifting the burden away from wage income can reduce total distortions on employment decisions and leads to an increase in employment and output. It also improves competitiveness and mimics the effects of a currency devaluation on the terms of trade ('fiscal devaluation').

Real wage costs fall only temporarily in these simulations. Nevertheless, there is a positive effect on employment and GDP. A temporary increase in employment leads to an increase in the capital stock in the medium term, until the pre-existing capital-labour ratio is re-established. At this point, however, the marginal product of labour returns to its initial level and therefore real wages that firms are willing to pay return to the baseline level at a higher level of employment and capital.[5]

In our benchmarking approach, we define the benchmark in terms of the ratio of labour to consumption tax revenues. Rather than moving Member States towards the lowest labour tax rates in the EU, the reforms are designed to move them towards the lowest labour to consumption tax revenue ratio by increasing indirect tax rates and using the fiscal space to reduce personal income tax rates accordingly (i.e. ex-ante budgetary neutrality).[6] It should be stressed that the effects of a switch from labour to consumption taxation will depend on how different income groups are compensated for the consumption tax increase. In particular, if unemployment benefits and other transfers are indexed to consumer prices, the output and employment effects will be smaller.

4.3.3 Unemployment Benefit Reform

A reduction in the benefit replacement rate acts in the model like a reduction in the reservation wage, which puts downward pressure on wages and so boosts labour supply.[7] The calibration of the wage elasticity to unemployment benefits is based

[5]In our model the long-term output effect is greater than the increase in employment and capital accumulation, due to an endogenous R&D increase. Employment in the R&D sector is higher and the increase in output ('ideas/patents') leads to an increase in total productivity.

[6]The skill-specific implicit labour tax rates are obtained from EUROMOD, European Commission, Joint Research Center.

[7]The target is defined as the EU average replacement rate; this scenario is not included for Member States below the average.

on information from regression studies on the link between the unemployment rate and the benefit replacement rate.[8]

As the employment rate is lowest for the low-skilled group, the same increase in employment means a proportionally smaller reduction in leisure for this group and this puts less upward pressure on their wages. As a result, the decline in wages for the low skilled is larger than that for other skill groups, and the increase in their employment is also greater.

As regards the impact on other variables, the effects of lowering benefit transfers are similar to those of reducing wages. Lower benefits would reduce consumption by liquidity-constrained households, but this is more than offset by an increase in consumption by non-constrained households due to higher permanent income. The benefit reduction acts like a negative shock to wages, which increases the demand for labour and reduces labour productivity initially. Wages and productivity increase over time and return to their baseline values as investment picks up. Unlike in a model with exogenous technical progress, there is a small positive long-term productivity effect due to higher employment of high-skilled workers in the R&D sector and increased demand for new patents from the entry of new firms in the intermediate sector. The government balance improves directly as a result of the reduction in benefits and additionally as a result of indirect effects as the economy improves (i.e. higher GDP, consumption and employment).

4.3.4 Other Labour Market Reforms

Rising participation rates for women, low-skilled male workers and 55–64 year-olds increase the labour force. Such reforms form an important part of our simulated packages and yield significant improvements in GDP. They have different budgetary implications: improving childcare facilities to raise female participation rates has budgetary costs, while raising the retirement age reduces pension payments and provides budgetary savings.

Active labour market policies (ALMPs) affect labour market outcomes by improving the matching process, thus favourably affecting employment. Firms can perceive ALMPs as a reduction in non-wage costs, e.g. training costs borne by government (employment subsidy). ALMPs have direct negative fiscal effects on the government budget balance. However, as the positive effects of better training for the unemployed gradually translate into improved matching, such policies can rely on a certain amount of self-financing, though the net effect on the budget balance remains negative as ALMPs are modelled as intensifying over the simulation

[8] For example, results from Bassanini and Duval (2006) and Orlandi (2012) point to an average effect for a panel of OECD/EU countries of somewhat less than 0.2% from a 1 pp reduction in the unemployment benefit replacement rate. We obtain results at a similar order of magnitude, but somewhat differentiated across countries.

horizon to reach their target gradually. We calibrate this shock to match the panel regression estimates in Orlandi (2012) on the effect of ALMP expenditures on the unemployment rate.

4.3.5 Human Capital Investment

Changes in the quality of education and their effects on the quality of the labour force can be captured in the model as changes in the skill composition. Thus, in this exercise human capital investment is modelled as changing the relative weights of the different skill categories (or participation rates within categories). The increase of the average skill level in the economy (e.g. reducing the proportion of low-skilled) is modelled as a gradual change, accounting for the substantial lags in achieving that objective, including lags in reforming the education system and the gradual passing through of new cohorts onto the labour market. The reform cost is modelled as an increase in education-related expenditure.

As regards the impact of such a measure, the results of the model are in line with previous empirical estimates.[9] Other effects in the model imply that, given imperfect substitutability between worker types, an increase in the share of medium-skilled workers would have positive wage effects on other types, especially low-skilled workers.

Policies aimed specifically at increasing the share of high-skilled workers (engaged in R&D activities) are also modelled. Initially, a fraction of the additional high-skilled labour will be employed in the production of final goods (replacing less efficient medium-skilled workers). Over time, however, there is a dynamic increase in employment in the R&D sector because of a decline in the wage of high-skilled workers. This reduces the price of patents and stimulates the entry of new firms. In the medium and long term, increasing the high-skilled share results in a strong 'real' R&D effect in terms of R&D employment and patent growth, yielding the highest output effect as compared with other human capital investment scenarios.

4.3.6 R&D Investment

Firms undertake tangible and intangible (or R&D) investment. Policy can affect R&D investment; e.g. R&D tax credits reduce the capital costs of intangibles and increase R&D activities, resulting in the production of more patents, which can be used to open up new product lines. On the labour side, this is accompanied by reallocating high-skilled workers from production to research activities and

[9] In particular, de la Fuente (2003) estimates the impact of an extra year's schooling in the EU on long-term productivity at 9.3%, which is close to the result yielded by our model.

by increasing the demand for high-skilled workers. The size of the output effect will therefore depend crucially on high-skilled labour supply elasticity. Because of reallocation of high-skilled workers, the effects on GDP are small in the short term and positive output effects will materialise only in the longer term, once the R&D activities have been successfully transformed into marketable products. For countries with limited high-skilled labour and limited scope for substituting high-skilled for medium-skilled workers in production, the crowding-out effect of R&D subsidies will be greater. It is also important to note that R&D tax credits are not self-financing, but lead to a deterioration of the government balance in the short and medium term.

The model can simulate only the effect of public subsidies to private R&D, e.g. in the form of tax incentives. Subsidies to R&D in public research institutes or universities could have different transmission channels and less of a crowding-out effect because business-financed R&D programmes typically focus on applied research, while public institutes and universities typically concentrate on basic research programmes which are too costly or less profitable for private R&D firms.[10]

4.3.7 *Stand-Alone Implementation*

Model simulations of structural reforms that close only half the gap with best performers show that even such modest reforms can have significant macroeconomic effects. In order to quantify the spillover effects, the sets of reform shocks are first run through the model for each country separately, keeping all variables in other countries constant. This yields the impact of reforms when each country acts on its own, without spillover effects. In a second stage, spillover effects are taken into account by simulating the shocks for all countries simultaneously. Estimated in this way, the growth impact per Member State will be composed of growth spurred both by domestic reform and by a 'spillover' component resulting from other Member States reforming at the same time.

The first panel in Fig. 4.2 shows the impact of structural reforms on GDP for Member States when acting on their own after 5, 10 and 20 years. The other panels show the results for labour productivity, employment, and trade balance. Results are presented in the standard format as deviations from a 'no-reform' baseline. The simulated reform shocks boost GDP levels in the EA (EU) by 3.3% (3.0%) after 5 years, 6.3% (5.8%) after 10 years, and 11.0% (10.0%) after 20 years. Employment shows similarly high increases, up to 6.8% (6.4%) after 10 years.

Output and employment differences across countries closely reflect the size of the reform gaps as compared with best practice. Output effects are largest in those countries for which the benchmarking methodology shows the largest potential

[10]The model is calibrated on total R&D expenditure by taking into account the new ESA 2010 accounting framework. All R&D is undertaken by an aggregate R&D sector.

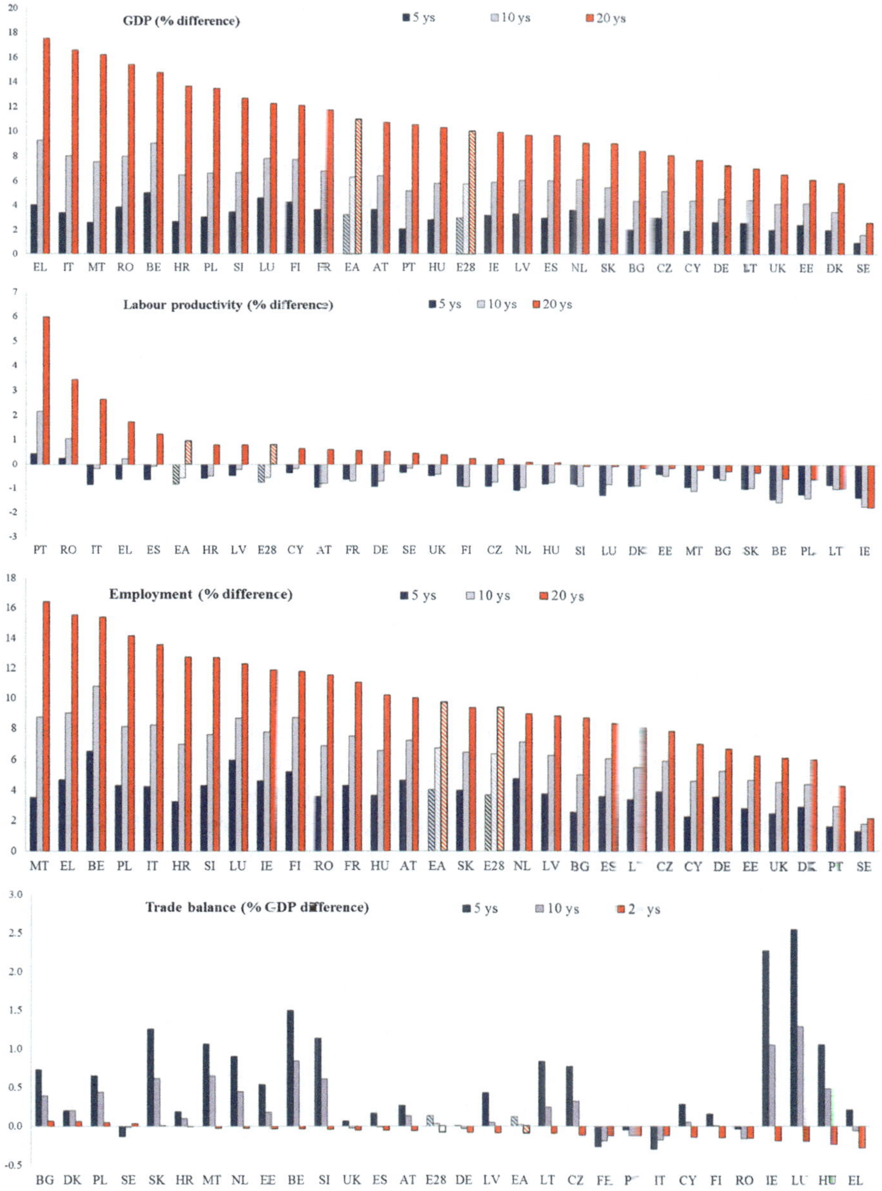

Fig. 4.2 Macroeconomic impact structural reforms: Stand-alone reforms. Difference from baseline. Source: Model simulations

for reforms, even when only half of the identified gaps are closed. To some extent, however, differences also reflect the degree to which the simulated reforms are biased towards measures which have a faster short-term impact on growth.

Education reforms improving skill distribution and participation rates yield positive results only in the longer term, with smaller GDP effects in the first 5–10 years, but up-front budgetary costs. Other reforms, such as shifting the tax burden from labour to consumption, can yield faster growth effects. However, as emphasised above, these scenarios may underestimate the timescale over which reforms can be expected to deliver positive growth effects, and more weight should be given to the medium to long-term effects. The effects after 10 years indicate that significant GDP and employment improvements can be realised in all countries if reforms are implemented.

The long-run gains are largest for Greece, due to the considerable scope for reforms identified in all areas by the distance-to-frontier approach (see Fig. 4.1). GDP is 17.5% higher after 20 years (9.2% after 10 years), even when only half of the gap is closed. Italy, Malta and Romania show similar large gains of between 17 and 15% after 20 years. Countries closest to the best performance frontier have the smallest output gains, although even there benefits from further reforms can be significant. For Sweden, GDP is 2.6% higher after 20 years, for Denmark, Estonia, and the UK between 5–7%. Other countries lie between these two extremes, with their output gains roughly proportional to the identified structural gaps.

There are some differences across countries in how output gains are related to employment gains. In those countries in which the main identified gap is labour force participation (e.g. Belgium), reforms have a proportionally larger employment effect. Labour productivity actually declines as participation of low-skilled workers increases. The largest gains in labour productivity are obtained in Portugal, Romania and Italy. Trade balance effects are positive in the short run when reforms are considered in each country acting on its own, and largest in countries where the identified gap is in e.g. the tax structure, where a larger shift in the tax burden from labour to consumption taxes improves competitiveness in the short run (e.g. Luxembourg). In the medium and longer run the demand effect comes to dominate as higher GDP raises imports and the improvement in trade balances evaporates.

Higher growth raises tax revenue and reduces transfer payments, and hence improves the government's budget balance. Budgetary effects are strongest in countries with an old-age participation gap, where a higher participation rate in the 55–64 age group and reduced pension payments can significantly improve the budget.[11] Costs of reforms can partly offset the benefits from higher tax revenues in the short term. For instance, the increase in female participation rates and improved skill structures are assumed to be accompanied by increased spending on childcare facilities and education, both measures involving frontloaded costs and yielding

[11] The baseline does not include pension reforms that have already been announced but will take effect later. To the extent that these will lead to higher participation rates and lower overall pension payments in future years, budgetary improvements can be expected.

sizeable benefits only in the medium/long term.[12] The standard fiscal closure rule in the model targets the initial debt-to-GDP ratio and the additional fiscal space created by reforms is used to reduce labour income taxes. This enhances the effects on growth. But the improvements in budget balances show the role structural reforms could play in restoring fiscal positions and reducing public indebtedness.

4.3.8 Jointly Implemented Reforms

While the above scenarios assumed that each country acts on its own demand effects will be larger when all EU countries would undertake reforms together while competitiveness gains will be much reduced. When considering simultaneous reforms in all EU member states, different types of spillovers can be examined

1. Demand spillovers whereby policy actions in one country (e.g. growth-enhancing structural reforms) influence import and/or export flows with partner economies. As structural reforms boost growth and domestic demand, reforms in one country lead to positive demand spillovers on others.
2. Competitiveness effects, e.g. resulting from measures that reduce labour costs or mark-ups in one country and improve its competitiveness. As these measures make other countries relatively less competitive, these effects reduce the positive demand spillover effect.
3. International financial flows caused by reforms in one country can have effects on others. For example, reforms that increase the rate of return on capital can lead to capital inflows until rates of return are equalised internationally. Exchange rate changes associated with international capital flows can induce further trade flows.
4. Knowledge spillovers resulting from the international diffusion of innovations will generally lead to a positive transmission of reforms that foster intangible capital formation. While these spillovers are less important in the short term, they play a longer-term role in the model for reforms that promote R&D. Based on empirical studies, we model domestic knowledge production (intangible capital) as resulting from domestic R&D efforts plus knowledge gained in the rest of the world.

These four types of spillovers are captured endogenously in model simulations of jointly implemented reform measures. The first two effects are the most important, and as the demand and competitiveness effects are counterbalancing each other the overall net macroeconomic effects are typically found to be relatively small.

A possible additional spillover effect that is not endogenously captured in the simulations relates to the contagion of risk premia. If structural reforms are

[12]In practice, however, alternative policy tools and financing strategies could be used to enact these reforms, thereby limiting the budgetary impact even in the short term.

successful in raising potential growth rates, this could change financial markets' perception of long-term debt sustainability and lead to a gradual reduction of sovereign risk premia.[13] While this is captured in the model, the sovereign risk premium depends on each country's own debt-to-GDP ratio and the model includes no additional cross-correlations of risk premia. Improving fiscal positions in other countries could reduce fears of defaults or debt restructuring and/or reduce liabilities through joint institutions such as the European Stability Mechanism, and may lead to an additional decline in risk premia. However, it should be recognised that these risk spillovers can also be negatively correlated (e.g. a reversal of earlier 'flight to safety' could raise bond yields in AAA-rated countries). All in all, the model may underestimate the impact on risk premia and disregards possible cross-country spillovers relating to this.

How are the results affected when all countries jointly introduce reforms? Figure 4.3 shows the GDP, productivity, employment, and trade balance effects for 'simultaneous' reforms. Compared to the 'acting alone' scenario in Fig. 4.2, results are very similar.

While simultaneous reforms lead to larger demand spillovers, improvements in competitiveness, by definition, have opposing effects across countries. As discussed above, the net spillover effect is the outcome of different channels partly offsetting each other.[14] Demand spillovers can boost exports in other countries and raise GDP, but competitiveness-improving reforms can have a negative impact. Trade balance effects are generally smaller. Lower net exports are partly compensated by higher consumption growth with simultaneous reforms, due to a shallower decline in the terms of trade.

In the case of simultaneous reforms, long-run productivity effects are larger, even in countries where most of the GDP gains were due to higher participation rates. The positive cross-country spillovers of R&D investment more than offset the negative productivity effects from higher participation of low-skilled workers.

Figure 4.4 summaries the GDP effects for the two different scenarios. Due to the counterbalancing channels the GDP effects after 5 and 10 years are almost identical to the 'acting alone' case in the previous section. After 20 years GDP is somewhat higher in the simultaneous reforms case (11.0 vs. 10.0 in the EU).

Which reforms have the largest impact? This is obviously related to the identified performance gaps. The relative contribution of different reforms also changes

[13]In the model, government bond yields depend on the current debt-to-GDP ratio. To the extent that structural reforms improve fiscal positions and reduce debt-to-GDP ratios, risk premia decline by three basis points for a one percentage point decline in the government debt-to-GDP ratio. While this is within the range of empirical estimates over longer horizons, in recent years there have been much larger swings in sovereign spreads.

[14]The direction of the impact of structural reforms on the current account is ambiguous from a theoretical point of view (see, for example, Vogel 2011 and Fournier and Koske 2010). Empirical evidence is also mixed. Jaumotte and Sodsriwiboon (2010) report a positive effect of labour productivity on current accounts, while the empirical results in Kerdrain et al. (2010) imply that such reforms have a negative impact on the current account position.

Fig. 4.3 Macroeconomic impact structural reforms: Jointly implemented reforms. Difference from baseline. Source: Model simulations

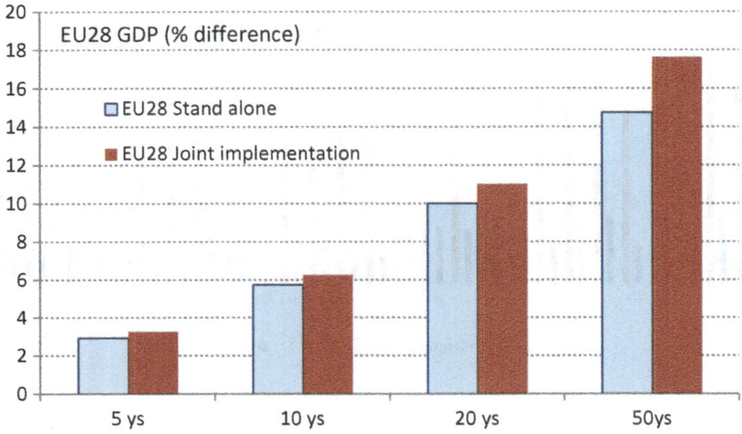

Fig. 4.4 Macroeconomic impact structural reforms: spillovers from simultaneous reforms. Difference from baseline. Source: Model simulations

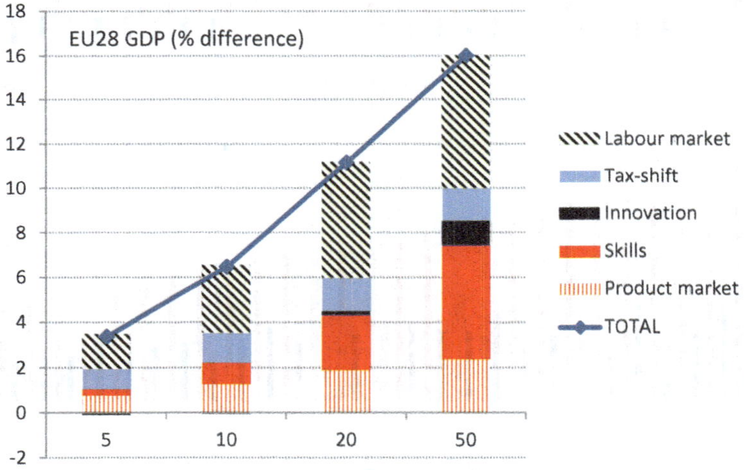

Fig. 4.5 GDP effects after 5, 10, 20, and 50 years, by reform areas. Difference from baseline. Source: Model simulations

over time, as Fig. 4.5 shows. In the short run, labour market reforms (increased participation, active labour market policies, and benefit reforms), tax reforms (shifting taxation towards indirect taxes) and product market reforms (higher competition in services sector and lower entry costs) have the largest effects. Which of these can deliver the fastest growth effects is not something that can be unequivocally answered by these model simulations, as it would crucially depend on implementation assumptions. In these scenarios, changes in structural indicators are introduced gradually and 'speed limits' are applied, as described in Sect. 4.2.

Larger output effects may be attainable in the short run if implementation could be speeded-up, and if product market reforms could be introduced quicker than labour market reforms then the relative ranking would be different. But it is clear that education/training (or skills enhancing) reforms cannot be expected to deliver significant growth effects in the short run. In the medium to long run though the effects of these reforms become sizeable. This also holds for innovation reforms (R&D promoting policies), which may not have a significant impact in the short to medium run, but can make a considerable contribution to higher output in the very long run (the final bar in Fig. 4.5 shows the effects after 50 years).

Concerning the distribution of GDP and productivity effects across countries, the largest GDP effects are found for Greece, Italy and Romania, the smallest gains for Sweden, Denmark and the UK. Productivity gains are largest in Portugal and Romania. The potential GDP gains would go some way in closing income gaps in the EU. In Varga et al. (2014) we use the model for a full closure of the performance gaps and find that this could account for between 67% and 99% of the current GDP-per-capita gaps between Mediterranean countries and the average of the three best euro-area performers. In the current exercise, reforms are undertaken in all countries and in a wider range of areas, and as best performers in one area can also improve in other areas, incomes are raised in all countries. Hence, convergence is lower in this exercise. Central and Eastern European countries tend to have a generally more favourable tax structure (higher share of indirect taxes) and higher participation rates, and can benefit less from reforms in these areas. The normal catching-up process and diffusion of technological progress can lead to further convergence in GDP-per-capita terms for these countries.

4.4 Impact Assessment of Actual Reforms

While the closing-of-the-gap simulations in the above exercise show the potential that reforms could deliver, it does not tell us much about the impact of measures that have actually been undertaken in recent years. This section summarises results from a study in which the impact of selected measures in Italy, France, Spain and Portugal is quantified. This uses detailed information on reform measures adopted and/or planned in each Member State, which are then mapped onto model variables and their impact simulated with the model.[15]

The exercise started with the reform measures put forward by these four Member States in their National Reform Programmes (NRPs). Reform measures were translated into quantitative shocks that could be simulated with the Commission's QUEST model. While some measures have been directly translated into model parameters, in other cases the translation was done through intermediary indicators that were then in a second step translated into model parameters. This is notably

[15]For detailed information, see European Commission (2016).

the case for some product and labour market reforms that have been quantified as changes in the OECD's Product Market Regulation (PMR) and Employment Protection Legislation (EPL) indicators and subsequently translated into mark-up or productivity shocks.[16,17]

Not all announced measures were quantified in this exercise. Translation of measures into quantified shocks was considered not feasible for some reforms, as the information provided was overall insufficient in terms of the quantitative elements and substantiation of the expected impacts or the description of the country-specific institutional details, timeframe and implementation strategies. In a few cases appropriate methodologies and reform indicators were also missing.

The simulated impact of the shocks is also sensitive to model assumptions. When monetary policy is operating at the effective lower bound, interest rates cannot be lowered to support structural reforms, and the effects may be smaller in the short run (see Jacquinot et al. 2017). As the interest rate effect for a single country in a monetary union will be small anyway, this would only make a significant difference when all countries were simultaneously undertaking reforms. At the current juncture, with high indebtedness of households and firms, the contractionary short run effects of structural reforms due to their deflationary effects may also imply smaller benefits in the short run. All this warrants extreme caution when interpreting these estimates, as these impact assessments are surrounded by large range of uncertainties.

Italy For Italy, measures included in respective National Reform Programmes from 2013, 2014 and 2015 were assessed. Italy's 2012 liberalisation package included measures to reform both the professional services sector and the energy sector. The implied reductions in the PMR indicators were translated into reductions in the mark-up. The professional services reform also increases labour productivity through improved allocative efficiency. The 2012–2013 simplification of public administration reform and the 2014 public administration reform included a range of measures facilitating the setting-up of businesses and the digitalization and simplification of bureaucracy. These provisions are expected to reduce administrative costs. The 2015 annual competition law and privatisation plan included the partial privatisation of the electricity company (ENEL), reforms to the telecommunication sector, changes in the monopoly position of Poste Italiane and a reduction in state ownership of the company. These measures were assessed through their impact on the PMR indicator.

Labour markets reforms in 2012–2013 targeted the rigidities and segmentation of the labour market by: (a) improving exit flexibility by modifying the legal framework on open-ended contracts and by introducing disincentives to use (or abuse) temporary and atypical contracts; and (b) strengthening active labour market policies. The first was captured through its impact on the EPL indicator, and the

[16]Based on elasticities provided in Thum-Thysen and Canton (2015), Canton et al. (2014) and European Commission (2013b).

[17]Based on elasticities provided in Bassanini et al. (2009) and Martin and Scarpetta (2011).

second, directly through the estimated increase in ALMP spending. The 2014–2015 reform of the labour market (Jobs Act) provides for a broad reform of the labour market, including revisions to labour protection legislation, the unemployment benefit system, the wage supplementation scheme, active labour market policies, and labour market contract types. Only the measures concerning labour protection legislation were considered in this exercise. In particular, the Jobs Act revises dismissal rules for new hires under open-ended contracts. This is captured through its impact on the EPL (EPR component) indicator. The other provisions of the act are not mapped in the exercise, because of the large uncertainties and difficulties in estimating their potential impact. Furthermore, the measures taken to ease the rules for temporary contracts were also not considered. The methodology adopted in this exercise to assess EPL reforms is based on Bassanini et al. (2009). The authors find evidence that the protection of workers with open-ended contracts has an effect on productivity growth but they do not find an effect of the regulations concerning temporary contracts. For this reason, the assessment of EPL reforms is based on the OECD indicator of the employment protection of regular workers. These measures of temporary contracts do not affect this indicator. The 2015 Education reform aims at improving the quality of the education system and reducing the dropout rate by, for example, increasing the number of permanent teachers. This reform is translated into a gradual shift in the skill distribution of the labour force.

Since 2012, Italy adopted a number of provisions affecting the tax structure. The main interventions involved an overall decrease in the labour tax wedge. In this exercise, we focus on the structural component of the tax reform and simulate tax measures in a budgetary neutral way with compensatory tax changes across the board. Overall, the tax reforms have a positive effect on GDP.

All in all, the reform measures should raise GDP by an estimated 1.3% by 2020 and raise employment levels by an estimated 1.5% (see Table 4.1). The measures also help to improve the government budget balance by 0.5 pps by 2020, in our simulation. A word of caution is needed concerning the short-term dynamic effects. According to these simulations, GDP in 2015 would already be 0.5% higher compared to a no-reform baseline, which seems hard to reconcile with the low GDP growth figures of recent years. This may indicate that our assumptions on the implementation of reforms are too optimistic and lead to an overestimation of the speed in which reforms have positive effects. While the short-run impact may be overestimated, this should not affect the long-run effects, which are clearly sizeable. The estimated GDP impact is smaller than the estimates from a benchmarking exercise in which half of the gap with best performers is closed as shown in the previous section. Under such further reaching reforms, GDP could be boosted by 4% after 5 years and 8.5% after 10 years. This indicates that the reform measures considered in the current exercise are going some way to closing these gaps with best practice, but still more could be done.

France For France, this exercise focuses exclusively on reforms contained in the 2015 NRP. On product market reforms, the quantification exercise includes the partial privatisation of network sectors (gas and telecom), which is captured in

Table 4.1 Simulated aggregate effects of selected reform measures

Italy									
Years	2013	2014	2015	2016	2017	2018	2019	2020	2025
GDP	0.11	0.28	0.54	0.80	0.95	0.99	1.10	1.29	2.07
Employment	0.03	0.27	0.66	0.97	1.18	1.29	1.39	1.47	2.10
Trade balance (% of GDP)	0.00	0.00	−0.06	−0.10	−0.08	0.01	0.06	0.07	0.07
Gov. balance (% of GDP)	0.06	0.11	0.26	0.32	0.39	0.36	0.37	0.45	0.69
France									
Years		2014	2015	2016	2017	2018	2019	2020	2025
GDP		0.11	0.20	0.25	0.26	0.30	0.32	0.35	0.40
Employment		0.14	0.25	0.29	0.29	0.30	0.31	0.31	0.34
Trade balance (% of GDP)		−0.03	−0.02	0.00	0.02	0.03	0.03	0.03	0.03
Gov. balance (% of GDP)		0.07	0.12	0.18	0.19	0.22	0.24	0.27	0.37
Spain									
Years	2013	2014	2015	2016	2017	2018	2019	2020	2025
GDP	0.17	0.37	0.59	0.72	0.86	1.01	1.16	1.31	2.06
Employment	0.31	0.58	0.78	0.89	0.98	1.07	1.18	1.29	1.90
Trade balance (% of GDP)	0.23	0.26	0.22	0.23	0.23	0.23	0.24	0.25	0.29
Gov. balance (% of GDP)	0.72	0.97	1.20	1.33	1.48	1.64	1.81	1.98	3.00
Portugal									
Years	2013	2014	2015	2016	2017	2018	2019	2020	2025
GDP	0.28	0.64	0.94	1.19	1.44	1.66	1.87	2.08	2.93
Employment	0.15	0.44	0.67	0.80	0.89	0.96	1.02	1.08	1.35
Trade balance (% of GDP)	0.21	0.32	0.34	0.35	0.35	0.34	0.34	0.34	0.34
Gov. balance (% of GDP)	0.75	1.06	1.28	1.46	1.65	1.84	2.03	2.23	3.28

Note: GDP and employment effects are expressed in %-difference from baseline; trade and government balance effects are expressed in pp. difference from baseline

the model through its effect on the public ownership sub-indicator of the PMR. Second, it includes the reform of the Sunday and evening openings in the Macron Law, through its effect on the overall PMR in retail. Third, reforms of regulated professions included in the Macron Law are captured through their impact on the PMR for professional services and their estimated effect on allocative efficiency. Fourth, the reform of regulated electricity tariffs is modelled as a reduction in the mark-up in energy. In addition, the authorities have launched an innovation tax credit for SMEs and given exemptions for innovative start-ups to stimulate research and development activity in France. These schemes are translated into a permanent increase in R&D-related tax credits.

The French authorities have started two programmes for fostering the employment of young and low-skilled workers. These measures were introduced as additional increases in ALMP spending. The French authorities also announced the creation of 60,000 additional jobs in education in the form of various measures including the reform of the priority education, for the most economically disadvantaged, the reform of secondary education system (collège), and the reform of study programmes etc. These measures should contribute towards improving the skills of the labour force, and boosting productivity in the longer run but their effects in the short run are negligible.

A reduction in the social contributions of firms is taking place over the period 2013–2017 through the 'Competitiveness and employment tax credit' (CICE) and the 'Responsibility and solidarity pact'. Both measures aim to reduce the cost of labour and improve the profit margins of firms, thereby boosting employment and competitiveness in the medium term. The CICE is a corporate income tax credit based on the salaries of low and middle-income earners. The Responsibility and solidarity pact cuts both employers' social contributions for low and middle-income earners, and also includes a reduction in corporate taxation. Reducing the tax wedge on labour and capital has a positive impact on employment and growth. What is taken into account here is the impact of the reform on the structure of the tax system, and the reduction in the ITR on labour is compensated by corresponding increases in other tax rates.

All in all, the simulated measures raise GDP by 0.4% by 2020 (see Table 4.1). There is also an improvement in the government's budget balance. While the short-term dynamic effects may be sensitive to assumptions on implementation speeds, the medium and long-run effects are clear. And given that this is only a partial assessment of reform measures undertaken in France, the effects are not insignificant. But for comparison, our estimates from a benchmarking exercise in which half of the gap with best performers is closed as in the previous section suggest that GDP could be boosted by 4% after 5 years, and 7.7% after 10 years. This indicates that the reform potential in France is large and that the measures quantified in this exercise are only going part of the way towards closing these gaps with best practice and therefore, that more could be done.

Spain Spain's 'market unity' law aimed at removing measures that may directly or indirectly obstruct the free movement of goods and services and the establishment of new operators throughout Spain. This is simulated as a reduction in the barriers for start-ups (entry costs) by 35%, which stimulates new entry, reduces fixed costs and leads to a reduction in mark-ups, so boosting GDP and employment. The 2012 retail reform made shop-opening hours more flexible, liberalised sales periods, and simplified licensing procedures for small retail outlets. Through a reverse engineering exercise we calculate the reduction in the OECD PMR indicator for retail and simulate the decrease in the mark-up.

The 2012 reform of unemployment benefits reduced the amount paid out to beneficiaries after more than 6 months from 60% of their last salary to 50%. In the model, this leads to an increase in labour supply and boosts growth and employment, with a corresponding improvement in the government balance as the reform affects both the expenditure (lower benefits) and revenue side (higher revenues from taxes). Reforms to employment protection legislation in 2012 led to a small decrease in the OECD indicator for the strictness of employment protection. This was mapped to a productivity shock with an overall positive but small effect on GDP and the government balance.

The 2013 pension reforms in Spain have: (i) restricted access to early and partial retirement, (ii) introduced as of 2019 a sustainability factor, which will curtail the initial pension benefit in line with expected changes in life expectancy and (iii) introduced a new indexation mechanism for pensions. These reforms were translated into an increase in the labour participation of older people progressively over time, which boosts growth and employment, particularly in the medium and long term. The reforms also lead to a sizeable improvement in the government balance in the medium and long term.

The 2012 tax reforms in Spain shifted the overall tax burden from labour to consumption, with positive GDP and employment effects. The 2014 tax reform cuts personal income taxes (PIT) and corporate income taxes (CIT) and has an expansionary effect in the model.

All in all, the aggregate effects of these measures are positive even in the short term. By 2020, GDP is 1.3% higher than in the baseline (Table 4.1). Similar effects are found for employment, while the government balance improves by about 2% of GDP, mainly due to the reform of unemployment benefits. There is also a small positive effect on the trade balance. The gains in output are significant and imply that on average up to 0.2 pps. is added to growth rates over the next 5 years. These estimates can be compared to those in the previous section where we reported a GDP gain of 3.2% after 5 years if, for all structural indicators, half the gaps with best performers are closed, and 6.1% after 10 years. This indicates that the reform measures quantified here go some way in closing the gaps with best practice, but could still be done.

Portugal Portugal has liberalised some of its highly regulated professional services, eliminating excessive restrictions and facilitating access to professions. The reforms have been gradually implemented since 2013, but some legal restrictions remain to the access of a number of regulated professions that in practice reduce the importance of the reforms. Thus the overall impact on the PMR indicators that cover these professions (legal, accounting, architectural and engineering services) is limited, and so is the corresponding reduction of the mark-up. During its EU/IMF adjustment programme, Portugal took measures to complete the liberalisation of services, facilitating market entry and competition. The reforms cover many different service sectors in areas such as retail and wholesale, tourism, business services, services related to the maintenance of equipment or real estate. Based on earlier work on the economic impact of the Services Directive, we estimate the impact on sectoral labour productivity in the affected service sectors at 1.8%. Administrative simplification through the Simplificar initiative is estimated to lead to a reduction in overhead labour cost, which is translated into a reduction in fixed labour costs in the model. Reforms in network industries include privatisations in the communication sector (post and telecom), and rail freight. These are captured through their impact on the PMR indicators and then translated into a mark-up reduction.

The Portuguese reforms to employment protection legislation in 2011 and 2012 have reduced the discrepancy between the protection of temporary and permanent employment contracts. We assess the impact using the OECD EPL indicator for regular workers (individual dismissals) and map this to a productivity shock based on the empirical study of Bassanini et al. (2009). The 2012 reform of unemployment benefits increased the coverage of the system and work incentives while reducing the maximum duration and generosity of the benefits after 6 months, which in the model reduces job search disincentives. This reform has a large positive impact on the government budget balance.

Tax reforms in 2012, 2013 and 2014 have led in most cases to increases in implicit tax rates, but in structural terms there has been a shift towards less distortive taxes with a positive effect on growth.

All in all, the reform measures assessed here raise GDP by 2.1% by 2020, and employment levels by 1.1%. It also leads to an improvement in the government's budgetary position of 2.2 pps., mainly through the decrease in unemployment benefits. Note that according to these simulations GDP was 0.9% higher by 2015 due to reforms undertaken in previous years. This may indicate an overestimation of the speed of implementation, and there is considerable uncertainty on this. But that would not affect the medium and long run effects, and these are sizeable.

The estimated GDP impact is in fact close to what was estimated in a benchmarking exercise in which half the gap with best performers is closed. Under such reforms, it was found that GDP could be boosted by 2.4% after 5 years, and 5.5% after 10 years. While this suggests that some progress has been made in closing these gaps with best practice, it also indicates the gap remains large at longer horizons and that more could be done to remove remaining structural rigidities, improve education, upgrade the labour force, and improve the skills distribution.

4.5 Concluding Remarks

The model simulations reported here show that large potential gains could be reaped from structural reforms. Euro-area GDP could be around 6% higher after 10 years if Member States adopt measures to halve the gap vis-à-vis the average of the three best-performing Member States in each of the reform areas considered. As it is based on only half the gap being closed, the simulated reform package should be seen as neither overly ambitious nor unrealistic for

Member States. A further closure of the gap would have proportionally larger impacts.

We also presented an impact assessment of actual reform measures taken in four countries in recent years. This complements other studies which typically use more stylised approaches. While these latter studies give estimates on the potential impact of structural reforms, the present analysis gives a more realistic assessment of the benefits of the reforms implemented or planned in selected Member States.

Appendix: Model Description

The model assumes the economy consists of households, final and intermediate goods producing firms, a research industry, a monetary and a fiscal authority. In the final goods sector, firms produce differentiated goods which are imperfect substitutes for goods produced abroad. Final good producers use a composite of intermediate goods and three types of labour, i.e. low-, medium-, and high-skilled labour. Non-liquidity constrained households buy the patents of designs produced by the R&D sector and license them to the intermediate goods producing firms. The intermediate sector is composed of monopolistically competitive firms which produce intermediate products from rented capital input using the designs licensed from the household sector. The production of new designs takes place in research labs, employing high-skilled labour and making use of the commonly available domestic and foreign stock of knowledge. Technological change is modelled as increasing product variety in the tradition of Dixit and Stiglitz (1977).

Households The household sector consists of a continuum of households $h \in [0,1]$. A share $(1 - \varepsilon)$ of these households is not liquidity constrained and indexed by $i \in [0, 1 - \varepsilon]$. They have access to financial markets where they can buy and sell domestic assets (government bonds), accumulate physical capital which they rent out to the intermediate sector, and they also buy the patents of designs produced by the R&D sector and license them to the intermediate goods producing firms.[18] The remaining share ε of households is liquidity constrained and indexed by $k \in (1 - \varepsilon, 1]$. These households cannot trade in financial and physical assets and consume their disposable income each period. For each skill group we assume that households (liquidity and non-liquidity constrained) supply differentiated labour services to unions which act as wage setters in monopolistically

[18]It is important to note that in a semi-endogenous model the number of intermediate goods varieties (A_t) can be interpreted in multiple ways. It corresponds to the total number of designs (or patents) invented by the R&D sector but at the same time it can be interpreted as the stock of ideas or as the stock of knowledge (or intangible) capital in the economy. It can be interpreted as an endogenous total factor productivity element as well.

competitive labour markets. The unions pool wage income and distribute it in equal proportions among their members. Nominal rigidity in wage setting is introduced by assuming that the households face adjustment costs for changing wages.

Non-liquidity-constrained households Non-liquidity-constrained households maximise an intertemporal utility function in consumption and leisure subject to a budget constraint. These households make decisions about consumption ($C_{i,t}$), and labour supply ($L_{i,s,t}$), the purchases of investment good ($J_{i,t}$) and government bonds ($B_{i,t}$), the renting of physical capital stock ($K_{i,t}$), the purchases of new patents from the R&D sector ($J_{A,i,t}$), and the licensing of existing patents ($A_{i,t}$), and receive wage income ($W_{s,t}$), unemployment benefits[19] ($bW_{s,t}$), transfer income from the government ($TR_{i,t}$), and interest income (i_t, $i_{K,t}$ and $i_{A,t}$) Hence, non-liquidity constrained households face the following Lagrangian

$$\max_{\left\{\begin{matrix} C_{i,t}, L_{i,s,t}, B_{i,t} \\ J_{i,t}, K_{i,t} \\ J_{A,i,t}, A_{i,t} \end{matrix}\right\}_{t=0}^{\infty}} V_{i,0} = E_0 \sum_{t=0}^{\infty} \beta^t \left(U\left(C_{i,t}\right) + \sum_{s\in\{L,M,H\}} V\left(1 - L_{i,s,t}\right) \right)$$
$$- E_0 \sum_{t=0}^{\infty} \lambda_{i,t} \frac{\beta^t}{P_t} \begin{pmatrix} \left(1 + t_{C,t}\right) P_{C,t} C_{i,t} + B_{i,t} + P_{I,t}\left(J_{i,t} + \Gamma_J\left(J_{i,t}\right)\right) + P_{A,t} J_{A,i,t} \\ - \left(1 + i_{t-1}\right) B_{i,t-1} \\ - \sum_s \left(1 - t_{w,s,t}\right) W_{s,t} L_{i,s,t} - bW_{s,t}\left(1 - NPART_{i,s,t} - L_{i,s,t}\right) \\ - \left(1 - t_K\right)\left(i_{K,t-1} - rp_K\right) P_{I,t-1} K_{i,t-1} - t_K \delta_K P_{I,t-1} K_{i,t-1} \\ - \left(1 - t_K\right)\left(i_{A,t-1} - rp_A\right) P_{A,t-1} A_{i,t-1} - t_K \delta_A P_{A,t-1} A_{i,t-1} - \tau_A P_{A,t} J_{A,i,t} \\ - TR_{i,t} - \sum_{j=1}^{N} PR_{fin,j,i,t} - \int_0^{A,t} PR_{\text{int},\ m,i,t}\, dm \end{pmatrix}$$
$$- E_0 \sum_{t=0}^{\infty} \lambda_{i,t} \xi_{i,t} \beta^t \left(K_{i,t} - J_{i,t} - \left(1 - \delta_K\right) K_{i,t-1}\right) - E_0 \sum_{t=0}^{\infty} \lambda_{i,t} \Psi_{i,t} \beta^t \left(A_{i,t} - J_{A,i,t} - \left(1 - \delta_A\right) A_{i,t-1}\right) \tag{4.1}$$

where s is the index for the corresponding low- (L), medium- (M) and high-skilled (H) labour type respectively ($s\in\{L,M,H\}$). The budget constraints are written in real terms with the price for consumption, investment and patents ($P_{C,t}$,$P_{I,t}$,$P_{A,t}$) and wages ($W_{s,t}$) divided by GDP deflator (P_t). All firms of the economy are owned by non-liquidity constrained households who share the total profit of the final and intermediate sector firms, $\sum_{j=1}^{N} PR_{fin,j,i,t}$ and $\int_0^{A,t} PR_{\text{int},\ m,i,t}\, dm$, where N and A_t denote the number of firms in the final and intermediate sector respectively. As shown by the budget constraints, all households pay consumption taxes ($t_{C,t}$), wage income taxes ($t_{w,s,t}$) and t_K capital income taxes less tax credits (τ_K and τ_A) and depreciation allowances ($t_K \delta_K$ and $t_K \delta_A$) after their earnings on physical capital and

[19]Households only make a decision about the level of employment but there is no distinction on the part of households between unemployment and non-participation. It is assumed that the government makes a decision how to classify the non-working part of the population into unemployed and non-participants. The non-participation rate (NPART) must therefore be seen as a policy variable characterising the generosity of the benefit system.

patents. When investing into tangible and intangible capital the household requires premium rp_K and rp_A in order to cover the increased risk on the return related to these assets.

The utility function is additively separable in consumption ($C_{i,t}$) and leisure ($1 - L_{i,s,t}$). We assume log-utility for consumption and allow for habit persistence.

$$U\left(C_{i,t}\right) = (1 - habc)\log\left(C_{i,t} - habcC_{t-1}\right) \tag{4.2}$$

We assume CES preferences with common elasticity but a skill specific weight (ω_s) on leisure. This is necessary in order to capture differences in employment levels across skill groups. Thus preferences for leisure are given by

$$V\left(1 - L_{i,s,t}\right) = \frac{\omega_s}{1-\kappa}\left(1 - NPART_{i,s,t} - L_{i,s,t}\right)^{1-\kappa}, \tag{4.3}$$

with $\kappa > 0$ and $NPART_{i,s,t}$ is the non-participation rate. Capital investment decisions are subject to convex adjustment costs, which are given by

$$\Gamma_J\left(J_{i,t}\right) = \frac{\gamma_K}{2}\frac{\left(J_{i,t}\right)^2}{K_{i,t-1}} + \frac{\gamma_I}{2}\left(\Delta J_{i,t}\right)^2. \tag{4.4}$$

The first order conditions of the household with respect to consumption, financial and real assets are given by the following equations:

$$\frac{\partial V_0}{\partial C_{i,t}} => U_{C,i,t} - \lambda_{i,t}\left(1 + t_{C,t}\right)\frac{P_{C,t}}{P_t} = 0 \tag{4.5a}$$

$$\frac{\partial V_0}{\partial B_{i,t}} => -\lambda_{i,t} + E_t\left(\lambda_{i,t+1}\beta\left(1 + i_t\right)\frac{P_t}{P_{t+1}}\right) = 0 \tag{4.5b}$$

$$\begin{aligned}\frac{\partial V_0}{\partial K_{i,t}} => &E_t\left(\lambda_{i,t+1}\frac{\beta P_{I,t}}{P_{t+1}}\left(\left(1 - t_K\right)\left(i_{K,t} - rp_K\right) + t_K\delta_K\right)\right)\\ &-\lambda_{i,t}\xi_{i,t} + E_t\left(\lambda_{i,t+1}\xi_{i,t+1}\beta\left(1 - \delta_K\right)\right) = 0\end{aligned} \tag{4.5c}$$

$$\begin{aligned}\frac{\partial V_0}{\partial J_{i,t}} => &-\left(\left(1 + \gamma_K\left(\frac{J_{i,t}}{K_{i,t-1}}\right) + \gamma_I\Delta J_{i,t}\right)\right)\\ &+E_t\left(\frac{1}{1+i_t}\frac{P_{I,t+1}}{P_{I,t}}\gamma_I\Delta J_{i,t+1}\right) + \xi_{i,t}\frac{P_t}{P_{I,t}} = 0.\end{aligned} \tag{4.5d}$$

Non-liquidity constrained households buy new patents of designs produced by the R&D sector ($J_{A,t}$) and rent their total stock of design (A_t) at rental rate $i_{A,t}$ to intermediate goods producers in period t. Households pay income tax at rate t_K on the period return of intangibles and they receive tax subsidies at rate τ_A. Hence, the first order conditions with respect to R&D investments are given by

$$\frac{\partial V_0}{\partial A_{i,t}} => E_t\left(\lambda_{i,t+1}\frac{\beta P_{A,t}}{P_{t+1}}\left(\left(1-t_K\right)\left(i_{A,t}-rp_A\right)+t_K\delta_A\right)\right)-\lambda_{i,t}\psi_{i,t} + E_t\left(\lambda_{i,t+1}\psi_{i,t+1}\beta\left(1-\delta_A\right)\right)=0 \tag{4.6a}$$

$$\frac{\partial V_0}{\partial J_{A,i,t}} => -\frac{P_{A,t}}{P_t}\left(1-\tau_A\right)+\psi_{i,t}=0. \tag{4.5b}$$

Therefore, the rental rate can be obtained from (4.6a), (4.6b) and (4.5b):

$$i_{A,t}=E_t\left(\frac{\left(1-\tau_A\right)\left(i_t-\pi_{A,t+1}+\delta_A+\delta_A\pi_{A,t+1}\right)-t_K\delta_A}{1-t_K}\right)+rp_A \tag{4.5c}$$

where $1+\pi_{A,t+1}=\frac{P_{A,t+1}}{P_{A,t}}$.

Equation (4.6c) states that households require a rate of return on intangible capital which is equal to the nominal interest rate minus the rate of change of the value of intangible assets and also covers the cost of economic depreciation plus a risk premium. Governments can affect investment decisions in intangible capital by giving tax incentives in the form of tax credits and depreciation allowances or by lowering the tax on the return from patents.

Liquidity-constrained households Liquidity-constrained households do not optimize but simply consume their current income at each date. Real consumption of household k is thus determined by the net wage income plus benefits and net transfers:

$$\left(1+t_{C,t}\right)P_{C,t}C_{k,t}=\sum_{s\in\{L,M,H\}}\left(\left(1-t_{w,s,t}\right)W_{s,t}L_{k,s,t}+bW_{s,t}\left(1-NPART_{k,s,t}-L_{k,s,t}\right)\right) + TR_{k,t}. \tag{4.7}$$

Wage setting Within each skill group a variety of labour services are supplied which are imperfect substitutes to each other. Thus, trade unions can charge a wage mark-up ($1/\eta_{s,t}$) over the reservation wage.[20] The reservation wage is given

[20]The mark-up depends on the intratemporal elasticity of substitution between differentiated labour services within each skill groups (σ_s) and fluctuations in the mark-up arise because of wage adjustment costs and the fact that a fraction ($1-sfw$) of workers is indexing the growth rate of wages π_W to wage inflation in the previous period $\eta_{s,t}=1-1/\sigma_s-\gamma_W/\sigma_s(\beta(sfw\,\pi_{W,t+1}-(1-sfw)\,\pi_{W,t-1})-\pi_{W,t})$.

as the marginal utility of leisure divided by the corresponding marginal utility of consumption. The relevant net real wage to which the mark up adjusted reservation wage is equated is the gross wage adjusted for labour taxes, consumption taxes and unemployment benefits, which act as a subsidy to leisure. Thus, the wage equation is given as

$$\frac{U_{1-L,h,s,t}}{U_{C,h,s,t}}\frac{1}{\eta_{W,s,t}}=\frac{W_{s,t}\left(1-t_{w,s,t}-b\right)}{P_{C,t}\left(1+t_{C,t}\right)}\quad \text{for } s\in\{L,M,H\}\,, \tag{4.8}$$

where b is the benefit replacement rate and $U_{1-L,h,s,t}$ and $U_{C,h,s,t}$ are the aggregate marginal utility of liquidity and non-liquidity constrained households with respect to leisure and consumption.

Aggregation The aggregate of any household specific variable $X_{h,t}$ in per capita terms is given by

$$X_t=\int_0^1 X_{h,t}dh=(1-\varepsilon)\,X_{i,t}+\varepsilon X_{k,t}. \tag{4.9}$$

Hence, aggregate consumption and employment is given by

$$C_t=(1-\varepsilon)\,C_{i,t}+\varepsilon C_{k,t} \tag{4.10}$$

and

$$L_t=(1-\varepsilon)\,L_{i,t}+\varepsilon L_{k,t}. \tag{4.11}$$

Firms: final output producers Since each firm produces a variety of the domestic good which is an imperfect substitute for the varieties produced by other firms, it acts as a monopolistic competitor facing a demand function with a price elasticity given by σ_d. Final output (Y_t) is produced using A_t varieties of intermediate inputs ($x_{m,t}$) with an elasticity of substitution $1/(1-\theta)>1$. The final good sector uses labour aggregate ($L_{Y,t}$) and intermediate goods in a Cobb-Douglas technology, subject to a fixed cost FC and overhead labour cost FC_L

$$Y_t=(L_{Y,t}-FC_L)^{\alpha}\left(\int_0^{A_t}(x_{m,t})^{\theta}dm\right)^{\frac{1-\alpha}{\theta}}K_G^{\alpha_G}-FC \tag{4.12}$$

with

$$L_{Y,t}=\left(\Lambda_L^{\frac{1}{\mu}}(\chi_L L_{L,t})^{\frac{\mu-1}{\mu}}+\Lambda_M^{\frac{1}{\mu}}(\chi_M L_{M,t})^{\frac{\mu-1}{\mu}}+\Lambda_{HY}^{\frac{1}{\mu}}(\chi_{HY} L_{HY,t})^{\frac{\mu-1}{\mu}}\right)^{\frac{\mu}{\mu-1}}, \tag{4.13}$$

$L_{L,t}$, $L_{M,t}$ and $L_{HY,t}$ denote the employment of low, medium and high-skilled in final goods production, respectively. Parameter Λ_z is the corresponding share parameter

($z \in \{L,M,HY\}$), χ_z is the efficiency unit, and μ is the elasticity of substitution between different labour types. Note that high-skilled workers can work in the final goods and the R&D sector as well, therefore the total number of high-skilled ($L_{H,t}$) should be equal to the number of high-skilled employed in the final goods ($L_{HY,t}$) and in the R&D sector respectively ($L_{RD,t}$):

$$L_{H,t} = L_{HY,t} + L_{RD,t}. \tag{4.14}$$

Our formulation assumes that investment in public capital stock (K_G) increases total factor productivity with an exponent of α_G set to 0.10. In a symmetric equilibrium, the demand for labour and intermediate inputs is given by

$$\alpha \frac{Y_t + FC}{L_{Y,t} - FC_L} \left(\frac{L_{Y,t} - FC_L}{L_{z,t}} \right)^{\frac{1}{\mu}} \Lambda_z^{\frac{1}{\mu}} \chi_z^{\frac{\mu-1}{\mu}} \eta = W_{z,t} - \psi_{almp,z} \quad z \in \{L, M, HY\} \tag{4.15}$$

$$px_{m,t} = \eta \, (1 - \alpha) \, (Y_t + FC) \left(\int_0^{A_t} (x_{m,t})^{\theta} dm \right)^{-1} (x_{m,t})^{\theta-1} \tag{4.16}$$

where $\eta = 1 - 1/\sigma_d$ is the inverse mark-up, $px_{m,t}$ stands for the price of intermediate goods and $\psi_{almp,\,z}$ is a shock variable to capture the effect of ALMP expenditures.

Firms: intermediate goods producers The intermediate sector consists of monopolistically competitive firms which have entered the market by licensing a design from domestic households and by making an initial payment FC_A to overcome administrative entry barriers. Capital inputs are also rented from the household sector for a rental rate of $i_{K,t}$. Firms which have acquired a design can transform each unit of capital into a single unit of an intermediate input. In a symmetric equilibrium, the respective inverse demand functions of intermediate goods producing firms are given as Eq. (4.16), therefore the first order condition is

$$\theta \eta \, (1 - \alpha) \, (Y_t + FC) \left(\int_0^{A_t} (x_{m,t})^{\theta} dm \right)^{-1} (x_{m,t})^{\theta-1} = i_{K,t}. \tag{4.17}$$

Intermediate goods producers set prices with a mark-up over marginal cost. Therefore intermediate goods prices are given by:

$$px_{m,t} = \frac{i_{K,t}}{\theta}. \tag{4.18}$$

The no-arbitrage condition requires that entry into the intermediate goods producing sector takes place until

$$PR_{\text{int},m,t} = I_{A,t}P_{A,t} + (i_{A,t} + \pi_{A,t+1})\,FC_A, \quad \forall m. \tag{4.19}$$

For an intermediate producer, entry costs consist of the licensing fee $i_{A,t}P_{A,t}$ for the design or patent which is a prerequisite of production of innovative intermediate goods and a fixed administrative entry cost FC_A.

R&D sector Innovation corresponds to the discovery of a new variety of producer durables that provides an alternative way of producing the final good. The R&D sector hires high-skilled labour ($L_{RD,t}$) and generates new designs according to the following knowledge production function:

$$\dot{A}_t = \nu A_{t-1}^{*\;\varpi} A_{t-1}^{\phi} (L_{RD,t})^{\lambda}. \tag{4.20}$$

In this framework we allow for international R&D spillovers following Bottazzi and Peri (2007). Parameters ϖ and ϕ measure the foreign and domestic spillover effects from the aggregate international and domestic stock of knowledge ($A^{*}{}_t$ and A_t) respectively. Negative value for these parameters can be interpreted as the "fishing out" effect, i.e. when innovation decreases with the level of knowledge, while positive values refer to the "standing on shoulders" effect and imply positive research spillovers. Note that $\phi = 1$ would yield the strong scale effect feature of endogenous growth models with respect to the domestic level of knowledge. Parameter ν can be interpreted as total factor efficiency of R&D production, while λ measures the elasticity of R&D production on the number of researchers ($L_{RD,t}$). The international stock of knowledge grows exogenously at rate g_{A*}We assume that the R&D sector is operated by a research institute which employs high-skilled labour at their market wage, $W_{H,t}$. We also assume that the research institute faces an adjustment cost (γ_A) of hiring new employees and maximizes the following discounted profit-stream:

$$\max_{L_{RD,t}} \sum_{t=0}^{\infty} d_t \left(P_{A,t}\Delta A_t - W_{H,t}L_{RD,t} - \frac{\gamma_A}{2} W_{H,t}(\Delta L_{RD,t})^2 \right) \tag{4.21}$$

where d_t is the discount factor. High-skilled workers are paid the same wages across sectors: $W_{H,t} = W_{HY,t}$.

Policy On the expenditure side we distinguish between government consumption (G_t), government investment (IG_t), government transfers (TR_t) and unemployment benefits (BEN_t), where

$$BEN_t = \sum_{s\in\{L,M,H\}} bW_{s,t}\,(1 - NPART_{s,t} - L_{s,t})\,. \tag{4.22}$$

The government provides subsidies (SUB_t) on physical capital and R&D investments in the form of a tax-credit and depreciation allowances

$$SUB_t = t_K \left(\delta_K P_{I,t-1} K_{i,t-1} + \delta_A P_{A,t-1} A_{i,t-1}\right) + \tau_K P_{I,t} J_{i,t} + \tau_A P_{A,t} J_{A,i,t}. \quad (4.23)$$

Government revenues ${R^G}_t$ are made up of taxes on consumption as well as capital and labour income. Government debt (B_t) evolves according to

$$B_t = (1 + i_t) B_{t-1} + G_t + IG_t + TR_t + BEN_t + SUB_t - R_t^G. \quad (4.24)$$

The labour tax ($t_{w,t}$) used for controlling the debt-to-GDP ratio according to the following rule

$$\Delta t_{w,t} = \tau_E \left(\frac{B_{t-1}}{Y_{t-1}} - b^T\right) + \tau_{DEF} \Delta \left(\frac{B_t}{Y_t}\right), \quad (4.25)$$

where τ_B captures the sensitivity with respect to deviations from b^T, the government debt target and τ_{DEF} controls the sensitivity of the tax-rule w.r.t. changes in the debt-to-output ratio.

Monetary policy is modelled via the following Taylor rule, which allows for some smoothness of the interest rate response (i_t) to the inflation and output gap.

$$i_t = \gamma_{ilag} i_{t-1} + \left(1 - \gamma_{ilag}\right) \left(r_{EQ} + \pi_{TAR} + \gamma_{\inf} \left(\pi_{C,t} - \pi_{TAR}\right) + \gamma_{ygap} \widehat{y}_t\right). \quad (4.26)$$

The central bank has a constant inflation target (π_{TAR}) and it adjusts interest rates whenever actual consumer price inflation ($\pi_{C,t}$) deviates from the target and it also responds to the output gap $\left(\widehat{y}_t\right)$ via the corresponding $\gamma_{\inf}$ and γ_{ygap} coefficients. There is also some inertia in nominal interest rate setting over the equilibrium real interest rate r_{EQ} determined by γ_{ilag}. The output gap is defined as deviation of capital and labour utilisation from their long run trends. Note that in our multicountry setting, members of the euro area do not have independent monetary policy. We assume that the European Central Bank sets interest rates by taking into account the euro area wide aggregate inflation and output gap changes in its Taylor-rule.

Trade In order to facilitate aggregation we assume that households, the government and the final goods sector have identical preferences across goods used for private consumption, investment and public expenditure. Let $Z_t \in \{C_t, I_t, G_t, IG_t\}$ be the demand of households, investors or the government as defined in the previous section, then their preferences are given by the following utility function:

$$Z_t = \left((1-\rho)^{\frac{1}{\sigma_{im}}} Z_{d,t}^{\frac{\sigma_{im}-1}{\sigma_{im}}} + \rho^{\frac{1}{\sigma_{im}}} Z_{f,t}^{\frac{\sigma_{im}-1}{\sigma_{im}}} \right)^{\frac{\sigma_{im}}{\sigma_{im}-1}}. \tag{4.27}$$

where ρ is the share parameter and σ_{im} is the elasticity of substitution between domestic ($Z_{d,t}$) and foreign produced goods ($Z_{m,t}$).

Calibration We calibrate our model in a multi-country setting for the member states. We select behavioural and technological parameters for the individual countries such that the model can replicate important empirical ratios, such as labour productivity, investment, consumption to GDP ratios, the wage share, the employment rate and the R&D share, given a set of structural indicators describing market frictions in goods and labour markets, tax wedges and skill endowments. Most of the variables and parameters are taken from available statistical or empirical sources and the remaining parameters are tied down by the mathematical relationship of the model equations.

We identify the intermediate sector as the manufacturing sector and the final goods sector as the aggregate of all remaining market sectors. The manufacturing sector resembles the intermediate sector along various dimensions. This sector is more R&D and patent-intensive, while a large fraction of manufacturing supplies innovative goods (in the form of investment goods but also innovative consumer goods). Final goods sectors, including services, on the other hand are typically not subject to large (patented) innovations but rely on organisational changes possibly in relation to new technologies supplied by the manufacturing sector. Also the two sectors differ in the degree of competition, with manufacturing showing smaller mark-ups compared to final goods sectors. Our calibration of mark-ups is based on Thum-Thysen and Canton (2015) using the method suggested by Roeger (1995). Using the most recent EU KLEMS databank the average mark-up for manufacturing is around 9%, while for final goods/service sector it is around 15% in the Euro Area. Concerning entry barriers we rely on estimates provided by the World Bank's *Doing Business Report.*

Database Empirical evidence on output elasticities has been provided by Bottazzi and Peri (2007) and Pessoa (2005). The growth rate of ideas has been obtained from Pessoa (2005) with the assumption of a 5% obsolescence rate. In our model, the R&D elasticity of research labour (λ) is determined by the wage cost share in the total R&D spending. We rely on Bottazzi and Peri (2007) to calibrate the knowledge elasticity parameters w. r. t. domestic and foreign knowledge capital. The authors do not estimate directly ϕ and ϖ, only the ratio between these coefficients and between ϕ and λ. These estimates together with the long-run growth rate of intangible capital and λ pin down the corresponding elasticities.

The calibration of the adjustment parameters in the labour market is based on estimates in Ratto et al. (2009). Labour force is disaggregated into three skill-groups: low-, medium- and high-skilled labour. We define high-skilled workers as that segment of labour force that can potentially be employed in the R&D sector, i.e.

engineers and natural scientists. Our definition of low-skilled workers corresponds to the standard classification of ISCED 0–2 education levels; the rest of the labour force is considered as medium-skilled. Data on skill-specific population shares, participation rates and wages are obtained from the Labour Force Survey, SES, and the Science and Technology databases of EUROSTAT. The elasticity of substitution between different labour types (μ) is one of the major parameters addressed in the labour-economics literature. We rely on Acemoglu and Autor (2011) who updated the seminal reference for this elasticity parameter by Katz and Murphy (1992, "KM" hereafter). While KM estimated that the elasticity of substitution between skilled and unskilled labour is about 1.4, Acemoglu and Autor (2011) argue for somewhat higher estimates in the range of 1.6–1.8 on the extended data sample of KM (from 1963 to 2008 as opposed to 1968–1987). We take 1.7 as our baseline value. The efficiency units are restricted by the labour demand equations which imply the following relationship between wages, skill-specific population and employment ratios, and efficiency units:

$$\chi_M = \left(\frac{W_{M,t}}{W_{L,t}}\right)^{\frac{\mu}{\mu-1}} \left(\frac{\Lambda_M}{\Lambda_L}\right)^{\frac{1}{1-\mu}} \left(\frac{L_{M,t}}{L_{L,t}}\right)^{\frac{1}{\mu-1}} \chi_L$$

$$\chi_H = \left(\frac{W_{H,t}}{W_{M,t}}\right)^{\frac{\mu}{\mu-1}} \left(\frac{\Lambda_{HY}}{\Lambda_M}\right)^{\frac{1}{1-\mu}} \left(\frac{L_{HY,t}}{L_{M,t}}\right)^{\frac{1}{\mu-1}} \chi_M.$$

In our baseline calibration low-skilled wages are obtained from the annual earnings of employees with low educational attainment (ISCED 0–2) irrespective of their occupation. High-skilled wages are approximated by the annual earnings of scientists and engineers with tertiary educational attainment employed as professionals or associate professionals in physical, mathematical, engineering, life science or health occupations (ISCO-08 occupations 21, 22, 31, 32). Earnings data of employees with tertiary educational attainment not working as scientists and engineers and employees with medium educational attainment (ISCED 3–4) irrespective of their occupation are taken to calculate wages for our medium-skilled workers in the model.

We use EUROSTAT for the breakdown of government spending into consumption, investment and transfers and we use effective tax rates on labour, capital and consumption to determine government revenues. In addition, we use estimates of R&D tax credits from Warda (2009) and OECD (2013). Monetary policy parameters are adopted from Ratto et al. (2009) while the bilateral trade data is obtained from the EUROSTAT/COMEXT database. Table 4.2 gives an overview of the major structural parameters discussed here.

Table 4.2 Calibration of main structural parameters

Variable/Parameter	AT	BE	BG	CY	CZ	DE	DK	EE	EL	ES	FI	FR	HR	HU	Source
R&D sector															
L_{RD}	1.5	1.5	0.6	0.3	1.2	1.5	2.1	0.9	1.0	1.2	2.2	1.6	0.7	0.9	EUROSTAT
R&D intensity (% GDP)	3.2	2.5	0.7	0.5	2.1	3.3	3.5	2.5	0.8	1.4	4.1	2.7	0.9	1.5	EUROSTAT
λ	0.4	0.5	0.7	0.5	0.5	0.4	0.5	0.3	0.9	0.7	0.4	0.6	0.9	0.6	Constrained by equations
ϕ	0.6	0.5	0.4	0.6	0.5	0.6	0.6	0.7	0.2	0.3	0.6	0.5	0.3	0.4	Bottazzi-Peri (2007)
ϖ	0.4	0.5	0.6	0.4	0.5	0.4	0.4	0.3	0.8	0.7	0.4	0.5	0.7	0.6	Bottazzi-Peri (2007)
ν	0.2	0.4	2.2	0.8	0.4	0.3	0.3	0.2	4.6	1.3	0.2	0.5	4.2	0.9	Constrained by equations
Final and intermediate goods sector															
Final goods mark-up	15.0	12.7	11.3	13.2	15.1	13.6	12.0	14.2	18.0	13.2	16.4	13.4	14.5	14.1	Commission services
Intermediate goods mark-up	9.1	9.1	6.5	9.1	9.1	9.1	9.1	9.1	9.1	9.1	9.1	6.5	6.5	9.1	Commission services
Risk-premia on intangibles	0.9	1.8	6.0	5.4	2.4	0.4	0.4	3.1	2.6	3.6	0.7	1.3	4.0	3.5	Constrained by equations
Fixed entry costs	11.7	6.3	5.9	14.3	12.6	9.1	1.8	3.3	23.8	12.3	4.9	2.7	9.2	9.5	www.doingbusiness.org
Labour, skills distribution															
s_L	16.9	27.2	18.2	21.5	7.2	13.7	21.7	9.4	32.8	44.5	14.1	24.9	18.7	17.5	EUROSTAT
s_M	76.7	64.8	75.4	69.4	86.8	77.2	70.7	79.2	59.9	45.6	73.7	66.6	76.8	77.6	EUROSTAT
s_H	6.4	7.9	6.4	9.1	6.0	9.2	7.5	11.4	7.3	9.8	12.2	8.5	4.5	4.9	EUROSTAT
μ (elasticity of substitution between skills)	1.7	1.7	1.7	1.7	1.7	1.7	1.7	1.7	1.7	1.7	1.7	1.7	1.7	1.7	Acemoglu and Autor (2011)
Skill premium % (high vs. medium)	32.5	25.9	45.6	40.1	54.3	56.5	17.3	45.4	34.4	37.2	18.9	41.8	59.3	72.9	EUROSTAT
Skill premium % (medium vs. low)	76.0	31.2	45.4	49.2	50.8	80.7	28.6	44.4	16.4	38.1	19.9	31.0	69.0	56.5	EUROSTAT
Frisch elasticity of labour supply	−0.3	−0.3	−0.4	−0.3	−0.3	−0.3	−0.2	−0.3	−0.4	−0.4	−0.4	−0.4	−0.4	−0.4	Chetty (2012)

Taxes and subsidies															
R&D tax-credit	0.12	0.15	0.15	0.18	0.18	−0.02	−0.01	0.18	0.01	0.34	0.25	0.38	0.15	0.25	Warda (2009); OECD (2013)
Labour taxes	27.1	26.8	27.5	21.3	29.0	24.7	44.7	35.2	19.3	16.3	36.0	24.6	41.1	39.0	EUROSTAT
Consumption taxes	41.5	42.8	24.5	28.8	38.8	37.8	34.4	35.0	38.0	33.5	40.1	39.5	29.2	39.8	EUROSTAT
Variable/Parameter	**IE**	**IT**	**LT**	**LU**	**LV**	**MT**	**NL**	**PL**	**PT**	**RO**	**SE**	**SI**	**SK**	**UK**	**Source**
R&D sector															
L_{RD}	1.2	1.0	0.8	2.4	0.6	0.9	1.4	0.6	1.2	0.3	1.8	1.7	0.8	1.2	EUROSTAT
R&D intensity (% GDP)	1.9	1.5	1.0	1.6	0.7	1.0	2.4	1.0	1.8	0.6	4.3	3.2	0.9	2.0	EUROSTAT
λ	0.5	0.7	0.5	1.1	0.7	0.7	0.5	0.4	0.8	0.6	0.3	0.5	0.6	0.5	Constrained by equations
ϕ	0.5	0.3	0.5	0.0	0.4	0.4	0.5	0.6	0.3	0.5	0.7	0.5	0.4	0.5	Bottazzi-Peri (2007)
ϖ	0.4	0.7	0.5	1.0	0.6	0.6	0.5	0.4	0.7	0.5	0.3	0.4	0.5	0.5	Bottazzi-Peri (2007)
ν	0.4	1.5	0.6	2.7	1.4	1.4	0.4	0.3	1.5	1.4	0.1	0.3	1.1	0.4	Constrained by equations
Final and intermediate goods sector															
Final goods mark-up	20.5	12.3	18.0	17.1	16.1	11.1	13.1	13.8	13.3	19.6	14.0	13.2	17.8	11.5	Commission services
Intermediate goods mark-up	9.1	9.1	7.4	9.1	6.1	9.1	9.1	10.7	9.1	9.1	9.9	9.1	6.5	6.5	Commission services
Risk-premia on intangibles	3.1	2.6	4.8	2.7	5.4	3.7	1.8	3.2	3.8	13.5	0.4	1.1	4.5	1.0	Constrained by equations
Fixed entry costs	2.6	18.0	6.2	4.8	6.5	20.3	6.4	22.1	3.2	5.3	5.0	1.6	5.4	3.9	www.doingbusiness.org
Labour, skills distribution															
s_L	23.3	41.8	6.6	19.5	10.6	59.4	24.2	9.9	60.2	23.7	16.8	14.6	8.1	21.6	EUROSTAT
s_M	67.3	54.0	83.3	72.3	82.2	37.1	69.3	84.2	35.7	71.4	74.2	78.8	86.6	69.0	EUROSTAT
s_H	9.3	4.2	9.9	8.2	7.2	3.5	6.3	6.0	4.1	4.9	9.0	6.7	5.2	9.4	EUROSTAT
μ (elasticity of substitution between skills)	1.7	1.7	1.7	1.7	1.7	1.7	1.7	1.7	1.7	1.7	1.7	1.7	1.7	1.7	Acemoglu and Autor (2011)
Skill premium % (high vs. medium)	34.6	54.7	33.3	21.0	49.8	20.5	26.7	45.9	35.8	71.3	16.8	29.5	55.8	16.2	EUROSTAT

(continued)

Table 4.2 (continued)

Variable/Parameter	IE	IT	LT	LU	LV	MT	NL	PL	PT	RO	SE	SI	SK	UK	Source
Skill premium % (medium vs. low)	34.2	38.2	44.6	70.6	39.8	30.4	40.7	40.8	94.7	45.4	15.1	84.9	61.9	34.3	EUROSTAT
Frisch elasticity of labour supply	−0.4	−0.4	−0.4	−0.4	−0.4	−0.4	−0.3	−0.4	−0.4	−0.4	−0.1	−0.3	−0.3	−0.3	Chetty (2012)
Taxes and subsidies															
R&D tax-credit	0.26	0.12	0.15	−0.01	0.18	0.18	0.23	0.00	0.49	0.15	−0.01	0.16	−0.01	0.18	Warda (2009); OECD (2013)
Labour taxes	28.0	21.5	21.0	40.7	21.1	23.0	32.5	23.9	22.1	26.4	36.1	30.5	20.1	23.5	EUROSTAT
Consumption taxes	28.7	42.8	31.9	32.9	33.0	23.3	38.5	33.9	25.4	30.4	38.6	35.6	32.3	25.2	EUROSTAT

References

Acemoglu D, Autor D (2011) Skills, tasks and technologies: implications for employment and earnings. In: Ashenfelter O, Card D (eds) Handbook of labour economics, vol 4b. Elsevier, Amsterdam, pp 1043–1171

Barkbu B, Rahman J, Valdes R (2012) Fostering growth in Europe now. IMF staff note 12/07

Bassanini A, Duval R (2006) Employment patterns in OECD countries: reassessing the roles of policies and institutions. OECD Economics Department Working Paper 486

Bassanini A, Nunziata L, Venn D (2009) Job protection legislation and productivity growth in OECD countries. Econ Policy 24(58):349–402

Bottazzi L, Peri G (2007) The international dynamics of R&D and innovation in the long run and in the short run. Econ J 117:486–511

Bouis R, Duval R (2011) Raising potential growth after the crisis: a quantitative assessment of the potential gains from various structural reforms in the OECD area and beyond. OECD Economics Department Working Paper 835

Canton E, Ciriaci D, Solera I (2014) The economic impact of professional services liberalisation. European Economy Economic Papers 533

Causa O, Hermansen M, Ruiz N (2016) The distributional impact of structural reforms. OECD Economics Department Working Paper 1342

Chetty R (2012) Bounds on elasticities with optimization frictions: a synthesis of micro and macro evidence on labor supply. Econometrica 80(3):969–1018

Christopoulou R, Vermeulen P (2012) Markups in the Euro area and the US over the period 1981–2004: a comparison of 50 sectors. Empir Econ 42(1):53–77

D'Auria F, Pagano A, Ratto M, Varga J (2009) A comparison of structural reform scenarios across the EU member states: simulation-based analysis using the QUEST model with endogenous growth. European Economy Economic Papers 392

De la Fuente A (2003) Human capital in a global and knowledge-based economy, part II: assessment at the EU country level. Barcelona Graduate School of Economics Working Paper 98

Dixit A, Stiglitz J (1977) Monopolistic competition and optimum product diversity. Am Econ Rev 67(3):297–308

Eggertsson G, Ferrero A, Raffo A (2014) Can structural reforms help Europe? J Monet Econ 61(C):2–22

European Commission (2013a) The growth impact of structural reforms. QREA 12(4):17–27

European Commission (2013b) Product market review 2013: financing the real economy. European Economy 8/2013

European Commission (2014) Structural reforms at the zero lower bound. QREA 13(3):21–25

European Commission (2016) The economic impact of selected structural reform measures in Italy, France, Spain and Portugal. European Economy Institutional Paper 23

Fournier J, Koske I (2010). A simple model of the relationship between productivity, saving and the current account. OECD Economics Department Working Paper 816

Jacquinot P, Savsek S, Tóth M, Vetlov I (2017) Structural reforms at the effective lower bound – insights from the EAGLE model. In: Structural reforms: moving the economy forward. Springer, Cham

Jaumotte F, Sodsriwiboon P (2010) Current account imbalances in the southern euro area. IMF Working Paper 10/139

Jones CI (1995) R&D-based models of economic growth. J Polit Econ 103(4):759–784

Jones CI (2005) Growth and ideas. In: Aghion P, Durlauf S (eds) Handbook of economic growth, vol 1, part B. North-Holland, Amsterdam, pp 1063–1111

Katz L, Murphy K (1992) Changes in relative wages, 1963-1987: supply and demand factors. Q J Econ 107(1):35–78

Kerdrain C, Koske I, Wanner I (2010) The impact of structural policies on saving, investment and current accounts. OECD Economics Department Working Paper 815

Martin JP, Scarpetta S (2011) Setting it right: employment protection, labour reallocation and productivity. IZA policy paper 27
OECD (2013) Science and technology scoreboard 2013. Innovation for growth. OECD Publishing, Paris
Orlandi F (2012) Structural unemployment and its determinants in the EU countries. European Economy Economic Papers 455
Pessoa A (2005) 'Ideas' driven growth: the OECD evidence. Port Econ J 4(1):46–67
Ratto M, Roeger W, in't Veld J (2009) QUEST III: an estimated DSGE model of the euro area with fiscal and monetary policy. Econ Model 26(1):222–233
Roeger W (1995) Can imperfect competition explain the difference between primal and dual productivity? J Polit Econ 103(2):316–330
Roeger W, Varga J, in't Veld J (2008) Structural reforms in the EU: a simulation-based analysis using the QUEST model with endogenous growth. European Economy Economic Papers 351
Roeger W, Varga J, in't Veld J, Vogel L (2017) The impact of structural reforms on the functional income distribution: a model-based assessment. European Economy Discussion Papers (forthcoming)
Thum-Thysen A, Canton E (2015) Estimation of service sector mark-ups determined by structural reform indicators. European Economy Economic Papers 547
Varga J, Roeger W, in't Veld J (2014) Growth effects of structural reforms in Southern Europe: the case of Greece, Italy, Spain and Portugal. Empirica 41(2):323–363
Vogel L (2011) Structural reforms and external rebalancing in the euro area: a model-based analysis. European Economy Economic Papers 443
Warda J (2009) An update of R&D tax treatment in OECD countries and selected emerging economies, 2008–2009. Mimeo

Chapter 5
Simulating the Impact of a Comprehensive Policy Package for Italy and Germany

Beatrice Pierluigi and Igor Vetlov

5.1 Introduction

Following the introduction of the euro, Italy and Germany experienced 8 years of a very similar growth. However, the two countries started to see a major disconnect from 2007 onwards, with Germany outperforming Italy also thanks to a set of structural reforms undertaken in early 2000s. At the same time, inflation in Germany was considerably lower than in Italy and a large price competitiveness gap between the two countries emerged. Looking forward, both countries need to undertake some rebalancing in order to return to a sustainable growth path. Subdued domestic demand and a strong reliance on exports make Germany particularly vulnerable to the external environment whereas Italy, constrained by on-going retrenchment in the public sector and dismal productivity growth, needs to improve its international competitiveness.

This chapter investigates by means of model-based simulations to which extent a package of reform measures for Italy and Germany—which are consistent with those recommended by international institutions—can help achieving a sustainable rebalancing in these countries. The package consists of the following measures:

The chapter benefited from comments provided by Günter Coenen, Geoff Kenny, Hans-Joachim Klöckers and Isabel Vansteenkiste. The views expressed in the chapter are those of the authors and do not necessarily reflect the views of the ECB.

B. Pierluigi (✉)
Economics Department, European Central Bank, Frankfurt am Main, Germany
e-mail: beatrice.pierluigi@ecb.europa.eu

I. Vetlov
European Central Bank, Frankfurt am Main, Germany

J. de Haan, J. Parlevliet (eds.), *Structural Reforms*,
https://doi.org/10.1007/978-3-319-74400-1_5

1. A set of TFP-enhancing policies in Italy targeting both the tradable and non-tradable sectors. These policies include the reduction of licencing procedures; improved functioning of the judicial system and enhanced efficiency of public and tax administration and public procurement rules.
2. A set of competition and investment-enhancing policies in Italy. These policies include the effective implementation of the new competition law, a strengthening of privatisation; a strengthening of insolvency procedures and debt collection.
3. A reduction of the tax wedge in Italy compensated by an increase in consumption taxes.
4. A set of TFP and investment-enhancing policies in Germany targeting mainly the non-tradable sector. These policies include the reduction of barriers to competition in retail trade, professional services and network industries, the reduction of bottlenecks in administrative capacity and a more efficient use of public procurement rules.
5. Higher infrastructure investment in Germany.
6. A reduction of the income tax wedge in Germany. This reduction is compensated by an increase in consumption taxes, as the fiscal space is assumed to be used for infrastructure investment.
7. The investment package (Juncker plan).[1] The implementation is carried out on the basis of the currently available information, which sees Italy gaining 0.4% of GDP, Germany 0.1% of GDP and the rest of the euro area 0.3% of GDP for the period 2017–2021.

To this end the chapter is divided in three parts. The first part presents some key stylised facts on demand and supply developments in the two countries over the past 16 years. The stylised facts, which have the purpose of informing the simulation baseline and the policy package, can be summarised as follows: The dismal productivity performance of Italy is significantly more severe in the non-tradable sector than in the tradable sector. In Germany, the strong productivity performance relies uniquely on the tradable sector. The productivity performance of the non-tradable sector has been as poor as that of Italy during the past 16 years. However, significantly more constrained wage developments in Germany than in Italy led to a more competitive non-tradable sector in Germany. Germany's productivity performance in the tradable sector has been significantly higher than that of Italy and the rest of the euro area. Since nominal wage developments have been significantly falling behind productivity developments, this translated in strong competitiveness gains. In Germany public investment as a share of GDP is

[1]https://ec.europa.eu/commission/sites/beta-political/files/2-years-on-investment-plan_en_2.pdf. At the time of writing this chapter, the Juncker plan was expected to use a small fraction of the EU budget as a guarantee for projects of the European Investment Bank that would be riskier and more innovative than the usual ones. These projects were expected to generate a total of €315 billion of investment. The resources used for the guarantee come from a reshuffling of the European Union budgets from 2015 to 2020 and are mainly taken from Horizon 2020 (i.e. research and innovation) and the Connecting Europe facility (i.e. transport infrastructure) budget lines.

significantly below that of the rest of the euro area, at the same time the quality of infrastructure investment has been deteriorating during the past 10 years. In Italy, the share of public investment over GDP is equal to that of Germany, with a significantly lower level of quality of infrastructure. In both countries the level of income taxes is relatively high compared to the rest of the euro area and the OECD average, while consumption taxes are generally lower than that of the rest of the euro area.

Against this background, the second part of the chapter describes the reform packages and how they can be implemented within a structural macroeconomic model. The packages consist of reforms which are expected to affect TFP growth, investment efficiency, price mark-ups, risk premia, infrastructure investment and the tax structure. In particular, in Italy structural reforms are associated with lighter licencing procedures, a better functioning of the judicial system, enhanced efficiency of public and tax administration and public procurement rules, stronger insolvency regimes, and an efficient enforcement of the competition law; and in Germany with the reduction of barriers to competition in retail trade, professional services and network industries, a reduction of bottlenecks in administrative capacity and a more efficient application of public procurement rules.

The impact of the policy packages is analysed with the 4-country block version of the ECB's EAGLE model, including Germany, Italy, the rest of the euro area and the rest of the world. Like in the case of other macroeconomic models used for the analysis of structural reforms, two key difficulties are related to: (1) the matching between the needed policy change and the type of shock that is best able to reproduce this policy change, and (2) the calibration of the size of the shock that corresponds to the implementation of the policy change. While a certain degree of judgement is unavoidable, to overcome both challenges the chapter relies as much as possible on existing empirical analysis. In particular, the chapter uses the information coming from recent empirical studies that test how structural reforms affect intermediate target variables (in our case productivity, price mark-ups and investment) and derive the gains from reforms by computing how much these intermediate target variables will be improved if certain structural indicators close the distance with best performers.

As done in other similar works and to add realism to the exercises, it is assumed that closing the distance with best practices takes time and that agents are not able to anticipate immediately the outcome of future changes in structural parameters. Thus, we assume that structural reforms are implemented over 5 years and are gradually bringing about productivity and investment gains. However, in the case of public investment and for the tax shifts it is more difficult to adopt the approach of closing the gap with best practices, as there is no obvious benchmark. Thus, we assume that Germany increases its ratio of public investment to GDP to that of the rest of euro area average (i.e. by 1% of GDP) in 2 years. Finally, we assume a 1% reduction in the tax wedge, compensated by a 1% of GDP increase in consumption taxes in both countries. This broadly corresponds to bringing consumption taxes towards the euro area average level.

The final part of the chapter presents the outcome of the simulation exercises. It reports the impact of the packages on real GDP and inflation for the two countries and for the euro area as a whole. It shows that the implementation of the packages is not only consistent with higher long-term growth but also with a rebalancing within the euro area, with price competitiveness gains in Italy and higher inflation in Germany. However, the size of the policy package is not able to bring about higher inflation swiftly.

Overall, the figures reported in this chapter are in line with findings of other studies. Nevertheless, while clearly highlighting the scope for achieving rebalancing through well-designed policy packages, the simulations results should be taken with caution as they entail a number of assumptions. These are related in particular to the degree of realism of the assumed implementation rate of structural policies and the ability of the model to capture all the channels through which structural changes can affect an economy.

5.2 Key Supply and Demand Developments in Italy and Germany

During the past 16 years Italy and Germany experienced 8 years of very similar growth and 8 years of increasing divergence (Fig. 5.1; see also Appendix 1). Between 1999 and 2007 both countries largely underperformed the rest of the euro area. However, since 2007 Italy has continued to underperform while Germany became the growth-engine of the euro area (Fig. 5.1). In Germany, the combination of a series of important reforms (e.g. Hartz reforms; see Chap. 10) and favourable economic developments (e.g. exchange rate depreciation, low oil prices, immigration wave, favourable geographical composition of exports) has helped a strong

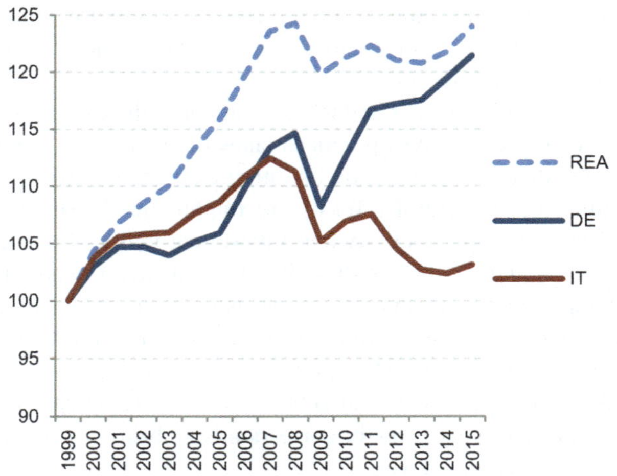

Fig. 5.1 Real GDP in Italy, Germany and the rest of the euro area (1999 = 100). Source: European Commission, Ameco database

export-led recovery since 2009. By contrast in Italy, long standing vulnerabilities (such as very high public debt and low productivity growth), coupled with rigidities in the labour and product markets and low administrative capacity which had remained unaddressed for many years, have largely affected the country's ability to properly recover from the financial crisis, and have exposed Italy to the euro area sovereign crisis from 2011 onwards. High and increasing non-performing loans have also greatly reduced the ability of the financial sector to support the economic recovery.

While the decoupling of domestic demand dynamics between the two countries started in 2007, TFP divergences started already in 2001. Domestic demand in Italy has been on a continuous downward path since 2007, with a cumulated fall of 13% until 2015. By contrast, the export-led recovery in Germany has been followed by a pick-up in domestic demand from 2009 onwards: in cumulative terms domestic demand grew by 5% between 1999 and 2009 and by 10% between 2009 and 2015 (Fig. 5.2). On the supply side, since the early 2000s Italy's TFP has been on a continuous declining path underperforming significantly Germany and the rest of the euro area (Fig. 5.3). Italy's TFP was also not able to recover from the 2009 drop. By contrast, in Germany, TFP recovered quickly after the 2009 drop and in 2011 it was back to its pre-crisis level. However, since then, the data suggests that TFP has been stagnant. While Germany appears much better placed than Italy both in terms of TFP growth and domestic demand recovery, the significant inaction on the reform side during the past decade increases the risks of falling back onto a low growth path.

The tradable versus non-tradable goods distinction can shed some lights on the sources of the productivity differentials in Germany and Italy. While this distinction has been shown to be often overly simplistic, as all sectors contain a certain degree

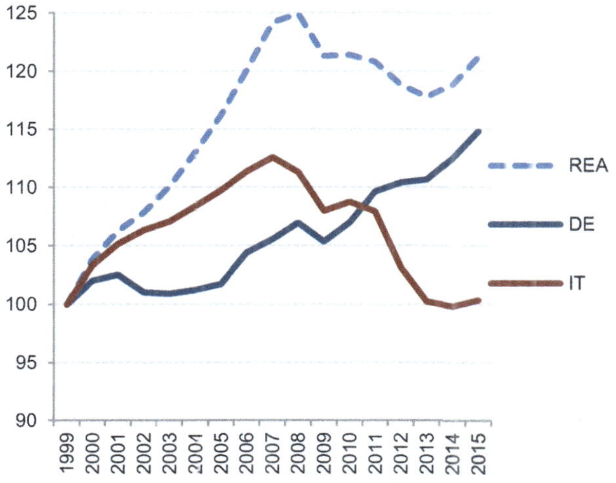

Fig. 5.2 Domestic demand in Italy, Germany and the rest of the euro area (1999 = 100). Source: European Commission, Ameco database

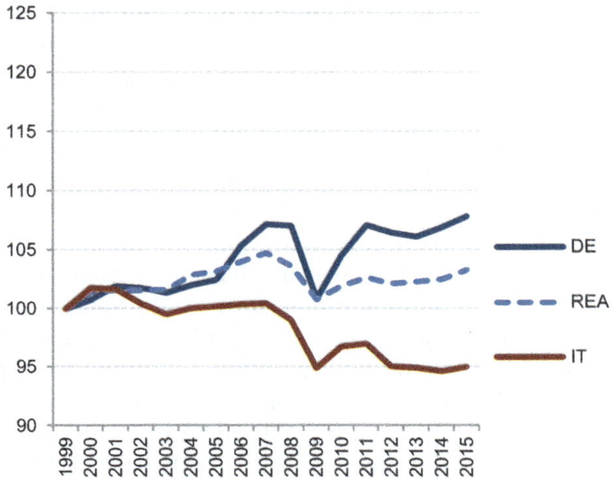

Fig. 5.3 TFP in Germany, Italy and the rest of the euro area (1999 = 100). Source: European Commission, Ameco database

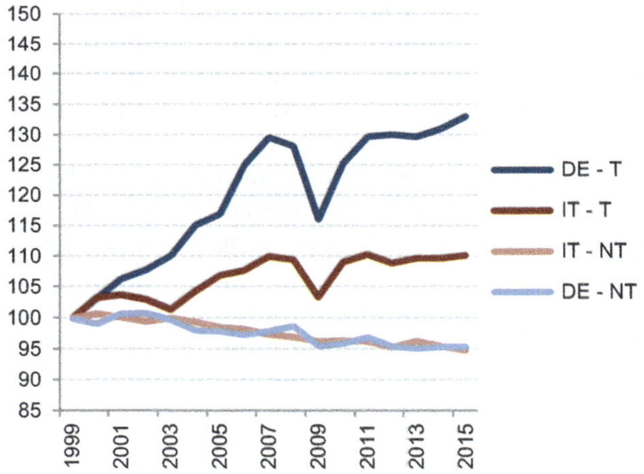

Fig. 5.4 Labour productivity in Italy and Germany: tradable (T) and non-tradable (NT) goods (1999 = 100). Notes: Tradable (T) = ISIC: A_E, G_I (Agriculture and fishing, mining and manufacturing, Trade, hotels, transport and similar). Non-Tradable (NT) = ISIC: F, J_P (Construction, Financial and Real Estate, Public and social services). Source: European Commission, Ameco database

of tradability, at the aggregate level it can still provide some important hints for understanding certain economic developments. Given the challenges of measuring TFP at the sectoral level, here we refer to labour productivity.

In Italy, productivity and price competitiveness problems have been larger in the sectors which typically produce the highest share of non-tradable goods (hereafter non-tradable sector) compared to the sectors which typically produce the highest share of tradable goods (hereafter tradable sector) (see Figs. 5.4 and 5.5).

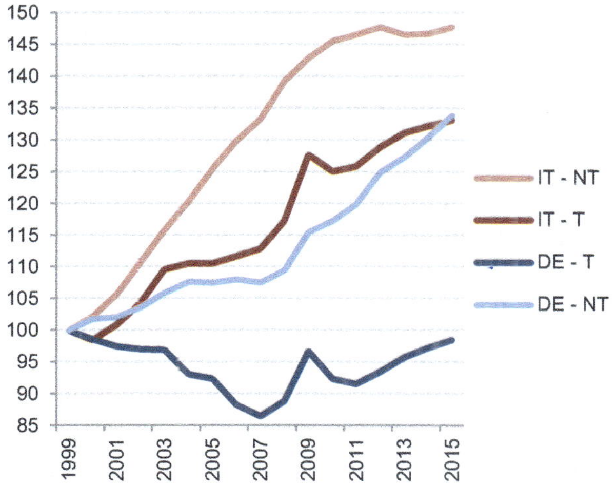

Fig. 5.5 Unit labour cost in Italy and Germany: tradable (T) and non-tradable (NT) goods (1999 = 100). See notes to Fig. 5.4. Source: European Commission, Ameco database

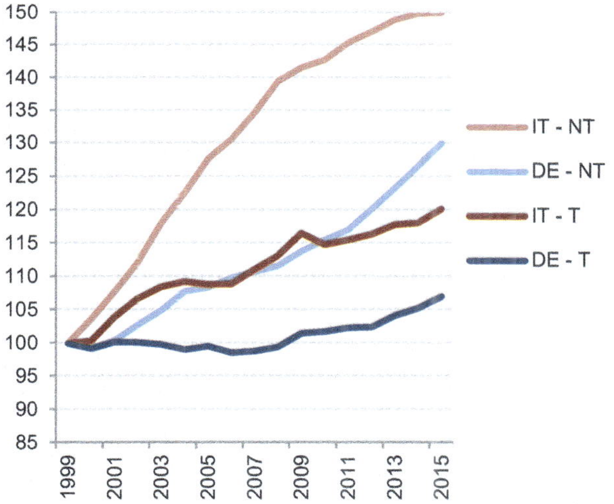

Fig. 5.6 Value added deflator in Italy and Germany: tradable (T) and non-tradable (NT) goods (1999 = 100). See notes to Fig. 5.4. Source: European Commission, Ameco database

Italy's output prices grew by 30% more in the non-tradable than in the tradable sector in cumulative terms during the past 16 years. At an average rate of increase of 2.6% per year since 1999, Italy's output prices in the non-tradable sector have been largely responsible for the observed price competitiveness losses (Fig. 5.6).

Also in Germany, there is a very large productivity gap between the tradable and non-tradable sectors: during the past 16 years productivity growth has been 37% higher (in cumulative terms) in the tradable than in the non-tradable sector. This compares with a 15% gap in Italy and a 19% gap in the rest of the euro area.

Germany's output prices grew by 23% more in the non-tradable than in the tradable sector in cumulative terms during the past 16 years. This translated in an average rate of increase of the GDP deflator in the tradable sector of 0.4% per year and in the non-tradable sector of 1.2% per year (Fig. 5.6).

5.3 The Policy Package

The above information on aggregate demand and supply developments is used to inform the baseline for the model-based simulations and to justify the choice of the policy packages. The model used in the simulations is the 4-country block version of the ECB's Euro Area and Global Economy (EAGLE) model, calibrated to reflect the fundamentals of Italy, Germany, the rest of the euro area and the rest of the world. The EAGLE model is particularly well suited for policy simulations related to rebalancing as it entails both a monetary union dimension (Italy and Germany vis-à-vis the rest of the euro area) and a global dimension (the euro area vis-à-vis the rest of the world). Given that the model also contains a rich set of supply-side features, including a distinction between tradable and non-tradable goods, it appears also well suited to construct and evaluate the impact of structural reforms.[2]

5.3.1 Measures to Boost Productivity and Competition

There are a number of important policies that would help increasing productivity, private investment and reduce price differentials in the tradable and non-tradable sectors in Italy and Germany. These policies have been spelled out in the EC Country Specific Recommendations, as well as in IMF Article IV consultations or OECD country reports. The list for Italy includes: licencing; civil justice; public procurement law; reform of the public administration; control of corruption;

[2]In addition, the model features two different types of households: credit constrained and non-credit constrained ones, and nominal and real rigidities. As to the nominal rigidities, these stem from the fact that there is monopolistic competition in product and labour markets. The degree of competition in the two markets is captured by a mark-up between firms' marginal costs and final prices, and between the households' marginal rate of substitution between consumption and leisure and wages. As to real rigidities, they are captured by the presence of habit persistence in consumption and adjustment costs in investment and in the import content of demand components. For a reference to the key characteristics of the EAGLE model see Gomes et al. (2012). The key parameters used for simulations reported in the chapter are shown in Appendix 2.

implementation of the competition law; liberalisation of regulated professions; privatisation; improvement of the insolvency system and debt collection mechanisms. In the case of Germany: public procurement law; efficiency in network industry; liberalisation of regulated professions; enhancement of PPPs and R&D spending.

However, it is not straightforward to implement these policy changes in the context of a structural macroeconomic model. Like in the case of other models, two key difficulties when analysing the impact of the above policies within the EAGLE model are related to: (1) the matching between the above policies and the type of shocks that are embedded in the model, and (2) the calibration of the size of the shock that would mimic the needed policy change. To overcome both challenges, a certain degree of judgement is needed. This judgment is based on the information coming from recent empirical studies that test how structural reforms affect intermediate target variables (i.e. variables that are explicitly included in our model such as productivity, price mark-ups and investment) and derive the gains from reforms by computing how much these intermediate target variables will be improved if certain structural indicators close the distance with best performers.

Focusing on TFP as an intermediate variable, various studies have shown that reforms targeting product markets and framework conditions can have a sizeable impact. Figure 5.7 shows the range of the estimated impact of reforms in product market and framework conditions on TFP in Germany and Italy according to different studies. It shows that the range is rather wide, from 1 to 5% in Germany and from 2.2 to 6% in Italy. The width of the range depends on the type of product market reforms analysed, the model used for the estimation, the sample period, the ambitiousness of the policy implemented (i.e. half of the gap with best performers closed or full gap). For both countries we calibrate the size of the TFP shock by taking the average point estimate of Fig. 5.7 and assume that TFP in both the tradable and non-tradable sectors can be increased by ½ of this average amount over a 5-year horizon. This gradual and partial closure of the gap is done to increase the realism of the reform package.

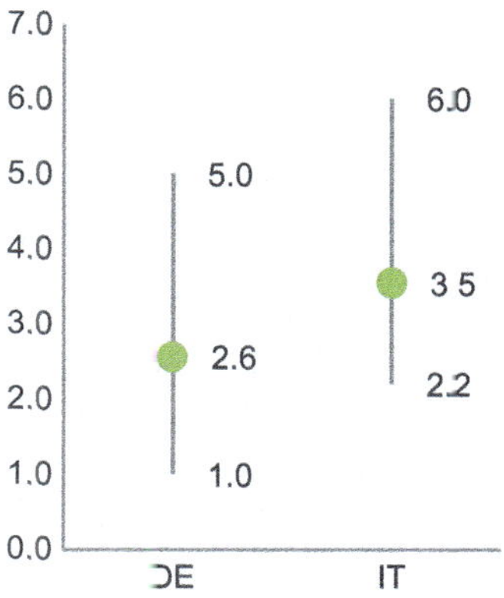

Fig. 5.7 Estimated ranges of impact of product market reforms on TFP. Note: green dots represent the average of the different estimates. Sources: Angelini et al. (2017), Cette et al. (2016), Bouis and Duval (2011), OECD (2015), Varga and in't Veld (2014)

For both countries it is assumed that the reforms that affect TFP also have an impact on investment efficiency. The latter captures the rate at which new investments add to the economy's capital stock used in production. This assumption derives from the evidence that policies, which are able to affect productivity, e.g. via higher innovation activity, are historically also found to affect the pace of capital accumulation (Moreno and Suriñach 2014).

In the case of Italy competition-enhancing reforms are also expected to affect the price mark-up in the non-tradable sector. The size of the fall in the price mark-up is based on closing half of the difference with the average of the EU 3 best performers in 5 years (Lusinyan and Muir 2013). Moreover, it is expected that improvement in the insolvency system and debt collection mechanisms induce a reduction of corporate borrowing costs. In the EAGLE model this cost reduction enters as a 25 bp reduction of the risk premium, which corresponds to the current average spread of NFCs lending rates between Italy and the euro area average.

It is finally assumed that the path of the above-mentioned structural reforms is not fully anticipated. In practical terms this means that every year agents observe and react only to the part of the reform which is being implemented and not to the full package. Households and firms adapt their behaviour incrementally as they learn about the full scale of the change over time. This feature of the simulation is included to add realism to the exercise; in particular, it captures unavoidable implementation lags (e.g. due to grandfathering and protection of insiders); uncertainty about timing of reform implementation (e.g. due to regional versus central government coordination problems); and imperfect credibility of policy announcements (e.g. related to changes in government and related policy agendas as well as reform fatigue).

5.3.2 Improving Infrastructure Investment

On top of productivity and competition-enhancing policies, the package includes a boost to infrastructure investment. It has been shown that for economies with clearly identified infrastructure needs, with efficient public investment processes and in the presence of economic slack and monetary accommodation, there is a strong case for increasing public infrastructure investment (see de Jong et al. 2017 and IMF 2014).

Government investment spending as a percentage of GDP is particularly low in Germany and it has been declining strongly in Italy since 2009 (Fig. 5.8). In both countries it is about 1 percentage-point below that in the rest of the euro area, thus from a pure cross-country perspective there seems to be scope for increasing government investment in both countries (Fig. 5.8). However, only in the case of Germany the fiscal situation would allow for a significant boost in public investment. Also, business executives' assessment of the overall quality of infrastructure has been steadily declining in Germany since 2006, possibly pointing to the need of

Fig. 5.8 Government investment (% of GDP). Source: European Commission, Ameco database

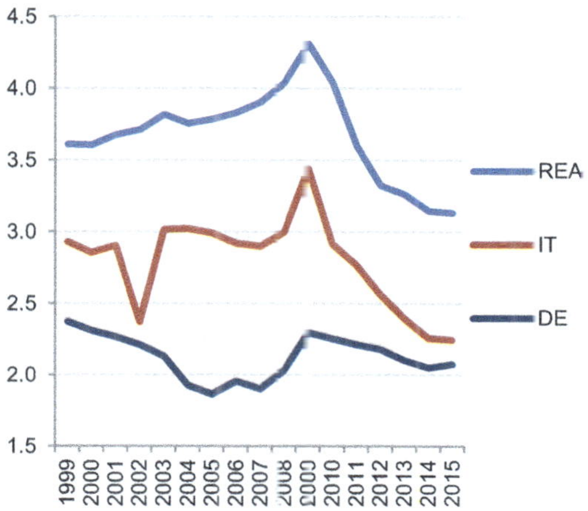

Fig. 5.9 Quality of infrastructure (index 0–7, higher values indicate better quality). Source: World Economic Forum, Global Competitiveness Indicator (2015–16 Edition)

investment to improve the quality of infrastructure. It should be noted that, despite its decline, the quality of infrastructure in Germany is significantly above that of Italy (Fig. 5.9). This suggests that Germany is better equipped than Italy to undertake spending in infrastructure investment in an efficient way.

An increase in public infrastructure investment can favourably affect the economy. In the short term, it boosts aggregate demand through the short-run fiscal multiplier, similar to other government spending, and also by potentially crowding-in private investment, given the highly complementary[3] nature of infrastructure

[3]As regards the complementarity nature of public investment spending vis-à-vis private investment spending in the context of the EAGLE model simulations, due to the substitutability assumption of public and private capital stock embedded in the Cobb-Douglas production function, the co-movement of public and private investment may only arise if the demand-side effect of raising public investment is sufficiently strong to compensate the direct supply-side substitution effects of higher capital stock on private capital stock. In this respect, the implied effect on private investment

services. Over time, there is also a supply-side effect of public infrastructure as the productive capacity of the economy increases with a higher infrastructure capital stock. The efficiency of investment is central to determine how large this supply-side effect will be. It is assumed that Germany is able to spend 1% of GDP in government investment in two consecutive years, an amount that would take this country to the rest-of-the-euro-area average. The simulations include also the implementation of the Juncker plan for Italy (0.4% of GDP between 2017 and 2021), Germany (0.1% of GDP) and the rest of the euro area (0.3% of GDP between 2017 and 2021). These figures reflect the current information set regarding the approved projects and relative financing (EFSI).[4] The implementation of the Juncker package is obtained by boosting public investment and investment efficiency. This is done to take into account the private component of the plan.

5.3.3 Shifting the Tax Structure Away from Labour Income

The simulations also entail a reduction of the tax burden, which in both countries is assumed to be (ex-ante) fiscal neutral, i.e. financed by an increase in consumption taxes.[5] The tax instrument is used to mimic the impact of a nominal devaluation in Italy[6] and to increase the take home wage in Germany. The case for reducing the tax burden on labour in Germany is evident from Fig. 5.10, which shows that the tax on labour income in percent of labour costs is extremely high in Germany compared to its euro area peers. In particular, the tax wedge at the level of the minimum wage

is sensitive to specific design characteristics of the policy scenario (e.g. duration of the shock, monetary policy stance, financing of the public spending, etc.).

[4]EFSI = European Fund for Strategic Investment. See http://www.eib.org/efsi/efsi-projects/index.htm?c=IT&se=

[5]Attinasi et al. (2016) assess the macroeconomic and welfare effects of budget-neutral reductions in the tax wedge using a New-Keynesian DSGE model for a sample of euro area countries including Italy and Germany. They find that while financing the labour tax wedge reduction by an increase in consumption taxation yields most favourable output effects, financing it by a reduction in government spending is more beneficial in terms of welfare as the latter does not imply a policy-induced increase in private consumption costs. When firms can adjust the extensive and intensive labour margin in response to policy changes, a reduction in the workers' and not the firms' burden is most beneficial.

[6]Similarly to exchange rate devaluation, a fiscal devaluation is expected to boost competitiveness and raise GDP growth and employment, at least in the short to medium-run. In the case of the fiscal devaluation this is achieved through the reduction in labour cost which reduces producer prices and ultimately export prices. As a result, the country gains competitiveness and export volumes increase. At the same time, the VAT rate increase only affects the prices of domestically produced goods, as exported goods are exempt. As imported tradable goods also face the increased VAT rates without however benefiting from the reduced production costs, there is also an incentive for consumers to shift to domestically produced goods thereby reducing imports. Both export and import effects should lead towards an improvement in the current account balances, thus contributing to an unwinding of external imbalances.

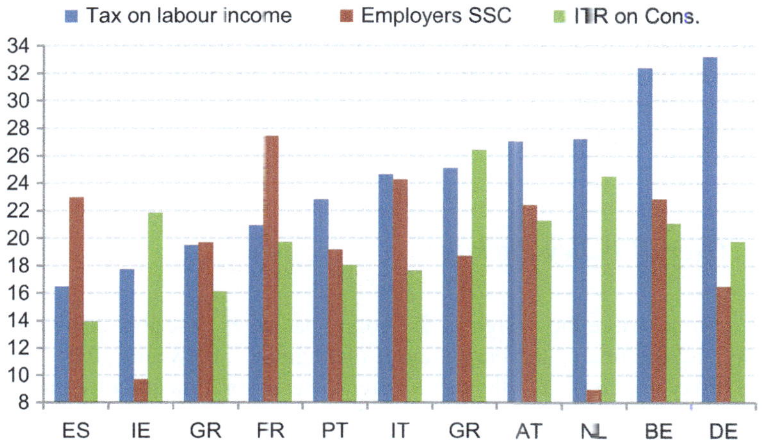

Fig. 5.10 Tax rate on labour income, employers' social security contributions (2015) and implicit tax rate (ITR) on consumption (2012). Notes: Tax on labour income and Employers SSC in % of labour cost. ITR on consumption in % of GDP. It should be noted that in 2013 the VAT rate in Italy (standard rate) was increased by 1pp, this increase has an impact on ITR which is not reflected in the chart. Sources: OECD Taxing Wages 2016; Eurostat, Taxation trends in the European Union, 2015

is high in comparison with other euro area countries, resulting in lower take-home income at the bottom of the wage scale. A reduction of the tax wedge for workers with lower income is one of the 2016 CSR recommendations and it is currently under discussion by the German government. In Italy, employers' social security contributions are amongst the highest in the euro area (Fig. 5.10). A reduction of the employers' tax wedge is expected to be translated in lower final prices and in an increase of competitiveness, employment creation and GDP growth. So far, there have been some attempts in Italy to reduce the tax burden on labour, but efforts have fallen mainly on the personal income tax, while the reductions in social security contributions only have been temporary.

From a cross-country perspective, there seems to be scope to increase taxes on consumption in both countries. These are generally less distortive than the taxes on labour income, thus the shift in taxation is not neutral for long-term GDP growth (Annichiarico et al. 2014). An increase in consumption taxes would bring about higher temporary inflation, with a negative impact on disposable income and thus on consumption. To the extent that the reduction of the labour tax wedge brings about higher employment, investment and growth this initial negative impact would be compensated. The simulations assume that the reduction of the tax wedge and the increase in consumption tax occur in two consecutive years in both countries. Similar to structural reforms, it is assumed that agents do not anticipate future tax changes. However, once a policy change is introduced, its duration is fully anticipated. Thus, a differentiation is made between reforms affecting product markets and framework conditions, where the implementation is imperfectly anticipated and agents learn about the exact path of the reforms as time pass-by, and reforms affecting the tax structure, where there are no ex-ante doubts about the size and duration of the undertaken policy change. In the proposed rebalancing policy package, the size of the tax shift is set at 1% of GDP. This would imply a level of consumption taxes that becomes closer to the euro area average.

5.3.4 Overall Policy Package

Table 5.1 summarises the design of the policy packages described above for Italy, Germany and the rest of the euro area. It distinguishes between reform areas, the model's proxy used to match the reform areas, the calibration and phasing-in of the policy change, and the degree of forward-lookingness (anticipation or not) of the agents affected by the reforms.

5.4 Results

The outcome of the simulation exercises is shown for a 5-year horizon, i.e. for the short to medium term. The simulations are carried out using a baseline which extends the observed historical developments for key macroeconomic variables until 2021. The baseline features a gradual unwinding of the effects of past shocks which implies a slow economic recovery and gradual pick-up in inflation. As a result, the monetary policy interest rate, governed endogenously by the policy rule, remains at its low level until end-2018 and increases gradually thereafter. The impact of the policy package is measured as deviations of the model-based scenario simulations (i.e. including the policy package) from the baseline simulations (i.e. excluding the policy package).

It is assumed that the policy package is implemented simultaneously. In other words, in each country all reforms start to be implemented at the same time. This assumption excludes the presence of administrative capacity bottlenecks; which are particularly important in Italy, a country with significant institutional weaknesses.

5.4.1 Reform Impact in Italy and Germany

The short-term GDP boost of the policy package is sizeable. Figure 5.11 shows the impact of the simulated package and the contribution from each individual policy measure on GDP. Assuming that the implementation of the reforms described above starts in 2017, the first-year impact is equal to 0.7% in both countries. The strong

Table 5.1 Design of the policy package

Reform areas	Model's proxy	Calibration and phasing in	Anticipation
Italy			
– Licencing procedures – Civil justice – Public procurement – Public administration – Corruption – Privatisation	Increase in TFP in non-tradables and tradables. Increase in investment efficiency	1.8% increase distributed in 5 years (1/2 average of the range of impact of product market reforms on TFP) 1.8% increase distributed in 5 years (assume same impact as for TFP)	No
– Competition law – Regulated professions	Fall in the price mark-up in the non-tradable sector	1.25% fall in 5 years (1/2 of the difference between IT and the average EU 3 best performers mark-ups)	No
– Insolvency system and debt collection	Lower corporate borrowing cost	Reduction of risk premia by 25bp (current average NFCs lending spread between IT and euro area average)	No
– Tax-wedge on labour	Reduction of employers social security contributions and increase in consumption taxes	1% of GDP cut in labour income tax and 1% of GDP increase in VAT in 2 years	Partial
– Juncker plan	Increase in investment efficiency and public investment	0.4% of GDP (available EFSI funds)	Yes
Germany			
– Public procurement – Efficiency in network industry – Education	Increase in TFP in non-tradables	1.3% increase distributed in 5 years (1/2 of the average of the range of impact of product market reforms on TFP)	No
– PPPs – R&D	Increase private investment efficiency	1.3% increase distributed in 5 years (assume same impact as for TFP)	No
– Investment in infrastructure	Increase public investment	1% of GDP in 2 years (based on the gap with rest of euro area)	Partial
– Tax-wedge on labour	Reduction of labour and corporate tax rates and increase in consumption taxes	1% of GDP cut in employers' social security contribution and 1% increase in VAT in 2 years	Partial
– Juncker plan	Increase in investment efficiency and public investment	0.1% of GDP (available EFSI funds)	Yes
Rest of the euro area			
– Juncker plan	Increase in investment efficiency and public investment	0.3% of GDP (available EFSI funds)	Yes

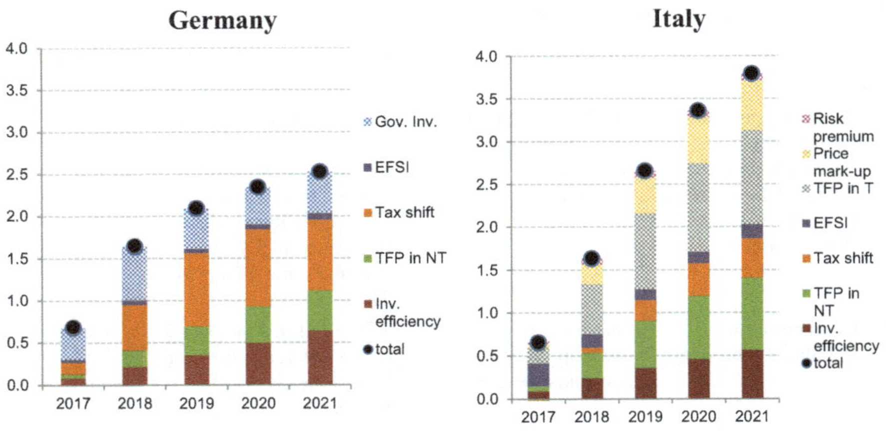

Fig. 5.11 Simulated impact of the package on GDP (deviations from baseline levels). Source: EAGLE simulations

impact on GDP, observed in the first year, is due to the large number of reforms[7] introduced, in particular in Italy, that are associated with the implementation of the policy package. Given the administrative capacity challenges of Italy, one might argue that starting the implementation process in all the areas mentioned in Table 5.1 simultaneously might be an optimistic assumption.

Across the different policies, government investment gives the strongest contribution to the GDP boost in Germany in 2017 (0.4%), whereas in Italy, the strongest contributions are due to the EFSI (0.25%) and TFP in the tradable sector (0.2%).[8] In Germany, the contributions from the increase in investment efficiency (0.1%), TFP in the non-tradable sector (0.1%) and the tax shift (0.1%) explain the rest of the GDP increase. In Italy, the remaining policy-induced changes (TFP in the non-tradable sector, investment efficiency, price mark-ups and risk premium) have also a marginal positive impact on GDP, while the tax shift has a marginal negative impact on GDP in 2017. This stems from the fact that the temporary increase in consumer prices reduces, in the short term, disposable income and thus private consumption.

[7]As argued in the literature, in case monetary policy faces zero lower bound constraint, structural reforms, by inducing downward pressure on prices, may imply negative output effects on impact via increasing real interest rate. In our simulations we assume that ex ante there is a high degree of uncertainty as regards the size and duration of the structural changes implied by the reforms. This implies a more gradual adjustment of the economy. The disinflation pressures associated with structural reforms are accordingly dampened and the potential negative effects of the real interest rate channel reduced, limiting, or even eliminating, short-run output losses.

[8]In all simulations, we apply a simple fiscal rule which gradually adjusts lump-sum taxes in response to the deviation of the government debt-to-GDP ratio from its target level. In case of the government investment shock, unfavourable implications of higher government spending on the government budget deficit are offset to the extent that larger public infrastructure boosts the economy-wide level of productivity and, hence, lifts private sector demand.

This reduction of disposable income is not compensated (as it is instead the case for Germany) by a reduction of the tax wedge, given that the latter favours employers and not employees.

By 2019, i.e. 3 years after the start of the reform package, the GDP level is 2.1% higher in Germany and 2.7% higher in Italy than in a no reform scenario. In Germany, the contribution of government investment declines while those of TFP, investment efficiency and the tax shift increase. In Italy, about half of the GDP increase is due to the contribution of TFP in the tradable and non-tradable sectors. A notable contribution is also coming from the reduction of the price mark-ups and investment efficiency. The contribution from the fall in the risk premium, the tax shift and the Juncker plan is instead less important.

By 2021, i.e. 5 years after the start of the reforms, the GDP level is 2.5% higher in Germany and 3.8% higher in Italy. In both countries, TFP and investment efficiency account for the largest part of the GDP gains. A country with largest reform needs has obviously more to gain from reforms, but even in a country like Germany, where the list of required reforms is certainly smaller than the one of Italy, the GDP gains from reforms appear very sizable. In both countries the reform package mainly works via a boost to private sector investment and employment (see Appendix 3).

In both countries higher investment efficiency implies higher return on investment as each unit of new investment leads to higher growth of the productive capital stock in the economy. It boosts investment demand in the short run and extends the economy's productive capacity over the long run. An improved utilisation of factors of production, or a positive TFP shock, leads to lower unit production costs and allows increasing output for given inputs of production. The excess supply induces downward pressure on prices. As prices fall, demand increases and the economy reaches a new equilibrium featuring higher output.

Overall, the outcome of the simulations is broadly in line with other model-based analysis. For example similar exercises conducted with the Commission's Quest model (Varga and in't Veld 2014) show an average impact in the euro area of about 3% on GDP in 5 years, while an IMF study on Italy (Lusinyan and Muir 2013) shows an impact of product market reforms of 4.4% on the Italian GDP in 5 years.

The package is consistent with inflation increasing in Germany and declining in Italy. Figure 5.12 shows that in 2017 and 2018 the tax shift is inflationary in both countries, as indirect taxation is passed through to final prices. Despite the fact that the size of the increase in indirect taxation (as a percent of GDP) is equal in Germany and Italy, the model's calibration implies a more sizable inflationary impact of the tax shift in Italy in the short term.[9] In Germany, the increase in public investment and the improvement in investment efficiency are also able to generate higher inflation via higher domestic demand. Thus, these policies are not only desirable because they would raise permanently the GDP level, but they can

[9]This is in part related to the fact that in Italy the GDP share of consumption is lower than in Germany. As a result, in order to raise tax revenues of 1% of GDP, the effective indirect tax rate in Italy has to be increased more than in Germany.

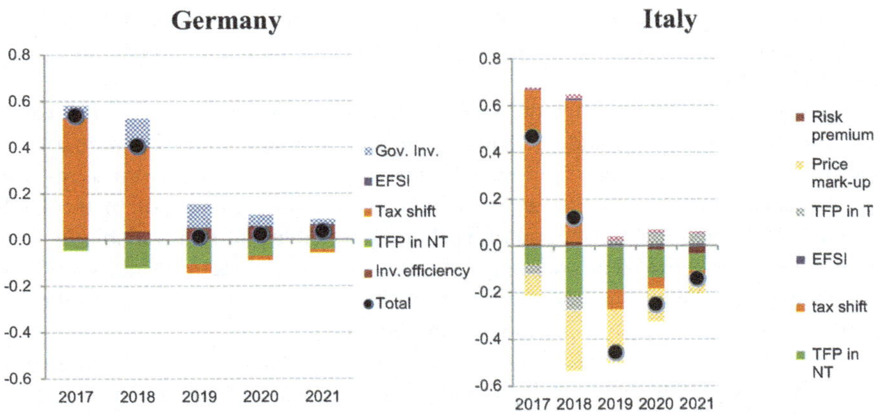

Fig. 5.12 Simulated impact of the package on inflation (deviation from baseline growth rates). Source: EAGLE simulations

also prevent a reduction of inflation in the short term. This effect is partially offset by the disinflationary impact caused by the increase in TFP in the non-tradable sector. Overall, in Germany inflation is higher by 0.55 percentage-points in 2017 and 0.4 percentage-points in 2018. In the medium term the temporary inflationary impact of the tax shift is reabsorbed and the impact of the other policies tends to diminish, resulting in 0.1 percentage-points higher inflation by 2021. In Italy, the TFP and price mark-up shocks exert significant downward pressures on inflation that partially compensate the temporary increase caused by the tax shift. Inflation is higher by 0.5 percentage-points in 2017, but lower by 0.5 percentage-points in 2019. As in the case of Germany, in the medium term the temporary inflationary impact of the tax shift is reabsorbed, while the impact of the other policies is slowly diminishing. In cumulative terms the inflation differential between Germany and Italy is reduced by 1.3% in 5 years as a result of this policy package.

5.4.2 Spillovers and the Euro Area Impact

Figure 5.13 compares the impact on GDP and consumer prices in Italy, Germany, the rest of the euro area and the euro area as a whole, in the short and medium term. It shows that the overall package is consistent with higher GDP and consumer price levels both in the short and in the medium term. The inflationary impact of the package, dominated by the supply-side measures, is rather limited and essentially confined to the measures related to the tax shift and public investment. Other models which feature market entry, due to the endogenous goods variety, are able to generate higher inflation from competition and productivity-enhancing reforms (Cacciatore et al. 2016).

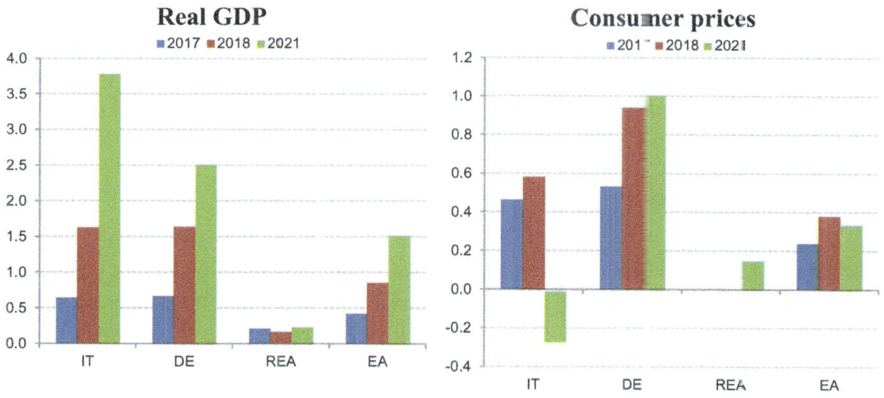

Fig. 5.13 Simulated impact of the overall package: Germany, Italy, Rest of the euro area (deviation from baseline levels). Source: EAGLE simulations

The GDP level in the rest of the euro area countries is 0.2% higher in 2021. Of this increase, 0.15% is explained by the implementation of the Juncker package. Given that the Juncker package is implemented also in the rest of the euro area the spillover part is very limited. It is, however, likely that the size of spillovers is underestimated in the EAGLE model as it relies only on the traditional transmission channels. In particular, TFP shocks can be forcefully transmitted through the sharing of common institutions, peer effects, mutual learning from best practices and confidence channels (see Coe et al. 2009).

While there is high uncertainty on the size of spillovers, the case for reforms remains very strong, given the impact in individual countries and in the euro area as a whole. The euro area would gain a 1.5% increase in real GDP by 2021, as the two reforming countries represent 45% of the euro area. As the type of reforms simulated in this exercise for Italy and Germany is needed in most euro area countries, the potential GDP increase in the euro area would be at least twice as big as the one obtained here, if all countries would simultaneously implement these reforms.

The package increases euro area inflation by 0.2 percentage-points in 2017, which cumulates to 0.3% higher consumer prices after 5 years. Overall, the simulations show that the reform package can be made consistent with higher inflation in the euro area. The tax shift and the boost in public investment in Germany are the main drivers of higher short-term inflation in this set-up. Later on in the horizon, the impact on inflation is reduced but the price level remains permanently higher. A more sizeable package of public investment and tax shift would lead to higher inflation in the short term. However, a very strong frontloading of public investment might not only be infeasible but also undesirable, given that very high public investment might not reflect infrastructure needs. In addition, very strong increases in indirect taxation might have the conflicting effect of depressing demand, via lower private consumption. Assuming a stronger frontloading of other inflationary structural policies, i.e. those affecting investment efficiency and the risk premia, seems unrealistic as well, as these reforms, even if they are fully credible, take time to unfold their impact. Other types of policies, e.g. an exogenous boost to wages obtained by an increase in the wage mark-up, have not been considered in this chapter, as it has been shown by many other works that the long-term impact of such a policy is negative on GDP and employment (Kollmann et al. 2015).

5.5 Conclusions

The model-based simulation results show that implementation of a policy package consistent with recent policy recommendations by international institutions for Italy and Germany can lead to a significantly higher growth in both countries, and particularly so in Italy. Assuming that the implementation of the reforms described above start in 2017, the first year impact on GDP level is 0.7% in both countries. This relatively large impact is due to the fact that all reforms are assumed to start to be implemented simultaneously, which, in countries with problems of administrative capacity, could be a rather optimistic assumption. Five years after the start of the reform package, the GDP level is 2.5% higher in Germany and 3.8% higher in Italy. The overall higher impact in Italy is due to the bigger gap with the best performers. In both countries higher TFP and investment efficiency accounts for the largest part of the GDP gains. Public investment helps the increase in GDP in Germany, and the Juncker plan helps the increase in GDP in Italy, albeit only marginally so.

The policy package brings about competitiveness gains in Italy, and higher inflation in Germany and in the euro area as a whole. Thus, it supports some rebalancing in the euro area. However, the achievements are relatively limited. In cumulative terms the price differential between Germany and Italy is reduced by 1.3% in 5 years. The euro area wide price level is 0.2% higher after 1 year and 0.35% higher after 5 years. The tax shift and the boost in public investment in Germany are the main drivers of higher short-term inflation in this set-up. Thus, these policies are not only desirable because they would raise permanently the GDP level, but they can counteract a reduction of inflation in the short term caused by other supply side policies, which, in an environment of low demand, could be misinterpreted as an undesirable outcome of structural reforms.

Overall, the simulation results should be taken only as an illustrative example on how a package of supply side reforms targeting product market, framework conditions, infrastructure investment and labour tax wedge could work out in the euro area. The numerical results entail many caveats related to the number of strong assumptions regarding the type, size and timing of the pass-through of the structural policies on TFP, investment efficiency, price mark-ups and risk premia. Also the implementation of the package did not take into consideration implementation obstacles related to administrative capacity, reform fatigue and political constraints. Moreover, there is no explicit modelling of the financial sector in the version of the EAGLE model applied in the analysis. Consequently, the model-based analysis may incompletely capture policy transmission mechanism due to a limited role of macro-financial linkages. Thus, while the main model results are reported in terms of point estimates, there is potentially large uncertainty attached to these estimates.

A.1 Appendix 1 Macroeconomic Developments in Italy and Germany

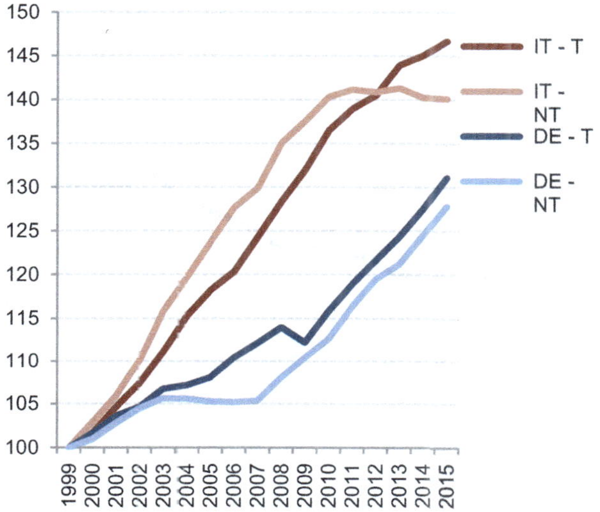

Fig. A.1 Compensation per employee in Italy and Germany: tradable (T) and non-tradable (NT) goods (1999 = 100). Source: European Commission, Ameco database

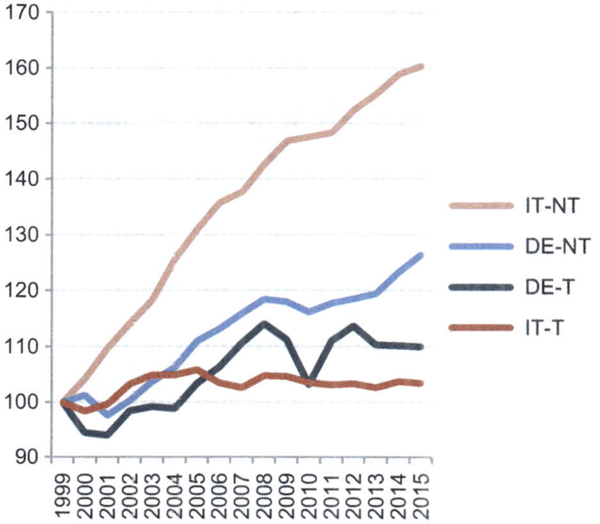

Fig. A.2 Unit profit in Italy and Germany: tradable (T) and non-tradable (NT) goods (1999 = 100). Source: European Commission, Ameco database

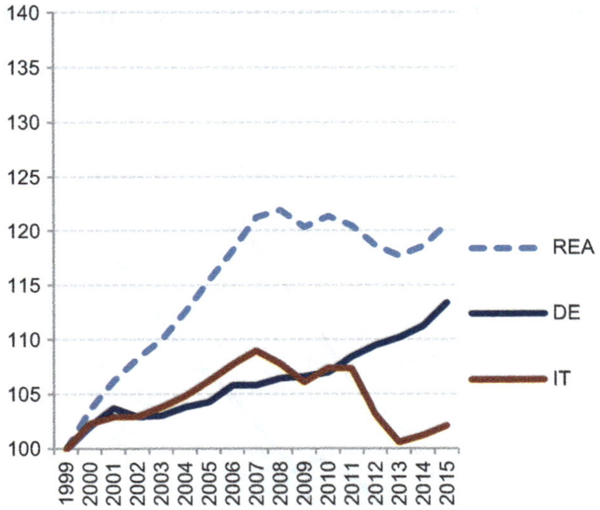

Fig. A.3 Private consumption (1999 = 100). Source: European Commission, Ameco database

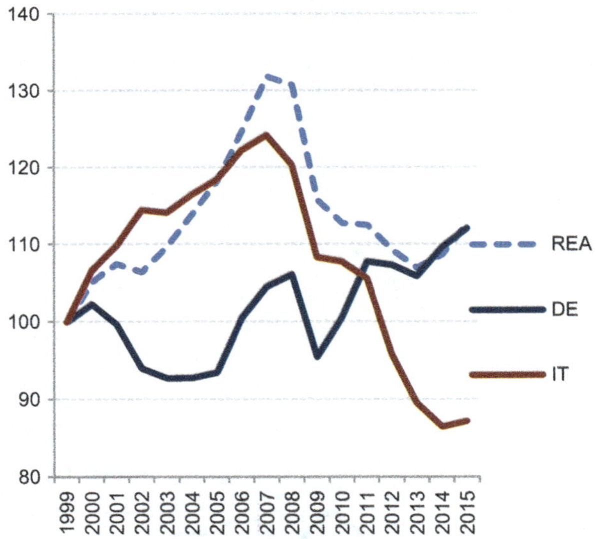

Fig. A.4 Total investment (1999 = 100). Source: European Commission, Ameco database

B.1 Appendix 2 Key Parameters of the EAGLE Model

Table B.1 Structural parameters

Parameters		Regions			
		DEU	ITA	REA	ROW
Share of world GDP		0.044	0.028	0.093	0.834
Demand					
Private consumption-to-GDP ratio		0.629	0.597	0.567	0.601
Private investment-to-GDP ratio		0.167	0.18	0.185	0.196
Public consumption-to-GDP ratio		0.165	0.177	0.197	0.162
Public investment-to-GDP ratio		0.041	0.044	0.049	0.041
Total import-to-GDP ratio		0.378	0.268	0.31	0.051
Imports of consumption goods-to-GDP ratio		0.19	0.147	0.157	0.027
Imports of investment goods-to-GDP ratio		0.086	0.04	0.06	0.016
Imports for export production-to-GDP ratio		0.102	0.08	0.093	0.008
Net foreign assets-to-GDP ratio		0.243	−0.217	−0.229	0.020
Intermediate-good production					
Gross steady-state growth rate, annualized	$\overline{g_z}$	1.012	1.012	1.012	1.012
Non-tradable goods-to-GDP ratio		0.562	0.601	0.57	0.616
Tradable goods-to-GDP ratio		0.438	0.399	0.43	0.384
Labour income-to-GDP ratio, non-tradables		0.405	0.431	0.389	0.523
Labour income-to-GDP ratio, tradables		0.507	0.478	0.486	0.556
Output elasticity of priv. capital, non-trad.	α_N	0.265	0.275	0.290	0.280
Output elasticity of priv. capital, tradables	α_T	0.265	0.275	0.290	0.280
Output elasticity of public capital	α_G	0.025	0.025	0.025	0.025
Depreciation rate of private capital stock	δ_P	0.020	0.020	0.020	0.020
Depreciation rate of public capital stock	δ_G	0.025	0.025	0.025	0.025
Dom. and imported input substitution, exports	μ_x	1.500	1.500	1.500	1.500
Domestic input bias in production of exports	ν_x	0.688	0.622	0.608	0.781
Price mark-up (non-tradables)	$\theta_N/(\theta_N - 1)$	1.500	1.368	1.500	1.278
Price mark-up (tradables sold domestically)	$\theta_T/(\theta_T - 1)$	1.200	1.234	1.200	1.200
Price mark-up (tradables sold abroad)	$\theta_x/(\theta_x - 1)$	1.200	1.234	1.200	1.200
Final-good production					
Substitution btw. dom. and imp. trad, goods	μ_{TC}	2.500	2.500	2.500	2.500
Bias towards domestic tradable goods	ν_{TC}	0.504	0.491	0.424	0.336
Substitution btw. trad, and non-trad. goods	μ_C	0.500	0.500	0.500	0.500
Bias towards tradable goods	ν_C	0.545	0.465	0.537	0.400
Substitution btw. dom. and imp. trad, goods	μ_{TI}	2.500	2.500	2.500	2.500
Bias towards domestic tradable goods	ν_{TI}	0.437	0.733	0.514	0.334
Substitution btw. trad, and non-trad. goods	μ_I	0.500	0.500	0.500	0.500
Bias towards tradable goods	ν_I	0.800	0.750	0.750	0.750

(continued)

Table B.1 (Continued)

Parameters		Regions			
		DEU	ITA	REA	ROW
Households					
Household discount factor, annualized rate	β^{-4}	1.008	1.008	1.008	1.008
Steady-state real gross interest rate, annual	$\overline{rr^4}$	1.020	1.020	1.020	1.020
Intertemporal elasticity of substitution	σ^{-4}	1.000	1.000	1.000	1.000
Habit formation in consumption	κ	0.600	0.600	0.600	0.600
Inverse of the Frisch elasticity of labor	ζ	2.000	2.000	2.000	2.000
Bias towards private consumption goods	ν_{CCI}	1.000	1.000	1.000	1.000
Bias towards private consumption goods	ν_{CCJ}	1.000	1.000	1.000	1.000
Elast. of subst. between priv. and pub. cons.	μ_{CCI}				
Elast. of subst. between priv. and pub. cons.	μ_{CCJ}				
Share of liquidity-constrained households	ω	0.250	0.323	0.308	0.250
Wage mark-up, unconstrained households	$\eta_I/(\eta_I - 1)$	1.300	1.300	1.300	1.160
Wage mark-up, constrained households	$\eta_J/(\eta_J - 1)$	1.300	1.300	1.300	1.160

Notes: *DEU* Germany, *ITA* Italy, *REA* Rest of Euro Area, *ROW* Rest of the World

Table B.2 Trade linkages

Parameters		Regions			
		DEU	ITA	REA	ROW
Trade matrix, ratios to domestic GDP					
Consumption-good imports from					
DEU			0.020	0.031	0.008
ITA		0.011		0.011	0.003
REA		0.064	0.047		0.015
ROW		0.115	0.08	0.115	
Investment-good imports from					
DEU			0.007	0.014	0.007
ITA		0.004		0.004	0.002
REA		0.025	0.011		0.007
ROW		0.057	0.022	0.042	
Re-exportable-good imports from					
DEU			0.012	0.019	0.003
ITA		0.005		0.007	0.001
REA		0.033	0.025		0.004
ROW		0.064	0.044	0.067	
Parameters of tradable bundles					
Consumption-good imports					
Substitution between consumption good imports	μ_{IMC}	2.500	2.500	2.500	2.500
Bias towards imports from					
DEU	$\upsilon_{IMC}^{H,CO}$		0.196	0.276	0.381
ITA	$\upsilon_{IMC}^{H,CO}$	0.08		0.091	0.137
REA	$\upsilon_{IMC}^{H,CO}$	0.36	0.325		0.483
ROW	$\upsilon_{IMC}^{H,CO}$	0.56	0.479	0.633	
Investment-good imports					
Substitution between investment good imports	μ_{IMI}	2.500	2.500	2.500	2.500
Bias towards imports from					
DEU	$\upsilon_{IMI}^{H,CO}$		0.26	0.316	0.515
ITA	$\upsilon_{IMI}^{H,CO}$	0.057		0.088	0.135
REA	$\upsilon_{IMC}^{H,CO}$	0.322	0.269		0.350
ROW	$\upsilon_{IMI}^{H,CO}$	0.621	0.471	0.596	
Re-exportable-good imports					
Substitution between re-exportable imports	μ_{IMX}	2.5	2.5	2.5	2.500
Bias towards imports from					
DEU	$\upsilon_{IMX}^{H,CO}$		0.212	0.288	0.435
ITA	$\upsilon_{IMX}^{H,CO}$	0.072		0.090	0.140
REA	$\upsilon_{IMX}^{H,CO}$	0.348	0.311		0.425
ROW	$\upsilon_{IMX}^{H,CO}$	0.580	0.477	0.622	

Notes: *DEU* Germany, *ITA* Italy, *REA* Rest of Euro Area, *ROW* Rest of the World

Table B.3 Adjustment and policy parameters

Parameters		Regions			
		DEU	ITA	REA	ROW
Real adjustment costs					
Import content: private consumption	γ_{IMC}	2.000	2.000	2.000	2.000
Import content: private investment	γ_{IMC}	1.000	1.000	1.000	1.000
Import content: exports	γ_{IMX}	2.000	2.000	2.000	2.000
Investment adjustment cost	γ_{I}	3.000	6.000	6.000	4.000
Capital utilization	γ_{u}	1.000	1.000	1.000	1.000
Transaction cost function	γ_{v1}	0.029	0.029	0.029	0.029
Transaction cost function	γ_{v2}	0.154	0.154	0.154	0.154
Cross-border intermediation cost function	γ_{B}	0.010	0.010	0.010	
Price setting					
Price Calvo: nontadables	ξ_{N}	0.900	0.900	0.900	0.850
Price Calvo: tradables sold domestically	ξ_{H}	0.850	0.850	0.850	0.750
Price Calvo: tradables exported	ξ_{x}	0.800	0.800	0.800	0.750
Price indexation: nontadables	χ_{N}	0.500	0.500	0.500	0.500
Price indexation: tradables sold domestically	χ_{H}	0.500	0.500	0.500	0.500
Price indexation: tradables exported	χ_{X}	0.500	0.500	0.500	0.500
Wage setting					
Wage Calvo: unconstrained households	ξ_{I}	0.800	0.800	0.800	0.750
Wage Calvo: constrained households	ξ_{J}	0.800	0.800	0.800	0.750
Wage indexation: unconstrained households	χ_{I}	0.750	0.750	0.750	0.750
Wage indexation: constrained households	χ_{J}	0.750	0.750	0.750	0.750
Monetary authority					
Inflation target	$\overline{\Pi}$	1.020	1.020	1.020	1.020
Interest-rate smoothing	ϕ_{R}	0.850	0.850	0.850	0.850
Response to inflation	ϕ_{Π}	2.000	2.000	2.000	2.000
Response to output	ϕ_{Y}	0.100	0.100	0.100	0.100
Fiscal authority					
Government debt-to-GDP ratio	$\overline{B_{Y}}$	0.600	0.600	0.600	0.600
Response to government debt-to-GDP ratio	$\phi_{B_{Y}}$	0.100	0.100	0.100	0.100
Consumption tax rate	τ_{C}	0.178	0.203	0.192	0.101
Labor income tax rate	τ_{N}	0.173	0.15	0.114	0.127
Rate of soc. sec. contrib. paid by households	τ_{W_h}	0.174	0.070	0.095	0.073
Rate of soc. sec. contrib. paid by firms	τ_{W_f}	0.168	0.246	0.233	0.093
Capital income tax rate	τ_{K}	0.219	0.344	0.325	0.348
Dividend income tax rate	τ_{D}	0.000	0.000	0.000	0.000

Notes: *DEU* Germany, *ITA* Italy, *REA* Rest of Euro Area, *ROW* Rest of the World

C.1 Appendix 3 Simulation Results

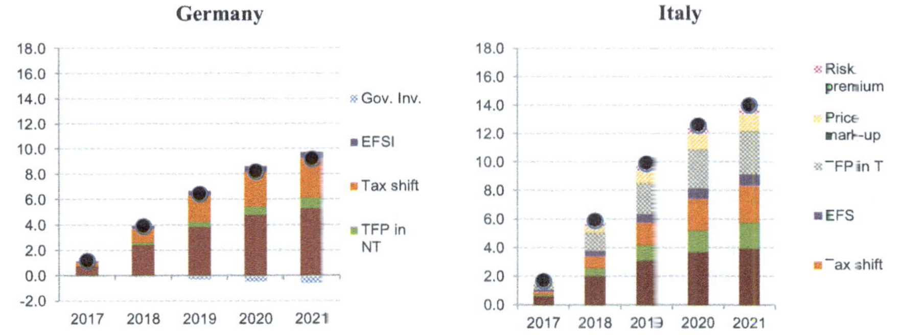

Fig. C.1 Investment (deviation from baseline levels). Source: EAGLE simulations

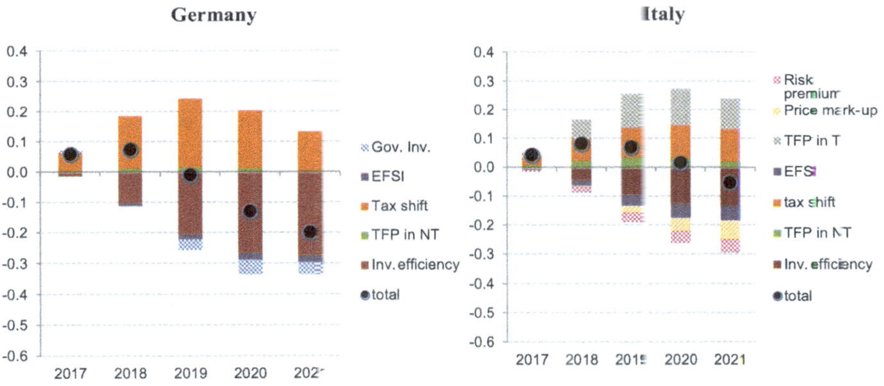

Fig. C.2 Trade Balance (deviation from baseline levels). Source: EAGLE simulations

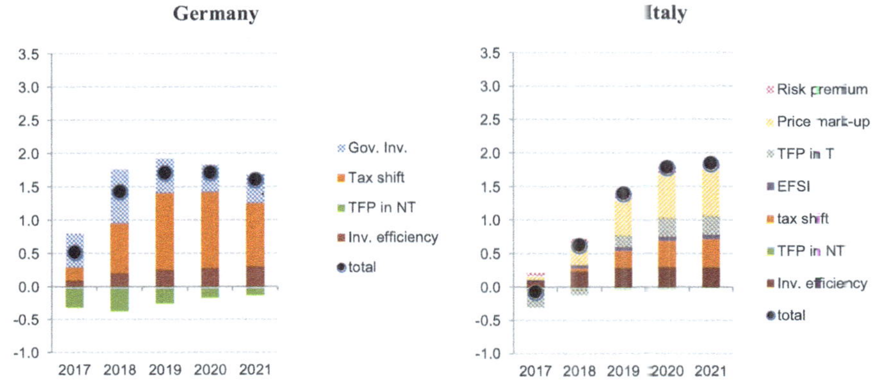

Fig. C.3 Total hours worked (deviation from baseline levels). Source: EAGLE simulations

References

Angelini E, Moshammer E, Pierluigi B (2017) Structural reforms, productivity and spillovers in the euro area. Mimeo

Annichiarico B, Di Dio F, Felici F (2014) Fiscal devaluation scenarios: a quantitative assessment for the Italian economy. Open Econ Rev 26:731–785

Attinasi M-G, Prammer D, Stähler N, Tasso M, van Parys S (2016) Budget-neutral labour tax wedge reductions: a simulation-based analysis for selected euro area countries. Bundesbank Discussion Paper 26

Bouis R, Duval R (2011) Raising potential growth after the crisis: a quantitative assessment of the potential gains from various structural reforms in the OECD and beyond. OECD Economic Department working paper 835

Cacciatore M, Duval R, Fiori G, Ghironi F (2016) Market reforms in the time of imbalance. NBER working paper 22128

Carton B, Herve K (2013) Is there any rebalancing in the euro area? CEPII working paper 2013-32

Cette G, Lopez J, Mairesse J (2016) Market regulations, prices and productivity. Am Econ Rev 106(5):104–108

Coe D, Helpman E (1995) International R&D spillovers. Eur Econ Rev 39(5):859–887

Coe D, Helpman E, Hoffmaister A (2009) International R&D spillovers and institutions. Eur Econ Rev 53(7):723–741

de Jong J, Ferdinandusse M, Funda J, Vetlov I (2017) The effect of public investment in Europe: a model-based assessment. ECB working paper 2021

Gomes S, Jacquinot P, Pisani M (2012) The EAGLE. A model for policy analysis of macroeconomic interdependence in the euro area. Econ Model 29(5):1686–1714

IMF (2014) Is it time for an infrastructure push? The macroeconomic effects of public investment. World Economic Outlook, Chapter 3, October

John J, Wu T (2016) Comprehensive, more balanced policies to strengthen the euro area. IMF Euro area policies, Selected issues, pp 80–94

Kollmann R, Ratto M, Roeger W, in't Veld J, Vogel L (2015) What drives the German current account? And how does it affect other EU member states? Econ Policy 30(81):47–93

Lusinyan L, Muir D (2013) Assessing the macroeconomic impact of structural reforms: the case of Italy. IMF working paper 13/22

Moreno R, Suriñach J (2014) Innovation adoption and productivity growth: evidence for Europe. Research Institute of Applied Economics working paper 2014/13

OECD (2015) Economic policy reforms 2015: going for growth. OECD Economic Department

Thum-Thysen A, Canton E (2015) Estimation of service sector mark-ups determined by structural reform indicators, European Economy. Economic Papers 547

Varga J, in't Veld J (2013) The growth impact of structural reforms. Quarterly Report on the Euro Area, European Commission 12/4, pp 17–27

Varga J, in't Veld J (2014) The potential growth impact of structural reforms in the EU: a benchmarking exercise. European Commission. Economic Papers 541

Chapter 6
Structural Reforms at the Effective Lower Bound: Insights from the EAGLE Model

Pascal Jacquinot, Simon Savsek, Máté Tóth, and Igor Vetlov

6.1 Introduction

Macroeconomic adjustment following the recent global financial crisis revealed structural weaknesses in a number of euro area economies. These weaknesses have also contributed to deeper and more prolonged recessions as well as slower correction of fiscal and external imbalances in a number of euro area countries. The euro area countries that were hit hardest by the crisis adopted a significant number of structural measures under circumstances where support from aggregate demand policies was not available or not even possible (see also ECB 2015a). Those measures included labour market reforms to increase labour market flexibility and boost employment by, for example, reducing labour market segmentation, decreasing employment protection for workers on permanent contracts, by employing less centralized wage bargaining systems or by adjusting employment/unemployment benefits. Examples include the 2012 labour market reform in Spain and labour market reforms in Portugal and Ireland (ECB 2015b). At the same time, a number of euro area countries implemented product market reforms to reduce the administrative burden for firms, to improve firms' access to finance and to increase competition

The authors would like to thank Robert Anderton, Günter Coenen, Geoff Kenny and Beatrice Pierluigi for their helpful comments. Simon Savsek was affiliated to the ECB during the project. The opinions expressed are those of the authors and do not reflect views of the ECB or the EIB. Any remaining errors are the sole responsibility of the authors.

P. Jacquinot (✉) · M. Tóth · I. Vetlov
European Central Bank, Frankfurt, Germany
e-mail: pascal.jacquiot@ecb.europa.eu

S. Savsek
European Investment Bank, Luxembourg, Luxembourg

J. de Haan, J. Parlevliet (eds.), *Structural Reforms*,
https://doi.org/10.1007/978-3-319-74400-1_6

in sheltered sectors. Indeed, Slovenia, Portugal, Lithuania and Cyprus implemented business-friendly reforms and a number of euro area countries moved towards more business-friendly environment. The importance of pension market reforms and reforms aimed at improving framework conditions also cannot be neglected (ECB 2016). Given the important role of structural policies in reinvigorating growth potential of the euro area, it can be expected that structural reform implementation will remain an issue in the foreseeable future.

There is a broad consensus in the literature as regards the long-term economic benefits of structural reforms (see Chap. 2 for a discussion). At the same time, it is often argued that the short-term outcome depends on how and when the structural reforms are implemented. In particular, it has been shown that for the reforms to succeed in the short run it is desirable to implement them in 'normal' times and ensure monetary and/or fiscal policy accommodation.[1] However, structural reforms are generally implemented during severe recessions. In the euro area the reform environment was characterized by malfunctioning financial markets, a sovereign debt crisis, and monetary policy being constrained by the effective lower bound (ELB). Such an environment requires a careful assessment of the interaction between various measures and policies.

In this chapter, we study macroeconomic effects of service sector liberalisation as well as reform combinations and different sequencing of product and labour reforms. Special emphasis of the analysis is put on the role of the ELB constraining monetary policy. To this end, we employ model-based simulations obtained using the Euro Area and Global Economy (EAGLE) model (Gomes et al. 2012)—a global extension of the New Area-Wide Model (NAWM, Coenen et al. 2008) with tradable and non-tradable sectors and a monetary union. It has been calibrated for a large euro area economy, the rest of the euro area, the US and the rest of world. In the EAGLE model, households supply labour services and set their wages in monopolistically competitive markets by charging a mark-up over their marginal rate of substitution between hours worked and consumption. Similarly, firms set prices on their differentiated goods by charging a mark-up over their marginal cost of production. The wage and output price mark-ups reflect the level of monopolistic powers in the economy and result in excessive rents and sub-optimal levels of labour utilization and production. Thus, in the context of this modelling framework, the implications of competition-enhancing reforms can be investigated by analysing the effects of a reduction in mark-ups.

Whereas the issue of the effective lower bound and its implications for the implementation of structural reforms in the euro area has already been discussed in the literature, the key contribution of this chapter is to provide insight into the design of reform measures such as sequencing, packaging and coordination. Our simulations introduce shocks mimicking the impact of ECB's non-standard monetary policy measures to provide insight into the complementarity or substitutability of structural

[1]See in particular Bayoumi et al. (2004), Forni et al. (2010) or Gomes et al. (2013) for the implementation in 'normal time' of reforms enhancing competition in Europe using global DSGE models.

and monetary policy measures. The simulations show that any type of easing that reduces the stringency of the effective lower bound constraint can be beneficial for reform implementation.

This chapter is structured as follows. Section 6.2 provides a critical literature review on several papers that investigated reform implementation under the effective lower bound. Section 6.3 presents the calibration of the model. Section 6.4 provides model-based simulations of various scenarios regarding sequencing and coordination of structural reforms. It also discusses issues of cross-border coordination and interaction with fiscal and non-standard monetary policy measures. Section 6.5 concludes.

6.2 Reforms Under the Effective Lower Bound

While the long-run macroeconomic impact of structural reforms is less debated in the literature, their short-run effects are more ambiguous. DSGE models are well suited to examine the short-run effects of structural reforms since in these frameworks the market imperfections targeted by reform measures, propagation mechanisms and policy interactions can be explicitly accounted for. The most widely used DSGE models typically feature a degree of monopolistic competition stemming from imperfect substitutability across types of goods and workers resulting in price and wage mark-ups. In these models structural reforms are typically captured as permanent negative shocks to the mark-ups, representing a higher degree of competition in product and labour markets, resulting in higher output/employment and a lower price/wage level. With the introduction of additional underlying rigidities the impact of more specific structural reforms can also be analysed.

DSGE frameworks have recently been used to examine the interaction of structural reforms and monetary policy, with the latter being constrained to react to the short-term effects of reforms. The constraint can come from a binding effective lower bound on nominal interest rates or membership in a monetary union, where common monetary policy only to a limited extent reacts to country-level developments. While the long-run effects of reforms typically remain unaffected, constrained monetary policy can have a bearing on their short-term impact. For example, if monetary policy is not able to react to the possible short-run deflationary effects of some reforms, the real interest rate increases which dampens the response of consumption and investment. The net short-run impact of reform shocks in the context of constrained monetary policy depends on the relative strength of the intertemporal substitution and permanent income effects.

The current debate about the short-term impact of reforms against the backdrop of constrained monetary policy started with Fernández-Villaverde et al. (2011). In a two-period new Keynesian model, the authors implement structural reforms as shocks to future productivity. A fully anticipated increase in future productivity generates wealth effects that increase present consumption. In their setup, monetary policy would normally increase interest rates in response to higher present consumption, which is not the case under the ELB constraint. Overall they find that anticipated future increases in productivity boost demand in the present and thus can, to some extent, substitute demand side policies when the latter are constrained.

Eggertsson et al. (2014) introduce structural reforms in a two-country monetary union as an immediate and permanent reduction in product (non-traded sector) and labour market mark-ups, with monetary policy being constrained by a lower bound on nominal interest rates. Since monetary policy cannot decrease nominal rates in response to the short-run deflationary impact of reforms, the real interest rate increases which more than counteracts positive permanent income effects and the depreciation of the terms-of-trade. So reforms become contractionary over the short run. This short-term negative effect on output is increasing with the magnitude of the reforms and becomes particularly large when reforms are not fully credible (i.e. if there is a chance of policy reversal at a later stage). Somewhat surprisingly, the authors find that temporarily granting higher monopoly power for firms and unions can be expansionary at the ELB by generating inflationary expectations. On the other hand, the credible announcement of structural reforms for some future period when the ELB is no longer binding can make the permanent income effects of reforms dominate over the short run.

In Fernandez-Villaverde's (2014) discussion of the results of Eggertsson et al. (2014)—which is mostly based on the two period model introduced in Fernandez-Villaverde et al. (2011)—three key points stand out. First, the timing of the reforms is important. Product and labour market reforms as currently under discussion in Europe are likely to be implemented with some lag, possibly beyond the period over which the ELB is binding. In this case—if they are perceived as credible—reforms implemented in the future can well be expansionary even in the short run. Second, the model of Eggertsson et al. (2014) does not include investment, thus a powerful forward-looking transmission channel of reforms is lacking. Third, solvency constraints in euro area periphery countries can matter a lot, but are unaccounted for in Eggertsson et al. (2014). Expected long-run gains in output due to structural reforms can reduce worries about debt sustainability, thereby lowering risk premia and increasing confidence, which can boost short-run growth.

Vogel (2014) uses a two sector, multi-region version of the European Commission's QUEST model to examine the effect of structural reforms (captured as 1 percentage points decreases in wage and price mark-ups in a region covering 30% of the euro area) at the ELB. He finds that compared to normal times an ELB constraint increases the short-term contractionary effect of reforms due to a decline in consumption and more muted increase of investments. However, the negative short-run effects are an order of magnitude smaller than in Eggertsson et al. (2014) due to a larger number of transmission channels, including investments. Short-term effects also depend on the specific reform measures. Vogel's results, furthermore, do not yield support to the idea that delaying structural reforms for the foreseeable future would improve economic conditions at the effective lower bound.

Gerali et al. (2015) assess the impact of structural reforms in a framework which is akin to the Eurosystem's EAGLE model. They examine the effects of a service sector reform, captured as lower non-traded sector mark-up, implemented in a small economy within a monetary union (calibrated to represent Italy). They find that even in the context of the ELB reform of the service sector increases GDP over the short-to-medium run and this effect critically hinges upon the response of investments. The latter react strongly to the permanent income effects induced by increased competition in the service sector, more than offsetting the contractionary impact of rising real interest rates stemming from monetary policy being unable to accommodate the deflationary impact of reforms under to the ELB. If investment does not respond—e.g. due to prohibitive financing constraints—the deflationary impact of reforms is strengthened.

Gomes (2018) also uses the EAGLE model to analyse the impact of product and labour market reforms in the context of a binding ELB in a two-bloc monetary union. His findings are similar to those of Gerali et al. (2015), but the author also analyses issues related to reform coordination and implementation. According to the author, structural reforms can help to alleviate the impact of the recession that drove the monetary union into the ELB, but reform coordination across member countries is necessary to reduce the time spent at the ELB. The short to medium-run impact of reforms depends on whether these were introduced gradually or not and if they are perceived as temporary or permanent.

Andres et al. (2014) model structural reforms as permanent reductions in desired price and wage mark-ups against the backdrop of a baseline deleveraging scenario, featuring a credit crunch shock in the context of collateral constraints and long-term debt. Since their set-up represents a single euro area country (calibrated to represent Spain) without autonomous monetary policy, the ELB problem is taken into account implicitly (i.e. there is no monetary policy reaction to the reform shocks). These authors find that their set of reforms can mitigate the short-run output and employment losses caused by the deleveraging shock. Under product market reform, stronger competition and the ensuing long-run gains in consumption and output lead (forward-looking) households and firms to increase their investment in the short run, vis-à-vis the baseline scenario without reform. Stronger investment demand, in turn, alleviates the fall in collateral values produced by the deleveraging shock. This can reinforce the short-run gains in investment in two related ways. First, borrowers anticipate higher collateral values from the period in which they regain access to credit onwards. Second, a faster recovery in collateral values allows borrowers to receive new credit at an earlier date. Thus, the reform brings forward the end of the deleveraging process, and hence of the recession, through the financial frictions. The latter effect is missing in the case of labour market reforms, where short-run effects are more sensitive to the response of trade flows and debt maturity.

Instead of simulating the impact of permanent price and wage mark-up shocks, Cacciatore et al. (2016) explicitly model underlying structural frictions (such as endogenous producer entry costs and search and matching frictions) allowing for more realistic structural reform shocks. The authors examine the impact of cutting barriers to entry, employment protection and unemployment benefit reforms. While reforms have a positive impact on GDP and consumption in the long run, they can be contractionary over shorter horizons due to the time it takes until benefits through increased firm entry and hiring materialize whereas reform-driven downsizing of incumbent firms and layoffs are immediate. Importantly, the kind of reforms they introduce do not have quantitatively important deflationary effects, thus being at the ELB does not change the results.

In sum, recent DSGE model-based studies suggest that structural reforms may imply transitory output costs, if the possibilities for an accommodative monetary policy are limited. The extent of short-term costs varies across models and is dependent on calibration and the underlying rigidities and frictions employed. There are still open questions regarding the interaction of various rigidities in response to reform shocks, and how the complementarities across different kinds of reforms and between structural and other policy areas can be used to minimise negative short-term impacts. In particular, under the prevailing conditions in the euro area, the interaction between structural reforms and non-standard monetary policy measures is of crucial importance. In the following we use the EAGLE model to create illustrative structural reform scenarios under different monetary policy settings in order to address the issues outlined above.

6.3 Model Calibration

EAGLE is a large-scale calibrated multi-country, micro-founded model. Explicit micro-foundations enable the identification of structural parameters and the proper analysis of the impact of structural changes, while the general equilibrium framework allows the effects of the behaviour of households and firms to be appropriately taken into account. The euro area regions are subject to a common monetary policy which reacts to a weighted average of the regional inflation rate and output. The theoretical foundation of the EAGLE model is similar to that of the NAWM.[2]

The model has been calibrated to match the key steady state and dynamic parameters of a large euro area country (the domestic economy). Great ratios, fiscal variables and trade linkages are based on actual data (taken from the OECD and national accounts) while structural parameters (utility function, production function, elasticity of substitution) and parameters driving the dynamics of the model are set according to empirical literature and existing evidence from similar models (mainly the NAWM and IMF's GEM model described in Bayouni 2004). To save space, we only report the calibration to the domestic economy (see Gomes et al. 2012 for the other blocks). Notice that the four economies are structurally identical but are calibrated differently.

The discount factor is calibrated so that the (annual) equilibrium real interest rate is about 3%. The habit persistence parameter is set to 0.75, the intertemporal elasticity of substitution to 1.0 and the Frisch elasticity to 0.50. The quarterly depreciation rate of private capital is set to 0.025, consistent with an annual

[2]See Gomes et al. (2012) for a more detailed description of the EAGLE model.

depreciation rate of 10%. Non-tradable and tradable intermediate goods are both produced using a Cobb-Douglas technology with productive public capital (as in Clancy et al. 2016). The elasticity of substitution between domestic tradable and imported goods is higher than that between tradable and non-tradable goods. The degree of substitutability between tradable and non-tradable goods is set to 0.50 while the substitutability between domestic and imported tradable goods is set to 2.50 (see Corbo and Osbat 2013; Imbs and Méjean 2009, 2010). Note that the elasticity for imported goods is lower in the short term, as imports are subject to adjustment costs. The bias toward the tradable bundle is lower in the consumption basket than in the investment basket. The elasticity of substitution between public and private consumption (Clancy et al. 2016) equals 0.30 as in Coenen et al. (2012) and Leeper et al. (2010).

We set Calvo price parameters in the domestic tradable and non-tradable sectors to 0.80. The indexation parameters on prices and wages are equal to 0.50 and 0.75, respectively, to get sufficiently hump-shaped response of wages and prices. For real rigidities, we set the parameters of the adjustment costs on investment changes to 6.0. Adjustment costs on consumption and investment imports are set to 2.0. Adjustment costs on capital utilisation are equal to 0.007 as in Smets and Wouters (2003).

The mark-up in the non-tradable sector (services) is higher than that in the labour market while the latter is higher than the mark-up in the tradable sector (manufacturing). The (net) price mark-up in the domestic economy is set to 50%, 30% and 20% in the service, labour and manufacturing sectors, respectively (Oliveira Martins et al. 1996; Oliveira Martins and Scarpetta 1999; Jean and Nicoletti 2002; Faruqee et al. 2007; Everaert and Schule 2008; Christopoulou and Vermeulen 2008).

Finally, the monetary authority follows a Taylor rule, where the interest rate reacts to the inertial component of the monetary policy, annual inflation and quarterly output growth. The fiscal rule ensures that the debt-to-GDP ratio is brought back to its baseline value and is calibrated as in the NAWM.

6.4 The EAGLE Model-Based Analysis of Structural Reforms

Consistent with EAGLE's modelling framework, in the simulations below, structural reform implementation is captured by a reduction in price or wage mark-ups reflecting a wedge between monopolistic and perfectly competitive concepts of equilibrium. For illustrative purposes, we consider a hypothetical permanent reduction in the non-tradable (service) sector price mark-up by 10 percentage points gradually over 2 years. Our benchmark simulation features a unilateral (country-specific) implementation of the reform in one of the euro area country (EA) assuming that the area-wide monetary policy is constrained by the ELB in the short run. In particular, we assume that, following the start of reform implementation the nominal interest rate is ex ante fixed for 2 years and it is fully anticipated by agents. Additional scenarios considered in the paper serve to illustrate sensitivity of the benchmark results to alternative model parameterization reflecting, for instance, historic structural heterogeneity of the euro area economies as well as to assess implications of alternative design of reform implementation by exploring various reform combination and coordination possibilities.

6.4.1 *The Role of Monetary Policy*

In order to investigate importance of monetary policy accommodation in shaping the macroeconomic response to structural reforms, we first consider a set of model simulations under alternative monetary policy reactions: (i) monetary policy constrained by the effective lower bound ('Benchmark'), (ii) unconstrained interest rate setting in line with the monetary policy rule ('Unconstrained standard monetary policy'), and (iii) fixed policy interest rate combined with the non-standard monetary policy measures ('Non-standard monetary policy at the ELB'). In the latter case, the non-standard monetary policy measures are calibrated in line with the available ECB staff estimates of impact of the ECB's non-standard monetary policy measures (excluding the March 2016 decisions) on the euro area GDP (Praet 2016).[3]

As simulations in Fig. 6.1 show, the unilateral implementation of the service sector reform may lead to transitional economic costs for some components of GDP, such as a fall in consumption, while investment rises in the short run (regardless of whether monetary policy is constrained by the ELB). Gradual reduction in the monopolistic power of firms implies downward adjustment of output prices and expansion in production levels. As a result, demand for factors of production increases and leads to higher investment and labour demand. A higher return on capital and labour services supports consumption over the long term. In the short run, however, substantial downward pressures on inflation, entailed by the reform, in the absence of effective monetary policy response, may induce a sharp rise in real interest rates and a transitory output loss, mainly via weakened domestic consumption. Indeed, the expected persistent decline in the relative price of consumption goods raises the return on current savings; hence, it is optimal to postpone consumption. In addition, while real wages of workers are boosted already in the short run, a significant share of households who own firms face sizable profit income losses due to decline in output prices. Indeed, simulations in Fig. 6.1 reveal potential

[3]In particular, the scenario assumes a reduction of the domestic risk premium (the wedge between the actual borrowing rate and the riskless interest rate set by the monetary authorities) in the euro area and a depreciation of the euro vis-à-vis the US dollar both designed to target a 1.5% extra benefit in terms of GDP growth, consistent with Praet (2016).

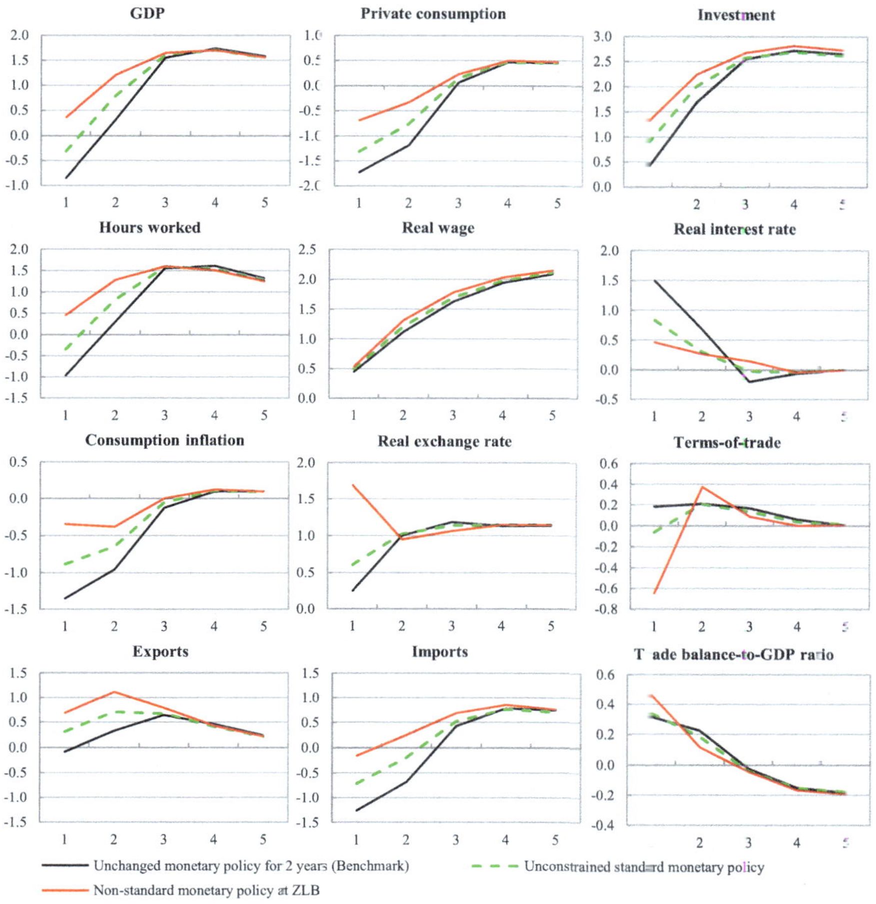

Fig. 6.1 Simulated impact of reform under alternative scenarios of monetary policy responses. Note: The figure depicts percentage (percentage point in case of inflation, interest rate and trade balance-to-GDP ratio) deviations from the baseline over a 5-year horizon

short-term adverse output effects for isolated reform implementation in individual countries even in cases when area-wide monetary policy is not constrained. If monetary policy is constrained by the ELB, the anticipated reduction in the inflation rate leads to a higher domestic real interest rate and a larger output loss in the short term. Nevertheless, under both scenarios, output growth is positive by the second year.

The interplay of the ELB constraint and non-standard monetary policy measures can substantially reduce transitional costs (Fig. 6.1). In this case, by lowering the risk premium, non-standard monetary policy helps reducing private sector borrowing costs which stimulates domestic demand. In addition, the implied depreciation of the euro exchange rate boosts domestic exports. As a result, the downward pressure on inflation associated with the structural reform implementation and the implied real interest rate increase is more limited, resulting in the benefits of the reforms being realized more rapidly when the non-standard measures are applied. Of course, the non-standard measures are applied across the euro area and therefore give larger positive offsetting impacts in comparison to the unconstrained monetary policy simulation where the latter policy response is limited as it is only reacting to conditions in one country. Nevertheless, the benign impacts of the reforms when combined with the non-standard measures show that the asset purchase policies create very favourable conditions for implementing reforms.

6.4.2 Impact of Rigidities

Price flexibility, which is directly linked to the frequency at which prices are re-optimized by firms, facilitates faster macroeconomic adjustment to shocks and, more importantly, implies lower relative price distortion and therefore higher output. In the benchmark scenario, a representative firm re-optimizes its output price on average every five quarters (in line with micro estimates).[4] If instead firms were able to set their prices optimally only every ten quarters, the reform would imply a considerably smaller reduction in domestic inflation in the first year (see Fig. 6.2). Slower price adjustment would facilitate weaker negative response in domestic demand in the short run. At the same time, the medium-term output gains will be realized at a slower pace. This is due to the fact that the implied increase in the real interest rate would be smaller, but more persistent and therefore would extend transitional costs of lower private consumption over a longer horizon.

Another key element to understand the dynamics of the economy, at least in the short term, is firms' ability to adapt their existing stock of capital to the new economic environment. More specifically, when adjustment costs of the capital utilization rate are high (that is, an increase in services of the existing capital stock comes at high costs) firms are forced to increase investment from the beginning of the period to adjust their production to the expected surge in aggregate demand. This additional stimulus in investment demand partly mitigates the initial decrease in consumption and allows for a limited output loss in the first year. This gain in economic activity brings higher inflation in the short term and lower increase in real interest rate.

---

[4]Due to presence of partial price indexation output prices are changed every period in line with the economy-wide level of inflation.

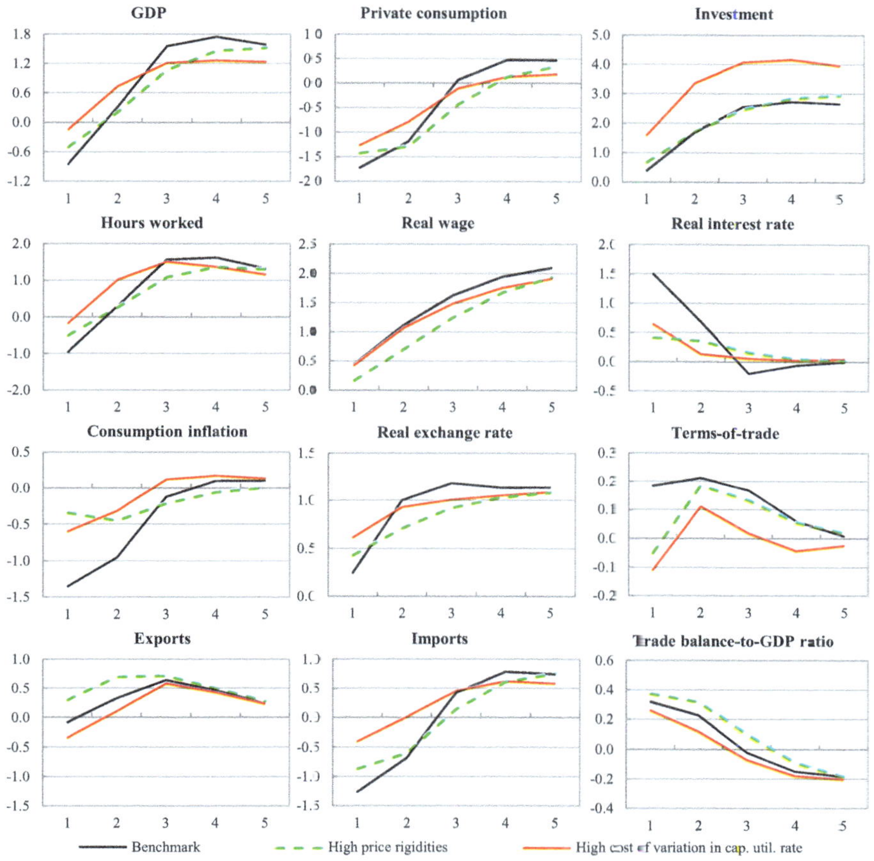

Fig. 6.2 Simulated impact of reform at the effective lower bound under alternative assumptions about economic flexibility. Notes: The figure depicts percentage (percentage point in case of inflation, interest rate and trade balance-to-GDP ratio) deviations from the baseline over a 5-year horizon. In this simulation, firms are able to set their prices optimally only every ten quarters

6.4.3 Delays in Reform Implementation

In the simulations above of the service sector reform there are no implementation delays. In the alternative scenarios below we consider reforms which are announced 2 years ahead of their implementation. It turns out that, at the effective lower bound, pre-announcement of the reform help limiting possible transitory costs of the reform associated with higher real interest rate, since reform implementation starts after the ELB stops being binding. This advantage, however, has to be weighed against considerable delays in realization of economic benefits of the reform.

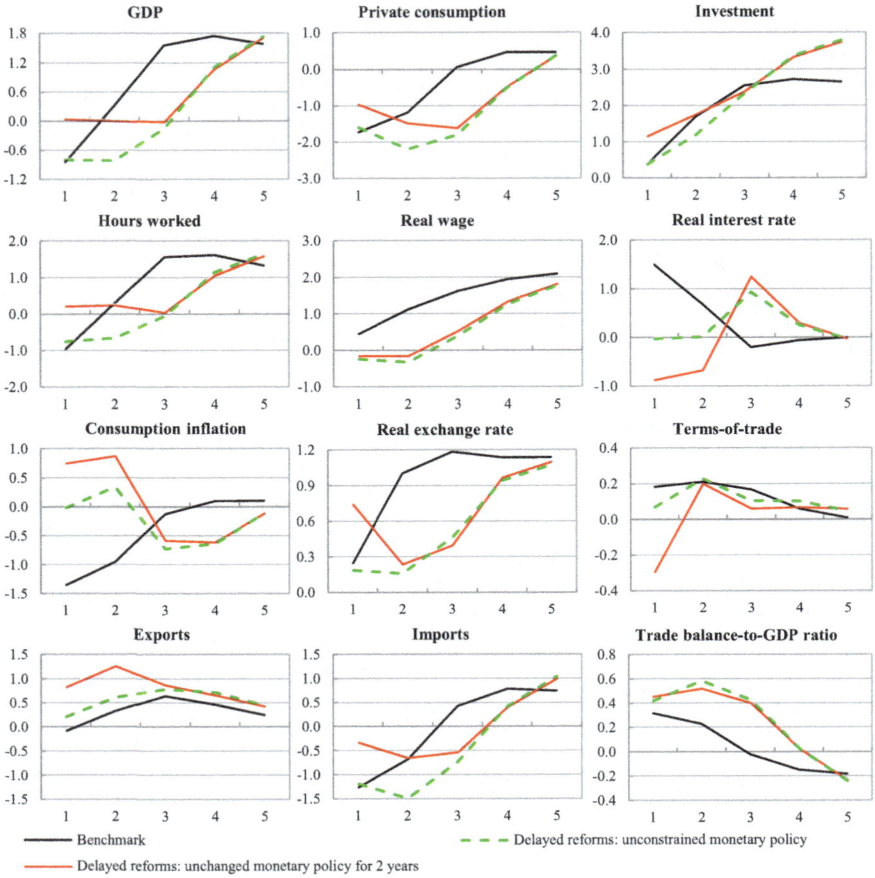

Fig. 6.3 Simulated impact of reform under alternative assumptions about the speed of implementation of the reform. Note: The figure depicts percentage (percentage point in case of inflation, interest rate and trade balance-to-GDP ratio) deviations from the baseline over a 5-year horizon

Let us first consider a 'normal times' scenario with an unconstrained monetary policy (see Fig. 6.3). Compared to the benchmark case, the short-term economic outlook is worsened as households are postponing their consumption plans for a longer period. In the short run, consumption drops more and investment increases less. The rebound appears later on when the reforms start to kick in. The inflation drop is now delayed by 2 years like the gain in competitiveness. Nevertheless, the trade balance improves further more in the short term mainly due to the contraction in the domestic demand.

In the second alternative scenario (see Fig. 6.3) the monetary policy rate is kept constant over a 2-year horizon. Firms fully anticipating a rise in long-term output would boost investment demand upon announcement of the planned reforms. As in the benchmark case, households postpone consumption until prices adjust. In the short run, the implied excess supply of goods is larger and leads to a stronger depreciation of the euro. The latter effect supports higher exports but also implies stronger inflationary pressures in the short run. Subsequently, the surge in inflation implies lower real interest rate which, in turn, stimulates domestic demand. Hence, compared to the active monetary policy case, consumption decreases less and investment is growing faster.

6.4.4 Reform Combination

In practice, structural reforms are rarely limited to some specific sectors of the economy. During the recent episode of structural reforms in Europe, both product and labour markets were targeted. Moreover, limiting the transmission channels of structural policy to just shrinking monopolistic mark-ups is, admittedly, a gross simplification of potential effects of structural reforms. In extending our analysis of the implications of structural reforms at the ELB, we first discuss model-based simulation results of scenarios where reform of the service sector is augmented by a contemporaneous labour market liberalisation. The latter is implemented via a permanent 10 percentage points reduction in the economy-wide wage mark-up gradually over 2 years. Next, we investigate the implications of the service sector reform which not only diminishes firms' monopolistic power but also facilitates an increase in productivity. Liberalization of the service sector can also be perceived as a positive productivity shock reflecting a related improvement in the general business environment. To this end, we assume total factor productivity in the service sector increases permanently by 1% gradually over 2 years.

The joint implementation of service sector and labour market reforms allows stronger long-term economic expansion and eliminates the short-run output losses even at the ELB (see Fig. 6.4). The labour market reform, by increasing competition in the labour market, lowers real wages which leads to an increase in labour demand. Higher employment helps mitigate labour income losses induced by lower real wages and supports consumption of liquidity-constrained households.[5] Liquidity unconstrained households boost consumption in response to elevated corporate profitability. In addition, driven by strong external competitiveness gains and large positive spill-over effects from the reforming country to the rest of the euro area, domestic exports rise substantially.

[5]The strength of the employment increase in the short run is dependent on the level of competition in the goods market, the degree of nominal price and wage rigidities, the price sensitivity of export demand, and the elasticity of substitution between domestic tradable goods and imports (WGEM 2012). Furthermore, employment frictions (i.e., search-matching costs) may significantly reduce short-run economic gains of labour market liberalisation. The EAGLE model does not account for the latter; hence, the simulations should be treated with caution.

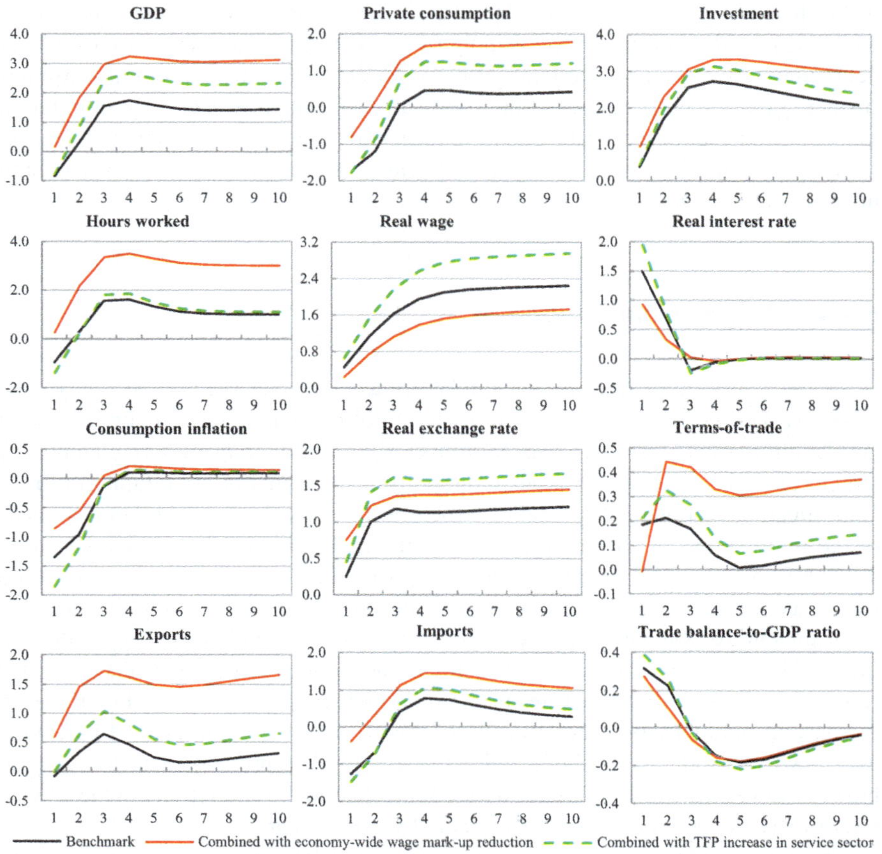

Fig. 6.4 Simulated impact of reform at the zero lower bound under alternative assumptions about the reform combination. Note: The figure depicts percentage (percentage point in case of inflation, interest rate and trade balance-to-GDP ratio) deviations from the baseline over a 5-year horizon

In comparison to the benchmark case, the terms-of-trade deteriorate reflecting lower prices of tradable goods. Import demand increases in line with stronger domestic income. Consequently, the improvement in the trade balance in the short run is slightly weaker than in the benchmark case. The long-term impact on the economy is significantly stronger. The most noticeable exception is real wages which increase by less than in the benchmark case due to the direct impact of labour market reforms. The GDP response is twice as large as in the benchmark case, and is always positive even in the short term, driven by the labour market reform which contributes to a proportionately greater response in consumption, employment and foreign trade flows.

As concerns productivity enhancing effects, the additional impact on growth in the very short term is estimated to be quite limited given the time required for the economy to fully benefit from this extra boost and also due to the fact that the positive effect on the economy of the future productivity prospect is partially counter-balanced by a less favourable real interest rates evolution due to lower inflation. When the two shocks are cumulated, inflation drops further implying higher real interest rates. At the same time, the overall impact on exports is positive as the domestic economy is gaining price competitiveness. Terms-of-trade vis-à-vis the rest of the euro area deteriorate more and subsequently boost domestic exports towards this region leading to a slight improvement in the trade balance.

6.4.5 Reform Sequencing

The EAGLE model-based simulation results shown in Fig. 6.4 suggest that simultaneously implementing labour and product market reforms is advantageous, as it facilitates positive expansion already in the short run in GDP, employment and real wages and results in faster stabilization of the economy around the new equilibrium.[6] In case of unsynchronised implementation of the reforms, the model-based simulations show that delaying service market reform may help to reduce the transitional output costs, though at the expense of a slower medium-term increase in demand, especially, investment (see Fig. 6.5). Delaying the service sector reforms, which generally feature considerably stronger downward pressure on inflation, reduces the room for the negative effects associated with the real interest rate channels at the effective lower bound in part because the period during which monetary policy is constrained is shorter. In contrast, delaying labour reforms worsens the short-term outlook which features lower GDP and higher downward pressure on inflation.

6.4.6 Domestic and Cross-Border Structural Policy Coordination

In the benchmark scenario fiscal authorities set their expenditures in line with actual GDP developments, i.e. fiscal policy is pro-cyclical. It implies that the transitory fall in GDP leads to lower government expenditures which, in turn, implies additional contribution to weaker output in the short run. Alternatively, fiscal authorities could set expenditures in line with potential output which is gradually rising as reforms

[6] This policy recommendation contrasts with Blanchard and Giavazzi (2003) who argue that one should start by deregulation of the product market.

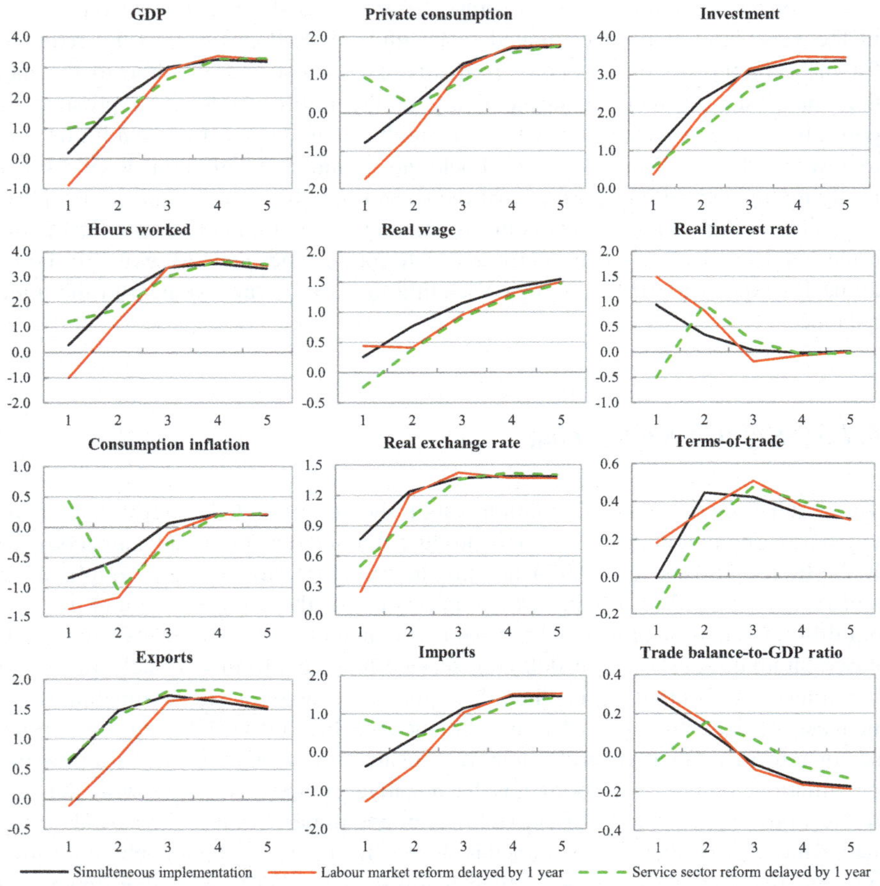

Fig. 6.5 Simulated impact of reform at the zero lower bound under alternative assumptions about the sequencing of labour and product market reforms. Note: The figure depicts percentage (percentage point in case of inflation, interest rate and trade balance-to-GDP ratio) deviations from the baseline over a 5-year horizon

being implemented. The implied contra-cyclical fiscal policy response (provided monetary policy is at the ELB) appears to be highly effective in largely averting output costs associated with the reforms (see Fig. 6.6). In this case, fiscal authorities would directly contribute to aggregate demand as well as indirectly support private consumption by reducing downward inflationary pressures, hence limiting the initial rise in the real interest rate.

Similarly, transitory output costs could be reduced significantly in case the reform is undertaken across the euro area. Relative to the individual country benchmark simulation, the coordinated area wide reform policy implementation ('Area-wide reform') facilitates quicker realization of the benefits of the reforms

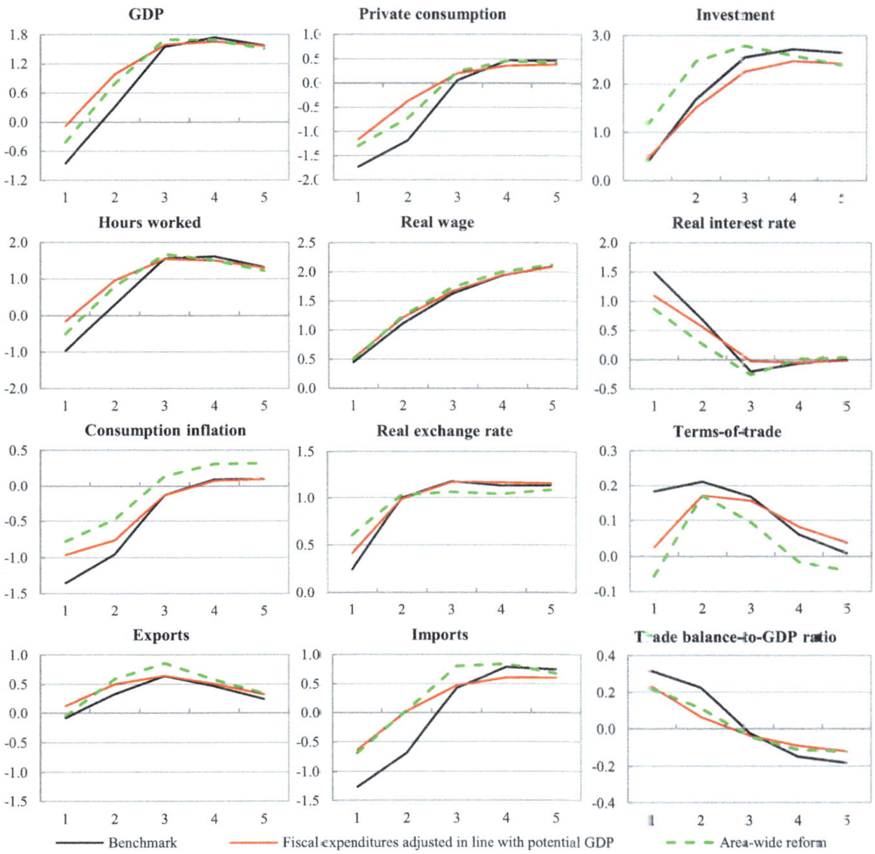

Fig. 6.6 Simulated impact of reform at the zero lower bound under alternative assumptions about policy coordination domestically and internationally. Note: The figure depicts percentage (percentage point in case of inflation, interest rate and trade balance-to-GDP ratio) deviations from the baseline over a 5-year horizon

through positive cross-border spill-over effects and stronger adjustment in the nominal exchange rate of the euro. These euro area-wide reforms support domestic output as the entire euro area now grows at a higher pace. This extra gain in aggregate demand, mainly driven by trade (exports are growing much faster), reduces the downward pressure on inflation and brings a more favourable domestic real interest rate evolution. As a consequence, the decrease in domestic consumption is also smaller compared to the benchmark scenario. In the short term, weaker consumption, combined with exports expansion, results in a foreign trade surplus which is, however, smaller than under the benchmark case. When reforms gradually kick in and euro area aggregate demand increases, the trade balance in each euro area region moves below its equilibrium level implying stronger real exchange rate depreciation. In the long run, the cross-border spill-over effects are estimated to be positive but quite limited, hence the long-run effect on the domestic economy when reforms are simultaneously implemented in the two euro area regions is similar to the benchmark case.

6.5 Conclusions

The model-based simulations of structural reforms in the service sector conducted using the baseline model specification indicate some possible potential costs that could be associated with monetary policy being constrained by the effective lower bound. However, it should be stressed, that in the case of single euro area countries, monetary policy response to any country specific shocks is limited even in normal times. Importantly, non-standard measures applied by the ECB seem to create favourable financial conditions for reform implementation diminishing constraints hindering resource reallocation across firms and over time.

In the light of macroeconomic instability induced by the global financial crisis and the euro area sovereign debt crisis, structural reform implementation took place in an environment which may be different from that associated with 'normal times'. In this regard, alternative scenarios featuring higher degree of nominal and real rigidities, and delays in implementation of the pre-announced reforms reveal outcomes of lower transitory output costs in cases where monetary policy has more difficulties in softening its stance in response to structural reform implementation. The implied lower transitory costs of the reforms, however, are associated with some significant delays in realization of the economic benefits of structural reforms and higher costs in the medium to long run.

In mitigating possible short-term costs of reforms under constrained monetary policy, it seems worthwhile to put more emphasis on a combination of reforms that have the least possible short-run negative impact or on measures that boost productivity in the long run without inflicting significant short-term economic costs, such as e.g. improving the overall business environment, boosting R&D spending, strengthening active labour market policies, and encouraging investment into knowledge based capital. Moreover, structural adjustment in the euro area should benefit from a greater coordination at the area-wide level as well as a supportive role of fiscal policy. With a proper policy mix, negative short-term effects can be sidestepped and long-term benefits maximized. Finally, policy makers should take into account the whole cost-benefit analysis of reforms and not only consider their short-term impacts, as reform benefits are mainly realized in the medium to longer run.

References

Andres J, Arce O, Thomas C (2014) Structural reforms in a debt overhang. Banco de España working paper 1421

Bayoumi T (2004) GEM: a new international macroeconomic model. IMF occasional paper 239

Bayoumi T, Laxton D, Pesenti P (2004) Benefits and spillovers of greater competition in Europe: a macroeconomic assessment. NBER working paper 10416

Blanchard O, Giavazzi F (2003) Macroeconomic effects of regulation and deregulation in goods and labour markets. Q J Econ 118(3):879–907

Cacciatore M, Duval R, Fiori G, Ghironi F (2016) Short-term pain for long-term gain? Market deregulation and monetary policy in small open economies. J Int Money Financ 68:358–385

Christopoulou R, Vermeulen P (2008) Mark-ups in the euro area and the US over the period 1981–2004: A comparison of 50 sectors. ECB working paper 856

Clancy D, Jacquinot P, Lozej M (2016) Government expenditure composition and fiscal policy spillovers in small open economies within a monetary union. J Macroecon 48:305–326

Coenen G, McAdam P, Straub R (2008) Tax reform and labour-market performance in the euro area: a simulation-based analysis using the New Area-Wide Model. J Econ Dyn Control 32(8):2543–2583

Coenen G, Straub R, Trabandt M (2012) Fiscal policy and the great recession in the EA. Am Econ Rev 102(3):71–76

Corbo V, Osbat C (2013) Trade adjustment in the European union—a structural estimation approach. ECB working paper 1535

Eggertson G, Ferrero A, Raffo A (2014) Can structural reforms help Europe? J Monet Econ 61:2–22

European Central Bank (2015a) Progress with structural reforms across the euro area and their possible impacts. ECB Econ Bull 2:59–71

European Central Bank (2015b) What is behind the recent rebound in euro area employment? ECB Econ Bull 8:54–72

European Central Bank (2016) Increasing resilience and long-term growth: the importance of sound institutions and economic structures for euro area countries and EMU. ECB Econ Bull 5:76–96

Everaert L, Schule W (2008) Why it pays to synchronize structural reforms in the euro area across markets and countries. IMF Staff Pap 55(2):356–366

Faruqee H, Laxton D, Muir D, Pesenti P (2007) Smooth landing or crash? Model-based scenarios of global current account rebalancing. In: Clarida R (ed) G7 current account imbalances: sustainability and adjustment. University of Chicago Press, Chicago

Fernández-Villaverde J (2014) Discussion of "Can structural reforms help Europe?" by Gauti Eggertsson, Andrea Ferrero, and Andrea Raffo. J Monet Econ 61(C):23–31

Fernández-Villaverde J, Guerrón-Quintana P, Rubio-Ramírez J (2011) Supply-side policies and the zero lower bound. NBER working paper 17543

Forni L, Gerali A, Pisani M (2010) Macroeconomic effects of greater competition in the service sector: the case of Italy. Macroecon Dyn 14(5):677–708

Gerali A, Notarpietro A, Pisani M (2015) Structural reforms and zero lower bound in a monetary union. Manch Sch 83(S3):120–139

Gomes S (2018) Euro area structural reforms in times of a global crisis. J Macroecon 55:28–45

Gomes S, Jacquinot P, Pisani M (2012) The EAGLE. A model for policy analysis of macroeconomic interdependence in the euro area. Econ Model 29(5):1686–1714

Gomes S, Jacquinot P, Mohr M, Pisani M (2013) Structural reforms and macroeconomic performance in the euro area countries: a model-based assessment. Int Fin 16(1):23–44

Imbs J, Méjean I (2009) Elasticities optimism. CEPR discussion paper 7177

Imbs J, Méjean I (2010) Trade elasticities. A final report for the European Commission. European Commission economic papers 432

Jean S, Nicoletti G (2002) Product market regulation and wage premia in Europe and North America: an empirical investigation. OECD working paper 419

Leeper EM, Walker TB, Yang S-CS (2010) Government investment and fiscal stimulus. J Monet Econ 57:1000–1012

Oliveira Martins J, Scarpetta S (1999) The levels and cyclical behaviour of mark-ups across countries and market structures. OECD working paper 213

Oliveira Martins J, Scarpetta S, Pilat D (1996) Mark-up ratios in manufacturing industries: estimates for 14 OECD countries. OECD working paper 162

Praet P (2016) Transmission channels of monetary policy in the current environment. Speech at the Financial Times Festival of Finance, London, 1 July 2016

Smets F, Wouters R (2003) An estimated dynamic stochastic general equilibrium model of the euro area. J Eur Econ Assoc 1(5):1123–1175

Vogel L, (2014) Structural reforms at the zero bound. European Commission, European Economy economic papers 537

WGEM (2012) Competitiveness and external imbalances within the euro area. ECB occasional paper 139

Chapter 7
When Do Structural Reforms Work? On the Role of the Business Cycle and Macroeconomic Policies

Anna Rose Bordon, Christian Ebeke, and Kazuko Shirono

7.1 Introduction

The effects of structural reforms are surprisingly difficult to pin down empirically for a variety of reasons. First, the effects of structural reforms may be endogenous to the economic environment in which reforms are conducted. For example, the impact of a reform implemented shortly before a cyclical upswing is difficult to be distinguished from the recovery itself. Figure 7.1 illustrates this point: the chart plots employment (as percentage of the labour force) in Germany. Employment appears to have risen after the so-called Hartz reforms implemented during the downturn in the early 2000s (shaded area), but one will need to untangle the impact of the reform on employment from the general improvement in the economic condition after the recession (gray-shaded area) in order to correctly capture the impact of the reforms. In this example, the possible endogeneity of the reform effort—that is, the fact that it was implemented when economic circumstances were about to turn—creates a possible upward bias in the estimates. There could also be a downward

The views expressed are those of the author(s) and do not necessarily represent the views of the IMF, its Executive Board, or IMF management. We are indebted to Helge Berger for his valuable inputs and guidance. We thank Romain Duval, Davide Furceri, participants at the IMF EUR surveillance meetings and SPR-RES Jobs and Growth seminar and participants at the IMF-DNB October 2015 Conference on Structural Reforms in Amsterdam for their comments and suggestions.

A. R. Bordon (✉) · K. Shirono
Strategy, Policy and Review Department, Washington, DC, USA
e-mail: ABordon@imf.org; KShirono@imf.org

C. Ebeke
European Department of the International Monetary Fund, Washington, DC, USA
e-mail: CEbeke@imf.org

J. de Haan, J. Parlevliet (eds.), *Structural Reforms*,
https://doi.org/10.1007/978-3-319-74400-1_7

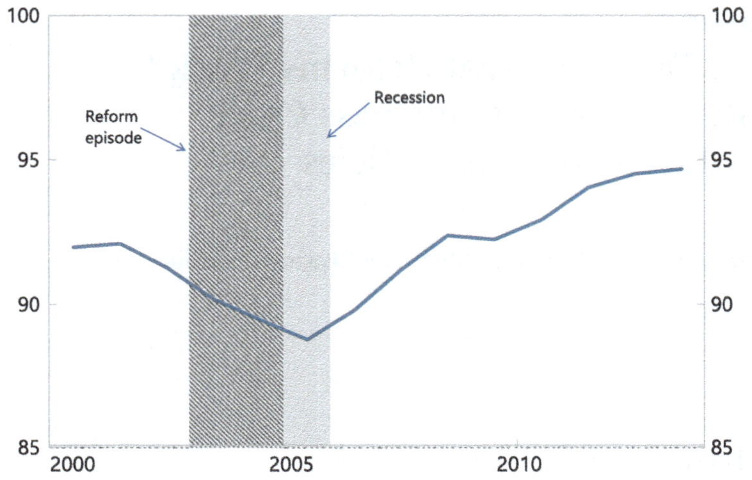

Fig. 7.1 Germany: employment rate (% labour force). Source: IMF WEO; OECD

bias, however. If, for example, countries implement structural reforms early during a downturn, this could create a downward bias in the estimate. In such a case, structural reforms will tend to be observed when employment or growth is low, and a simple regression will underestimate the impact of reforms on employment or growth.

Second, the business cycle could affect the magnitude of the impact of structural reforms. For example, structural reforms may free up resources that cannot be absorbed in more efficient sectors because excess capacity exists and aggregate demand is low. A reform launched during recessions could also add further uncertainty, for example, because of required legal clarification. In these cases, some structural reforms may not achieve the desired improvements, having small or even negative effects in depressed economies.

Third, the state of the cycle itself may not only affect the likelihood of a reform or shape the reform's impact on macroeconomic outcomes, but also prompt a macroeconomic policy response. Monetary or fiscal policy conducted with structural reforms could affect the estimated impact of the reform. By reducing the uncertainty and sustaining aggregate demand during the reform episode, supportive macroeconomic policies can increase the positive effects of reforms on macroeconomic outcomes. It is therefore crucial to account for the policy stance when examining the macroeconomic effects of reforms.

The large literature on estimating the impact of structural reforms is only beginning to address these issues (see Sect. 7.2). Existing studies have shown that the long-run effects of structural reforms on growth and employment are positive (see Chap. 2). However, the evidence on the short-run effects of structural reforms is rather mixed and limited. While some studies find that the impact of structural reforms may depend on the business cycle, these effects vary across studies in terms of size as well as direction.

This chapter contributes to this literature by presenting robust estimates of the impact of structural reforms by using local projection techniques while controlling for endogeneity and other biases. Local projections allow for estimating the dynamic effects of structural reform by computing the cumulative impact of a reform shock on the change of employment over a 5-year horizon. To address endogeneity, we adopt the augmented inverse probability weighting (AIPW) method which estimates the treatment effects of reforms while controlling for potential selection bias. The chapter also examines the role of the business cycle and macroeconomic policies by explicitly controlling for these variables.

The empirical results suggest that structural reforms have a lagged but positive impact on employment. This estimated positive effect remains even after the endogeneity of the decision to reform is taken into account. Both labour and product market reforms increase employment rates by about a little over 1% point over 5 years. Our analysis also suggests that supportive macroeconomic policy plays an important role in reaping the medium term benefit of labour and product market reforms by enhancing their impact on employment. This supports the view that some structural reforms are best initiated in conjunction with supportive fiscal or monetary policy if policy space so permits.

The rest of the chapter is organized as follows. The next section provides a brief overview of the existing literature. Section 7.3 discusses the data, including the definitions of various variables. Section 7.4 presents the methodologies used in the empirical analysis. Section 7.5 reports the empirical results, and Sect. 7.6 concludes.

7.2 Literature Review

Recent macro studies assessing the impact of structural reforms on the economy can be broadly classified into (i) those using simulations (typically based on DSGE models, such as the IMF's *Global Integrated Monetary and Fiscal model* (GIMF) or the EC's *QUarterly ESTimated macroeconomic model* (QUEST)); and (ii) those using empirical methods (typically based on cross-country data).[1] Many studies report that the long-run effects of structural reforms on output are positive. However, the short-run effects are ambiguous, and some recent studies find that the impact of structural reforms may depend on the business cycle.

Model-based analysis has an advantage of being able to run various scenarios and quantify the impact of structural reforms under different circumstances. For

[1]There is also a large literature that looks at micro evidence from a particular country on the effectiveness of structural reforms, such as trade liberalization, opening to FDI, and entry of large retail chains on firm productivity or employment. This section focuses on the empirical macro literature.

example, Hobza and Mourre (2010) quantify the impact of various structural reforms envisaged in the Europe 2020 strategy using the macroeconomic model QUEST III. They find that structural reforms could boost real GDP growth from 1.7% to 2.2% between 2010 and 2020, depending on the depth of the reforms while employment gains range from 1% to 4.5%. Anderson et al. (2014), using the GIMF model, report that structural reforms in the euro area can increase real GDP, but it will take time for the benefits to fully materialize.[2] Gomes et al. (2013) use a multi-country general equilibrium model of the euro area to assess the macroeconomic effects of increasing competition in the labour and services markets in Germany and the rest of the euro area. The paper concludes that such reforms would increase long-run output.

In empirical studies, the long-run effects on growth, employment, and productivity of product and labour market reforms are also often found to be positive. Bouis and Duval (2011) report on the impact of various structural reforms using estimated models from Bassanini and Duval (2006), Bassanini et al. (2009) and Bourlès et al. (2010).[3] They find that a gradual alignment of product market regulations with best practice in a broad range of non-manufacturing sectors could boost aggregate labour productivity by several percent over 10 years in many OECD countries and by more than 5% across most of continental Europe. They also conclude that labour market reforms in the areas of unemployment benefit systems, activation policies, labour taxes and pension systems could raise employment rates by several percentage points in many OECD countries over a 10-year horizon if these reforms are phased in faster. They also report that the impact of structural reforms is larger in the long run (10 years) than in the medium run (5 years).

There are varied views on the short-run impact of structural reforms, and empirical quantification is relatively limited. OECD (2012b) notes that benefits from structural reforms usually take time to fully materialize, but seldom involve significant losses and often deliver gains already in the short run (see also Cacciatore et al. 2012). However, some argue that short-run effects of structural reforms could be negative especially when slack in the economy is large.[4] Structural reforms may free up resources that cannot be absorbed in more efficient sectors, thus not achieving the desired productivity improvement.

In theory, unemployment benefits and activation policies are likely to boost employment rates relatively quickly and reduce employment because they increase the cost of being unemployed. Job protection reforms, however, can have ambiguous near-term effects, as layoffs are likely to rise in the short run if legal or regulatory constraints are relaxed. Product market reforms can also have ambiguous short-run

---

[2]See also Anderson et al. (2013) and Lusinyan and Muir (2013) who also use the GIMF model to assess the impact of the structural reforms.

[3]See also Barnes et al. (2011) who adopt a somewhat similar approach but cover slightly different reform areas.

[4]See, for example, "Europe's Way Out" by Dani Rodrik available at https://www.project-syndicate.org/commentary/saving-the-long-run-in-the-eurozone-by-dani-rodrik.

effects as inefficient firms may be forced to exit the market due to more competition. On the other hand, new entrants may invest more and create new jobs (OECD 2012a).

Some model-based studies show that short-run effects of some structural reforms can be indeed negative. Anderson et al. (2014) find that weak demand conditions could dampen the short-run impact of structural reform, and in some cases, structural reforms initiated in weaker initial demand conditions have very little positive and possibly negative impact on growth and employment even in the medium run.[5]

Empirical studies on the short-term effect of structural reforms are rather scarce. Bouis et al. (2012a) find that structural reforms deliver short-run benefits. For example, an increase in spending on ALMP employment incentives will raise employment even in the short run. Unemployment benefit reforms (especially a reduction in unemployment benefit duration) also boost employment relatively quickly. However, they also find tentative evidence that unemployment benefit (a reduction in the initial unemployment benefit replacement rate) and job protection reforms pay off more in good times than in bad times, and can entail short-term losses in severely depressed economies. Bouis et al. (2012b) report similar results for the impact of reducing unemployment benefits.

More recently, there has been an emerging view on the role of macroeconomic policies and structural reforms, particularly in the context of the debate on policy options to facilitate recovery from the European debt crisis. Eggertsson et al. (2014), using a standard dynamic stochastic general equilibrium model, show that structural reform do not increase output during a crisis. Their simulation also suggests that structural reforms may have negative impact when monetary policy is constrained by the effective lower bound (ELB). On the other hand, Decressin et al. (2015) find that structural reforms have a positive impact under quantitative easening.[6] Empirical studies, however, are rather limited in this area.

Building upon the existing studies, particularly Bouis et al. (2012a, b), the following sections estimate the impact of structural reforms on employment. It improves upon previous studies by attempting to correct for selection bias in the estimates and by examining the complementary role of demand policies.

[5]See also Cacciatore et al. (2016) who find that easing job protection implemented in a crisis time deepens and lengthens the recession using a dynamic general equilibrium model.

[6]Policy makers are also acknowledging the link between structural reforms and macro policies in the context of Europe. For example, ECB President Mario Draghi stated that QE will bring an "additional benefit" if "complemented by structural reforms" at the hearing of the European Parliament's Economic and Monetary Affairs Committee (https://www.ecb.europa.eu/press/key/date/2015/html/sp150323_1.en.html).

7.3 Measuring Structural Reform Shocks

The rest of the chapter estimates the dynamic impact of structural reforms on changes in the employment rate. This section explains how we derive the structural reform variable in the sample and discusses other variables used in the analysis.

7.3.1 Structural Reform Shocks

Structural reform shocks are identified based on OECD reform indicators. These range from 0 to 6 to capture the restrictiveness of regulation in labor and product markets. The indices are computed as a weighted sum of scores assigned to several underlying criteria.[7] A higher value indicates more restrictive regulation and the introduction of a reform would be represented by a fall of the index. Following Bouis et al. (2012a, b), a reform shock in this study is identified as a drop in the OECD index, and the reform variable is defined as a dummy variable which takes a value of one when a reform shock is observed.

More specifically, the reform variable used here has the following characteristics:

- *Large*. A change in an OECD index is considered a reform shock if it exceeds two standard deviations of the change in the indicator over all observations. There are, however, far fewer labour market reforms than product market reforms in the sample. Given that fewer observations complicate econometric analysis, the floor for labour market reforms was reduced to one standard deviation. The focus on large episodes allows us to treat them as a shock and to estimate impulse responses using a dynamic specification. This implies that a series of small reforms over several years may not be identified as reform shocks in this study.
- *Discrete*. A reform shock is represented by a dummy variable. While this approach neglects the intensity of a reform, it allows for identifying the impact of reform shocks using treatment evaluation techniques where information on the predicted probability to reform can be taken into account to address the endogeneity issues mentioned earlier. We will discuss the degree to which reform intensity might matter for the reform impact later on.
- *Unsequenced*. We do not address the issue of reform sequencing. This implies that we also do not capture reform reversals. Focusing on drops in the OECD indicators implies that our analysis will ignore episodes where the OECD indicator increases significantly (i.e. tightening of regulations), even after an initial decline in the indicator. Ignoring the presence of possible reform reversals down the road could be misleading and could create substantial biases, given

[7] See http://www.oecd.org/els/emp/EPL-Methodology.pdf and http://www.oecd.org/eco/reform/Schemata_PMR.xlsx on the derivation of labour and product market indices, respectively.

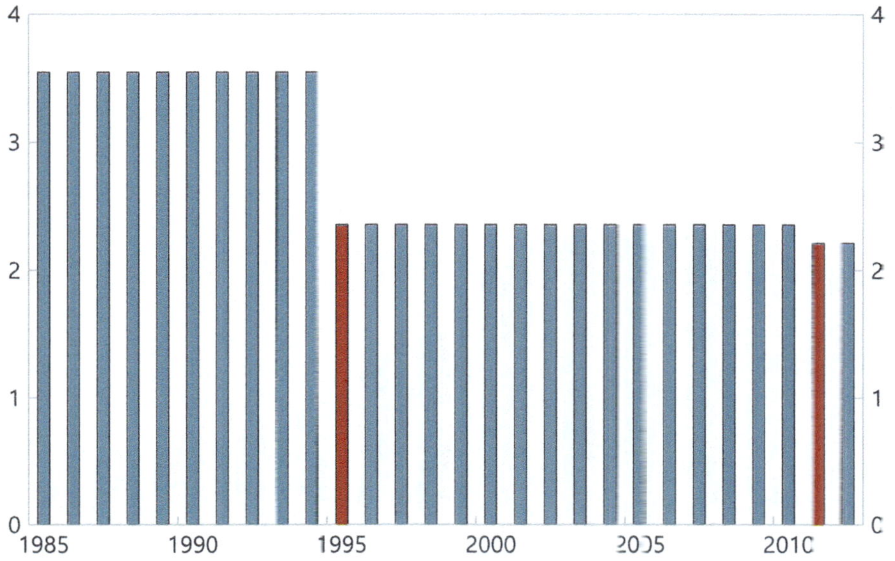

Fig. 7.2 Spain: OECD indicator of EPLR. Source: OECD

that the approach traces the dynamic effects of reform over time. However, a careful examination of the sample suggests that there are very few cases of reform reversals in practice.

- *Non-sectoral.* We do not examine sectoral effects of reform shocks which would require measuring reform shocks at the sectoral level and measuring outcomes at that level of disaggregation.

Figures 7.2 and 7.3 illustrate some of these characteristics. Figure 7.2 shows the OECD indicator on employment protection legislation on regular workers (EPLR) for Spain, and Fig. 7.3 shows the OECD indicator on product market reform (PMR) for the UK. The red bars indicate the years when the drop in the indicators exceed our threshold of two standard deviations and therefore appear with a dummy variable value of 1 in the data. The EPLR indicator for Spain captures labour market reforms applying to regular workers in 1995 and 2011. The changes in the indicator were large enough such that they were captured as reform episodes. The PMR indicator for the UK, on the other hand, shows the gradual implementation of privatization and liberalization in the UK economy. For almost every year from the early 1980s to early 2000s, the indicator declined but in small steps. As a result, only three reform episodes are picked up.

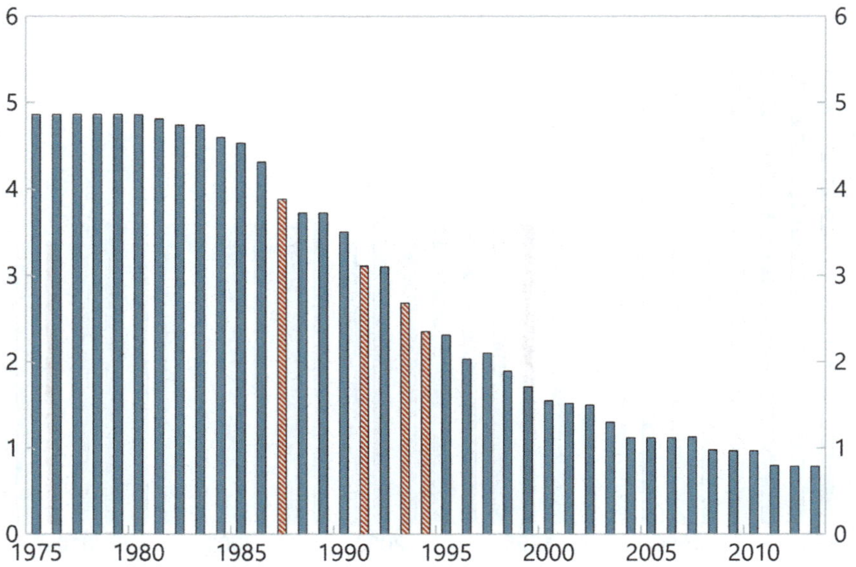

Fig. 7.3 United Kingdom: OECD indicator of PMR. Source: OECD

7.3.2 *Caveats*

The OECD indicators are among the few quantitative and comprehensive measures of reform effort but have a number of well-known limitations. These include the fact that the complexity of employment protection legislation can be difficult to summarize in an index. Also, interactions across reforms may not be well captured in these indicators. For example, several labour market reforms in the 1980s and 1990s that made it more difficult to dismiss regular workers but easier to hire temporary workers are captured as reforms in employment protection legislation on temporary workers. The product market indicator summarizes reforms in seven industries in the energy, communication, and transportation sectors. However, the OECD indicator does not capture any reform that occurs outside these industries.

With these caveats in mind, this chapter analyses the impact of EPLR and product market reforms at the aggregate macro level. All in all, we have data for 36 countries from 1960 to 2013, picking up 28 reforms in employment protection legislation for regular workers and 102 product market reforms (see Fig. 7.4). Limited data availability for several variables needed for the chosen empirical specification further restricts that sample to less than 30 countries (see Appendix 1).

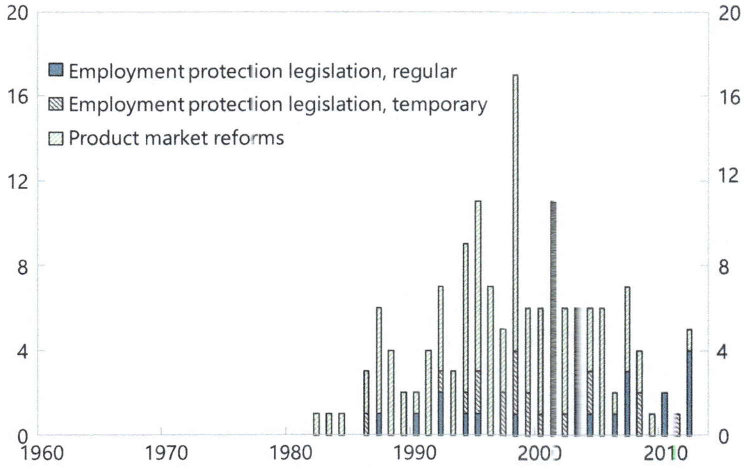

Fig. 7.4 Number of reforms. Source: OECD

7.4 Methodological Issues and Results

Estimating the impact of reforms is a difficult task. As discussed, several considerations should be taken into account. First, tracing the impact of a reform shock on a macro variable over time makes it sensitive to the internal dynamics of the business cycle itself. For instance, if labour market reforms tend to be implemented or launched during periods of substantial slack in the economy but close to a business cycle's turnaround, there is a risk of confounding the positive impact of the reform shocks on job creation with the recovery that follows a recession.

Second, even after cyclical conditions are controlled for, there could still be reasons why the effects of structural reforms could be biased. Reforms and macroeconomic outcomes could be jointly determined by third factors such as the economic and political cycle, the competencies of the leaders in charge of economic affairs, globalization or regional integration, etc. The risk of finding or not finding an impact of reforms on a given outcome will depend on the direction of the bias and its severity.

Third, there could be heterogenous effects in the sense that the marginal and dynamic effects of structural reforms are shaped by the macroeconomic environment and policy responses undertaken by decision makers, which are also strongly correlated.

The next subsection starts by discussing a baseline model. Then, several extensions are considered, including by reducing endogeneity issues and allowing for non-linearities in the effects of reforms.

7.4.1 The Local Projection Method

The key outcome variable of this chapter is the change in the employment rate, following Bouis et al. (2012a, b). Labour market reforms are likely to impact employment more directly while the transmission mechanism of product market reforms on employment may be more complex. The treatment variable is the reform shock and we are interested in estimating the impact of a reform shock in the following years. The employment rate is a more direct consequence of employment protection legislation reforms. The data on employment and real GDP growth are taken from the IMF World Economic Outlook (WEO) database.

The core econometric approach relies on local projection (LP) estimates (Jordà 2005). This follows recent work on estimating fiscal multipliers (Auerbach and Gorodnichecko 2013; Owyang et al. 2013; Jordà and Taylor 2013) where fiscal consolidation is treated as a shock whose impact on growth over several years is estimated via local projections. A key advantage of the LP technique is its flexibility. LP accommodates possibly non-linear or state-dependent impacts easily, which allows for investigating whether the effects of structural reforms can vary during booms or slumps, and in periods of supportive or non-supportive fiscal and monetary policies.

The LP technique is also flexible enough to robustly control for endogeneity issues, especially when the shock variable is not necessarily exogeneous. Later, we will be amending the LP framework to allow for an identification strategy which uses treatment effect methods as in Jordà and Taylor (2013) to reduce risks of endogeneity bias.

7.4.2 Baseline Specification

The first set of estimations aims at measuring the time-varying association between reform shocks and changes in employment rates while controlling for basic determinants, cyclical conditions, and time-invariant factors. More formally, the LP specification is as follows:

$$e_{i,t+h} = \theta_h R_{i,t} + \psi_h(L)e_{i,t+h-1} + X'_{i,t-1}\Gamma_h + u_i + \lambda_t + \epsilon_{i,t+h} \tag{7.1}$$

where $e_{i,\,t+h} = E_{i,\,t+h} - E_{i,\,t-1}$, and E_{it} is the employment rate in country i observed at year t. We estimate the model at each horizon $h = 0, 1, \ldots, 5$.[8] R is the reform variable and X is a matrix of control variables. Control variables include the lagged change in the employment rate, the output gap, output loss during financial crises, and country and year fixed effects to account for time-invariant

[8]The employment rate here is defined as the ratio of total employment to the labour force.

Table 7.1 Effect of reform on the employment rate (Baseline; dependent variable: deviation in employment rate relative to pre-reform year)

	Year 0	Year 1	Year 2	Year 3	Year 4	Year 5
Labour market reforms	−0.185	−0.311	0.103	0.705	1.233**	1.458**
	(−1.15)	(−0.97)	(0.19)	(1.55)	(2.59)	(2.53)
Observations	555	555	555	526	497	468
Number of countries	29	29	29	29	29	24
Product market reforms	0.134	0.261*	0.444*	0.645***	0.781***	0.954***
	(1.37)	(1.70)	(1.93)	(2.75)	(3.14)	(3.60)
Observations	709	709	709	683	657	631
Number of countries	26	26	26	26	26	26

Notes: t-statistics from Driscoll-Kraay standard errors in parentheses. Additional controls: Lagged annual change in employment rates (3 lags), lagged output gap, output loss during a financial crisis (Laeven and Valencia 2013)
***$p < 0.01$, **$p < 0.05$, *$p < 0.1$

country-specific factors and common time effects across countries (e.g., the global business cycle), respectively.[9] The output gap is included to control for cyclical conditions while the output loss during financial crises aims at capturing possible structural breaks at the country level arising from large financial instability. Except for the output loss due to a financial crisis, which is taken from Laeven and Valencia (2013), all variables are from the IMF WEO database.[10] The coefficients of interest are θ_h which measure the impact of reforms on the cumulative change in the employment rate at each horizon starting in year $h = 0$ (the year of the reform) up to 5 years after the reform is identified. Driscoll and Kraay (1998) standard errors are computed to account for correlations in the error terms. The models are estimated using a sample of 29 or 26 OECD countries (see Appendix 1 for details) observed over the period 1980–2013.

Table 7.1 reflects the cumulative impact of the reform on the employment rate on years 0–5. For labour market reforms, proxied by changes in the EPLR indicator, the impact is not significantly different from zero in years 0–3. It becomes significantly positive in year 4–5. By year 5, the reform increases the employment rate by 1.5% points. This is the same order of magnitude that Bouis et al. (2012a, b) find. For product market reforms, the impact is positive and statistically significant in years 1–5, with the employment rate rising by about 1% point by year 5.

These results are consistent with other empirical work: in the near term, the impact of reforms on the change in employment is not significant. The positive impact is felt in the medium term.

[9]There may be other factors that affect employment (e.g. social benefits and pensions, labour market income tax). Country fixed effects capture these institutional differences to the extent that these policies are time-invariant.

[10]WEO data is as of February 2014. Alternative specifications that we tried include the labour force participation rate and its various lags as additional control variables.

7.4.3 *State-Dependent Reform Multipliers: Initial Conditions Could Matter*

Initial conditions could matter for structural reforms, and the effects of these reforms may be affected by the state of the business cycle. Assume, for example, that two countries with otherwise similar characteristics launch structural reforms in good and bad times, as measured by the size of the output gap, respectively. The interesting question is whether the resulting employment rate paths will be the same. Analytical results on this question are not clear cut as discussed in Sect. 7.2. In this part of the chapter, we propose a formal test of the interaction between reforms and employment rate, conditional on business cycle conditions at the time of the inception of structural reforms.

To measure the effects, we amend the baseline LP model to include an interaction of the reform variable interacted with a measure of the business cycle at the time of the introduction of the reform. The cyclical variable is a dummy variable taking the value 1 in each year in which the output gap as percentage of potential output (extracted from the IMF WEO database and based on desk estimates) is lower than -1% ("bad times"), and 0 otherwise ("good times").[11]

To ensure that we correctly identify the contribution of the state of the business cycle to the marginal effect of structural reforms on employment, we need to take into account the fact that the state of the business cycle is likely to prompt a policy response in the form of demand-supporting policies in the short-term. The risk is therefore to confound the effect of the interaction of reforms with the business cycle variable, with the effect of policy changes put in place to respond to the economic cycle. To gauge this possible effect, we control in the model for indicators of fiscal and monetary policy stances (P).[12] Following the work by Alesina and Perotti (1995), we define a fiscal consolidation event within countries as a period where the annual change in the cyclically-adjusted primary balance-to-potential GDP exceeds 1% point.[13] Monetary stance (here a restrictive monetary stance) is defined as country-year observations corresponding to positive annual changes in countries' specific short-term nominal interest rates. Data on short-term nominal interest rate are from the IMF WEO database.

---

[11]The results are unchanged when we use more or less restrictive thresholds for the output gap (-1.5% or 0%). Results are available from the authors upon request.

[12]As for fiscal policy, we do not control for the composition of government policies (expenditure vs. revenue) beside the overall stance. Admittedly, tax increases or spending cuts may have differential impacts on the cycle.

[13]Data on cyclically-adjusted primary balance ratio are drawn from the IMF WEO database. We also explore the same question but focusing on the narrow measure of fiscal consolidation episodes identified using the IMF narrative approach and borrowed from Guajardo et al. (2011). The results do not differ substantially.

The model takes the following form:

$$e_{i,t+h} = (\theta_{1h} + \theta_{2h} I_{i,t}) R_{i,t} + \sigma_h P_{i,t} + \phi_h I_{i,t} + \psi_h(L) e_{i,t+h-1} + X'_{i,t-1}\Gamma_h + u_i + \lambda_t + \epsilon_{i,t+h} \quad (7.2)$$

where I is a dummy variable capturing periods of economic slack and defined as:

$$I_{i,t} = \mathbf{1}\,[Output\ gap < -1]$$

and P is a dummy variable capturing fiscal or monetary policy stances:

$$P_{i,t} = \mathbf{1}\,[\Delta\ CAPB \geq 1] \text{ or } P_{i,t} = \mathbf{1}\,[\Delta\ INT \geq 0]\,.$$

The coefficients of interest are θ_{1h} and $(\theta_{1h} + \theta_{2h})$. They measure the association of reforms with cumulative changes in employment rates at each horizon in good and bad times, respectively. The model is estimated using the LP method with corrected standard errors.

Table 7.2 shows that the estimated impact of labour and product market reforms is affected by the cyclical position of the economy, but the effect differs depending on the type of reforms. More specifically, the effect of labour market reforms (here a significant decline in the employment protection of regular workers) launched during bad times is negative and statistically significant, and these effects are felt

Table 7.2 Effect of reform on the employment rate, accounting for the economic cycle (Dependent variable: deviation in employment rate relative to pre-reform year)

	Year 0	Year 1	Year 2	Year 3	Year 4	Year 5
Labour market reform, no slack	−0.0373	0.529**	1.069**	1.243**	1.344**	1.886***
	(−0.133)	(2.194)	(2.148)	(2.276)	(2.095)	(3.287)
Labour market reform, slack	−0.436**	−1.563***	−1.853***	−1.027**	−0.024	0.193
	(−2.23)	(−3.92)	(−3.19)	(−2.33)	(−0.03)	(0.24)
Observations	442	442	442	421	400	379
Number of countries	21	21	21	21	21	20
Product market reform, no slack	0.180*	0.245*	0.365**	0.696**	0.755**	0.953**
	(1.780)	(1.826)	(2.166)	(2.744)	(2.526)	(2.702)
Product market reform, slack	0.143	0.051	−0.143	−0.145	−0.034	−0.032
	(0.80)	(0.15)	(−0.27)	(−0.23)	(−0.07)	(−0.12)
Observations	430	430	404	379	354	329
Number of countries	26	26	25	25	25	25

Notes: t-statistics from Driscoll-Kraay standard errors in parentheses. Additional controls: Lagged annual change in employment rates (3 lags), lagged output gap, output loss during a financial crisis (Laeven and Valencia 2013), fiscal and monetary stance dummy variables
$^{***}p < 0.01$, $^{**}p < 0.05$, $^{*}p < 0.1$

almost immediately after the reform is implemented. The negative and statistically significant coefficients found from year 0 to year 3 are in line with the view that a reduction in the protection of regular workers during periods of slack in the economy leads to more job destruction, and the effect is almost immediate and sizable. This result arises as removing excessive job protection makes it easier for firms to lay off employees in periods of significant slack in the economy. In contrast, our econometric results show that product market reforms launched during bad times do not necessarily lead to negative and significant employment losses—a somewhat surprising result as it is often thought that the additional supply capacity created by structural reforms will not be absorbed when aggregate demand is weak, leading to deflationary pressures. In fact, the traditional argument would suggest that the additional capacity created by the reforms will initially remain unmatched by demand and could further only worsen the unemployment rate—the opposite of what our results for product market reforms suggest. This is an interesting result as this suggests that different mechanisms may be at play when different types of structural reforms are implemented. The next subsection explores this possibility by examining the intensity of reforms.

7.4.4 The Intensity of Reforms

The seriousness of reform implementation, which is not controlled for in the model above, may differ depending on when the reform is implemented. Reforms initiated during periods of slack may be more or less ambitious depending on a number of considerations including political economy ones.

On the one hand, in periods of slack, with their backs against the wall, policymakers may be more determined to adopt bigger—and likely more difficult—reforms that also could have a stronger impact on growth and employment. This could then offset a possible negative impact of additional excess capacity freed up by structural reforms. On the other hand, leaders can also pass weaker reform bills in bad times because of fear of uncertainty and political backclash following an unpopular reform in the public opinion. In that context, bold, ambitious and significant reforms could be less likely during downturns.

To investigate these aspects, we compare the size of reforms, as captured by the average decline in the OECD indicator, implemented during good and bad times as defined before using the output gap threshold. With labour market reforms, the average decline in the OECD indicator is larger when the reform is initiated during good times. The same is also found for product market reforms, suggesting that more serious product market reforms tend to be implemented during non-slack periods (Fig. 7.5). These results are also consistent with the econometric regressions of Table 7.2 which show that both labour and product market reforms have a positive medium-term effect on job creation in a relatively less demand-constrained environment. At the same time, these results suggest that various factors may play a role in determining the timing of reform implementation. The next section proposes

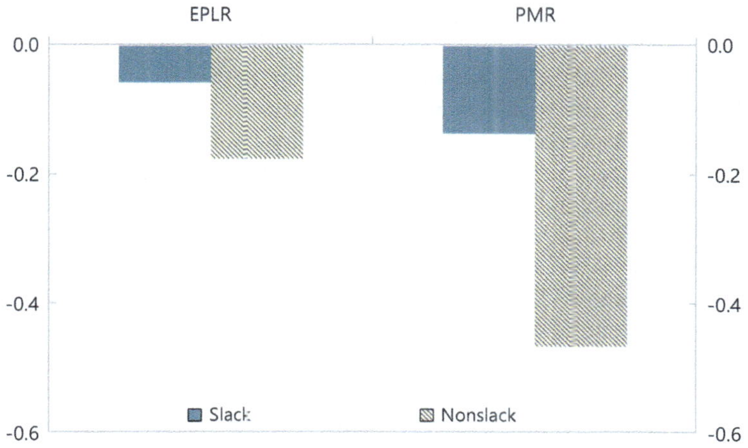

Fig. 7.5 Average change in the OECD indicator during reform episodes. Bigger reforms are implemented during good times (non-slack periods). Sources: OECD; IMF staff calculations

a more robust approach to assess the effect of structural reforms, taking into account the underlying economic and political forces behind the reform adoption.

7.5 A More Robust Approach to Measure the Impact of Reforms

7.5.1 Baseline Specification

The results so far suggest that the occurrence of structural reforms may not be random and the non-exogeneity of the reform shock could potentially bias the results obtained from the LP technique. The LP approach in Sect. 7.4 tried to control for the impact of business cycle movements and the associated macroeconomic policies and added several time-varying and time-invariant factors including country-fixed effects. However, this may not be enough. Countries that do (or do not) reform could share other characteristics beyond their cyclical position that also determine employment changes. For example, some countries might be more or less inclined or able to accompany structural reforms during crises periods with macroeconomic demand support measures. In addition, political factors might play a role and impact, among other things, the effectiveness of a given reform approach.

To more robustly assess the link between reforms and outcomes, the rest of the chapter adopts treatment effect techniques, which have been used extensively in micro and medical studies. An alternative approach to address endogeneity is to use an instrumental variable (an exogeneous source of variation) for the reform variable. However, finding such an instrument is not easy and particularly difficult with macro data. Instead, the treatment effect approach allows us to implement doubly robust matching estimates (Imbens 2004; Lunceford and Davidian 2004; Kreif et al. 2013; Jordà and Taylor 2013) where the treatment group (in this case, countries engaged in reforms) is compared to the counterfactual group.

These methods proceed in several steps. First, policy propensity scores are derived from a latent model which, in our context, explains the probability of implementing a structural reform based on a number of possible factors, including cyclical, structural and political variables. Any predictor of policy should be included, regardless of whether that predictor is a fundamental variable in a macroeconomic model. These propensity scores are then used in the next step to correct for selection bias and to achieve a quasi-random distribution of treatment and control observations via reweighting.[14] Second, a regression model—the LP model in our context—is used to fit or project the outcome variables (at each horizon in our case) in the treatment group and in the control group (countries which did not reform) on a number of determinants to obtain conditional means. Finally, differences in weighted conditional means (where weights are represented by the inverse propensity scores of each observation) at each horizon between the treatment and control groups are computed and give an approximation of average treatment effects (ATEs).

Specifically, we use the (locally) semi-parametric efficient estimator (Lunceford and Davidian 2004), the Augmented Inverse Propensity-Score Weighting (AIPW) which adds an adjustment factor to the ATE to stabilize the estimator when the propensity scores get close to zero or one. Jordà and Taylor (2013) use the methodology to estimate the fiscal multiplier, given that consolidation (the treatment) is determined by many factors that also impact growth (the outcome).

The first stage regression is presented in Appendix 2. It employs a probit regression to estimate the probability of implementing structural reform. The second stage follows the baseline LP model discussed in Sect. 7.4.2. The average treatment effect is computed as the difference of the estimated weighted mean change in employment rate between the reformers and non-reformers where the weight of each observation is the inverse of the propensity to reform as estimated in the first stage logit regressions.

As a benchmark, Table 7.3 first reports the baseline model estimated using the AIPW approach. Similar to the results of the baseline LP model reported in Table 7.1, the positive impact of reforms emerges only in the medium term. However, the impact of PMR identified by the more robust AIPW approach is now estimated to be larger than the estimate in Table 7.1. Labour and product market reforms increase the employment rate by 1.3% and 1.2% points, respectively, by the fifth year. These results confirm that structural reforms have a lagged but positive impact on employment, in line with earlier studies.

[14]Weighting by the inverse of the propensity score shifts weight away from the oversampled toward the undersampled region of the distribution. This shift of probability mass reconstructs

Table 7.3 Effect of reform on the employment rate (AIPW; dependent variable: deviation in employment rate relative to pre-reform year)

	Year 0	Year 1	Year 2	Year 3	Year 4	Year 5
Labour market reform	0.014	−0.162	−0.149	0.296	1.123**	1.275**
	(0.09)	(−0.77)	(−0.36)	(0.53)	(2.20)	(2.15)
Observations	555	555	555	526	497	468
Product market reform	−0.019	0.115	0.457*	0.750**	0.866***	1.183***
	(−0.20)	(0.66)	(1.85)	(2.42)	(2.66)	(3.27)
Observations	709	709	709	683	657	631

Notes: t-statistics in parentheses. Conditional mean controls: Lagged annual change in employment rates (3 lags), lagged output gap, output loss during a financial crisis (Laeven and Valencia 2013). Propensity score based on the probit model as described in the text and includes: lagged GDP growth, legislative election dummy, forward EU accession dummy, age dependency ratio, and political leader's education background. AIPW estimates do not impose restrictions on the weights of the propensity score

***$p < 0.01$, **$p < 0.05$, *$p < 0.1$

7.5.2 *State-Dependent Reform Multipliers: The Role of the Business Cycle*

Do structural reforms deliver different results if implemented in periods of slack or non-slack? We revisit this question by re-estimating the state-dependent reform parameters using the AIPW approach outlined in the previous section. In the AIPW approach, the first stage estimates the joint probability of implementing structural reforms and a specific business cycle position (e.g. slack versus non-slack). The second stage then estimates the effect of state-dependent structural reforms on changes in the employment rate. As the model allows for reducing the selection bias that possibly affects the estimates, we would interpret the results as robustness checks of the effect of reforms depending on the state of the business cycle. However, unlike in Table 7.2, the AIPW approach does not allow us to control for macroeconomic policy variables in this specific context: If we control for macroeconomic policies, the sample size reduces, and this makes it difficult to find convergence in the first-stage probit models. Thus the results below will not be directly comparable with the results in Table 7.2, but still give us some sense about the possible impact of selection bias. We will further examine the role of macroeconomic policies in the next subsection.

Table 7.4 presents the results of the effects of labour market and product market reforms dummies interacted with the slack or non-slack dummy variables. The impact of labour and product market reforms on employment is positive and statistically significant when these reforms are launched when there is limited slack in the economy. However, when labour market reforms are launched in periods of slack,

the appropriate frequency weights of the underlying true distribution of outcomes under treatment and control.

Table 7.4 Effect of reforms on the employment rate, accounting for the business cycle (AIPW; dependent variable: deviation in employment rate relative to pre-reform year)

	Year 0	Year 1	Year 2	Year 3	Year 4	Year 5
Labour market reform, slack	−0.831	−2.196	−4.674*	−4.951	−7.957*	−11.94*
	(−0.640)	(−0.968)	(−1.838)	(−1.406)	(−1.939)	(−1.907)
Observations	557	557	557	528	499	470
Labour market reform, no slack	−0.00324	0.00188	0.584	1.637*	2.391**	2.778**
	(−0.0224)	(0.00635)	(0.848)	(1.686)	(2.112)	(1.961)
Observations	557	557	557	528	499	470
Product market reform, slack	−0.448	−0.374	0.208	0.594	0.730	1.330
	(−1.467)	(−0.742)	(0.312)	(0.736)	(0.876)	(1.535)
Observations	709	709	709	683	657	631
Product market reform, no slack	0.105	0.306	0.590	0.826*	0.758*	1.020**
	(0.794)	(1.096)	(1.426)	(1.678)	(1.660)	(2.014)
Observations	709	709	709	683	657	631

Notes: t-statistics in parentheses. Conditional mean controls: Lagged annual change in employment rates (3 lags), lagged output gap, output loss during a financial crisis (Laeven and Valencia 2013). Propensity score based on the probit models as described in the text and include: lagged GDP growth, legislative election dummy, forward EU accession dummy, age dependency ratio, and political leader's education background. AIPW estimates do not impose restrictions on the weights of the propensity score

***$p < 0.01$, **$p < 0.05$, *$p < 0.1$

our results indicate a negative effect on employment. The estimated coefficients are large, but these results need to be interpreted with caution because the number of episodes of reform shocks during slack (12 labour market reforms-slack occurrences versus 16 labour market reforms-non slack occurrences) is relatively limited, and this is likely to affect the first stage probit regressions in the AIPW approach.[15] Despite these limitations, the results suggest that structural reforms (both labour and product market reforms) are most effective when implemented in period of limited slack. A natural question, however, is to what extent supportive macroeconomic policies in place can also enhance the effectiveness of the reform implementation and impact. The next section specifically addresses this question using the AIPW framework.

7.5.3 *State-Dependent Reform Multipliers: The Role of Macroeconomic Policies*

Do structural reforms deliver better results if implemented in periods of supportive macroeconomic policies? This is an important question, as several countries had to

[15]For product market reforms, we have maximum of 34 product market-slack occurrences versus 63 product market-non slack occurrences.

implement reforms in conjunction with fiscal consolidations. Not all reforms have been implemented in periods of neutral or expansionary fiscal or monetary policies. As noted earlier, understanding the role of macroeconomic policy for structural reforms may require a more robust approach than the simple LP technique, as different factors seem to affect the occurrence of different reforms.

We employ the AIPW technique which focuses on exogenous changes in the structural reform variable to revisit the role of macroeconomic policy for structural reforms. In this approach, the first stage estimates the joint probability of implementing structural reforms and a specific policy stance (e.g. restrictive/non-restrictive fiscal/monetary policy). The second stage then estimates the effect of structural reforms on employment.

Ideally, one would estimate the structural reform impact conditional on the state of the business cycle and, separately, the stance of monetary and fiscal policy for both labour and product market reforms. However, since the number of structural reform shocks interacted with the fiscal consolidation dummy is limited, a complete approach quickly runs into data constraints. What is feasible, however, is estimating a model asking whether the impact of exogenous structural reforms varies with the fiscal and monetary stance, given the availability of sufficient non-zero observations to run first-stage probit models for the occurrence of a structural reform interacted with fiscal and monetary stances. For product market reforms, we were able to estimate the impact of reform shocks under various fiscal and monetary policy stances. However, for labour market reforms, we were only able to robustly estimate the effect of reforms conditional on the monetary policy stance (we have enough positive observations to run the associated first-stage probit models in this particular case, but not for the fiscal poliy stance).

Tables 7.5, 7.6, and 7.7 present the results of the interaction between product market reforms and the fiscal stance and between labour and product market reforms

Table 7.5 Effect of reform on the employment rate, accounting for the fiscal policy stance (AIPW: dependent variable: deviation in employment rate relative to pre-reform year)

	Year 0	Year 1	Year 2	Year 3	Year 4	Year 5
PMR, non-restrictive fiscal policy	−0.0962	−0.108	0.258	0.633**	0.668**	1.113***
	(−0.800)	(−0.483)	(0.919)	(1.981)	(1.995)	(2.764)
Observations	429	429	429	404	379	354
PMR, restrictive fiscal policy	0.325	−0.104	−0.524	−1.097	−1.667**	−2.271***
	(0.791)	(−0.206)	(−0.761)	(−1.300)	(−1.970)	(−2.318)
Observations	429	429	429	404	379	354

Notes: t-statistics in parentheses. Conditional mean controls: Lagged annual change in employment rates (3 lags), lagged output gap, output loss during a financial crisis (Laeven and Valencia 2013). Propensity score based on the probit model as described in the text and includes: lagged GDP growth, legislative election dummy, forward EU accession dummy, age dependency ratio, and political leader's education background. AIPW estimates do not impose restrictions on the weights of the propensity score

***$p < 0.01$, **$p < 0.05$, *$p < 0.1$

Table 7.6 Effect of reform on the employment rate, accounting for the monetary policy stance (AIPW; dependent variable: deviation in employment rate relative to pre-reform year)

	Year 0	Year 1	Year 2	Year 3	Year 4	Year 5
LMR, non-restrictive monetary policy	−0.471**	−0.723***	−0.294	0.513*	1.540***	2.897***
	(−2.214)	(−3.735)	(−1.233)	(1.770)	(3.682)	(6.026)
Observations	551	551	551	522	493	464
LMR, restrictive monetary policy	0.163	0.204	−0.0234	−0.887**	−0.543	−0.666
	(0.672)	(0.475)	(−0.0299)	(−2.013)	(−1.089)	(−0.977)
Observations	551	551	551	522	493	464

Notes: t-statistics in parentheses. Conditional mean controls: Lagged annual change in employment rates (3 lags), lagged output gap, output loss during a financial crisis (Laeven and Valencia 2013). Propensity score based on the probit model as described in the text and includes: lagged GDP growth, legislative election dummy, forward EU accession dummy, age dependency ratio, and political leader's education background. AIPW estimates do not impose restrictions on the weights of the propensity score

***$p < 0.01$, **$p < 0.05$, *$p < 0.1$

Table 7.7 Effect of reform on the employment rate, accounting for the monetary policy stance (AIPW; dependent variable: deviation in employment rate relative to pre-reform year)

	Year 0	Year 1	Year 2	Year 3	Year 4	Year 5
PMR, non-restrictive monetary policy	−0.017	0.199	0.563**	0.956***	0.999***	1.191***
	(−0.16)	(1.05)	(2.25)	(2.96)	(2.88)	(2.81)
Observations	689	689	689	663	637	611
PMR, restrictive monetary policy	−0.084	−0.049	−0.006	−0.132	0.012	0.390
	(−0.59)	(−0.26)	(−0.03)	(−0.53)	(0.04)	(1.06)
Observations	689	689	689	663	637	611

Notes: t-statistics in parentheses. Conditional mean controls: Lagged annual change in employment rates (3 lags), lagged output gap, output loss during a financial crisis (Laeven and Valencia 2013). Propensity score based on the probit model as described in the text and includes: lagged GDP growth, legislative election dummy, forward EU accession dummy, age dependency ratio, and political leader's education background. AIPW estimates do not impose restrictions on the weights of the propensity score

***$p < 0.01$, **$p < 0.05$, *$p < 0.1$

and the monetary stance, respectively. Note that Table 7.5 shows the results of two regressions: one where the first stage regression outcome variable is non-restrictive fiscal policy interacted with the probability of product market reform and the other where the outcome variable is restrictive fiscal policy interacted with the probability of product market reform. A similar structure is used in Tables 7.6 and 7.7 but with monetary policy.

The impact of product market reforms on employment when initiated with non-restrictive fiscal policy is positive and significant in the medium term (starting in the third year after the reform is launched). The employment rate rises starting in year 3 and has increased by more than 1% point 5 years after the reform. On the other hand, when the fiscal policy stance is restrictive, the impact of product market reforms on the employment rate is negative and statistically significant 4 and 5 years after the reform has been launched.

The results for the interaction of labour and product market reforms and supportive monetary policy are similar in nature (Tables 7.6 and 7.7). The employment rate rises significantly for reforms occurring along with non-restrictive monetary policy, after the reform. In the case of non-accommodative monetary policies, the positive effect of reforms disappears fully.

The results suggest that structural reforms are most effective when supported by non-restrictive macroeconomic policy. Similar to the robust baseline model in Sect. 7.5.1, the reform impact gathers strength in the medium term. While the short-term impact is limited, the benefit of structural reforms materializes in the second or third year. This time pattern is consistent with the simulation studies: when monetary policy is restrictive, which is effectively the case in a binding effective lower bound (ELB) environment absent effective non-conventional measures, simulation results predict that the impact of structural reforms on output will be small or even negative (Eggertsson et al. 2014). When monetary policy is non-restrictive, however, for example, in the presence of active asset purchasing programs in an ELB environment, theoretical results tend to predict that the impact of structural reforms on output will be positive (Decressin et al. 2015).

7.6 Conclusion

This chapter has investigated the impact of structural reforms on employment, using more robust methods to control for potential biases including endogeneity. The empirical results suggest that structural reforms have a lagged but positive impact on employment, which confirm results reported elsewhere. This positive effect, however, tends to be larger once the endogeneity of the decision to reform is taken into account. Using the local projection (LP) approach with treatment effect techniques, our estimates suggest that labour and both product market reforms tend to increase employment rates by about 1% point over a 5-year horizon.

The chapter also examined the interplay between structural reforms, the macroeconomic environment, and fiscal and monetary policies. Data limitations can make a full discussion of these interactions difficult. However, we find suggestive evidence that the effects of labour market reforms tend to be negative if they are implemented in a period of economic distress. We also find that supportive macroeconomic policy enhances the positive impact of structural reforms in the medium term, suggesting that structural reforms are best initiated in conjunction with supportive fiscal or monetary policy if policy space is available.

While our findings contribute to the current debate on the role of structural reforms and growth, they are far from the final word on this important topic. One important caveat is that a fuller investigation would require a richer data set of reforms—something likely to be more available at the sectoral level than at the macro level focused on here. The chapter also does not address the important questions which reform should be implemented in what order, how structural reforms will impact different sectors, and how different structural reforms interact with each other.

Appendix 1: Country Sample

The sample covers OECD countries with population of more than 5 million, with large episodes of labour market reforms for regular workers (EPLR) and product market reforms (PMR). Additional restrictions, such as non-missing output gap and employment rate variables with at least 3 lags, are also imposed, given the specification used in estimation. Finally, the first stage AIPW regression required some political variables, the unavailability of which constricts the sample further. All in all, the baseline EPLR regressions, reflected in Tables 7.1 and 7.3, include 555 observations from 29 countries (see Table 7.8 for the list of countries). The baseline PMR regression, reflected in Tables 7.1 and 7.3, include 709 observations from 26 countries. Regressions in Tables 7.2 and 7.4–7.6 that include policy variables further restrict the sample.

Table 7.8 Sample of countries

Australia	France	Korea	South Africa
Austria	Germany	Mexico	Spain
Belgium	Hungary	Netherlands	Sweden
Canada	Indonesia[a]	Poland	Switzerland
Chile	Israel	Portugal	Turkey
Czech Republic	Italy	Russia[a]	United Kingdom
Denmark	Japan	Slovak Republic	United States[a]
Finland			

[a]Dropped in the PMR regression sample owing to the absence of any large reform episode

Appendix 2: Determinants of Labor and Product Market Reforms

In the first stage, propensity scores to implement reforms are estimated using a probit regression of the probability of implementing either a labour or product market reform on lagged GDP growth (to account for cyclical conditions), a legislative election dummy (political variable), an EU accession dummy (economic integration factor), the age dependency ratio (demographic developments), and the political leader's educational background (either captures the competency of the leaders or their proximity with liberal views).[16]

Lagged GDP growth is included to capture the notion that countries in a recession may be more likely to implement reforms.

A legislative election dummy is 1 when there is a legislative election in that year. The variable is drawn from the database on political institutions (DPI). It helps capture previous findings that reforms are often times implemented early in the political cycle (Tompson 2009).

The EU accession dummy is 1 if the country is in the EU. External pressures from the EU or from other member countries can induce countries to implement reforms.

The reform implementation literature also includes the age dependency ratio—capturing the notion that the population aged 65 and older will tend to push for more pro-competitive labor market reforms to beef up pensions and social security contributions.

The political leader's educational background variable is drawn from Hallerberg and Wehner (2016) and takes the value 1 whenever the Prime Minister or the Minister of Finance has a degree in economics. It represents the idea that more technocratic leaders with a background in economics are more likely to initiate reforms. For instance, one of the main finding of Hallerberg and Wehner (2016) is that leaders that take office during a banking crisis in advanced economies are more likely to have an economics background.

Table 7.9 shows the regression results of the probit model. Results are based on the estimation of a pooled panel or random effect probit model where key determinants of the probability of observing labor and product market reforms are identified, respectively. The results for labour market reforms show that structural reforms are more likely to be implemented following periods of lower growth, off election cycles, and in countries with EU accession commitments. Product market reforms tend to occur in good times, in countries with a high dependency ratio and where key political leaders (Prime Minister or Minister of Finance) have an economic background.

[16]More recently, IMF (2016) and Duval et al. (2017) have examined the drivers of structural reforms in OECD countries where structural reforms are also defined as a large change in the OECD indicators but also with additional criteria. They also consider similar variables used in our probit regression in addition to many other potential determinants.

Table 7.9 Determinants of structural reforms (pooled probit regression; dependent variable: probability of adopting a reform)

	Labour market reform	Product market reform
Lagged GDP growth	−0.0493*	0.0653***
	(−1.660)	(4.053)
Legislative election dummy	−0.450*	−0.0226
	(−1.738)	(−0.189)
EU accession dummy, 1 year ahead	0.644**	0.00966
	(2.155)	(0.0780)
Aged 65 up	−0.0382	0.0396**
	(−0.947)	(2.539)
Technocratic leader dummy	−0.0309	0.254**
	(−0.168)	(2.366)
Observations	688	1105

***$p < 0.001$, **$p < 0.05$, *$p < 0.1$

References

Anderson D, Hunt B, Snudden S (2013) Fiscal consolidation in the Euro area: how much can structural reforms ease the pain? IMF working paper 13/211

Anderson D, Barkbu B, Lusinyan L, Muir D (2014) Macroeconomic impact of structural reforms in the Euro area. In: Jobs and growth: supporting the European recovery, April. IMF, Washington

Alesina A, Perotti R (1995) Fiscal expansions and fiscal adjustments in OECD countries. NBER working paper 5214, Aug 1995

Auerbach AJ, Gorodnichenko Y (2013) Output spillovers from fiscal policy. Am Econ Rev 103(3):141–146

Barnes S, Bouis R, Briard P, Dougherty S, Eris M (2011) The GDP impact of reform: a simple simulation framework. OECD Economics Department working paper 834

Bassanini A, Duval R (2006) Employment patterns in OECD countries: reassessing the role of policies and institutions. OECD Economics Department working paper 486

Bassanini A, Nunziata L, Venn D (2009) Job protection legislation and productivity growth in OECD countries. Econ Policy 24(58):349–402

Bouis R, Duval R (2011) Raising potential growth after the crisis: a quantitative assessment of the potential gains from various structural reforms in the OECD area and beyond. OECD Economics Department working paper 835

Bouis R, Causa O, Demmou L, Duval R, Zdzienicka A (2012a) The short-term effects of structural reforms: an empirical analysis. OECD Economics Department working paper 949

Bouis R, Causa O, Demmou L, Duval R, Zdzienicka A (2012b) How quickly does structural reform pay off? An empirical analysis of the short-term effects of unemployment benefit reform. IZA J Labor Policy 1:1–12

Bourlès R, Cette G, Lopez J, Mairesse J, Nicoletti G (2010) The impact on growth of easing regulations in upstream sectors. CESifo Dice Report J Int Comparisons 8(3):8–12

Cacciatore M, Duval R, Fiori G (2012) Short-term gain or pain? A DSGE model-based analysis of the short-term effects of structural reforms in labour and product markets. OECD Economics Department working paper 948

Cacciatore M, Duval R, Fiori G, Ghironi F (2016) Market reforms in the time of imbalance. J Econ Dyn Control 72:69–93

Decressin J, Espinoza R, Halikias I, Kumhof M, Leigh D, Loungani P, Meda P, Mursula S, Schindler M, Spilimbergo A, Teng Xu T (2015) Wage moderation in crises: policy considerations and applications to the Euro area. IMF staff discussion note 15/22

Driscoll J, Kraay AC (1998) Consistent covariance matrix estimation with spatially dependent data. Rev Econ Stat 80:549–560

Duval R, Furceri D, Miethe J (2017) The needle in the haystack: establishing the drivers of structural reforms in OECD countries. International Monetary Fund (forthcoming)

Eggertsson G, Ferrero A, Raffo A (2014) Can structural reforms help Europe? J Monet Econ 61:2–22

Gomes S, Jacquinot P, Mohr M, Pisani M (2013) Structural reforms and macroeconomic performance in the Euro Area countries: a model-based assessment. Int Fin 16(1):23–44

Guajardo J, Leigh D, Pescatori A (2011) Expansionary austerity: new international evidence. IMF working paper 11/158

Hallerberg M, Wehner J (2016) When do you get economists as policy-makers? Available at SSRN. https://ssrn.com/abstract=2191490, doi:https://doi.org/10.2139/ssrn.2191490

Hobza A, Mourre G (2010) Quantifying the potential macroeconomic effects of the Europe 2020 Strategy: stylized scenarios. ECFIN economic paper 424

Imbens G (2004) Nonparametric estimation of average treatment effects under exogeneity: a review. Rev Econ Stat 86(1):4–29

International Monetary Fund (2016) World economic outlook, April 2016

Jordà Ò (2005) Estimation and inference of impulse responses by local projections. Am Econ Rev 95(1):161–182

Jordà Ò, Taylor A (2013) The time for austerity: estimating the average treatment effect of fiscal policy. NBER working paper 19414

Lusinyan L, Muir D (2013) Assessing the macroeconomic impact of structural reforms: the case of Italy. IMF working paper WP/13/22, Jan 2013

Kreif N, Grieve R, Radice R, Sekhon J (2013) Regression-adjusted matching and double-robust methods for estimating average treatment effects in health economic evaluation. Health Serv Outcome Res Methodol 3:174–202

Laeven L, Valencia F (2013) Systemic banking crises database. IMF Econ Rev 61:225–270

Lunceford J, Davidian M (2004) Stratification and weighting via the propensity score in estimation of causal treatment effects: a comparative study. Stat Med 23:2937–2960

Organization for Economic Cooperation and Development (2012a) Economic surveys Euro area. OECD, Paris

Organization for Economic Cooperation and Development (2012b) Going for growth. OECD, Paris

Tompson W (2009) The political economy of reform: lessons from pensions, product markets and labour markets in ten OECD countries. OECD, Paris

Owyang MT, Ramey VA, Zubairy S (2013) Are government spending multipliers greater during periods of slack? Evidence from 20th century historical data. NBER working paper 18769, Feb 2013

Chapter 8
Labour Market Resilience: The Role of Structural and Macroeconomic Policies

Alexander Hijzen, Andreas Kappeler, Mathilde Pak, and Cyrille Schwellnus

8.1 Introduction

The Great Recession of 2008–2009 and the slow pace of the subsequent recovery have highlighted how large economic downturns can have long-lasting economic and social costs. Some public policies that reduce the ex-ante risk of downturns also reduce growth and employment in the long term (Caldera-Sánchez et al. 2016). However, this is not the case with public policies that enhance labour market resilience, i.e. an economy's capacity to limit fluctuations in employment and to quickly rebound in the wake of economic shocks. These policies are key not only

---

This is an adaptation of the OECD publication OECD (2017), "Labour market resilience: The role of structural and macroeconomic policies", in OECD Employment Outlook 2017, OECD Publishing, Paris. https://doi.org/10.1787/empl_outlook-2017-6-en.

A. Hijzen (✉)
Directorate for Employment, Labour and Social Affairs, OECD, Paris, France
e-mail: Alexander.Hijzen@OECD.org

A. Kappeler
Department of Economics, European Investment Bank, Luxembourg, Luxembourg
e-mail: a.kappeler@eib.org

M. Pak
Economics Department, OECD, Paris, France
e-mail: Mathilde.Pak@OECD.org

C. Schwellnus
Economics Department, OECD, Paris, France
e-mail: Cyrille.Schwellnus@OECD.org

J. de Haan, J. Parlevliet (eds.), *Structural Reforms*,
https://doi.org/10.1007/978-3-319-74400-1_8

to limiting the short-term social cost of economic downturns but also to supporting labour market and economic performance in the medium to long term, by mitigating the knock-on effects of their cyclical impact on higher structural unemployment ("hysteresis").

This chapter provides an overview of labour market resilience in OECD countries in the wake of the Great Recession of 2008–2009 and empirically assesses the role played by macroeconomic and labour market policies. Drawing on the experience from economic cycles since the mid-1980s, the chapter analyses how structural policies and institutions shape the labour market response to aggregate shocks and the extent to which macroeconomic policies can stabilise aggregate demand during economic downturns. It further analyses how labour market and fiscal policies affect the extent to which an economic downturn continues to have an impact on labour market performance through hysteresis effects that persist even once cyclical effects have faded.

The remainder of the chapter is organised as follows. Section 8.2 describes the conceptual framework and assesses labour market resilience in the wake of the Great Recession. Section 8.3 analyses how various labour market policies shape the effect of a given aggregate shock on labour market outcomes and assesses the effects of fiscal policy on labour market performance during economic downturns. Section 8.4 uses the resulting estimates to quantify the role of labour market and fiscal policies for labour market resilience during and in the wake of the Great Recession. The final section contains some concluding remarks.

8.2 Resilience in the Wake of the Great Recession

Resilience in this chapter is defined in terms of the social and economic costs of economic downturns, i.e. the capacity of an economy to limit persistent deviations in output and labour market outcomes from pre-crisis trends in the aftermath of adverse aggregate shocks (i.e. recessions). This definition encompasses the avoidance of excessive fluctuations in output and labour market outcomes as well as the swiftness of the rebound. In the descriptive analysis of resilience in this section, labour market outcomes are not expressed directly in relation to the size of the initial shock, but output and labour market resilience are analysed jointly to allow gauging the labour market response to output developments. In the econometric analysis in the subsequent sections, the size of the initial shock is explicitly taken into account.

In operational terms, *output* resilience refers to the cumulative deviation of output from a counterfactual trend following an adverse aggregate shock, while *labour market* resilience refers to the cumulative deviation of unemployment from its pre-crisis structural rate. The structural rate of unemployment is approximated by the non-accelerating inflation rate of unemployment (NAIRU). The counterfactual output trend in this chapter is based on Ollivaud and Turner (2015), who calculate it using the growth rate of trend labour productivity (the ratio of potential output to potential employment) over the period 2000–2007 and counterfactual potential employment growth over 2008–2015. Counterfactual potential employment growth is obtained by using pre-crisis trends in potential employment rates (the ratio of potential employment to the working-age population) by age cohort but allowing for observed demographic developments over 2008–2015. The advantage of focusing on pre-crisis trend labour productivity growth rather than pre-crisis observed labour productivity growth is that it is less sensitive to unsustainable booms in the run-up to the Great Recession. Accounting for actual demographic developments over 2008–2015 for the calculation of counterfactual potential employment growth reduces the risk that declines in potential output that would have occurred in the absence of the crisis, are erroneously attributed to the crisis.

Resilience can be decomposed into cyclical and structural components, with the latter obtained as cumulative deviations of potential output from the counterfactual output trend and the NAIRU from the pre-crisis rate. A small cyclical component implies limited deviations of output and unemployment from potential output and the NAIRU in terms of amplitude and duration. A small structural component implies limited *hysteresis* as potential output and the NAIRU remain close to their counterfactual. The decomposition thus allows assessing the extent to which output losses and unemployment increases in the wake of the crisis reflected transitory or persistent developments and the extent to which developments in potential output were reflected in structural unemployment.

As estimates of potential output and the NAIRU are surrounded by considerable uncertainty, the decomposition is used exclusively for descriptive purposes in the present section. By contrast, the econometric analysis in Sect. 8.3 does not rely on potential output and the NAIRU to distinguish between cyclical and structural effects.

OECD output has deviated significantly from the pre-crisis trend in the wake of the Great Recession (Fig. 8.1, Panel A).[1] By the second quarter of 2016, output per capita was about 6% below the pre-crisis trend, but the cumulative loss in output per capita since the Great Recession amounted to almost 6 months of income (6% of output per capita over 8 years). This predominantly reflects the structural component of output resilience as measured by the deviation of potential output from the pre-crisis trend rather than its cyclical component as measured by the cumulative output gap. According to current estimates, the main impact of the crisis was therefore to change the growth rate of potential output, which implies that the effects of the crisis on output are likely to continue to be felt for a long time.

The impact of the Great Recession on unemployment has also been substantial, but in contrast to output, the unemployment rate for the OECD as a whole has returned to close to the pre-crisis level, with no significant increase in structural

[1]The timing and duration of the Great Recession differed across OECD countries and a number of countries did not experience a technical recession defined as at least two consecutive quarters of output contraction (e.g. Korea, Poland and Australia).

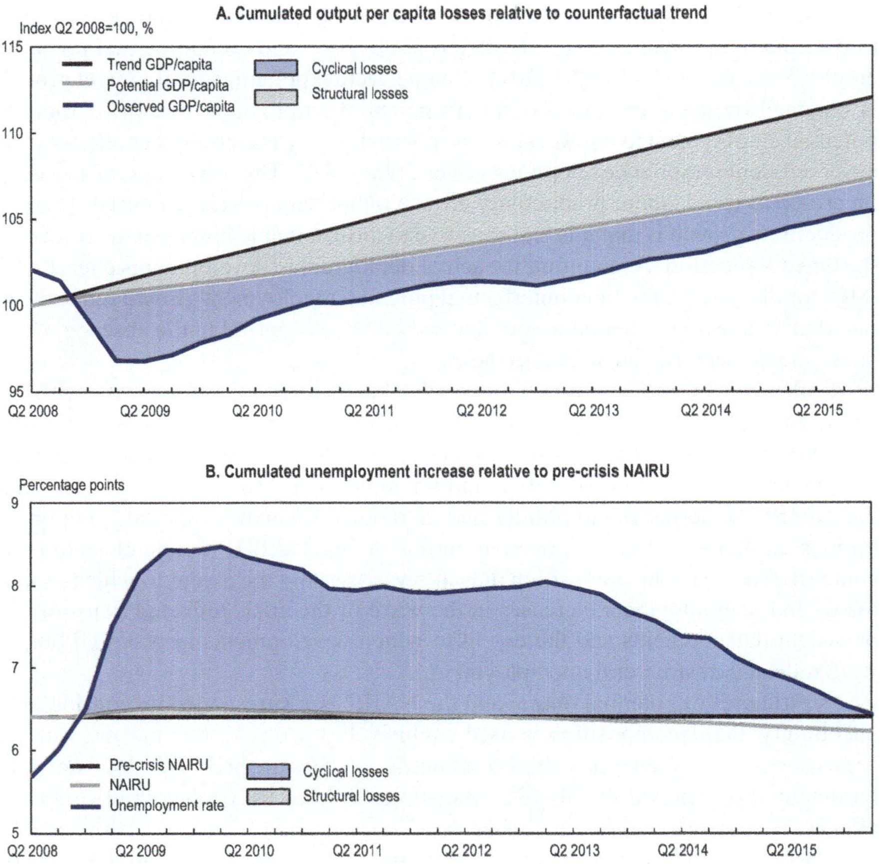

Fig. 8.1 Output and unemployment developments in the OECD since the onset of the Great Recession, 2008–2015. Notes: The intercept of the counter-factual trend in Panel A is normalised to 100 and corresponds to the level of potential output per capita in Q2 2008. Its slope is the counter-factual potential output per capita growth rate in Ollivaud and Turner (2015). The pre-crisis NAIRU in Panel B is the NAIRU in Q2 2008. The area between the black and blue lines gives an indication of the total cost of the crisis in terms of the cumulative impacts on output and unemployment. The blue area gives an indication of the cyclical component, whereas the grey area gives an indication of its structural component. Source: OECD calculations based on the OECD Economic Outlook No. 100, https://stats.oecd.org/index.aspx?DataSetCode=EO

unemployment (Fig. 8.1, Panel B). The cost of the crisis as measured by the cumulative increase in unemployment amounted to around 8 percentage points (average deviation of around 1 percentage point from the pre-crisis NAIRU over 8 years), but structural losses have been limited. This partly reflects good structural outcomes in a number of large countries that receive a large weight in the OECD average, including Germany, Japan, the United Kingdom and the United States. In many other OECD countries, the annualised deviation of structural unemployment from the pre-crisis rate was positive over the period 2008–2015 (see below). There is no indication that the Great Recession has led to a persistent decline in effective labour supply. The aggregate OECD labour force participation rate has remained close to its pre-crisis value of 65%.

The absence of an increase in the rate of structural unemployment or a decline in the rate of labour force participation in the OECD area indicates that the slowdown in potential output growth is largely unrelated to labour market developments. This is consistent with evidence suggesting that the slowdown in potential output growth reflects declines in capital deepening and a slowdown in multi-factor productivity growth (Ollivaud et al. 2016). While the decline in capital deepening largely reflects increased financial frictions and persistent shortfalls in aggregate demand related to the economic downturn, the slowdown in multi-factor productivity growth began before the Great Recession and is therefore at best only partly related to the economic downturn (Andrews et al. 2016).

There are large differences in the overall degree of output resilience across OECD countries (Fig. 8.2). In countries with annualised output per capita losses of 12% or more, including Estonia, Greece and Latvia, cumulative losses over the period 2008–2015 amount to at least a year of lost income (Panel A). Several other countries either were little affected by the Great Recession (e.g. Israel) or have partly made up for output losses relative to trend in the wake of the Great Recession through above-trend growth in later years (e.g. Germany).

Differences in output resilience translate to an important extent into differences in labour market resilience (Panel B). Countries with large deviations of output per capita from the pre-crisis trend, such as Greece and Ireland, which were hit by major banking and sovereign debt crises, typically experienced large deviations of unemployment from the pre-crisis rate. The opposite is true for countries with small deviations of output per capita from the pre-crisis trend, such as Germany and Japan, which experienced transitory declines in external demand. Overall, around half of the variance in unemployment resilience is explained by output developments.

There are also large cross-country differences in the relative importance of the structural component of labour market resilience, but increases in the NAIRU were limited compared to the large deviations of potential output from pre-crisis trends. In the majority of countries, the annualised deviation of unemployment from the pre-crisis NAIRU was positive over the period 2008–2015, and in 2015 the deviation remained positive in more than half of these countries (Panel C). The average annual deviation from the pre-crisis NAIRU amounted to over 5 percentage points in Greece and Spain, where structural unemployment increased, but was negative in Germany where structural unemployment continuously declined during most of the period. However, compared to the large number of countries that experienced average deviations of potential output per capita from pre-crisis trends of more than 5 percentage points, only few countries experienced average deviations of the NAIRU from the pre-crisis rate of more than 1 percentage point.

A high degree of resilience in terms of unemployment compared to output reflects adjustments in labour productivity, working time and labour force participation. Figure 8.3 decomposes the annualised deviation of output from the counterfactual

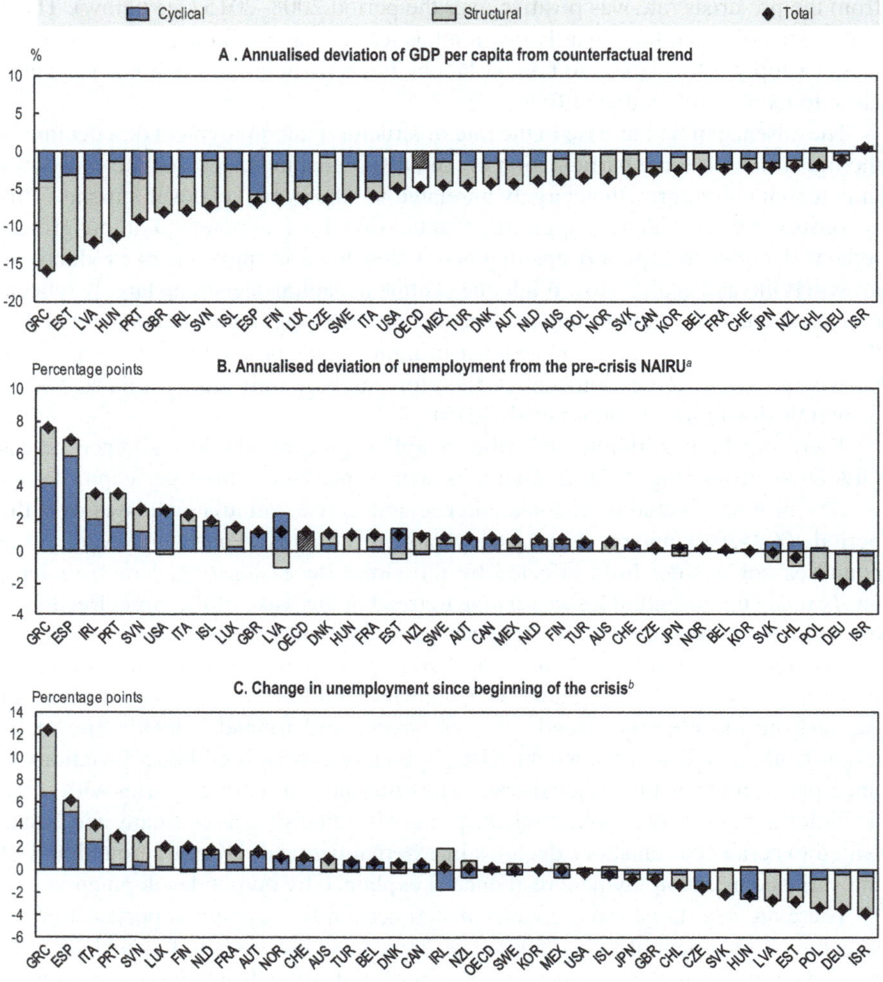

Fig. 8.2 A number of OECD countries experienced persistent deviations of unemployment from the pre-crisis NAIRU, 2008–2015. (a) The total height of the bars in Panel B denotes the deviation of the unemployment rate from the pre-crisis NAIRU, with the part in grey denoting the deviation of the NAIRU from the pre-crisis NAIRU. (b) The total height of the bars in Panel C denotes the change in the unemployment rate over 2008–2015 with respect to the pre-crisis NAIRU. Source: OECD calculations based on the OECD Economic Outlook No. 100, https://stats.oecd.org/index.aspx?DataSetCode=EO

trend into the annualised deviations of unemployment and working time from their pre-crisis rates and the annualised deviations of hourly labour productivity and labour force participation from their counterfactual trends. This decomposition can be used to explain—in an accounting sense—how developments in output were reflected in adjustments along different margins. For example, it reveals that

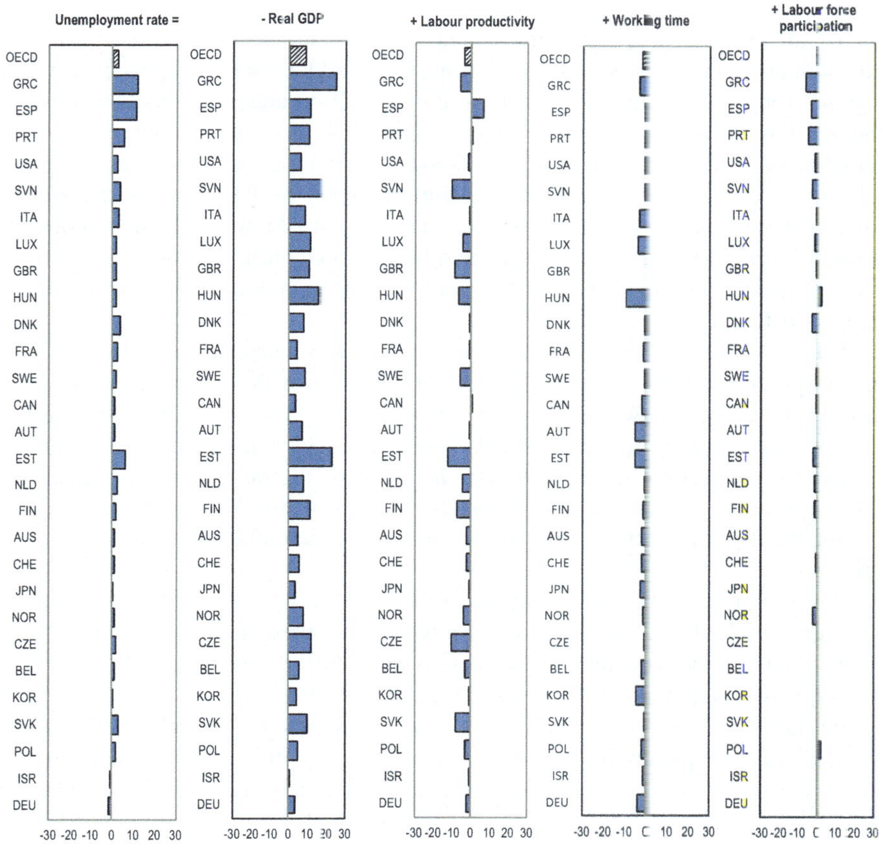

Fig. 8.3 Declines in productivity, working time and participation dampened the impact on unemployment (Decomposition of the annualised deviation of unemployment from the pre-crisis rate), 2008–2015. Notes: The decomposition is based on the approximation $u - u^* \approx [-(y - y^*)] + [(y - y^*) - (n + h - (n^* + h^*))] + [h - h^*] + [lf - n^*]$, where the right hand-side variables are expressed in logarithms and denote GDP (y), the number of employees (n), hours worked per employee (h) and the labour force (lf). $u - u^*$ is the percentage point deviation of unemployment from the pre-crisis rate; the first right hand-side term in square brackets is the percentage deviation of GDP from the counterfactual trend in Ollivaud and Turner (2015); the second term is the percentage deviation of labour productivity from the pre-crisis trend; the third term is the percentage deviation of hours per worker from the pre-crisis level; and the fourth term is the percentage change in labour force participation in deviation from the counterfactual employment trend. In contrast to Fig. 8.2, the reported deviations of unemployment and real GDP from the pre-crisis counterfactual rates and trends are computed relative to actual unemployment and output in Q2 2008 rather than the corresponding unemployment and output gaps. Given that unemployment and output gaps were typically positive in Q2 2008, the deviations in Fig. 8.3 are typically larger than those in Fig. 8.2. Source: OECD calculations based on the OECD Economic Outlook No. 100, https://stats.oecd.org/index.aspx?DataSetCode=EO

for the OECD as a whole almost 30% of the decline in output was accounted for by an increase in the unemployment rate. It can also be used to show how adjustments in labour productivity, working time and labour force participation can account for cross-country differences in the annualised unemployment response to the annualised decline in output. For the OECD as a whole, labour hoarding—which was reflected in lower hourly labour productivity growth—was the main adjustment margin that dampened the impact of the decline in GDP growth on unemployment, accounting for over 40% of the adjustment to the decline in output. Average adjustments in working time and labour force participation were typically more muted, accounting for about 25% and 10% of the decline in output on average across the OECD.

The slowdown in labour productivity growth was reflected in a slowdown in real wage growth rather than a slowdown in profit growth (Fig. 8.4). At constant real wage trends, a slowdown in labour productivity growth would be reflected in a lower capital share in value added. While a number of countries experienced declines in the capital share, typically the brunt of the downward adjustment in labour productivity was borne by workers in terms of lower real wages.[2] In other words, the flip side of the high resilience in terms of unemployment was lower job quality.

To summarise, in the wake of the Great Recession, there were large cross-country differences in labour market resilience when measured in terms of unemployment. To a significant extent, these cross-country differences reflected differences in output developments, which were related to the nature and the size of the initial aggregate shock and the effects of macroeconomic policies. For instance, unemployment typically increased more in countries with major housing, banking or sovereign debt crises. However, unemployment developments also reflected different margins of labour market adjustment, which in turn partly depended on labour market policies and institutions.

8.3 The Policy Determinants of Labour Market Resilience

8.3.1 The Role of Labour Market Policies and Institutions for Labour Market Resilience

Structural policies and institutions can affect labour market resilience through a number of different channels. First, structural policy settings affect the relative importance of different margins of labour input adjustment. In particular, they

[2]Note that since hours and wages in the above decomposition cover dependent employees only, the capital share is implicitly defined as 1—the share of wages of dependent employees in GDP so that it includes mixed income. An increase in the capital share may therefore partly reflect an increase in the number of self-employed rather than an increase in profits.

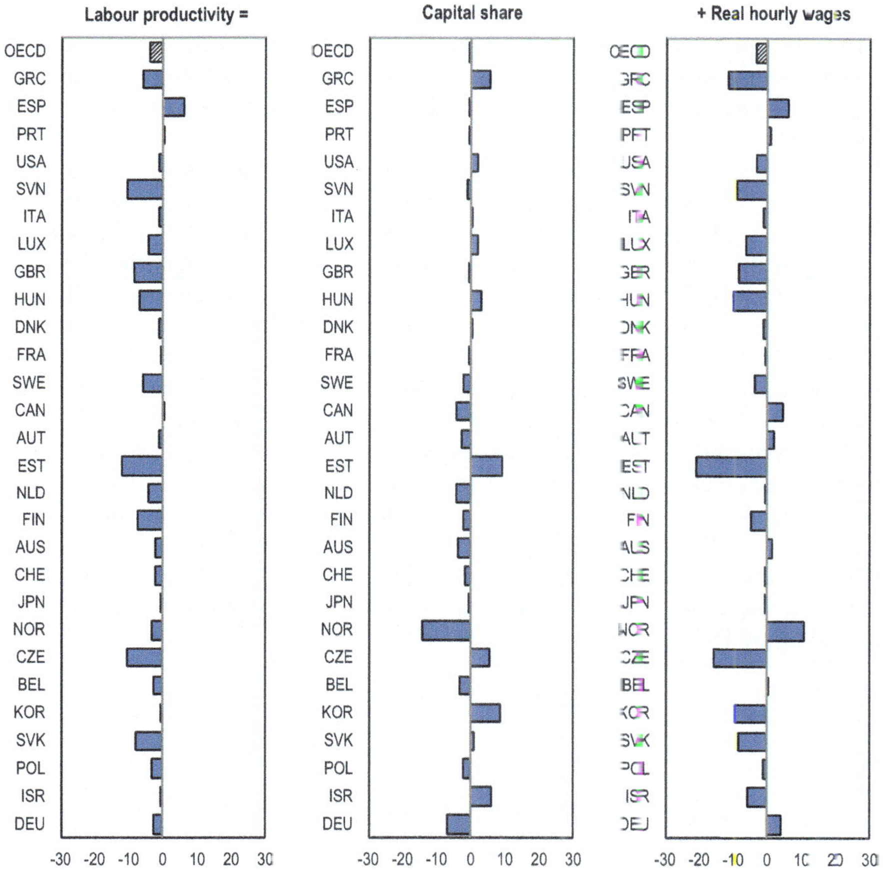

Fig. 8.4 Lower labour productivity growth translated into lower real wage growth (Decomposition of the annualised deviation of labour productivity from the pre-crisis trend), 2008–2015. Notes: The decomposition is based on the logarithmic identity: $(y - y^*) - (n + h - (n^* + h^*)) = [(y - y^*) - (n + h - (n^* + h^*)) - (w - w^*)] + (w - w^*)$. y is GDP, n is the number of employees, h is hours worked per employee and w is the real wage. The left hand side is the deviation of labour productivity from the pre-crisis trend, the first term in square brackets is the change in the capital share and $(w - w^*)$ is the deviation of real wage growth from the pre-crisis trend. Source: OECD calculations based on the OECD Economic Outlook No. 100, https://stats.oecd.org/index.aspx?DataSetCode=EO

determine the degree of labour hoarding and whether adjustment takes place along the intensive margin, in terms of working time and hourly wages, or along the extensive margin, in terms of the number of jobs. Second, structural policy can also affect the extent to which any cyclical rises in unemployment translate into higher structural levels of unemployment. For instance, unemployed people may gradually become less employable as their skills deteriorate the longer they stay unemployed. The jobs created in the recovery may also differ from those that were destroyed in the downturn in terms of their location or skill requirements. While such job churn may raise growth in the longer term, for instance, by generating better matches between job requirements and individuals' skills or moving labour to higher-productivity firms, it may also persistently raise unemployment if residential mobility is low or skills are not easily adaptable.

To analyse the short- to medium-term effects of labour market policies and institutions for labour market resilience, impulse response functions are estimated using the local projection method as proposed by Jordà (2005). This method allows for the robust estimation of impulse response functions by estimating their coefficients directly for each time horizon as opposed to deriving them indirectly from the estimates of a specific dynamic model, such as a vector auto-regression (VAR), which are typically more sensitive to misspecification.

The role of labour market policies and institutions for labour market resilience is examined by relating the response of labour market outcomes to output shocks to different policy settings across countries. Since most labour market policies cannot be deployed quickly to offset the negative effect of an aggregate shock on the labour market, the labour market policy that is in place at the time of the initial shock determines the labour market response. This means that the labour market response does not take account of reforms that took place in the wake of the crisis, including temporary measures taken in response to the crisis. More specifically, the following empirical model is used:

$$\begin{aligned} L_{ct+s} - L_{ct-1} &= \gamma^s Y_{ct} + \sum\nolimits_{j=1}^{J} \beta_j^s \left(Y_{ct} \cdot Str_{ct-1}^{j} \right) \\ &\quad + \sum_{i=1}^{2} \delta_i^s X_{ct-i} + \alpha_c^s + \alpha_t^s + \varepsilon_{ct+s} \forall s = 0, 1, \ldots, \mathrm{S} \end{aligned} \tag{8.1}$$

where L is the labour market outcome variable of interest; Y is the change in GDP; Str is the labour market policy setting in the year preceding the initial shock; X denotes a vector of controls including labour market policy to control for the independent effects of policies, GDP growth to control for the state of the business cycle and lags of the dependent variable to reduce serial correlation; and α_c^s and α_t^s are country- and year-fixed effects. β_j^s denotes the difference in the labour market response s periods after the initial shock under different labour market policy settings at the time of the initial shock.

The empirical analysis considers the following labour market policies and institutions: the stringency of employment protection provisions related to the dismissal of regular workers; the generosity of unemployment benefits using the average replacement rate which takes account of the level of benefits and their maximum duration; the coverage rate of collective bargaining agreements; and a measure of the degree of centralisation or co-ordination of the collective wage bargaining process. This is measured using an indicator which takes values 1 for decentralised and uncoordinated processes, and 2 and 3 for intermediate and high degrees of centralisation/co-ordination, respectively (Bassanini and Duval 2006).

The results are visualised by focusing on the impulse response function during the first 4 years following a 1% decline in GDP under different institutional settings. More specifically, it shows impulse response functions for a one standard deviation increase in the policy or institution of interest relative to the impulse response function that is obtained when all policies and institutions are kept at their OECD average. Results are not shown for policies or institutions that have no significant effect on any of the indicators of resilience considered.

Drawing on the experience from economic cycles since the mid-1980s for 22 OECD countries, the empirical analysis finds that only employment protection of regular workers and the centralisation/co-ordination of collective wage bargaining are significantly related with labour market resilience. The average replacement rate of unemployment benefits and collective bargaining coverage do not significantly dampen or amplify aggregate shocks in the near and medium term. The following more detailed conclusions can be drawn. The results are visualised by focusing on the impulse response function during the first 4 years following a 1% decline in GDP under different institutional settings (Fig. 8.5).

First, strict employment protection of regular workers tends to make labour markets less resilient. The analysis distinguishes between the effect of employment protection for regular workers on labour market resilience through its impact on hiring and firing of regular workers (the direct effect) and through its impact on the use of temporary workers (the indirect effect).[3] The direct effect of employment protection tends to dampen the negative effect on employment in the early phase of economic downturns when many jobs are at risk of being destroyed (Panel G). During the subsequent recovery the direct effect lowers the decline in unemployment by weakening incentives for hiring workers on permanent contracts (Panel A). Provisions that protect workers on regular contracts against the risk of job loss also affect labour market resilience indirectly by providing incentives for employers to rely more heavily on workers on temporary contracts. The combination of strict employment protection provisions for regular workers with lenient rules on the use of temporary workers tends to give rise to labour market segmentation. A high incidence of temporary work amplifies the unemployment response to aggregate demand shocks (Panels B and H). Results for employment are consistent with those for unemployment, while the wage response to aggregate shocks does not appear

[3]To this end, it exploits the well-known stylised fact in the literature that the average incidence of temporary work is closely related to the stringency of employment protection for regular workers across countries, but that they are not systematically related over time (Boeri and Van Ours 2013). Consequently, a country's average strictness of employment protection (the "between component") is used as an instrument for the average incidence of temporary work to give an indication of the indirect impact of employment protection on labour market resilience through its impact on labour market segmentation. The time-varying component of employment protection (the "within component") is used to capture the direct effect of employment protection on labour market resilience through its impact on hiring and firing.

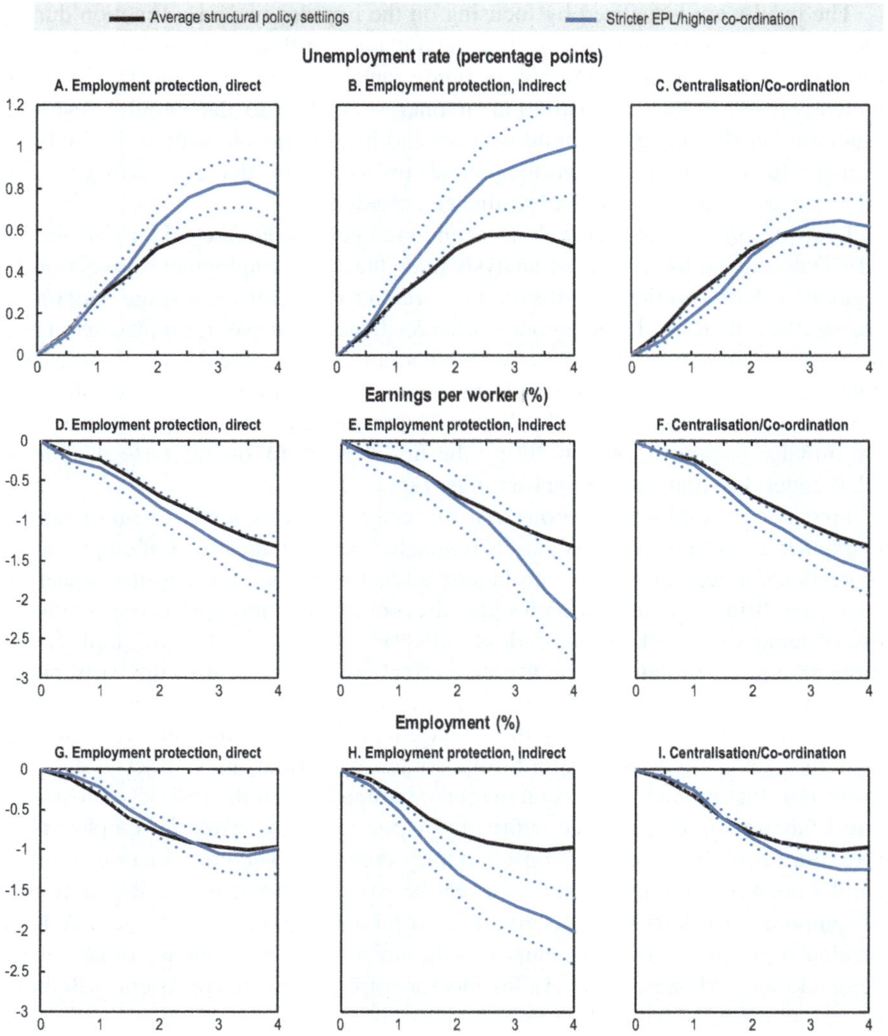

Fig. 8.5 The role of labour market policies and institutions for labour market resilience (The impact of a 1-percentage point decline in GDP under alternative labour market policy settings over the following 4 years). Note: The solid black line denotes the impact of a 1-percentage point decline in GDP on the unemployment rate under average structural policy settings. The solid blue line indicates the point estimate of a 1-percentage point decline in GDP on the unemployment rate when the structural policy setting of interest is increased by one standard deviation, while the dotted blue lines denote the corresponding 90% confidence interval around the blue line relative to the black line. Source: OECD calculations based on the OECD Economic Outlook No. 100, https://stats.oecd.org/index.aspx?DataSetCode=EO

to be significantly associated with employment protection for regular workers (Panel E).[4,5]

Second, centralised or co-ordinated wage bargaining systems may facilitate labour market adjustment in the short term, although their quantitative impact is rather small. In countries with highly centralised or co-ordinated wage bargaining systems, the initial adjustment on the employment margin is mitigated relative to countries with intermediate levels of centralisation and co-ordination and countries with decentralised or uncoordinated wage bargaining systems (Panels C and D) by promoting more adjustment on the earnings margin (Panel F).[6] Typically, this takes the form of reductions in working time with corresponding reductions in earnings and labour costs rather than reductions in hourly wages, which are likely to be more demoralising since they represent a devaluation of work. Having centralised or co-ordinated wage bargaining systems can help to make such adjustments more acceptable to workers by ensuring that they are broad-based and hence are more equally shared.[7] In some countries, working-time reductions are uncompensated so that they result in proportional reductions in earning (e.g. Sweden), while in others they may be partially compensated through the use of short-time work schemes (e.g. Germany, Japan). These schemes are typically more important in countries with relatively strict employment protection provisions and often require the involvement of the social partners (Hijzen and Venn 2011; Hijzen and Martin 2013).

8.3.2 *The Role of Fiscal Policy for Labour Market Resilience*

Fiscal policy affects labour market resilience directly by impacting aggregate demand, both through automatic fiscal stabilisers and through discretionary measures. Automatic fiscal stabilisers reflect adjustments in fiscal revenue and expenditure that are directly related to the business cycle, such as declines in income tax revenues and increases in unemployment benefit expenditure during recessions. Consequently, the effect of automatic fiscal multipliers on aggregate demand and labour market outcomes cannot be estimated econometrically. In order to estimate the effect of fiscal policy on labour market outcomes, the econometric analysis focuses on discretionary fiscal policy changes that are unrelated to the business

[4]The results are robust to the exclusion of countries with dual labour markets that were hit particularly hard by the crisis (e.g. Spain).

[5]The fact that in countries with strict employment protection of regular workers the employment and unemployment responses do not converge to those in countries with average strictness over a horizon of 4 years suggests that employment protection may give rise to labour market hysteresis in the wake of aggregate shocks.

[6]Decentralised and uncoordinated wage bargaining systems do not appear more or less resilient in terms of unemployment than countries with intermediate levels of centralisation or co-ordination.

[7]See Smith (2015) for a discussion of the welfare effects of individual versus broad-based reductions in earnings.

cycle. In Sect. 8.4 the resulting employment multiplier is then applied to actual changes in fiscal balances to approximate the effects of overall fiscal policy, including that of automatic stabilisers, on unemployment.

Discretionary fiscal policy changes that are unrelated to the business cycle are measured using forecast errors obtained by comparing the actual change in discretionary public spending with the corresponding forecast for the change in public spending that was made 6 months earlier (details are in the Appendix). Forecasts for public spending are taken from historical vintages of the OECD Economic Outlook. The assumption for identifying the causal effect of fiscal policy is thus that the implementation lag of public spending is at least 6 months. Fiscal shocks are calculated separately for public consumption and investment and are scaled by lagged GDP to allow for the direct interpretation of output and labour market effects as fiscal multipliers. The effects of spending on active labour market programmes (ALMPs) are also analysed. While there are no official OECD forecasts for these, forecast errors are constructed *ex post* by comparing actual active spending developments with forecasts for active spending based on the available information in the previous period.

As in the case of structural policies and institutions, the impact of fiscal shocks for labour market resilience is analysed by means of impulse response functions which document the evolution of GDP or unemployment in response to an impulse in public spending during the subsequent 4 years. Results are reported for the cross-country average impact over the business cycle as well as separately for the impact during economic downturns and expansions. While the impact of fiscal policy is likely to depend on the degree of trade openness, the level of public debt, the exchange rate regime, the monetary policy response and labour market policies and institutions, issues of cross-country heterogeneity in the labour market impact of fiscal policy are beyond the scope of this chapter.

On average over the business cycle, an increase in discretionary fiscal spending of 1% of GDP increases GDP by about 1% after 2 years (Fig. 8.6). This corresponds to a fiscal multiplier of about 1, which is within the range of typical estimates reported in the literature by Gechert (2015) and Ramey (2016). The estimated short-term impact of fiscal spending on GDP is strong during severe economic downturns (Panel A) but absent during large economic expansions (Panel B), which is consistent with previous evidence (Auerbach and Gorodnichenko 2012, 2013). While the fiscal multiplier during a severe economic downturn—around 2½ after 2 years—is in the upper range of previous estimates, a severe economic downturn in the context of the current methodology corresponds to the largest economic downturn across countries over the sample period. During more moderate economic downturns, the fiscal multiplier is closer to the reported average over the business cycle.

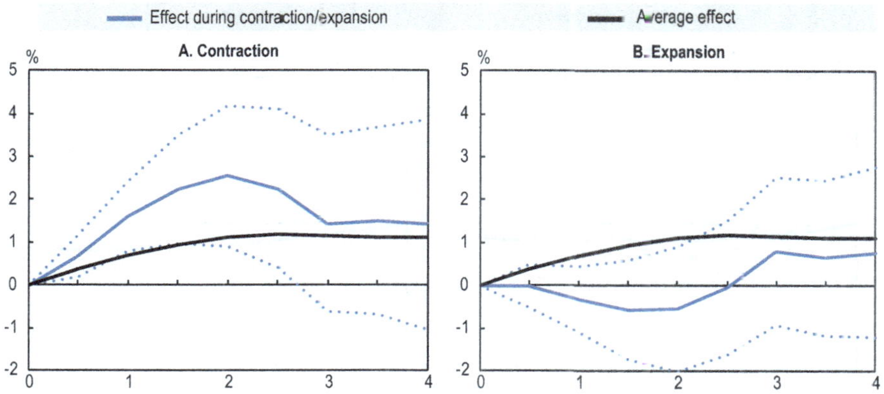

Fig. 8.6 Government spending stabilises aggregate demand during economic downturns (Impact of a fiscal spending shock of 1% of GDP on GDP over the following 4 years). Note: The solid blue line indicates the point estimate during economic contractions/expansions, while the dotted lines indicate the corresponding 90% confidence interval. The black line indicates the point estimate on average over the business cycle. Overall public spending is defined for the present purposes by the sum of consumption and investment spending. Source: OECD calculations based on the OECD Economic Outlook No. 100, https://stats.oecd.org/index.aspx?DataSetCode=EO

The differential impact of fiscal spending shocks over the business cycle reflects the possibility that public spending crowds out private spending to a lesser extent during economic downturns than during economic expansions or may even crowd in private spending by raising expectations of future growth. Moreover, monetary policy may not act to offset the fiscal stimulus if the policy interest rate is at the zero lower bound or expected inflation is below the target so that an increase in inflation expectations in response to the fiscal stimulus directly translates into lower real interest rates.

By stabilising aggregate demand, discretionary fiscal spending limits the increase in unemployment in the wake of negative aggregate shocks (Fig. 8.7). With regards to the impact of fiscal policy on unemployment the following key findings emerge. First, on average over the business cycle, a discretionary public spending shock of 1% of GDP reduces the unemployment rate by about half a percentage point (Panel A). Given a fiscal multiplier of about one, the implicit responsiveness of the unemployment rate to an increase in aggregate demand is about one half.

Second, the timing of public spending shocks matters for its effectiveness in promoting labour market resilience. An increase in overall fiscal spending reduces the unemployment rate during economic downturns but not during economic expansions (Panel A). The maximum impact during a severe economic downturn is reached after 2 years at which point a 1% increase in public spending is associated with an almost 1-percentage point reduction in the unemployment rate.

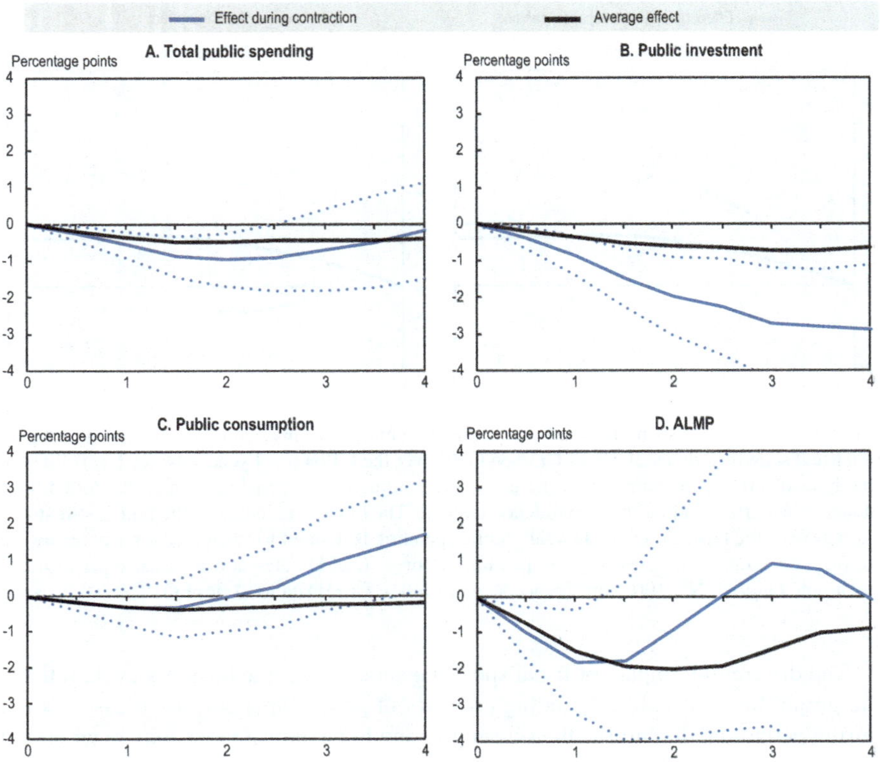

Fig. 8.7 Government spending reduces unemployment during economic downturns (Impact of a fiscal spending shock of 1% of GDP on the unemployment rate over the following 4 years). Note: The solid blue line indicates the point estimate during economic contractions, while the dotted lines indicate the corresponding 90% confidence interval. The black line indicates the point estimate on average over the business cycle. *Source*: OECD calculations based on the OECD Economic Outlook No. 100, https://stats.oecd.org/index.aspx?DataSetCode=EO and OECD Labour Market Programmes Database, https://stats.oecd.org/Index.aspx?DataSetCode=LMPEXP

Third, the composition of public spending matters (Panels B and C). The impact of public investment on unemployment tends to be both larger and more persistent than that of public consumption. Moreover, the impact of public investment on unemployment is also more sensitive to the business cycle, with its effect being much larger during severe downturns than in normal times. In principle, this could reflect the crowding in of private investment as firms raise investment in response to higher aggregate demand. However, there is considerable uncertainty about the exact size of the unemployment-reducing effects of public investment as can be seen from the wide confidence bands associated with the estimates.[8]

[8]These findings are qualitatively consistent with results in Abiad et al. (2016).

Finally, public spending on active labour market programmes (ALMP) significantly reduces unemployment in the short term (Panel D). After 1 year, an increase in active labour market spending of 1% of GDP would reduce the unemployment rate by almost 2 percentage points compared with less than half a percentage point for public spending overall.[9] Given the average share of active labour market spending in GDP in the OECD of around 0.5%, an increase of 1% of GDP is extremely large and may neither be desirable nor feasible. However, the result implies that even modest increases in active labour market spending can make a significant contribution to reducing unemployment in the short term. It also implies that an increase in active labour market spending could partially pay for itself by reducing the overall cost of unemployment benefits.[10]

By limiting the rise in unemployment during economic downturns, fiscal stimulus not only reduces the social cost of the crisis, but also the risk that the cyclical increase in unemployment becomes structural or translates into a semi-permanent reduction in labour supply. The long-term unemployment rate, i.e. the number of persons who are unemployed for 1 year or more as a share of the labour force, could signal changes in both the importance of structural barriers to employment and the risk that workers become discouraged searching for a job and drop out of the labour force. Figure 8.8 shows that total fiscal spending also reduces the long-term unemployment rate. The estimated impact of spending on active labour market programmes (ALMPs) is even larger and more persistent than for unemployment overall. This may reflect the possibility that active labour market programmes disproportionately benefit the long-term unemployed or unemployed persons at risk of long-term unemployment (Andrews and Saia 2017).[11]

[9]While the short-term impact of ALMP spending on the unemployment rate is statistically different from zero it is not statistically different from that of overall spending as there is considerable uncertainty about the exact size of the estimated effect of ALMP spending.

[10]Total spending on unemployment benefits as a share of GDP amounted to 0.9% for the OECD as a whole in 2009. Taking account of the actual OECD unemployment rate at the time (8%), it can be shown that a 1% increase in active labour market spending of GDP leads to a 0.2% reduction in the share of unemployment benefit spending in GDP. This implies a marginal cost of active labour market spending of 0.8. The marginal cost of active labour market spending is considerably smaller in countries with more comprehensive and generous unemployment benefits system such as Austria and the Netherlands where it is about 0.5.

[11]Similar results were found for the rate of labour force participation. This suggests that the positive impact of active labour market spending does not reflect the role of stricter activation systems for pushing unemployed workers out of the labour force and into inactivity.

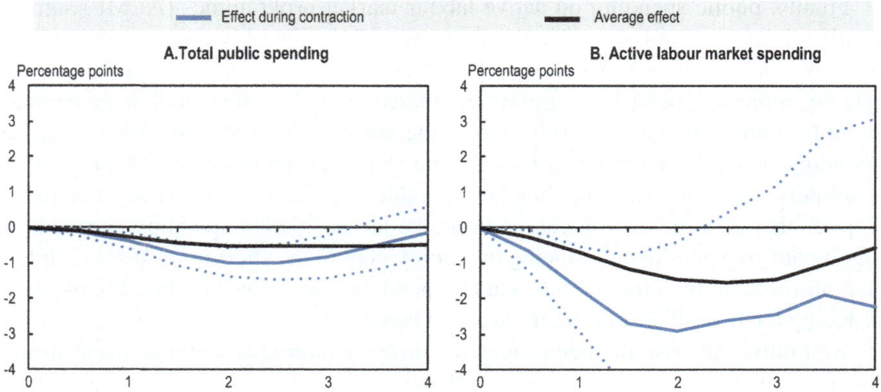

Fig. 8.8 Government spending reduces long-term unemployment during economic downturns (Impact of a fiscal spending shock of 1% of GDP on the long-term unemployment rate in the following 4 years). Note: The solid blue line indicates the point estimate during economic contractions, while the dotted lines indicate the corresponding 90% confidence interval. The black line indicates the point estimate on average over the business cycle. The long-term unemployment rate refers to the share of persons who are unemployed for 1 year or more in the labour force. Source: OECD calculations based on the OECD Economic Outlook No. 100, https://stats.oecd.org/index.aspx?DataSetCode=EO, OECD Labour Market Programmes Database, https://stats.oecd.org/Index.aspx?DataSetCode=LMPEXP and OECD Labour Force Statistics Database, http://www.oecd.org/employment/onlineoecdemploymentdatabase.htm

8.4 The Effects of Labour Market and Fiscal Policies for Labour Market Resilience Following the Great Recession

This section builds on estimates in the previous section to simulate the overall effect of structural and fiscal policies on labour market resilience in the aftermath of the Great Recession. In the labour market policy simulations, observed developments in GDP are applied to the coefficients estimated in the previous section under different assumptions on labour market policy settings at the onset of the Great Recession (actual or OECD average). In the fiscal policy simulations, observed developments in GDP are applied to the estimated fiscal multiplier of public expenditure under different assumptions on the evolution of the fiscal balance since the start of the Great Recession (constant versus actual). The fiscal policy simulations account for the fact that the fiscal multiplier is larger during economic downturns than economic expansions. Since the fiscal multiplier has been estimated using exogenous forecast errors, it is not affected by the endogeneity of the fiscal balance to the business cycle. However, since changes in the fiscal balance reflect both automatic fiscal stabilisers and discretionary measures, the overall effect of fiscal policy on unemployment will tend to be larger in countries with large economic downturns.

The simulations implicitly assume that the effects of labour market and fiscal policies are identical in all countries. This means that the analysis abstracts from country characteristics that may influence the country-specific impact of labour market and fiscal policies on resilience. Since the scenarios considered in the labour market and fiscal policy simulations are not comparable, they cannot be used to assess their relative importance for labour market resilience.

Figure 8.9 provides an indication of the role of labour market policies and institutions for labour market resilience by documenting the change in the annualised deviation of unemployment from the pre-crisis rate during the period 2008–2015 that would have occurred if labour market policy settings in each country had been equal to their average level in the OECD instead of the actual values.[12] The simulations account only for labour market policies and institutions that were found to play a statistically significant role for labour market resilience in Sect. 8.2, i.e. the stringency of employment protection provisions for regular workers and the nature of collective bargaining systems.

The simulation results suggest that adopting the average structural policy settings in the OECD before the crisis would have significantly reduced the unemployment impact of the Great Recession in Greece, Spain and Portugal, but would have significantly increased the unemployment cost of the crisis in Austria, Australia, the Czech Republic, the Slovak Republic and the United States (Panel A). The bulk of these changes reflect changes in the employment protection provisions of regular workers, both through their direct effect on hiring and firing and their indirect effect on the incidence of temporary work. The degree of co-ordination and centralisation of collective bargaining systems typically played a minor role.

The role of employment protection helps to explain some of the variation in labour market resilience across countries. Actual settings tended to reduce labour market resilience in countries where the unemployment impact of the crisis was very large (e.g. Greece, Spain), while they increased it in countries where the unemployment impact was small (e.g. Australia, the Czech Republic and the Slovak Republic) (Panel B).

The fiscal policy simulations take account of both discretionary fiscal policy measures and automatic stabilisers. This is done by using the estimated fiscal multipliers for discretionary spending shocks in combination with actual developments in the headline fiscal balance and the cyclically-adjusted fiscal balance over the period 2008–2015. This implicitly assumes that the estimated fiscal multiplier for discretionary spending is similar for other revenue and spending components, including discretionary changes in the tax system and automatic stabilisers. Previous studies typically show that the impact of these other components on aggregate demand tends to be somewhat weaker than that of discretionary fiscal spending (Alesina et al. 2016; Ramey 2016). Consequently, the simulations in this section may somewhat overstate the impact on unemployment of changes in the headline

[12]This choice of counterfactual necessarily implies that structural policies and institutions increased labour market resilience in about half of the countries and reduced it in the other half.

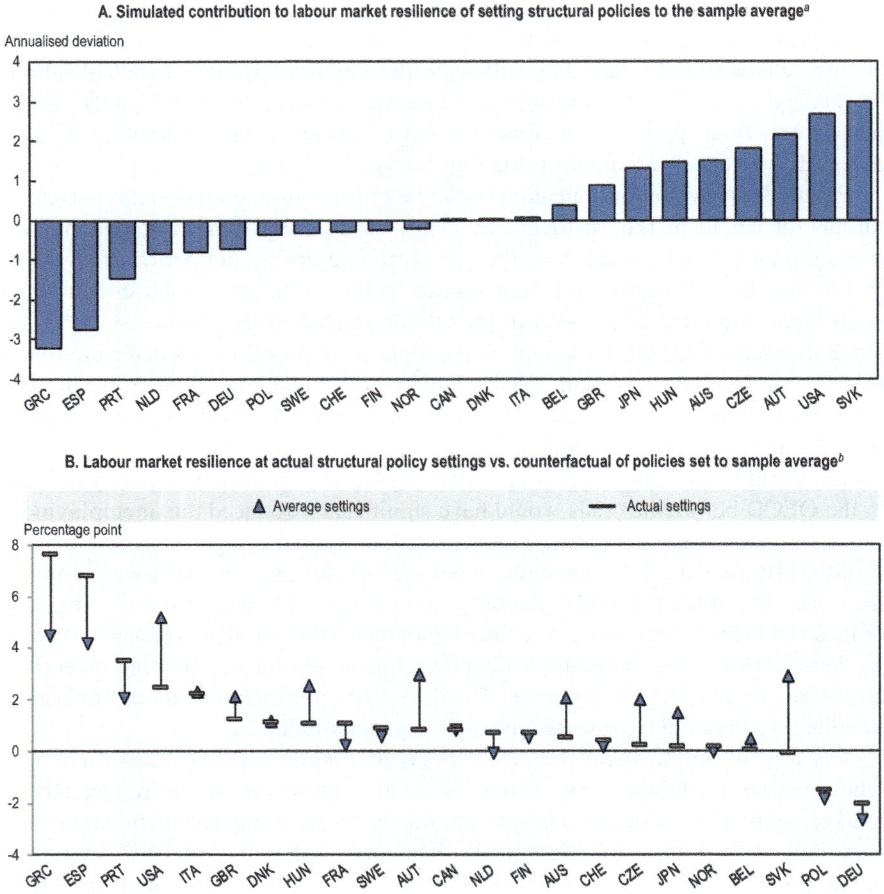

Fig. 8.9 Strict employment protection provisions for regular workers tended to reduce resilience (annualised deviation of unemployment from the pre-crisis NAIRU), 2008–2015. (a) Bars denote the change to the annualised deviation of unemployment that arises when replacing actual structural policy settings in 2007 by the sample average. The simulations take account of the direct effect of employment protection for regular workers on the hiring and firing of employees and its indirect effect on the incidence of temporary work as well as the role of more co-ordinated and more centralised collective bargaining systems. (b) "Actual settings" refers to the annualised deviation of unemployment from the pre-crisis NAIRU as reported in Fig. 8.2; "Average settings" refers to the counterfactual outcome that would be obtained in the event that structural settings had been equal to the sample average instead. In practical terms, this involves adding the simulated contribution of this policy change as documented in Panel A of this figure to the annualised deviation of unemployment obtained with actual settings. Source: OECD calculations based on the OECD Economic Outlook No. 100, https://stats.oecd.org/index.aspx?DataSetCode=EO

and cyclically-adjusted fiscal balance. Moreover, the cross-country variation in the role of fiscal policy should only be considered as indicative since the simulations do not account for cross-country differences in the effectiveness of fiscal policy.

In most countries, the headline fiscal balance was allowed to deteriorate during the Great Recession, thereby supporting aggregate demand and contributing to labour market resilience (Fig. 8.10, Panel A). This was largely driven by automatic stabilisers while discretionary fiscal policy—measured in terms of the cyclically adjusted fiscal balance—either complemented or partially offset them. A number of countries, such as New Zealand and the United States, took discretionary measures to stimulate aggregate demand either by raising public spending or reducing government revenue during the downturn. In these countries, the headline fiscal balance deteriorated by more than implied by the free operation of the automatic stabilisers, which contributed to labour market resilience. In countries with modestly contractionary discretionary fiscal policy during the crisis, such as the Slovak Republic or Portugal, automatic stabilisers more than offset the upward effect of discretionary measures on the unemployment rate. While many euro area countries tightened discretionary fiscal policy over 2011–2012, in most of these countries the tightening only partly offset the downward effect on the unemployment rate of fiscal expansions during the downturn. In part, this reflects the fact that the estimated fiscal multiplier during downturns is larger than during recoveries. Only Greece, Hungary and Italy did not allow the automatic stabilisers to operate at all by fully offsetting automatic declines in the headline fiscal balance via discretionary fiscal tightening.

Fiscal policy significantly contributed to labour market resilience on average but was not systematically related to its cross-country pattern (Fig. 8.10, Panel B). The simulation results suggest that fiscal policy reduced the annualised deviation of unemployment from the pre-crisis NAIRU during the period 2008–2015 from over 4 to about 1 percentage point for the OECD as a whole. In a number of countries that were particularly hard hit by the crisis, including Greece, Italy and Portugal, automatic stabilisers were not allowed to operate fully. However, in a number of other countries that were hard hit by the crisis automatic stabilisers were allowed to operate, which contributed to labour market resilience. Overall, similar levels of labour market resilience despite large differences in fiscal policy suggest that other factors played a larger role than fiscal policy in explaining cross-country patterns in labour market resilience.

While structural and fiscal policies explain some of the cross-country variation in labour market resilience, a considerable part remains unexplained. The most important reason for this is probably that no account is taken of the nature of the shock, i.e. whether it reflected largely domestic problems related to finance, housing and construction (e.g. Spain and the United States), was compounded with a sovereign debt crisis (e.g. Greece, Portugal and Italy) or originated largely from abroad, with a sharp but short-lived impact on export demand (e.g. Germany and Japan). A second issue is that the simulations do not take account of the composition of public revenue and expenditure, even though this was shown to be important in Sect. 8.3. Third, the analysis does not take account of all structural policy developments such as the progressive implementation of activation strategies

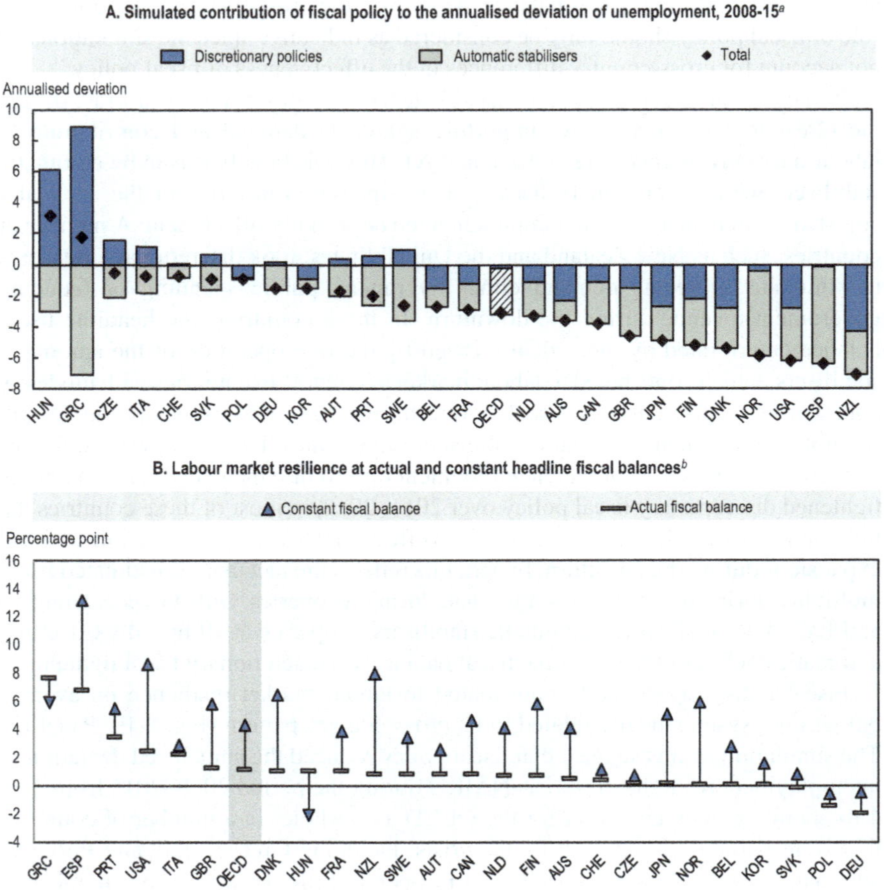

Fig. 8.10 Automatic fiscal stabilisers contributed to labour market resilience (Annualised deviation of unemployment from the pre-crisis NAIRU), 2008–2015. (a) The diamond denotes the estimated effect of changes in the headline fiscal balance on the annualised deviation of unemployment from the pre-crisis NAIRU. The blue bar denotes the estimated effect of discretionary fiscal policy changes measured in terms of the cyclically adjusted fiscal balance on the annualised deviation of unemployment from the pre-crisis NAIRU. The grey bar denotes the estimated effect of automatic stabilisers on the annualised deviation of unemployment from the pre-crisis NAIRU in the absence of discretionary fiscal policy changes. This is obtained by subtracting the discretionary fiscal policy effect from the total fiscal policy effect. The simulations are based on the estimates reported in Panel A of Fig. 8.7. (b) "Actual fiscal balance" refers to the annualised deviation of unemployment from the pre-crisis NAIRU as reported in Fig. 8.2; "Constant fiscal balance" refers to the counterfactual outcome that would be obtained in the absence of any changes in the headline fiscal balance since the start of the Great Recession. In practical terms, this involves subtracting the simulated contribution of fiscal policy as documented in Panel A of this figure to the annualised deviation of unemployment obtained with actual fiscal balances. Source: OECD calculations based on the OECD Economic Outlook No. 100, https://stats.oecd.org/index.aspx?DataSetCode=EO

in many OECD countries. Not only is this likely to have contributed to achieving record-low unemployment rates at the onset of the crisis, it also likely to have helped job-losers get back into work more quickly during the crisis than otherwise would have been the case (e.g. Germany, Sweden and the United Kingdom).

8.5 Conclusions

The analysis presented in this chapter suggests that fiscal policy played an important role in stabilising the labour market and preventing hysteresis following the Great Recession of 2008–2009. Fiscal policy appears to be particularly effective during recessions, which implies that allowing automatic fiscal stabilisers to operate and complementing them with additional discretionary measures during deep economic downturns can go some way toward promoting labour market resilience. However, the use of fiscal policy as a stabilisation tool requires that sufficient fiscal space be available during recessions. Lack of fiscal space explains why a number of countries hit particularly hard by the crisis could not allow automatic stabilisers to operate fully. This highlights the importance of keeping public debt at prudent levels during expansions and building sufficient flexibility into institutional fiscal rules.

Structural policies and institutions also have a role to play in promoting labour market resilience, both by directly sustaining employment during downturns and by supporting aggregate demand. A well-designed social protection system for workers (i.e. one which combines effective protection with effective activation policies) and activation policies that respond strongly to cyclical increases in unemployment can be particularly effective. Not only do they directly reduce the social cost of economic downturns by providing income support to people who have lost their job and facilitating their return to work, but they also strengthen automatic fiscal stabilisers by sustaining the consumption levels of unemployed people. Well-designed short-term work schemes and collective bargaining systems can promote labour market resilience by facilitating adjustments in wages and working time. In particular, better co-ordination of collective bargaining outcomes across sectors and firms can help making collective bargaining systems more responsive to economic conditions. Avoiding large gaps in the degree of employment protection between those on permanent and temporary contracts reduces dualism in the labour market by limiting the overuse of temporary contracts which in turns contributes to labour market resilience.

While structural and fiscal policies play an important role for labour market resilience, they cannot fully offset the effects of large aggregate shocks on employment. For instance, the countries with the largest losses in terms of unemployment in the wake of the Great Recession of 2008–2009 were typically hit by severe housing, banking and sovereign debt crises that resulted in large and persistent declines in aggregate demand and employment, whereas the countries with the smallest losses typically experienced transitory shocks in external demand. This demonstrates that structural policies that are not directly related to the labour market, especially regulations that reduce the risk of financial crises, can have large effects on labour market resilience.

Structural and fiscal policies that promote labour market resilience also have beneficial effects for long-run growth, employment performance as well as inclusiveness. Stabilising labour market outcomes during large economic downturns not only reduces the social cost of such downturns, but also reduces the risk that transitory increases in unemployment translate into semi-permanent increases in unemployment and decreases in labour force participation. Moreover, the benefits of higher labour market resilience are likely to accrue disproportionately to the most vulnerable workers, including young people, the long-term unemployed and workers on temporary contracts.

Appendix 1: Fiscal Policy: The Empirical Model

Identifying the causal effect of fiscal policy on output and unemployment requires isolating changes in fiscal policy that are exogenous to the business cycle. Previous studies have used either a narrative approach (Romer and Romer 2010; Ramey 2011) or an approach based on fiscal forecast errors (Blanchard and Perotti 2002; Auerbach and Gorodnichenko 2012). The narrative approach uses detailed background information on the motivation behind legislated policy changes, while the approach based on forecast errors interprets fiscal policy changes that are unanticipated by professional forecasters as exogenous. The interpretation of fiscal policy surprises as exogenous hinges on the assumption that fiscal policy cannot adjust to the business cycle instantaneously, because of implementation lags (e.g. a specific measure has to be identified, budgetary approval needs to be obtained and arrangements have to be made for its effective implementation). This assumption requires focusing on government consumption, public investment and active labour market spending, since government transfers and taxes adjust automatically to the business cycle.

The econometric analysis in this chapter adopts the approach based on fiscal forecast errors. The fiscal shock is constructed as the error in forecast public spending changes scaled by lagged GDP. For government consumption and public investment, the forecast error can be constructed from historical vintages of the *OECD Economic Outlook* database as follows:

$$Fis_t = (\Delta G_t - E_{t-1}[\Delta G_t]) / GDP_{t-1},$$

where G_t denotes the final national account figures for real fiscal expenditure (government consumption or public investment); $E_{t-1}[\Delta G_t]$ denotes the forecasted change in real fiscal expenditure for period t from the OECD Economic Outlook vintage in period $t - 1$; and GDP_{t-1} denotes the final national account figure for GDP in period $t - 1$. Scaling the forecast error in public spending by GDP allows interpreting the estimated coefficients on the fiscal shock directly as fiscal multipliers (Hall 2009).

Forecasts for active labour market spending are not available in the OECD Economic Outlook Database. However, it is possible to isolate the discretionary part of active labour market spending by generating a series of out-of-sample forecasts for this spending category for period t using regression models that use all information in period $t-1$, including the forecasts of GDP and unemployment from the OECD Economic Outlook vintage for period t. This is in the spirit of previous work by Darby and Melitz (2008) and Furceri and Zdzienicka (2012).

The response of output and the labour market to exogenous fiscal policy shocks during the business cycle is modelled using the local projection method as follows

$$R_{ct+s} - R_{ct-1} = \beta_L^s g(z_{ct}) Fis_{ct} + \beta_H^s [1 - g(z_{ct})] Fis_{ct} + \sum_{i=1}^{2} \delta_i^s X_{ct-i} + \alpha_c^s + \alpha_t^s + \varepsilon_{ct+s} \forall s = 0, 1, \ldots, S,$$

where R denotes real GDP or labour market outcomes; Fis is a measure of the fiscal shock; $g(z)$ is a smooth transition function between states of the business cycle which takes the form $g(z_{ct}) = \frac{\exp(-\gamma z_{ct})}{(1+\exp(\gamma z_{ct}))}$, with $\gamma = 1.5$. z_{ct} is the forecast of GDP growth from the OECD Economic Outlook vintage released in $t-1$; X denotes a vector of controls which include lags of the dependent variable, actual GDP growth and actual public spending; and β_L^s and β_H^s denote the response of the labour market to the discretionary fiscal shock evaluated at the most extreme busts and booms in the sample. As in the case of structural policies and institutions, the analysis is based on an unbalanced panel of semi-annual data for the period 1986–2015 for 22 OECD countries.

References

Abiad A, Furceri D, Topalova P (2016) The macro-economic effects of public investment: evidence from advanced economies. J Macroecon 50:224–240

Alesina A, Azzalini G, Favero C, Giavazzi F, Miano A (2016) Is it the 'how' or the 'when' that matters in fiscal adjustments? NBER working paper 22863

Andrews D, Saia A (2017) Coping with creative destruction: reducing the costs of firm exit. OECD Economics Department working paper 1353

Andrews D, Criscuolo C, Gal P (2016) The best versus the rest: the global productivity slowdown, divergence across firms and the role of public policy. OECD productivity working paper 05

Auerbach A, Gorodnichenko Y (2012) Measuring the output responses to fiscal policy. Am Econ J Econ Policy 4(2):1–27

Auerbach A, Gorodnichenko Y (2013) Output spillovers from fiscal policy. Am Econ Rev 103(3):141–146

Bassanini A, Duval R (2006) Employment patterns in OECD countries: reassessing the role of policies and institutions. OECD social, employment and migration working paper 35

Blanchard O, Perotti R (2002) An empirical characterization of the dynamic effects of changes in government spending and taxes on output. Q J Econ 117(4):1329–1368

Boeri T, Van Ours J (2013) The economics of imperfect labor markets, 2nd edn. Economics Books\Princeton University Press, Princeton
Caldera-Sánchez A, de Serres A, Gori F, Hermansen M, Röhn O (2016) Strengthening economic resilience: insights from the post-1970 record of severe recessions and financial crises. OECD economics policy paper 20
Darby J, Melitz J (2008) Social expenditure and automatic stabilisers in the OECD. Econ Policy 23(56):715–756
Furceri D, Zdzienicka A (2012) How costly are debt crises? J Int Money Financ 31(4):726–742
Gechert S (2015) What fiscal policy is most effective? A meta-regression analysis. Oxf Econ Pap 67(3):553–580
Hall RE (2009) By how much does GDP rise if the government buys more output? NBER working paper 15496
Hijzen A, Martin S (2013) The role of short-time working schemes during the global financial crisis and early recovery: a cross-country analysis. IZA J Labor Policy 2(1):1–31
Hijzen A, Venn D (2011) The role of short-time work schemes during the 2008-09 recession. OECD social, employment and migration working paper 115
Jordà Ò (2005) Estimation and inference of impulse responses by local projections. Am Econ Rev 95(1):161–182
OECD (2017) OECD employment outlook 2017. OECD Publishing, Paris
Ollivaud P, Turner D (2015) The effect of the global financial crisis on OECD potential output. OECD J Econ Stud 2014(1):41–60
Ollivaud P, Guillemette Y, Turner D (2016) Links between weak investment and the slowdown in productivity and potential output growth across the OECD. OECD Economics Department working paper 1304
Ramey V (2011) Identifying government spending shocks: it's all in the timing. Q J Econ 126(1):1–50
Ramey V (2016) Macro-economic shocks and their propagation. NBER working papers 21978
Romer CD, Romer DH (2010) The macro-economic effects of tax changes: estimates based on a new measure of fiscal shocks. Am Econ Rev 100(3):763–801
Smith JC (2015) Pay growth, fairness, and job satisfaction: implications for nominal and real wage rigidity. Scand J Econ 117(3):852–877

Chapter 9
Structural Reforms and Endogenous Market Structures

Andrea Colciago

9.1 Introduction

This chapter studies the interaction between structural reforms and the form and extent of competition in the goods market. Building on Colciago and Etro (2010b) and Colciago and Rossi (2011, 2015), I consider an economy with distinct sectors, each one characterized by many firms supplying goods that can be imperfectly substitutable to a different degree, taking strategic interactions into account and competing either in prices (Bertrand competition) or in quantities (Cournot competition). As in Bilbiie et al. (2012, BGM henceforth), sunk entry costs allow to endogenize entry in each sector. Therefore, the degree of market power depends endogenously on the form of competition, on the degree of substitutability between goods and on the number of firms. The labour market is characterized by Mortensen and Pissarides-style search and matching frictions.

Firms are large and workers may separate from a job for two reasons: either because the firm where the job is located exits from the market or because the match is destroyed. As in the bulk of the literature, wages and individual hours

I thank the Editors Jante Parlevliet and Jakob de Haan for encouraging me to write this chapter. The views expressed here do not necessarily reflect the views of DNB or the Eurosystem.

A. Colciago (✉)
Research Department, De Nederlandsche Bank, Amsterdam, Netherlands

Department of Economics, University of Milano, Milano, Italy
e-mail: a.colciago@dnb.nl

J. de Haan, J. Parlevliet (eds.), *Structural Reforms*,
https://doi.org/10.1007/978-3-319-74400-1_9

are determined according to Nash bargaining. The government provides a tax-financed unemployment insurance to unemployed workers. Market structures are said to be endogenous since the number of producers and price markups are endogenously determined in each period. Similarly, search frictions endogenize the rate of unemployment.

In this framework, I study the dynamics of the main macroeconomic variables in response to two specific structural reforms. The first one is a reduction in sunk entry costs for new firms due to deregulation. The second one is a reduction in the unemployment benefits for unemployed workers. I compare the effects of the reforms under oligopolistic competition to those under monopolistic competition, where strategic interactions between firms are neglected and markups are constant.

A reduction in entry costs leads to entry of new firms, higher output, consumption and lower unemployment in the long run under all market structures considered. There is a short-run cost in terms of consumption attached to the reform. Namely, consumption decreases in the short run to finance the creation of new firms.

Under oligopolistic competition, entry of firms strengthens competition and, via strategic interactions, reduces price markups. The dynamics response of the price markup has relevant implications for the evolution of factors' share. Indeed, under Bertrand and Cournot competition we observe a long-run increase in the labour share of income, coupled with a decrease in the profit share. A lower markup implies that a larger fraction of the marginal revenue product of labour is distributed to workers in the form of wages. Under monopolistic competition, where the price markup is a constant, we observe a permanent decrease in the labour share of income. This suggests that the form of competition in the goods market could affect the evolution of the distribution of income between capital and labour in the aftermath of reforms.

Over the past quarter century, labor's share of income in the United States has trended downward, reaching its lowest level in the postwar period after the Great Recession, as noticed by Elsby et al. (2013). The IMF World Economic Outlook (2017) reports that a similar pattern can be observed in emerging market and developing economies since the early 1990s. Notice that capital and firms' profits tends to be concentrated in the upper ends of the income distribution, thus a redistribution of income in favor of capital could affect inequality. Thus, structural reforms, by affecting the distribution of income between labor and profits, could also potentially affect income inequality.

Turning to the second reform, a reduction in unemployment benefits leads to similar long-run effects with respect to the reduction in the entry cost. Namely, we observe an increase in the output, consumption and competition together with a decrease in unemployment. There are, however, some relevant differences with respect to the earlier case. The first one is that the reform has no short-run costs in terms of consumption. This results echoes that in Cacciatore et al. (2016a,b). While in the case of a reduction in entry costs we observed a short-run reduction in aggregate consumption, necessary to finance the higher investment required to create new firms, in the case of lower unemployment benefits consumption increases from the outset of the reform. This is so since lower unemployment benefits bring about a reduction in the taxes required to finance them. The resulting positive income effect allows consumption and investment to grow together. The two reforms have also different effects on factor shares. A reduction in unemployment benefits implies a permanent reduction in the real wage. This results in a lower labour share of income and a mirror increase in the profit share. Notice that the reduction in the labour share of income is higher the more competitive is the structure of the goods market. In particular, it is higher under Bertrand and monopolistic competition than under Cournot competition. This is due to the response of the price markup. The elasticity of the price markup to the number of producers is higher under Cournot competition than under Bertrand competition. A stronger reduction of the markup under Cournot competition implies that a larger fraction of the marginal product of labour is distributed to workers in the form of wages, mitigating the negative effect on the labour share of income spreading from the reduction in real wages.

Several recent papers study the effects of structural reforms in a General equilibrium framework. Most of the existing studies model an increase in competition in the relevant market through an exogenous reduction in markups. In this spirit, Eggertson et al. (2014) find that structural reforms in a crisis that pushes the nominal interest rate to its effective lower bound, do not support economic activity in the short run and may be contractionary. This is so since reforms, by reducing firms' marginal costs, create deflation, raise real interest rate, and depress demand. Gomes et al. (2011) simulate the effects of supply side reforms in a multicountry general equilibrium model of the Euro Area. They find that reforms implemented individually by each country in the euro area produce positive effects, and that cross-country coordination produces larger and more evenly distributed beneficial effects.

In the framework presented in this paper markups and the extent of competition are, instead, endogenous as well as the rate of unemployment. For these reasons the model economy just outlined represents an ideal laboratory to study the aggregate short and long-run effects of reforms in both goods and labour markets, an issue of central interest in the aftermath of the Great Recession.

Other works have, instead, a similar approach to that in this chapter. Hebel and Haefke (2009) consider a labour search model with firms' entry and study whether lower entry barriers translate into higher employment. In the same spirit Cacciatore and Fiori (2016) consider a model with endogenous entry and imperfect competition, and focus on the macroeconomics effects of structural reforms in goods and labour markets. They show that structural reforms are beneficial in the long run, but are associated to output losses in the short-run. In their framework the relationship between the number of goods and their substitutability can be microfounded through the translog preferences introduced by Feenstra (2003), which are characterized by demand-side pricing complementarities. While driven by different mechanisms, both the demand side explanation by Cacciatore and Fiori (2016) and the supply side explanation presented in this chapter deliver endogenous responses of price mark ups to a change in the number of competitors in the market. Cacciatore et al. (2016a,b) evaluate the effects of structural reforms in goods and labour markets in an open economy model with firms heterogeneity. They study the effects of reforms in good and bad times. They find that business cycle conditions affects adjustment dynamics in response to reforms.

The remainder of the chapter is organized as follows. Section 9.2 presents the Model economy; Sect. 9.3 describes the calibration strategy; Sect. 9.4 contains the main results and Sect. 9.5 concludes.

9.2 The Model

The economy features a continuum of atomistics sectors, or industries, on the unit interval. Each sector is characterized by different firms producing a good in different varieties, using labour as the only input. In turn, the sectoral goods are imperfect substitutes for each other and are aggregated into a final good. Households use the final good for consumption and investment purposes. Price competition and endogenous firms' entry is modeled at the sectoral level, where firms also face search and matching frictions in hiring workers.

9.2.1 *Labour and Goods Markets*

At the beginning of each period N^e_{jt} new firms enter into sector $j \in (0, 1)$, while at the end of the period a fraction $\delta \in (0, 1)$ of market participants exits from the market for exogenous reasons.[1] As a result, the number of firms in a sector N_{jt}, follows the equation of motion:

$$N_{jt+1} = (1 - \delta)(N_{jt} + N^e_{jt}) \tag{9.1}$$

where N^e_{jt} is the number of new entrants in sector j at time t. Following BGM (2012) we assume that new entrants at time t will only start producing at time $t + 1$ and that the probability of exit from the market, δ, is independent of the period of entry and identical across sectors. The assumption of an exogenous constant exit rate in adopted for tractability, but it also has empirical support. Using U.S. annual data on manufacturing, Lee and Mukoyama (2007) find that, while the entry rate is procyclical, annual exit rates are similar across booms and recessions. Below we describe the entry process and the mode of competition within in each sector in detail. For simplicity, we assume that entry requires a fixed cost ψ in units of the final good, which is common across sectors.[2] The labour market is characterized by search and matching frictions, as in Andolfatto (1996) and Merz (1995). Firms producing in t need to post vacancies in order to hire new workers.

---

[1]As discussed in BGM (2012), if macroeconomic shocks are small enough $N^e_{j,t}$ is positive in every period. New entrants finance entry on the stock market.

[2]Our results are unchanged, both qualitatively and quantitatively, if we assume that new entrants do not exit from the market.

Unemployed workers and vacancies combine according to a CRS matching function and deliver m_t new hires, or matches, in each period. The matching function reads as $m_t = \gamma_m \left(v_t^{tot}\right)^{1-\gamma} u_t^{\gamma}$, where γ_m reflects the efficiency of the matching process, v_t^{tot} is the total number of vacancies created at time t and u_t is the unemployment rate. The probability that a firm fills a vacancy is given by $q_t = \frac{m_t}{v_t^{tot}}$, while the probability to find a job for an unemployed worker reads as $z_t = \frac{m_t}{u}$. Firms and individuals take both probabilities as given. Matches become productive in the same period in which they are formed. Each firm separates exogenously from a fraction $1 - \varrho$ of existing workers each period, where ϱ is the probability that a worker stays with a firm until the next period. As a result, a worker may separate from a job for two reasons: either because the firm where the job is located exits from the market or because the match is destroyed. Since these sources of separation are independent, the evolution of aggregate employment, L_t, is given by

$$L_t = (1 - \delta)\, \varrho L_{t-1} + m_t \tag{9.2}$$

Notice that $u_t = 1 - L_{t-1}$ also represents the fraction of agents searching for a job.[3]

9.2.2 Households

Using the family construct of Merz (1995) we can refer to a representative household consisting of a continuum of individuals of mass one. Members of the household insure each other against the risk of being unemployed. The representative family has lifetime utility:

$$U = E_0 \sum_{t=0}^{\infty} \beta^t \left(\log C_t - \chi L_t \frac{h_t^{1+1/\varphi}}{1 + 1/\varphi} \right) \quad \chi, \varphi \geq 0 \tag{9.3}$$

where $\beta \in (0, 1)$ is the discount factor, the variable h_t represents individual hours worked and C_t is the consumption of the final good. The family receives real labour income $w_t h_t L_t$, where w_t is the real wage, and profits Π_t from the ownership of firms. Unemployed individuals receive a real unemployment benefit b, hence the overall benefit for the household is $b\,(1 - L_t)$. This is financed through lump sum taxation by the government. Notice that the household recognizes that employment is determined by the flows of its members into and out of employment according to

$$L_t = (1 - \delta)\, \varrho L_{t-1} + z_t u_t \tag{9.4}$$

[3]Given that population is normalized to one, the number of unemployed workers and the unemployment rate are identical.

The household chooses how much to save in riskless bonds and in the creation of new firms through the stock market according to standard Euler and asset pricing equations. The first order condition (FOC) with respect to employment, L_t, is

$$\Gamma_t = \frac{1}{C_t} w_t h_t - \chi \frac{h_t^{1+1/\varphi}}{1+1/\varphi} - \frac{b}{C_t} + \beta E_t \left[(1-\delta)\, \rho - z_{t+1} \right] \Gamma_{t+1} \tag{9.5}$$

where Γ_t is the marginal value to the household of having one member employed rather than unemployed and $1/C_t$ is the marginal utility of consumption. Equation (9.5) indicates that the household's shadow value of one additional employed member (the left hand side) has four components: first, the increase in utility generated by having an additional member employed, given by the real wage expressed in utils; second, the decrease in utility due to more hours dedicated to work, given by the marginal disutility of employment; third the foregone utility value of the unemployment benefit b/C_t; fourth, the continuation utility value, given by the contribution of a current match to next period household's employment.

9.2.3 *Firms and Technology*

The final good is produced aggregating a continuum of measure one of sectoral goods according to the function

$$Y_t = \left[\int_0^1 \ln Y_{jt}^{\frac{\omega-1}{\omega}} dj \right]^{\frac{\omega}{\omega-1}} \tag{9.6}$$

where Y_{jt} denotes output of sector j and ω is the elasticity of substitution between any two different sectoral goods. The final good producer behave competitively. In each sector j, there are $N_{jt} > 1$ firms producing differentiated goods that are aggregated into a sectoral good by a CES aggregating function defined as

$$Y_{jt} = \left[\sum_{i=1}^{N_{jt}} y_{jt}(i)^{\frac{\varepsilon-1}{\varepsilon}} \right]^{\frac{\varepsilon}{\varepsilon-1}} \tag{9.7}$$

where $y_{jt}(i)$ is the production of good i in sector j, $\varepsilon > 1$ is the elasticity of substitution between sectoral goods. As in Colciago and Etro (2010a), we assume a unit elasticity of substitution between goods belonging to different sectors. This allows to realistically separate limited substitutability at the aggregated level, and high substitutability at the disaggregated level. Each firm i in sector j produces a differentiated good with the following production function

$$y_{jt}(i) = A_t n_{jt}(i)\, h_{jt}(i) \tag{9.8}$$

where A_t represents technology which is common across sectors and evolves exogenously over time. Variable $n_{jt}(i)$ is firm i's time-t workforce and $h_{jt}(i)$ represents hours per employee. Period-t real profits of a firm are defined as

$$\pi_{jt}(i) = \rho_{jt}(i)\, y_{jt}(i) - w_{jt} n_{jt}(i)\, h_{jt}(i) - \kappa v_{jt}(i) \tag{9.9}$$

where $w_{jt}(i)$ is the real wage paid by firm i, $v_{jt}(i)$ represents the number of vacancies posted at time t and κ is the output cost of keeping a vacancy open. Notice that $\rho_{jt}(i)$ is the price of firm i's output expressed in units of the final good. The value of a firm is the expected discounted value of its future profits

$$V_{jt}(i) = E_t \sum_{s=t+1}^{\infty} \Lambda_{t,s}\pi_{js}(i) \tag{9.10}$$

where $\Lambda_{t,t+1} = (1-\delta)\,\beta\left(\frac{C_{t+1}}{C_t}\right)^{-1}$ is the households' stochastic discount factor which takes into account that firms' survival probability is $1-\delta$. Firms which do not exit from the market have a time-t individual workforce given by

$$n_{jt}(i) = \varrho n_{jt-1}(i) + v_{jt}(i)\, q_t \tag{9.11}$$

The unit intersectoral elasticity of substitution implies that the nominal expenditure, EXP_t, is identical across sectors. Thus, the final producer's demand for each sectoral good is

$$P_{jt} Y_{jt} = P_t Y_t = EXP_t. \tag{9.12}$$

where P_{jt} is the price index of sector j and P_t is the price of the final good at period t. Denoting with $p_{jt}(i)$ the price of good i in sector j, the demand faced by the producer of each variant is

$$y_{jt}(i) = \left(\frac{p_{jt}(i)}{P_{jt}}\right)^{-\varepsilon} Y_{jt} \tag{9.13}$$

where P_{jt} is defined as

$$P_{jt} = \left[\sum_{i=1}^{N_{jt}} \left(p_{jt}(i)\right)^{1-\varepsilon}\right]^{\frac{1}{1-\varepsilon}} \tag{9.14}$$

Using (9.13) and (9.12) the individual demand of good i can be written as a function of aggregate expenditure,

$$y_{jt}(i) = \frac{p_{jt}^{-\varepsilon}(i)}{P_{jt}^{1-\varepsilon}} EXP_t \tag{9.15}$$

As technology, the entry cost and the exit probability are identical across sectors, in what follows we drop the index j and refer to a representative sector. As a result

$$N_{jt} = N_t, P_{jt} = P_t, n_{jt}(i) = n_t(i), h_{jt}(i) = h_t(i), v_{jt}(i) = v_t(i)$$

and

$$p_{jt}(i) = p_t(i), \pi_{jt}(i) = \pi_t(i), V_{jt} = V_t(i)$$

9.2.4 Bertrand Competition

Let us consider competition in prices. Contrary to the traditional Dixit-Stiglitz approach which neglects strategic interactions between firms, we take these into consideration and derive the exact Bertrand equilibrium. Each firm i chooses $p_t(i)$, $n_t(i)$ and $v_t(i)$ to maximize $\pi_t(i) + V_t(i)$, taking as given the price of the other firms in the sector. The problem is subject to two constraints, namely Eqs. (9.15) and (9.11). The variable $\phi_t(i)$ is the Lagrange multiplier of the first constraint, and represents the time-t value of an additional worker to the firm; $mc_t(i)$ denotes the time-t real marginal cost faced by firm i and represents the Lagrange multiplier on the second constraint. Given sectors are atomistics, firms consider the effect of their price choices on the sectoral price index, but they take the aggregate expenditure and the aggregate price level as given.

In what follows we distinguish between producers according to their period of entry. We define as *new firms* those producing units which entered the market in period $t-1$ and at time t produce for the first time.[4] The term *incumbent firms* refers, instead, to producers which entered the market in period $t-2$ or prior. The distinction is relevant because new firms have no beginning of period workforce. Nevertheless Colciago and Rossi (2011) show that all producing firms in the Bertrand equilibrium, independently of the period of entry, have the same size, impose the same markup over a common marginal cost and have the same individual level of production. For this reason in what follows we drop the index i denoting variables relative to the individual firm. Optimal pricing implies that the relative price chosen by firms is

$$\rho_t(\varepsilon, N_t) = \mu_t mc_t \tag{9.16}$$

[4]Recall that just a fraction $(1-\delta)$ of time t-1 entrants start producing in period t.

where the markup over the marginal cost is given by

$$\mu_t^B(\varepsilon, N_t) = \frac{\varepsilon (N_t - 1) + 1}{(\varepsilon - 1)(N_t - 1)} \tag{9.17}$$

The latter is decreasing in the number of firms in the sector, with an elasticity $\epsilon_N^B = \frac{N_t}{(1+\varepsilon(N_t-1))(N_t-1)}$. Further, when $N_t \to \infty$ the markup tends to $\mu_t^{MC} = \varepsilon/(\varepsilon - 1)$, i.e. the traditional one under monopolistic competition. Also, it is decreasing in the degree of substitutability between products ε, with an elasticity $\epsilon_\varepsilon^B = \frac{\varepsilon N_t}{(1-\varepsilon+\varepsilon N_t)(\varepsilon-1)}$, and vanishes in case of perfect substitutability: $\lim_{\varepsilon \to \infty} \mu_t^B(\varepsilon, N_t) = 1$. In equilibrium firms set the same prices, hence Eq. (9.14) implies that the relative price is also identical across producers and reads as $\rho_t(\varepsilon, N_t) = \frac{p_t}{P_t} = N_t^{\frac{1}{\varepsilon - 1}}$.

9.2.5 *Cournot Competition*

The main difference between Bertrand and Cournot competition is that profit maximization must take the inverse demand function as a constraint. The latter is

$$p_t(i) = \frac{y_t(i)^{-\frac{1}{\varepsilon}} EXP_t}{\sum_{i=1}^{N_t} y_t(i)^{\frac{\varepsilon-1}{\varepsilon}}} \tag{9.18}$$

which implies that period profits can be written as

$$\pi_t = \frac{y_t(i)^{1-\frac{1}{\varepsilon}}}{\sum_{i=1}^{N_t} y_t(i)^{\frac{\varepsilon-1}{\varepsilon}}} \frac{EXP_t}{P_t} - w_t(i) n_t(i) h_t(i) - k v_t(i) \tag{9.19}$$

and the constraint (9.15) is replaced by $A_t n_t(i) h_t(i) = y_t(i)$. As in the Bertrand equilibrium all producing firms have the same size, impose the same markup over a common marginal cost and have the same individual level of production.[5]

Optimal pricing implies

$$p_t = \mu_t^C MC_t \tag{9.20}$$

where

$$\mu_t^C = \frac{\varepsilon}{(\varepsilon - 1)} \frac{N_t}{(N_t - 1)} \tag{9.21}$$

[5] See Colciago and Rossi (2011) for a formal derivation.

For a given number of firms, the markup under Cournot competition is always larger than the one obtained before under Bertrand competition, as well known for models of product differentiation (see, for instance, Vives (1999)). Notice that the mark up is decreasing in the degree of substitutability between products θ, with an elasticity $\epsilon_{\theta}^{C} = 1/(\theta - 1)$, which is always smaller than ϵ_{θ}^{B}: higher substitutability reduces mark ups faster under competition in prices than under competition in quantities.

In the Cournot equilibrium, the markup remains positive for any degree of substitutability, since even in the case of homogenous goods, we have $\lim_{\varepsilon \to \infty} \mu^{C}(\theta, N_t) = N_t/(N_t - 1)$. When $N_t \to \infty$ the markup tends, as in the Bertrand case, to $\mu_t^{MC} = \varepsilon/(\varepsilon - 1)$, i.e. the one under monopolistic competition.

9.2.6 Job Creation Condition

Under both market structures the first order condition (FOC) with respect to vacancies reads as

$$\phi_t = \frac{\kappa}{q_t} \tag{9.22}$$

Thus, the firm sets the value of the marginal worker, ϕ_t, equal to the expected cost of hiring the worker, $\frac{\kappa}{q_t}$. The FOC with respect to employment reads as

$$\phi_t = (mc_t A_t h_t - w_t h_t) + \varrho E_t \Lambda_{t,t+1} \phi_{t+1} \tag{9.23}$$

Condition (9.23) implies that the value of the marginal worker is represented by the profits associated to the additional worker, the term in brackets, plus the continuation value. Next period, with probability ϱ the match is not severed. In this event the firm obtains the future expected value of a job. Combining the latter two equations delivers the Job Creation Condition (JCC)

$$\frac{\kappa}{q_t} = \left(\frac{\rho_t}{\mu_t^i} A_t h_t - w_t h_t \right) + \varrho E_t \Lambda_{t,t+1} \frac{\kappa}{q_{t+1}} \tag{9.24}$$

where we used the pricing condition to substitute for $mc_t = \frac{\rho_t}{\mu_t^i}$ where $i = B, C$.[6] Since the ratio $\frac{\rho_t}{\mu_t^i}$ increases in the number of firms, it follows that competition leads to a rise in the marginal cost and hence in the equilibrium marginal revenue. For this reason the marginal revenue product of labour (MRP), given by $\frac{\rho_t}{\mu_t^i} A_t h_t$, also rises

---

[6]For simplicity, we slightly abuse the notation indexing uniquely the price markup. Clearly, the equilibrium number of firms and hence the relative price also differ across market structures.

with competition. Thus, stronger competition promotes the creation of vacancies and employment due to its positive effect on the MRP of labour.

9.2.7 Hiring Policy

Let π_t^{new} and v_t^{new} be, respectively, the real profits and the number of vacancies posted by a new firm. Symmetrically, π_t and v_t define, respectively, the individual profits and vacancies posted by an incumbent producer. New firms and incumbent firms are characterized by the same size, n_t. Thus, the optimal hiring policy of new firms, which have no initial workforce, consists in posting at time t as many vacancies as required to hire n_t workers. As a result $v_t^{new} = \frac{n_t}{q_t}$. Since $n_t = \varrho n_{t-1} + v_t q_t$, it has to be the case that

$$v_t^{new} = v_t + \varrho \frac{n_{t-1}}{q_t} \tag{9.25}$$

Hence, a new firm posts more vacancies than an incumbent producer. For this reason, and given vacancy posting is costly, the profit of new firms are lower than those of incumbent firms. To see this, notice that

$$\pi_t^{new} = \rho_t y_t - w_t h_t n_t - k v_t^{new} \tag{9.26}$$

Substituting Eq. (9.25) in the latter delivers

$$\pi_t^{new} = (\rho_t y_t - w_t h_t n_t - \kappa v_t) - k \frac{\varrho n_{t-1}}{q_t} = \pi_t - k \frac{\varrho n_{t-1}}{q_t} \tag{9.27}$$

The last equality follows from the fact that the term in the round bracket represents the profits of an incumbent producer, π_t. Consistently with the U.S. empirical evidence in Haltiwanger et al. (2010) and Cooley and Quadrini (2001), a young firm creates on average more new jobs than a mature firm and distributes lower dividends.

9.2.8 Endogenous Entry

In each period the level of entry is determined endogenously to equate the value of a new entrant, V_t^e, to the entry cost

$$V_t^e = \psi \tag{9.28}$$

Notice that perspective new entrants have lower value than producing firms because they will have, in case they do not exit from the market before starting production, to set up a workforce in their first period of activity. The difference in the value between a firm which is already producing and a perspective entrant is, in fact, the discounted value of the higher vacancy posting cost that the latter will suffer, with respect to the former, in the first period of activity. Formally

$$V_t = V_t^e + \kappa \varrho E_t \Lambda_{t,t+1} \frac{n_t}{q_{t+1}} \tag{9.29}$$

where V_t is the value of a producing firm (both new firms and incumbent firms) at time t.

9.2.9 Bargaining Over Wages and Hours

As in Trigari (2009), bargaining takes place along two dimensions: the real wage and the hours of work. We assume Nash bargaining. That is, the firm and the worker choose the wage w_t and the hours of work h_t to maximize the Nash product

$$(\phi_t)^{1-\eta} (\Gamma_t C_t)^{\eta} \tag{9.30}$$

where ϕ_t is firm value of having an additional worker, while $\Gamma_t C_t$ is the household's surplus expressed in units of consumption. The parameter η reflects the parties' relative bargaining power. The FOC with respect to the real wage is

$$\eta \phi_t = (1-\eta) \Gamma_t C_t \tag{9.31}$$

Using the definition of ϕ_t in Eq. (9.23) and that of Γ_t given by Eq. (9.5), after some manipulations, yields the wage equation

$$w_t h_t = \eta \left(\frac{\rho_t}{\mu_t^i} A_t h_t + \frac{\kappa}{(1-\delta)} E_t \Lambda_{t,t+1} \theta_{t+1} \right) + (1-\eta) \left(b + \chi C_t \frac{h_t^{1+1/\varphi}}{1+1/\varphi} \right) \tag{9.32}$$

where we use $\frac{z_t}{q_t} = \theta_t$, $\Lambda_{t,t+1} = (1-\delta)\beta \left(\frac{C_{t+1}}{C_t}\right)^{-1}$ and $mc_t = \frac{\rho_t}{\mu_t^i}$, for $i = B, C$. The wage shares costs and benefits associated to the match according to the parameter η. The worker is rewarded for a fraction η of the firm's revenues and savings of hiring costs and compensated for a fraction $1-\eta$ of the disutility he suffers from supplying labour and the foregone unemployment benefits. A distinguishing feature of our approach is that the wage depends on the degree of competition in the goods market. The direct effect of competition on the real wage is captured through the term $\eta \frac{\rho_t}{\mu_t} A_t h_t$, which represents the share of the MRP which goes to workers. As discussed above, entry leads to an increase in the ratio $\frac{\rho_t}{\mu_t^i}$ and hence in the MRP.

Thus, everything else equal, stronger competition shifts the wage curve up. This result is similar to that in Blanchard and Giavazzi (2003), who find a positive effect of competition on the real wage. The FOC with respect to h_t yields

$$\chi C_t h_t^{1/\varphi} = \frac{\rho_t}{\mu_t^i} A_t \quad \text{for} i = B, C \tag{9.33}$$

Because the firm and the worker bargain simultaneously about wages and hours, the outcome is (privately) efficient and the wage does not play an allocational role for hours. Stronger competition leads to an increase in hours bargained between the workers and firms for the same reasons for which competition positively affects the wage schedule.

9.2.10 Aggregation and Market Clearing

Considering that sectors are symmetric and have a unit mass, the sectoral number of firms and new entrants also represents their aggregate counterpart. Thus, the dynamics of the aggregate number of firms is

$$N_t = (1-\delta)\left(N_t + N_t^e\right)$$

The firms' individual workforce, n_t, is identical across producers, hence $L_t = N_t n_t$. As aggregate expenditure and sectoral expenditure are identical, it follows that $EXP_t = \sum_{i=1}^{N_t} p_t y_t = N_t p_t y_t$. Considering $\rho_t = \frac{p_t}{P_t}$ and the individual production function we obtain

$$Y_t = \rho_t N_t y_t = \rho_t A_t L_t h_t \tag{9.34}$$

where $\rho_t = N_t^{\frac{1}{\varepsilon-1}}$. As a result, the aggregate production function features a form of increasing returns. In this case a productivity shock impacts directly on output, but also through the firm creation channel. Total vacancies posted at period t are $v_t^{tot} = (1-\delta) N_{t-1} v_t + (1-\delta) N_{t-1}^e v_{t-1}^{new}$, where $(1-\delta) N_{t-1}$ is the number of incumbent producers and $(1-\delta) N_{t-1}^e$ is the number of new firms. Aggregating the budget constraints of households we obtain the aggregate resource constraint of the economy

$$C_t + \psi N_t^e + \kappa v_t^{tot} = w_t h_t L_t + \Pi_t \tag{9.35}$$

which states that the sum of consumption and investment in new entrants must equal the sum between labour income and aggregate profits, Π_t, distributed to households at time t. Aggregate profits are defined as

$$\Pi_t = (1-\delta) N_{t-1}\pi_t + (1-\delta) N^e_{t-1}\pi^{new}_t \qquad (9.36)$$

Goods' market clearing requires

$$Y_t = C_t + N^e_t \psi + \kappa v^{tot}_t \qquad (9.37)$$

Finally, the dynamics of aggregate employment reads as

$$L_t = (1-\delta)\,\varrho L_{t-1} + q_t v^{tot}_t \qquad (9.38)$$

which shows that workers employed into a firm which exits the market join the mass of unemployed.

9.3 Steady State and Calibration

Calibration is conducted on a quarterly basis as in Shimer (2005) and Blanchard and Galì (2010) among others. The discount factor, β, is set to the standard value of 0.99, while the rate of business destruction, δ, equals 0.025 as in BGM (2012).

The entry cost, ψ, and the monetary unemployment benefit, b, are two key parameters in light of the reforms designed below. I choose the baseline calibration for these two parameters in order to mimic the macroeconomic data relative to peripheral Euro area member countries. This is so since the structural reforms characterized below will amount to a change in these parameters in order to bring them in line with those relative to the core Euro area member countries.

The baseline calibration for entry costs is chosen as follows. Ebell and Haefke (2009) estimate the regulation cost of market entry for 17 advanced countries in the year 1997. They measure the average number of months of output lost due to administrative delays and fees. Cacciatore et al. (2016a,b) update the measure of Ebell and Haefke (2009) to 2013 by making use of the OECD's barriers to entrepreneurship indicators, which are available for the years 1998 and 2013. I set the baseline value of the entry cost, ψ, at the weighted average value computed by Cacciatore et al. (2016a,b) for euro area peripheral member countries. Weights are equal to the contributions of individual countries' GDPs to euro area total GDP. Cacciatore et al. (2016a,b) report that it takes the equivalent of 2.94 months of lost output to start a business in the peripheral euro area countries. This implies a value $\psi = 0.94$. The value of the baseline unemployment benefit, b, is such that the monetary replacement rate equals 34.9%, the average for euro area peripheral member countries reported by Cacciatore et al. (2016a,b). Since we consider a labour-leisure choice, the overall replacement rate is given by the sum between the unemployment insurance benefit and the disutility cost of working. This equals 0.7 a value consistent with Costain and Reiter (2008) among others.

With no loss of generality, the value of χ is such that steady state labour supply equals one. In this case the Frisch elasticity of labour supply reduces to φ, to which we assign a value of 1/2 in line with the existing micro-evidence in Card (1991) and Pencavel (1986). We take as the baseline value for the intersectoral elasticity of substitution $\varepsilon = 6$. This would lead to a steady state price markup equal to 20% under monopolistic competition, a value commonly used in the literature. As standard in the literature we set the steady state marginal productivity of labour, A, to 1. Next we turn to parameters that are specific to the search and matching framework. As mentioned above our baseline calibration attempts to capture the features of the sclerotic European labour market. The elasticity of matches to unemployment is $\gamma = \frac{1}{2}$, within the range of the plausible values of 0.5–0.7 reported by Petrongolo and Pissarides (2001) in their survey of the literature on the estimation of the matching function. In the baseline parameterization we impose symmetry in bargaining and set $\eta = \frac{1}{2}$, as in the bulk of the literature. We then set the efficiency parameter in matching, γ_m, and the steady state job market tightness to target an average job finding rate, z, equal to 0.25 and a vacancy filling rate, q, equal to 0.7. We draw the latter value from ECB (2002) and Weber (2000), while the former from Blanchard and Galì (2010). The cost of posting a vacancy κ is obtained by equating the steady state version of the JCC and the steady state wage setting equation. As in Blanchard and Galì (2010) we set the steady state unemployment rate to 10%.

9.4 Structural Reforms

We compute the effects on the main macroeconomic variables of two different structural reforms. The first one is a reform in the goods market aimed at fostering entry of new firms and competition. The reform consists in a reduction of entry costs from the baseline level, which was set as a weighted average of the entry costs relative to euro area peripheral member countries, to the average value relative to core European member countries. Cacciatore et al. (2016a,b) estimate the latter to be equivalent to 2.58 months of lost output in 2013. This implies a value $\psi = 0.86$, about 12% lower with respect to the pre-reform value.

The second reform instead is a labour market reform aimed at reducing the unemployment rate. The reform consists in a reduction of the monetary unemployment benefit, b, from the baseline level, which was set as a weighted average of the replacement ratio relative to euro area peripheral member countries, to the average value relative to core European member countries. Cacciatore et al. (2016a,b) estimate the latter to be equivalent to 29.4%. We compare the effects of the reforms across the alternative forms of competition we have outlined.

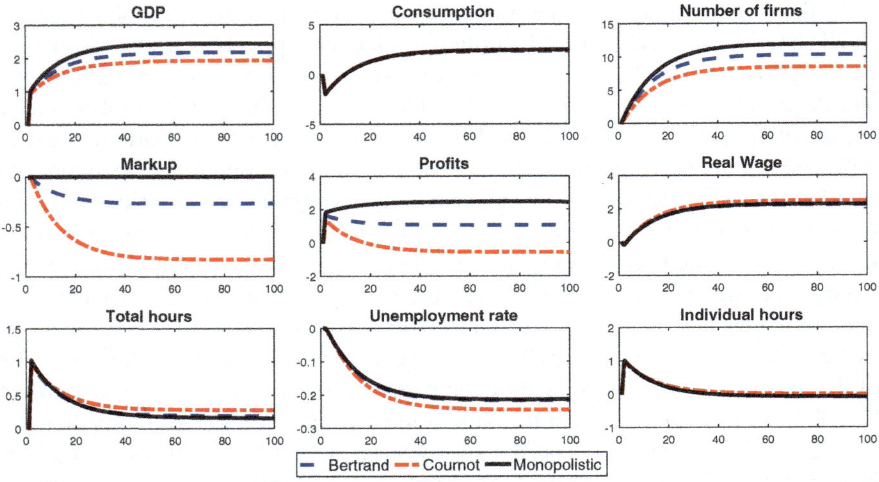

Fig. 9.1 Dynamics of the main macroeconomic variables in response to a permanent reduction in entry costs

9.4.1 Deregulation: Lower Entry Costs

Figures 9.1 and 9.2 display the effects of an unexpected permanent reduction in entry barriers in the final good markets, in the form of lower entry costs. The figures display exact non-linear transitional dynamics from the initial, pre-reform, steady state to the final, after-reform, steady state. The vertical axis reports percentage deviations from the initial steady state. Time on the horizontal axis is measured in quarters. Transitional dynamics are computed using the Newton-Rapson method implemented in Dynare.

We compare the dynamics of variables under the alternative competitive structures outlined above. Solid lines refer to the case of monopolistic competition, dashed lines to the case of Bertrand Competition and dotted lines to the Cournot case.

Lower entry costs provide firms with an incentive to enter into the market. The creation of new firms, however, requires investment by households who initially reduce consumption. Higher investment in new firms leads to a positive response of output. Entry of new firms fosters competition. Under oligopolistic competition this translates into a reduction in the price markup. As expected, stronger competition does not alter the price markup under monopolistic competition. Notice that dynamics under Bertrand competition are very close to those under monopolistic competition. This is not the case for Cournot competition. The difference dynamics under Cournot Competition are due to the dynamics of the price markup. Cournot competition features a higher elasticity of the price markup to the number of competitors in the market with respect to Bertrand. As a result, the decrease in the

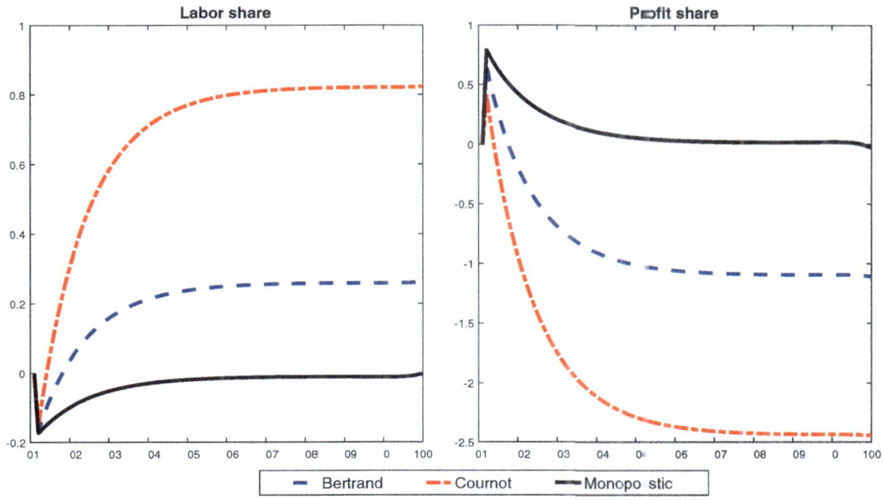

Fig. 9.2 Dynamics of factor shares in response to a permanent reduction in entry costs

price markup is quantitatively more relevant under this market structure. This has several implications in both the goods and the labour market.

In the goods market it implies that aggregate profits decrease in the long run. In turn, this leads to a lower increase in the number of producers compared to other market structures. Notice that profits initially increase also under Cournot competition. This is so since the number of firms is a state variable and its initial response is muted. As a result in the first period the markup stays at the initial level, and only gradually reduces to its new equilibrium value. As this happens, profits converge to their lower post-reform steady state level. Turning to the labour market, the larger change in the number of competitors under monopolistic competition and Bertrand does not translate into a stronger reduction in unemployment compared to Cournot competition. This is so since, as described above, a lower markup boosts the marginal revenue product of labour leading to a stronger hiring incentive. The reduction of the unemployment rate is in fact more relevant under Cournot competition which displays a strong markup reduction. Under all forms of competitions firms initially compensate for the higher demand resorting to the intensive margin of labour, leading to an increase in individual hours worked. As new matches are created the intensive margin of labour returns to the initial value, while we observe a permanent increase in the extensive margin and thus a permanent reduction in the unemployment rate. Notice that the response of the price markup has also implications for factor shares. The real wage increases under all market structures. Figure 9.2 shows transitional dynamics relative to the labour share and the profit share of income. Under oligopolistic competition the labour share of income initially decreases, but then reaches a permanently higher level. The initial decrease is again due to the initial muted response of the price markup. The mirror image of this is the permanent reduction in the profit share of income. Under oligopolistic competition, where the price markup is unchanged, we observe an opposite response. Thus, competition, and its effect on the dynamics of the price markup, has relevant implications for the distribution of income between labour and capital.

Summing up a reduction in entry costs leads to higher output, consumption and lower unemployment in the long run under all market structures considered. There is a short-run cost as consumption decreases in the short run to finance the creation of new firms.

Employment increases more under Cournot competition than under more competitive market structures. Under both forms of oligopolistic competition we also observe a long-run increase in the labour share of income, coupled with a decrease in the profit share. These effects are related to the dynamics of the price markup, which under oligopolistic competition, decreases as competition in the final good market becomes more intense.

9.4.2 *Lower Unemployment Benefits*

Figures 9.3 and 9.4 display the effects of an unexpected permanent reduction in unemployment benefits. As above, the figures display exact non-linear transitional dynamics from the initial, pre-reform, steady state to the final, after-reform, steady state. The vertical axis reports percentage deviations from the initial steady state. Time on the horizontal axis is measured in quarters.

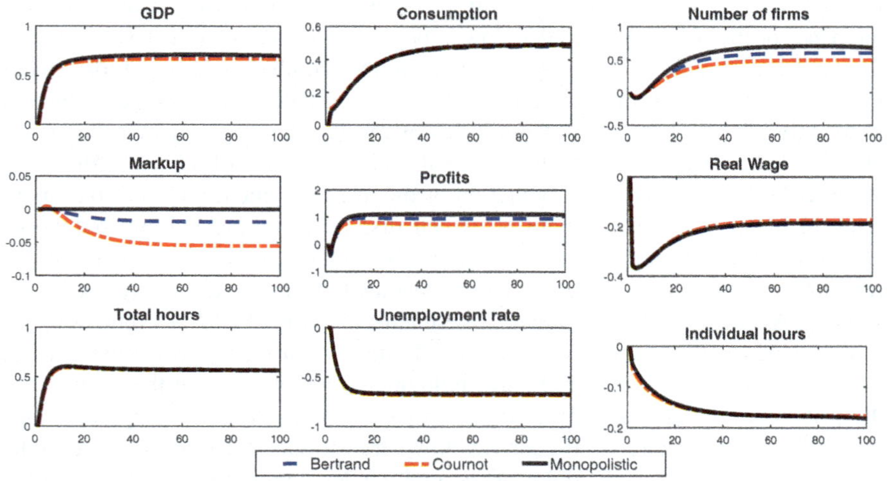

Fig. 9.3 Dynamics of the main macroeconomic variables in response to a permanent reduction in unemployment benefits

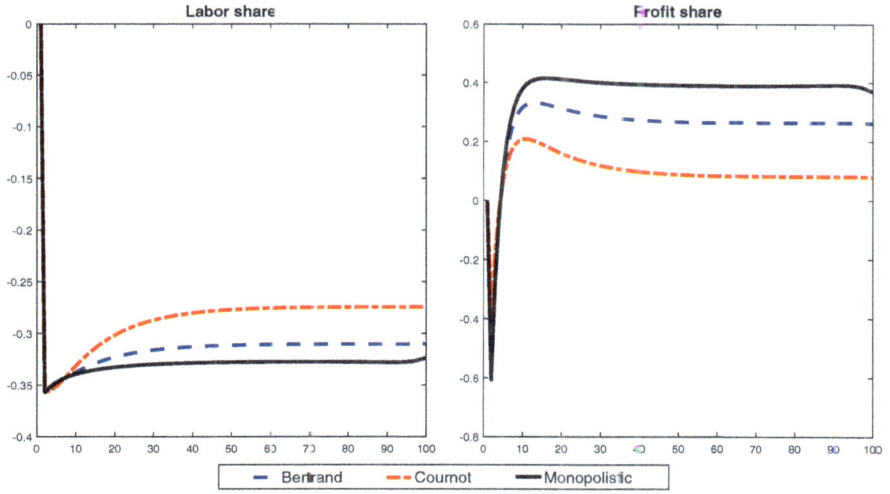

Fig. 9.4 Dynamics of factor shares in response to a permanent reduction in unemployment benefits

The reduction in the unemployment benefit for unemployed workers leads to similar long-run effects with respect to the reduction in the entry cost. Namely, we observe an increase in the output, consumption and the number of producers together with a decrease in unemployment. There are, however, some relevant differences with respect to the earlier case. The first one is that the reduction in the outside option for workers leads to a lower long-run real wage. The second one is that higher total hours of work in the post reform steady state is obtained through a reduction in unemployment coupled with a reduction in individual hours of work. Thus we observe an increase in the usage of the extensive margin of labour together with a reduction in the intensive one. The third one is that the reform has no short-run costs. This results echoes that in Cacciatore et al. (2016a,b). While in the case of a reduction in entry costs we observed a short-run reduction in aggregate consumption, necessary to finance the higher investment required to create new firms, in the case of lower unemployment benefits consumption increases from the outset of the reform. This is so since lower unemployment benefits bring about a reduction in the taxes required to finance them. The resulting positive income effect allows consumption and investment to growth together. The two reforms have also different effects on the dynamics of factor shares. Figure 9.4 shows that a reduction in unemployment benefits implies a permanent reduction in the labour share of income and a mirror increase in the profit share of income. Notice that the reduction in the labour share of income is higher the milder the reduction in the price markup. As discussed earlier, Cournot competition displays a higher price markup sensitivity to a change in the number of competitors in the market. For this reason the decrease in the labour share of income is milder under Cournot with respect to other market structures.

9.5 Conclusions

We study the effects of structural reforms in goods and labour market in the DSGE model provided by Colciago and Rossi (2011). In this framework, markups and the extent of competition are endogenous as well as the rate of unemployment. For these reasons the model economy represents an ideal laboratory to study the aggregate short and long-run effects of reforms in both the goods and labour markets, an issue of central interest in the aftermath of the Great Recession. Two specific structural reforms are considered. The first one is a reduction in sunk entry costs for new firms due to deregulation. The second one is a reduction in the unemployment benefits for unemployed workers. Both reforms boosts competition, output and employment in the long run. Lower entry costs boost competition in the final good market. Under oligopolistic competition this leads, via strategic interactions, to lower price markups. A lower price markup implies that a larger fraction of the marginal product of labour is distributed to workers in the form of wages. As a result, in the long run we observe an increase in the labour share of income, coupled with a decrease in the profit share. On the contrary, under monopolistic competition, where the price markup is a constant, we observe a permanent decrease in the labour share of income. This suggests that the form of competition in the goods market affects the evolution of the distribution of income between capital and labour in the aftermath of reforms. Lower unemployment benefits bring about a reduction in the taxes required to finance them. The result is a positive income effect which implies that the reform has no short-run costs attached to the transition period. A reduction in unemployment benefits leads to a permanent reduction in the real wage. This results in a permanently lower labour share of income and a mirror increase in the profit share.

References

Andolfatto D (1996) Business cycles and labour market search. Am Econ Rev 86:112–132

Bilbiie F, Ghironi F, Melitz M (2012) Endogenous entry, product variety, and business cycles. J Polit Econ 120:304–345

Blanchard O, Galì J (2010) Labour market frictions and monetary policy: a new Keynesian model with unemployment. Am Econ J Macroecon 2(2):1–30

Blanchard O, Giavazzi F (2003) Macroeconomic effects of regulation and deregulation in goods and labour markets. Q J Econ 118(3):879–907

Cacciatore M, Fiori G (2016) The Macroeconomic effects of goods and labour markets deregulation. Rev Econ Dyn 20:1–24

Cacciatore M, Fiori G, Duval R, Ghironi F (2016a) Short-term pain for long-term gain: market deregulation and monetary policy in small open economies. J Int Money Financ 68:358–385

Cacciatore M, Fiori G, Duval R, Ghironi F (2016b) Market reforms in the time of imbalance. J Econ Dyn Control 72:69–93

Colciago A, Etro F (2010a) Endogenous market structures and the business cycle. Econ J 120:1201–1233

Colciago A, Etro F (2010b) Real business cycle with Cournot competition and endogenous entry. J Macroecon 32:1101–1117

Colciago A, Rossi L (2011) Firms entry, oligopolistic competition and labour market dynamics. DNB Working Papers 465

Colciago A, Rossi L (2015) Firm dynamics, endogenous markups and the labour share of income. Macroecon Dyn 19(6): 1309–1331

Costain J, Reiter M (2008) Business cycles, unemployment insurance, and the calibration of matching models. J Econ Dyn Control 32(4):1120–1155

Cooley T, Quadrini V (2001) Financial markets and firm dynamics. Am Econ Rev 91(5):1286–1310

Ebell M, Haefke C (2009) Product market deregulation and the U.S. employment miracle. Rev Econ Dyn 12(3):479–504

Elsby M, Hobij B, Sahin A (2013) The decline of the U.S. labor share. Brook Pap Econ Act

Gomes S, Jacquinot P, Mohr M, Pisani M (2011) Structural reforms and macroeconomic performance in the Euro area countries. A model-based assessment. ECB Working paper 1323

Haltiwanger JC, Jarmin RS, Miranda J (2010) Who creates jobs? Small vs. large vs. young NBER Working Paper 16300

Lee Y, Mukoyama T (2007) Entry, exit and plant-level dynamics over the business cycle. Cleveland Fed Working Paper 07-18

Merz M (1995) Search in the labour market and the real business cycle. J Monet Econ 36:269–300

Petrongolo B, Pissarides C (2001) Looking into the black box: a survey of the matching function. J Econ Lit 39(2):390–431

Shimer R (2005) The cyclical behavior of equilibrium unemployment and vacancies. Am Econ Rev 95(1):25–49

Trigari A (2009) Equilibrium unemployment, job flows and inflation dynamics. J Money Credit Bank 41(1):1–33

Vives X (1999) Oligopoly pricing. Old ideas and new tools. The MIT Press, Cambridge

Chapter 10
Coordinated Structural Reforms: Insights from Fiscal and Labour Market Reforms in Germany

Oke Röhe and Nikolai Stähler

10.1 Introduction

The outbreak of the financial crisis and the subsequent escalation of the sovereign debt crisis brought severe financial and economic imbalances in the euro area to light, leading to the emergence of a general consensus that the implementation of structural reforms is indispensable both for restoring macroeconomic stability and for reducing the risk of a renewed build-up of unsustainable imbalances. Although several member countries enacted a range of ambitious reforms in the aftermath of the crisis, the reform process in the euro area has slowed noticeably over the past few years, while in many areas policies are still some considerable way from best practice (OECD 2016).

One explanation for the sluggish implementation of reforms can be found in the political economy literature. Despite overall long-term gains, structural reforms may have inherent unwanted distributional effects, at least for a period of time, constraining the implementation process (Leiner-Killinger et al. 2007; Parlevliet 2015). Against this backdrop, a number of theoretical studies have advocated the implementation of coordinated reform packages in order to mitigate adverse side effects and hence promote the adoption and implementation of structural reforms (see, for example, Blanchard and Giavazzi 2003). The need for careful prioritisation and sequencing of reforms has been emphasised, specifically with

The chapter has benefited from the useful comments and suggestions made by Johannes Hoffmann, Josef Hollmayr and Karsten Wendorff. The views expressed are those of the authors and do not necessarily reflect the opinions of the Deutsche Bundesbank.

O. Röhe (✉) · N. Stähler
Deutsche Bundesbank, Frankfurt, Germany
e-mail: oke.roehe@bundesbank.de; nikolai.staehler@bundesbank.de

J. de Haan, J. Parlevliet (eds.), *Structural Reforms*,
https://doi.org/10.1007/978-3-319-74400-1_10

respect to structural adjustments in the labour market (see, among others, Cacciatore et al. 2016a, b, c; Cacciatore and Fiori 2016; IMF 2016).

A practical example of this is the package of reforms adopted in Germany between 1999 and 2008, which involved the gradual implementation of fiscal and labour market reforms including tax shifts and reductions as well as a less generous unemployment insurance scheme (to be described in detail below).[1] In this chapter, a model-based analysis shows how a change in the composition of the tax mix, in conjunction with far-reaching labour market reforms, can boost output and employment while also alleviating potential adverse distributional effects.

However, employing expansionary fiscal measures to mitigate unwanted side effects does not come free of cost. In Germany, the reduction in the overall tax burden contributed to rising deficit-to-GDP ratios which may affect the risk premium on public debt. Hence, this chapter also considers the effects of the above-mentioned reform package on the risk premium on public debt. Furthermore, we outline how budget-neutral tax shifts (away from direct to indirect taxation) in conjunction with labour market reforms can still be used to boost output and employment while keeping negative distributional effects at a minimum.

The analysis presented in this chapter draws on a number of studies analysing the effects of German labour market reforms. Krause and Uhlig (2012) and Launov and Wälde (2013) focus on a reduction in unemployment benefits, while Krebs and Scheffel (2013, 2017) and Busl and Seymen (2013) additionally consider the effects of improved matching efficiency. All these papers focus on domestic effects except for Busl and Seymen (2013), who also analyse structural reform spillover effects on the euro area. Also, Dao (2013a) analyses international spillovers of reduced unemployment benefits in Germany within a dynamic stochastic general equilibrium (DSGE) model. With regard to the effects on domestic macroeconomic variables, particularly unemployment, the above-mentioned papers consistently find that structural labour market reforms tend to increase output and reduce unemployment. Nevertheless, the size of such effects differs, which can partly be attributed to differing assumptions about the magnitude of the decline in unemployment benefits and the increase in matching efficiency. Analyses taking the international dimension into account, such as Busl and Seymen (2013) and Dao (2013a), find positive spillover effects which appears to be consistent with the empirical and theoretical literature on the international effects of labour market reforms (Dao 2013b; Felbermayr et al. 2012, 2013; Gomes et al. 2013, 2016; Schwarzmüller and Stähler 2013). Cacciatore et al. (2016a, b, c; Cacciatore and Fiori 2016) provide a comprehensive overview of labour market reforms under several different sets of circumstances. However, these papers do not investigate distributional aspects.

Our analysis is also related to the literature dealing with tax shifts. Reductions in the labour tax wedge financed by higher consumption taxation (often referred to as "fiscal devaluation") have recently been discussed with a focus on international

[1]Although the German reform package implemented between 1999 and 2008 did not represent a fully coordinated programme in a strict sense, it provides a vivid example of the interaction of fiscal and labour market reforms.

competitiveness. Farhi et al. (2014) provide a formal analysis of fiscal devaluations in a New-Keynesian open economy DSGE model. They find that an intended nominal devaluation can be robustly replicated with a small set of fiscal instruments (namely, labour income and consumption taxes). Gadatsch et al. (2016) show that Germany's fiscal devaluation between 1999 and 2003 improved GDP, but only by a small amount. Similarly, Lipinska and von Thadden (2009, 2012), using a two-country DSGE model, show that fiscal devaluations generate only small quantitative effects. Engler et al. (2017) demonstrate that these effects can be increased when using payroll taxes levied on firms, while Attinasi et al. (2016) find that, where there is an intensive and extensive labour adjustment margin, personal labour income tax cuts may be more efficient. Further, Langot et al. (2014) also detect beneficial effects of a fiscal devaluation in France. Distributional effects of fiscal devaluation have, to our knowledge, largely been ignored so far in the theoretical literature. In a micro-simulation study, Picos-Sánchez and Thomas (2015) find that fiscal devaluations tend to be regressive.

The chapter is structured as follows. Section 10.2 describes the analytical framework used for our analysis. Section 10.3 describes the German reform agenda and its model implementation, while Sect. 10.4 shows how expansionary fiscal policy played a part in alleviating the negative distributional effects of the labour market reforms. Section 10.5 then contains a reassessment of the impact of such a policy taking risk premiums on public debt into consideration. There, we also propose a budget-neutral tax shift which can still help to generate positive output and employment effects, while keeping negative distributional consequences at a minimum. Section 10.6 concludes.

10.2 The Model

The impact of the reform package is evaluated using an extended version of the medium-scale open economy DSGE model FiMod originally developed by Banco de España and Deutsche Bundesbank staff (Stähler and Thomas 2012). Besides standard ingredients of New Keynesian DSGE frameworks, such as nominal price and wage rigidities, habit formation in consumption, and convex capital accumulation costs, the model features liquidity-constrained households, search and matching frictions in the labour market, and a comprehensive fiscal block, which together make it possible to mimic the respective policy changes in quite some detail within a two-country monetary union framework calibrated to Germany and the rest of the European Monetary Union. Figure 10.1 provides an overview of the model.[2]

More precisely, the model is set up as follows. To maximise expected discounted lifetime utility given their available funds, households make optimal choices regarding savings in physical capital as well as national and international financial

[2]A detailed description of the model is presented in Gadatsch et al. (2016).

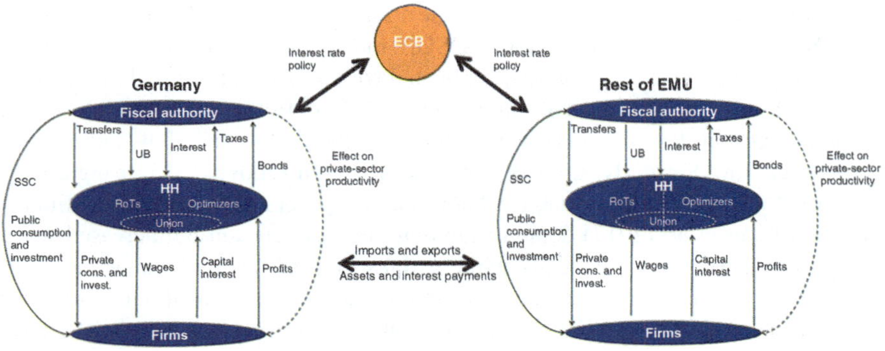

Fig. 10.1 Model overview. Note: The graph outlines the broad structure of the underlying DSGE model. UB denotes unemployment benefits. SSC refers to social security contributions

assets and purchases of consumption and investment goods. The latter add to the private sector capital stock, which is rented out to private firms. In our model, household members may find a job in the private sector or stay unemployed. We explicitly differentiate between short and long-term unemployment in line with Gadatsch et al. (2016), whose model serves as the basis for our analysis. Furthermore, household members may decide not to participate in the labour market at all. Following the literature with frictional labour markets, labour relations are determined according to a standard search and matching framework with Nash wage bargaining.[3] Households hence receive interest and wage payments, unemployment benefits and other fiscal transfers, and they pay taxes. In line with Galí et al. (2007), the model also assumes that an exogenously given percentage of households does not participate in asset markets. Thus, a household of this type consumes all of its income in each period. These households have become known as 'rule-of-thumb' (RoT) households in the literature. We assume that the share of RoT households amounts to 40%, following Le Blanc et al. (2014).

On the firms' side, monopolistic competitors in each region produce a variety of differentiated products and sell these to the domestic and foreign markets. No price discrimination between markets is assumed. Firms use labour and private capital as production inputs. A public capital stock is productivity enhancing as in Baxter and King (1993) or Leeper et al. (2010). Its provision is outside the firms' control and conducted by the fiscal authority. Cost minimisation determines the amount of labour and capital input per firm. Because firms enjoy monopolistic power, they are able to set their prices. Price and wage setting are staggered as in Calvo (1983).

The model, following Stähler and Thomas (2012), provides a relatively sophisticated public sector with multiple types of public revenue and expenditure. For

[3]For the standard setup of a typical New-Keynesian DSGE model, see Smets and Wouters (2003, 2007) or Christiano et al. (2005). Moyen and Sahuc (2005), Christoffel et al. (2009) and Boscá et al. (2011), among others, provide an overview of how to include a search labour market into a New- Keynesian DSGE framework.

instance, revenue comes from taxation on private consumption, on labour income (whereby a distinction is also made between taxes paid by employees and those paid by employers, the latter being termed "social security contributions") and on investment income. Public expenditure comprises unemployment benefits and other transfers, public consumption and public investment. As pointed out above, the public capital stock has a positive impact on the productivity of private firms. Furthermore, the fiscal authorities can issue debt on which they have to pay interest in the following periods. The model thus features a considerable number of feedback channels between fiscal policy, the government budget and the general economic situation. A fiscal policy rule that responds to the debt ratio ensures that, in the long run, the ratio converges towards a target value.

In the baseline model, sovereign default is ruled out. However, in order to include risk premiums for "overly indebted" economies, which will become relevant in Sect. 10.5, we follow Corsetti et al. (2013) and include an exogenously given fiscal limit. Whenever debt reaches this limit, the government is expected to default. In the initial steady state, the debt-to-GDP ratio is assumed to be sufficiently far away from this limit that the resulting annual default probability determining the risk premium demanded by financial agents endogenously does not exceed 4%. However, the more the actual debt-to-GDP level approaches this limit, the higher will be the default probability and, consequently, also the risk premium. Its evolution is approximated by a non-linear beta distribution function, implying that the closer the debt-to-GDP level is to the limit, the stronger will be the increase in the risk premium. Furthermore, it is assumed that this risk premium spills over to the financing conditions of firms in the private sector.

The monetary authority sets the nominal reference interest rate. In the euro area, monetary policy is conducted according to a Taylor-type rule that responds to measured euro-area-wide inflation and the output gap, which has become a common assumption in monetary DSGE models (see, for example, the New Area-Wide Model used by the European Central Bank, Christoffel et al. 2008; or Coenen et al. 2013).

10.3 The German Reform Package 1999–2008

In the late 1990s up to the early 2000s, the German economy was characterised by low GDP growth, a deteriorating labour market performance, and lack of international competitiveness, all of which motivated a comprehensive reform package. The centrepiece of the reform agenda was a set of extensive labour market reforms, commonly known as the "Hartz reforms" (named after Peter Hartz, the chairman of the independent committee which drew up the package of reforms).

The Hartz reforms were implemented through four laws, the first of which entered into force in 2003. Their objectives were to improve job matching efficiency and incentives to take up employment (Hartz I), promote the transition to self-employment and introduce more flexible arrangements for minor employment relationships (Hartz II), further support the matching process between firms and workers through a reorganisation of the Federal Labour Agency (Hartz III), and improve work incentives by reducing the reservation wage (Hartz IV). Specifically, the Hartz IV reform entailed a fundamental restructuring of the unemployment benefit system, significantly changing the level of benefits and their entitlement. As of January 2005, the unemployment and social assistance benefits were merged into a strongly means-tested unemployment benefits II—more or less at the lower social assistance level—and the maximum duration of the unemployment benefits was reduced to 12 months for recipients under the age of 55 (previously up to 26 months) and to 18 months for older workers (previously up to 32 months) as of 2006.[4] At the same time, former recipients of social assistance now gained much easier access to the overhauled set of active labour market policies which had hitherto been available only to recipients of unemployment benefits and unemployment assistance.[5]

The Hartz reforms were accompanied by a raft of fiscal reforms, including several tax changes. From 1999 to 2003, Germany raised energy taxes in order to finance a reduction in social security contributions and thus reduce the price of labour. In 2001, Germany lowered corporate taxes and, from 2001 to 2005, implemented a series of labour tax cuts in order to improve price and cost competitiveness, growth, and employment. In 2007 the standard rate of the value added tax was raised to ensure the sustainability of fiscal policy. However, one-third of the additional revenues was used to reduce the effective tax burden on labour by lowering social security contributions. Finally, in 2008 Germany cut corporate taxes in order avoid losses in the tax base.

To implement the fiscal reforms, the associated changes in the corresponding tax rates have to be identified. As described in Gadatsch et al. (2016), we take the official expected changes in the tax base and transform them into changes in the implied tax rate using the implied tax rates published by the European Commission (2014). With regard to the labour market reforms, we assume that they can be approximated by an improvement in matching efficiency (Hartz I to Hartz III), and an increase in the probability of becoming long-term unemployed plus the merger of unemployment and social assistance (Hartz IV).[6] Table 10.1 summarises how the reform agenda translates into changes in model parameters.

[4]From 2008 on, the maximum duration of unemployment benefit was extended to 24 months for workers aged 58 and above.

[5]Note that while the level of long-term unemployment assistance decreased with the introduction of Hartz IV, the level of social welfare assistance actually increased.

[6]The reduction in the entitlement duration for unemployment benefits is modelled as an increase in the probability of moving from short to long-term unemployment, while the merging of means-tested unemployment and social assistance benefits into unemployment benefits II is taken into account by reducing the replacement rate of long-term unemployed, with benefits designed as a fixed payment independent of previous wages, and increasing social assistance. With regard to Hartz III, the reform is simulated as a 10% increase in the aggregate matching function's efficiency which is in line with the recent empirical literature.

Table 10.1 Reform instruments and timing

Year	$\Delta\tau_{c\,(pp)}$	$\Delta\tau^{sc}_{employee}$(pp)	$\Delta\tau^{sc}_{employer}$(pp)	$\Delta\tau^{w}{}_{(pp)}$	$\Delta\tau^{k}{}_{(pp)}$	$\Delta\kappa^{p}_{e\,(\%)}$	$\Delta\vartheta_{(pp)}$	$\Delta rrl_{(pp)}$
1999	+0.51	−0.42	−0.42					
2000	+0.22	−0.15	−0.15					
2001	+0.23	−0.15	−0.15	−1.59	−1.08			
2002	+0.22	−0.15	−0.15					
2003	+0.22	−0.15	−0.15					
2004				−0.75		+10.00		
2005				−2.12			+11.67	−8
2006								
2007	+1.45	−0.35	−0.35					
2008					−0.64			

Notes: The table shows percentage (point) changes in fiscal instruments. To simulate the reforms, policy instruments and the timing of policy actions are chosen to closely match the actual scenario: From 1999 to 2003, Germany raised energy taxes (τ_c) in order to finance a reduction in social security contributions ($\tau^{sc}_{employee}$ and $\tau^{sc}_{employer}$). In 2001, Germany cut corporate taxes (τ^k) and from 2001 to 2005 labour taxes (τ^w). With regard to labour market reforms, the implementation of Hartz III in 2004 is modelled as an increase in matching efficiency (κ^p_e) between unemployed workers and vacancies. Hartz IV, put in place in 2005, consists of three measures. First, the duration of entitlement to unemployment benefits was reduced, which is reflected in a corresponding increase in the probability of becoming long-term unemployed (ϑ). Second, the replacement rate for long-term unemployed (*rrl*) is reduced. Finally, unemployment assistance for the long-term unemployed is merged into social welfare assistance. In 2007, value added tax (τ_c) was increased. One-third of the revenue was used to reduce the effective tax burden on labour by lowering social security contributions ($\tau^{sc}_{employee}$ and $\tau^{sc}_{employer}$). Finally, in 2008 Germany cut corporate taxes (τ^k)

Our simulation starts in 1999 from the initial steady state. For each reform measure, we change the relevant parameters as indicated in Table 10.1. We assume that individual reforms were not anticipated, which implies that anticipation effects are only relevant in the case of multi-year reforms (see Gadatsch et al. 2016 for technical details).

10.4 Model Simulations of the German Reform Agenda

Starting with an isolated investigation of the labour market reforms, the simulation results for Germany suggest an unambiguously favourable effect on output, consumption, investment, and employment, thereby confirming previous findings (see, for example, ECB 2015). Moreover, the Hartz reforms turn out to have noticeable positive spillover effects on the rest of the euro area, which is in line with the findings of Busl and Seyman (2013) and Dao (2013a).

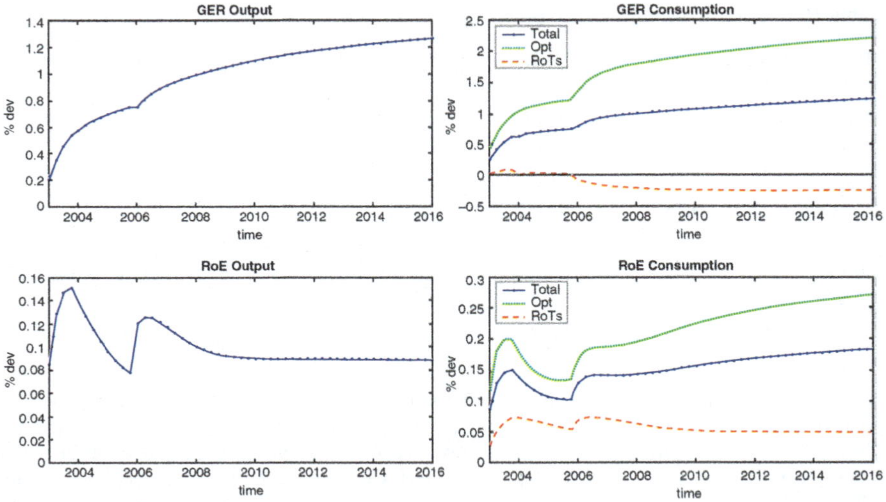

Fig. 10.2 Effects of German labour market reforms on output and consumption in Germany (GER) and the rest of the euro area (RoE). Note: Graphs depict deviations in percentage points from the variable's respective pre-reform long-run equilibrium level

A disaggregated analysis of German consumption, however, reveals marked differences between rule-of-thumb consumers and optimising households. The simulated labour market reforms not only increase consumption inequality but also lead to a Pareto-worsening of liquidity-constrained households by reducing their steady-state consumption level (see Fig. 10.2), which is an issue that has received little attention in the literature. The Pareto-worsening is explained by the fact that RoT consumers cannot derive the same type of benefit as optimising households from the improved labour market efficiency and the lower unit labour costs for German firms, since they do not receive dividends or capital income.[7] Hence, only the optimising households are able to overcompensate the negative effect on consumption originating from the loss in real wage income, which itself is primarily a result of the lower fall-back position in the wage bargaining process between households and firms due to shorter entitlement duration and lower unemployment assistance payments (Hartz IV). Concerning the positive spillover effects on the rest of the euro area, the reform-induced increase in consumption is not evenly distributed either, although clearly Pareto-improving for both types of households.

Turning to the simulation of the full reform package implemented between 1999 and 2008 (i.e. fiscal and labour market reforms), the direction of effects on output, consumption, investment, and employment remains unaltered, although the medium to long-run gains are larger in terms of deviations from the variable's respective pre-

[7]Note that besides having unrestricted access to capital markets, only optimising households are assumed to own firms and hence to be entitled to dividends.

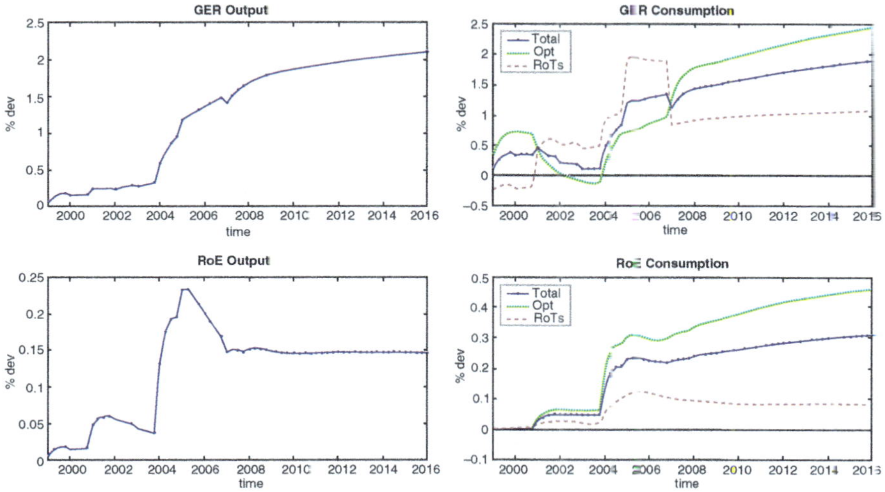

Fig. 10.3 Effects of German fiscal and labour market reforms on output and consumption in Germany (GER) and the rest of the euro area (RoE). Note: Graphs depict deviations in percentage points from the variable's respective pre-reform long-run equilibrium level

reform long-run equilibrium level for both Germany and the rest of the euro area (see Fig. 10.3). From a distributional perspective, however, noticeable differences show up when simulating the gradual implementation of German fiscal and labour market reforms. Specifically, the consumption inequality between the household types decreases profoundly in the course of the implementation process, implying a clear Pareto-improvement in the medium to long run for optimising households and rule-of-thumb consumers alike (see Table 10.2). The main reasons for the decrease in inequality—measured in terms of relative changes in consumption—can be found in the effective tax changes that reduce the tax burden on labour, which, in particular, increases available income and affects the consumption patterns of rule-of-thumb consumers due to their inability to smooth consumption.

With regard to the rest of the euro area, the spillover effects on consumption still lead to a Pareto-improvement for both types of households, while consumption inequality between the household types increases compared to the previous reform scenario.

The model-based case study of the 1999–2008 German reform package presented in this section emphasises the benefits of a careful prioritisation and sequencing of structural reforms. Specifically with respect to labour market reforms, it could be argued that a well-designed policy mix permits the mitigation of unintended distributional side effects.

Table 10.2 Long-run effects of German reforms

Variable	Percentage (point*) deviation from initial steady state	
	Labour market reforms	Labour market and fiscal reforms
Germany		
Output	1.38	2.29
Aggregate consumption	1.41	2.18
Optimiser's consumption	2.47	2.86
RoT's consumption	−0.18	1.16
Investment	1.16	2.56
Unemployment*	−1.56	−1.60
Rest of the Euro area		
Output	0.09	0.15
Aggregate consumption	0.20	0.33
Optimiser's consumption	0.30	0.49
RoT's consumption	0.05	0.08
Investment	0.18	0.30
Unemployment*	−0.04	−0.06

Note: Table shows long-run effects of the reform scenarios in percentage (point*) deviations relative to the initial steady state of the selected variables

10.5 The Impact of Risk Premiums on the Simulation Results and Budget-Neutral Reform Options

The findings of the previous section show that compensating (fiscal) measure after a structural labour market reform can be useful in alleviating income losses for some segments of the population. This might help to increase public support in euro area countries for which it is proposed to undertake similar labour market reforms. However, compensating measures in the form of tax relief, as was the case in Germany, are not free of cost. Figure 10.4 plots the simulation-based yearly deficit-to-GDP ratios from 1999 to 2016 in Germany for two scenarios: (1) implementation of labour market reforms only, and (2) implementation of the full reform agenda including fiscal reforms. It can easily be verified that especially the reductions in labour tax in 2001, 2004 and 2005 (see Table 10.1) under the full reform package expanded the deficit-to-GDP ratio by up to more than 0.4 percentage points relative to the scenario in which only labour market reforms were undertaken.[8]

Hence, given the tight fiscal situation of some member countries of the European Economic and Monetary Union (EMU), alleviating unwanted side effects of

[8] In this respect, it might be noted that the German deficit-to-GDP ratio actually exceeded the 3% threshold during the period from 2001 to 2005, which was also a time of major labour tax reductions. However, these developments can, first and foremost, be explained by an unexpected shortfall in taxes related to firms' profits and not by compensating measures to compensate those who lose from the labour market reform.

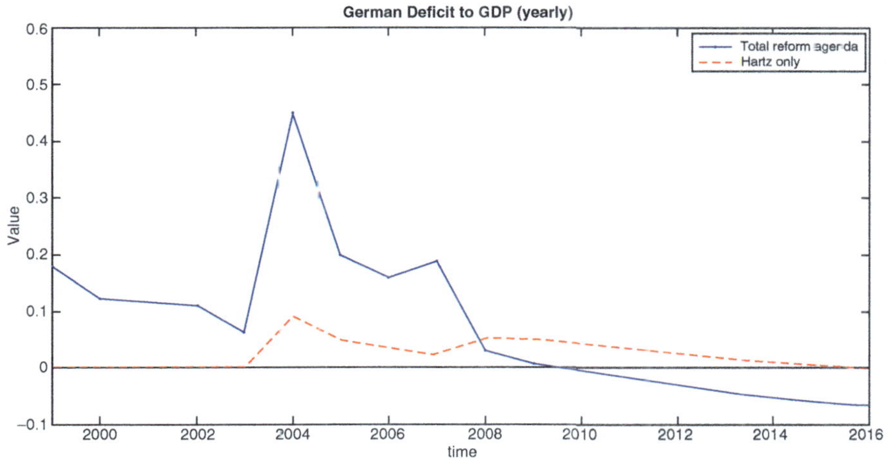

Fig. 10.4 Yearly model-based deficit-to-GDP ratio. Note: Graph depicts the simulation-based yearly deficit-to-GDP ratio from 1999 to 2016 in Germany when implementing only the labour market reforms (dashed red line) and when implementing the full reform agenda (bold blue line)

structural reforms might be more difficult today. In this section, we therefore show that when the fact is taken into account that financial markets nowadays price in risk premiums more quickly there may be favourable (budget-neutral) alternatives. For this purpose, we extend the baseline model by an endogenous risk premium on public debt that spills over to the private sector along the lines of Corsetti et al. (2013) and then re-simulate the entire reform agenda. Figure 10.5 shows the results.

Given the reform agenda described above, risk premiums on government debt raise public sector financing needs. This, in turn, significantly increases the deficit-to-GDP ratio (see Fig. 10.6; while the evolution of the deficit-to-GDP ratio is similar to the one shown in Fig. 10.4 excluding risk premiums, the magnitude increases considerably). Since the risk premium on public debt spills over to the private sector, the financing conditions of private firms deteriorate, too. This implies that domestic investment demand falls, which immediately reduces aggregate domestic demand relative to a setting without risk premiums both, directly and indirectly. The latter occurs through comparatively dampened increases in total factor productivity stemming from higher financing costs which, in turn, result in a relatively lower reduction in domestic goods prices and weaker improvements in international competitiveness, such that export demand for domestic goods is also suppressed in relative terms. Furthermore, for optimising households the public sector risk premium raises the cost of borrowing internationally, which further lowers their consumption perspectives. In summary, when taking into account risk premiums on public debt, improvements in GDP due to the entire reform agenda are about 1 percentage point lower relative to a situation without such premiums.

When comparing these results to the scenario analysis of structural labour market reforms only (see Table 10.2) described in the previous section, we see that the

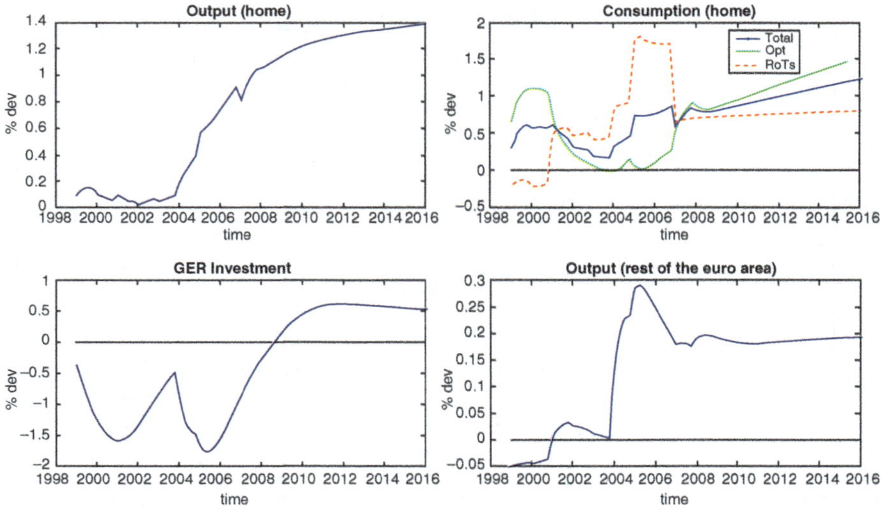

Fig. 10.5 Effects of German fiscal and labour market reforms on output and consumption in Germany (GER) and the rest of the euro area (RoE) when taking into account risk premiums. Note: Graphs depict deviations in percentage points from the variable's respective pre-reform long-run equilibrium level

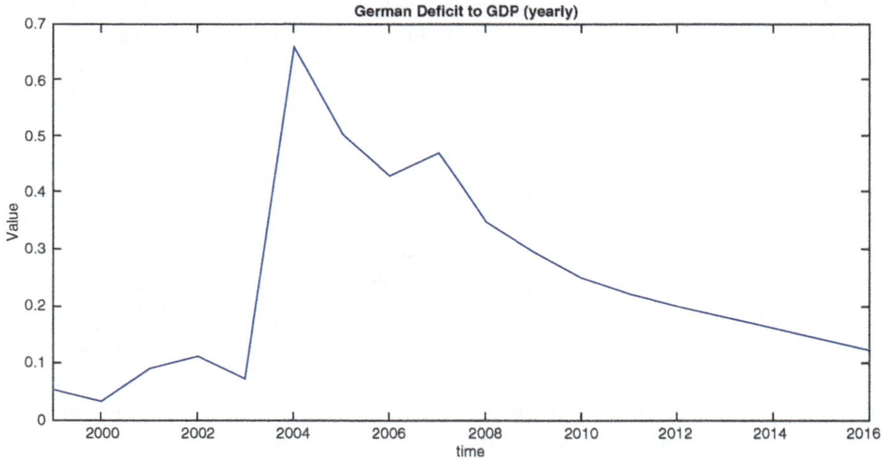

Fig. 10.6 Yearly model-based deficit-to-GDP ratio including risk premiums. Note: The graph depicts the simulation-based yearly deficit-to-GDP ratio from 1999 to 2016 in Germany when implementing the full reform agenda and taking into account risk premiums on public debt

contractionary effects of higher risk premiums on public debt basically eat up the positive macroeconomic effects of a labour tax reduction. However, the consumption gains and losses across both household types are distributed differently. While labour tax reductions still benefit the liquidity-constrained households, the optimisers suffer from deteriorating financing conditions. How strong this effect is, however, depends to a large extent on the exact calibration of the beta distribution function which determines the endogenously evolving default probability and, thus, the impact on the risk premium.

In order to avoid the surge in public sector risk premiums while still mitigating the unwanted redistributive side effects of a structural labour market reform alone, it therefore seems advisable to design the compensation measures in a budget-neutral way. One option for doing so is a tax shift away from direct labour taxation (to alleviate the direct income loss) towards more indirect consumption taxation. Since at least 2011, the European Commission's country specific recommendations have included such tax shifts, and since 2014, the Eurogroup has identified budget-neutral labour tax wedge reductions as one of their top priorities (see European Commission 2014, 2016).

In order to investigate what effects a labour market reform like the one described above might have when accompanied by a budget-neutral tax shift, we simulate the following scenario: the labour market reforms plus the labour income tax reductions used as a compensating measure described previously are introduced but the resulting public revenue losses are financed by an appropriate increase in the consumption tax rate.[9] The results are shown in Fig. 10.7.

It is apparent that, with a budget-neutral compensation of RoTs in the form of lower labour income and higher consumption tax rates, a labour market reform reducing the generosity of the unemployment insurance system along the lines of the Hartz reforms does not entail any consumption losses for the two types of households. This is because the gain in net income resulting from a reduction in the labour income tax rate overcompensates the increased consumption costs stemming from higher consumption taxes. Since the measure is fiscally budget-neutral, no adverse effects from higher financing costs occur. Furthermore, the reduction in gross wages as a result of workers' lower outside option due to the decreased generosity of the unemployment insurance system as well as lower labour income taxes (augmenting the net income directly) additionally fosters relative factor productivity, international competitiveness and exports. Overall, the simulation results indicate that such a measure even outperforms the entire reform agenda set out in Table 10.1 in the long run, when risk premiums on public debt are taken into account. The output effect, in this case, is about 0.2 percentage point higher.

The scenario simulated above should be considered as an example. There are probably many budget-neutral ways to compensate losers of a structural labour

[9]For simplicity, we refrain from decreasing the capital interest taxation in this simulation, which is present when simulating the entire reform agenda. However, the inclusion of lower capital interest taxes (when financed by higher consumption taxes) would increase the positive macroeconomic effects further and augment consumption, especially of optimising households, because capital taxes generally produce the largest distortions in this class of models (see Kempkes and Stähler 2016, for a more in-depth discussion). Still, liquidity-constrained households, who we want to be compensated for the losses resulting from the labour market reform, would only benefit indirectly.

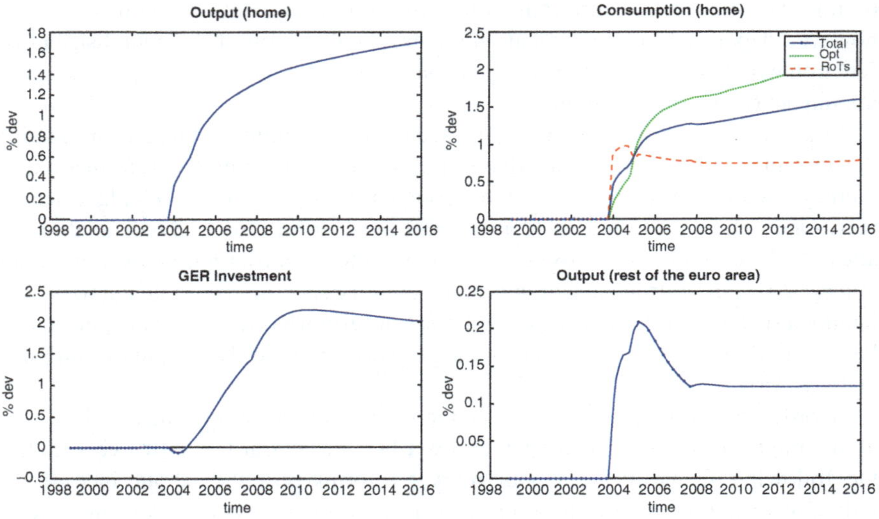

Fig. 10.7 Effects of German labour market reforms on output and consumption in Germany (GER) and the rest of the euro area (RoE) with budget-neutral labour tax reductions. Note: Graphs depict deviations in percentage points from the variable's respective pre-reform long-run equilibrium level

market reform which may even outperform the one presented here. Nevertheless, our analysis suggests that structural labour market reforms can be implemented without deficit-financed measures to compensate the losers of such reforms. First, there are budget-neutral compensation measures. Furthermore, in an environment where financial markets are stressed and may demand higher risk premiums quickly, deficit financing may even be the least desirable option.

10.6 Conclusion

By means of a simulation-based analysis using a New-Keynesian DSGE model, this chapter points out that structural labour market reforms, although clearly favourable from an aggregate perspective, are also likely to produce unwanted distributional side effects, especially when designed in such a way that the outside option of workers in the bargaining process is decreased. The German Hartz reforms, which brought about an improvement in labour market matching efficiency and a significant reduction in the generosity of the unemployment insurance system, were used as an example. Simulations indicate that the reform has a positive impact on GDP, consumption and employment.

However, such reforms entail aggregate wage income losses (which cannot be fully cushioned by higher aggregate employment) and only households which benefit from higher dividends and/or capital income gain as a result of the macroeconomic improvement. Especially liquidity-constrained households are, therefore, most likely to lose. To compensate such households for their income losses, tax cuts (which were part of the German reform agenda between 1999 and 2008) could be a useful instrument.

Nevertheless, tax relief is not costless as it may increase budget deficits. Given the current tight fiscal situation of many countries for which such labour market reforms are proposed, mitigating unwanted distributional effects may be more challenging today than it was in the early 2000s. Therefore, it could be argued that countries implementing structural labour market reforms should be granted more generous deficit targets/paths in the form of, for example, tolerated deviations from the agreed fiscal thresholds of the Stability and Growth Pact (SGP).[10]

Our analysis shows that there are at least two reasons why this may not be necessary. First, the tense situation on financial markets may imply that financial markets demand risk premiums on public debt more rapidly. If this is the case, deficit financing compensation measures could eat up the macroeconomic benefits of tax reductions through negative repercussions on the financial markets. Second, there are budget-neutral measures which can be used to compensation losers of reforms, such as a shift from labour income taxes towards consumption taxes. Such measures may even outperform deficit financed tax reductions when taking risk premiums into account.

While we consider our analysis to be a reasonable first step in examining the distributional aspects of coordinated fiscal and labour market reforms, a few caveats should be noted. Although taking into account two household types serves as a useful shorthand approach to analyse possible distributional effects, it only represents a coarse approximation of the “true” dimension of household heterogeneity. This is specifically relevant with regard to the expected effects of tax changes, which, for example, could affect households in very different ways. Correspondingly, the distributional effects of labour tax cuts might vary substantially among the respective households. Addressing these issues is, in our view, a vital task for future research.

References

Attinasi MG, Prammer D, Stähler N, Tasso M, van Parys S (2016) Budget-neutral labour tax wedge reductions: a simulation-based analysis for selected euro area countries. Deutsche Bundesbank discussion paper 26/2016

Baxter M, King RG (1993) Fiscal policy in general equilibrium. Am Econ Rev 83:315–334

[10] Note that the SGP already allows taking into account reform efforts in calculating the deficit path (see European Economy, 2016). As our analysis shows, further alleviations do not necessarily seem appropriate.

Blanchard O, Giavazzi F (2003) Macroeconomic effects of regulation and deregulation in goods and labor markets. Q J Econ 118:879–907

Boscá J, Doménech R, Ferri J (2011) Search, Nash bargaining and rule-of-thumb consumers. Eur Econ Rev 55:927–942

Busl C, Seymen A (2013) The German labour market reforms in a European context: a DSGE analysis. ZEW discussion paper 13-097.

Cacciatore M, Fiori G (2016) The macroeconomic effects of goods and labor market deregulation. Rev Econ Dyn 20:1–24

Cacciatore M, Duval R, Fiori G (2016a) Short-term pain for long-term gain: Market deregulation and monetary policy in small open economies. J Int Money Finance 68:358–385

Cacciatore M, Duval R, Fiori G, Ghironi F (2016b) Market deregulation and optimal monetary policy in a monetary union. J Int Econ 99:120–127

Cacciatore M, Duval R, Fiori G, Ghironi F (2016c) Market reform in the time of imbalance. J Econ Dyn Control 72:69–93

Calvo G (1983) Staggered prices in a utility-maximizing framework. J Monet Econ 12:383–398

Christiano L, Eichenbaum M, Evans C (2005) Nominal rigidities and the dynamic effects of a shock to monetary policy. J Polit Econ 113:1–45

Christoffel K, Coenen G, Warne A (2008) The new area-wide model of the euro area: a micro-founded open-economy model for forecasting and policy analysis. ECB working paper 944

Christoffel K, Kuester K, Linzert T (2009) The role of labor markets for euro area monetary policy. Eur Econ Rev 53:908–936

Coenen G, Straub R, Trabandt M (2013) Gauging the effects of fiscal stimulus packages in the euro area. J Econ Dyn Control 37:367–386

Corsetti G, Kuester K, Meier A, Müller G (2013) Sovereign risk, fiscal policy, and macroeconomic stability. Econ J 123:F99–F132

Dao M (2013a) International spillovers of labour market policies. Oxf Econ Pap 65:417–446

Dao (2013b) Foreign labor costs and domestic employment: what are the spillovers? J Int Econ 89:154–171

ECB (2015) Measurement of the costs and benefits of the German labour market reforms of the early 2000s. Econ Bull 7(November):65–68

Engler P, Ganelli G, Trevala J, Voigts S (2017) Fiscal devaluation in a monetary union. IMF Econ Rev 65:241–272

European Commission (2014) Taxation trends in the European Union, 2014 Edition

European Commission (2016) The economic impact of selected structural reform measures in Italy, France, Spain and Portugal. European economy, Institutional papers 23

Farhi E, Gopinath G, Itskhoki O (2014) Fiscal devaluations. Rev Econ Stud 81:725–760

Felbermayr GJ, Larch M, Lechthaler W (2012) The Shimer-puzzle of international trade: a quantitative analysis. Ifo working paper 134

Felbermayr GJ, Larch M, Lechthaler W (2013) Unemployment in an interdependent world. Am Econ J Econ Pol 5:262–301

Gadatsch N, Stähler N, Weigert B (2016) German labor market and fiscal reforms 1999–2008: can they be blamed for intra-euro area imbalances? J Macroecon 50:307–324

Galí J, Lopez-Salido JD, Valles J (2007) Understanding the effects of government spending on consumption. J Eur Econ Assoc 5:227–270

Gomes S, Jacquinot P, Mohr M, Pisani M (2013) Structural reforms and macroeconomic performance in the euro area countries: a model-based assessment. Int Finance 16:23–44

Gomes S, Jacquinot P, Pisani M (2016) Fiscal devaluation in the euro area: a model-based assessment. Econ Model 52:58–70

IMF (2016) Time for a supply-side boost? Macroeconomic effects of labor and product market reforms in advanced economies. World Economic Outlook, April 2016

Kempkes G, Stähler N (2016) A one-off wealth levy? Discussing the pros, the cons, and the importance of credibility. Fisc Stud 37:821–849

Krause M, Uhlig H (2012) Transitions in the German labor market: structure and crisis. J Monet Econ 59:64–79

Krebs T, Scheffel M (2013) Macroeconomic evaluation of labor market reform in Germany. IMF Econ Rev 61:664–701

Krebs T, Scheffel M (2017) Labor market institutions and the cost of recessions. IMF working paper 17/87

Langot F, Patureau L, Sopraseuth T (2014) Fiscal devaluation and structural gaps. Banque de France working paper 508

Launov A, Wälde K (2013) Estimating incentive and welfare effects of non-stationary unemployment benefits. Int Econ Rev 54:1159–1198

Le Blanc J, Porpiglia A, Teppa F, Zhu J, Ziegelmeyer M (2014) Household saving behavior and credit constraints in the euro area. Deutsche Bundesbank discussion paper 16/2014

Leeper E, Walker TB, Yang SCS (2010) Government investment and fiscal stimulus. J Monet Econ 57:1000–1012

Leiner-Killinger N, Lopéz Peréz V, Stiegert R, Vitale G (2007) Structural reforms in EMU and the role of monetary policy: a survey of the literature. ECB occasional paper 66

Lipinska A, von Thadden L (2009) Monetary and fiscal policy aspects of indirect tax changes in a monetary union. ECB working paper 1097

Lipinska A, von Thadden L (2012) On the (in)effectiveness of fiscal devaluations in a monetary union. Board of Governors of the Federal Reserve System Finance and Economics discussion paper 2012-71

Moyen S, Sahuc JG (2005) Incorporating labour market frictions into an optimising-based monetary policy model. Econ Model 22:159–186

OECD (2016) Economic policy reforms 2016. Going for growth interim report, February 2016

Parleviet J (2015) What drives public acceptance of reforms? Longitudinal evidence from the run-up of the increase of the Dutch retirement age. DNB working paper 492

Picos-Sánchez F, Thomas A (2015) A revenue-neutral shift from SSC to VAT: analysis of the distributional impact of 12 EU-OECD countries. FinanzArchiv/Public Financ Anal 71:278–298

Schwarzmüller T, Stähler N (2013) Reforming the labor market and improving competitiveness: an analysis for Spain using FiMod. J Span Econ Assoc 4:437–471

Smets F, Wouters R (2003) An estimated stochastic general equilibrium model of the euro area. J Eur Econ Assoc 1:1123–1175

Smets F, Wouters R (2007) Shocks and frictions in US business cycles: a Bayesian DSGE approach Am Econ Rev 97:586–606

Stähler N, Thomas C (2012) FiMod—A DSGE model for fiscal policy simulations. Econ Model 29:239–261

Chapter 11
Tax-Benefit Reforms and Structural Models for Labour Supply

Henk-Wim de Boer, Egbert Jongen, and Mauro Mastrogiacomo

11.1 Introduction

Faced with tight budget constraints, policymakers are reconsidering their tax-benefit policies and the trade-off between equity and efficiency (Mirrlees, 1971). Redistribution from rich to poor households, or from singles to couples, distorts the labour supply decision or effort more generally, and subgroups may respond differently to this redistribution. Understanding the heterogeneity in labour market responses of different groups, traditionally measured by the wage elasticity of labour supply,[1] is thus essential for an efficient design of tax incentives.

[1] A related literature studies the elasticity of taxable income to measure the distortions of taxation (Saez et al., 2012a). However, there is an active debate on whether the elasticity of taxable income is a sufficient statistics to measure the distortions from taxation (Chetty, 2009).

The views expressed in this chapter do not necessarily reflect the position of CPB Netherlands Bureau for Economic Policy Analysis, Leiden University, DNB, the Eurosystem, VU University Amsterdam or Netspar. This chapter draws on Jongen et al. (2014), CPB (2015), Mastrogiacomo et al. (2017) and De Boer and Jongen (2017).

H.-W. de Boer (✉)
CPB Netherlands Bureau for Policy Analysis, The Hague, Netherlands
e-mail: H.W.de.Boer@cpb.nl

E. Jongen
CPB Netherlands Bureau for Policy Analysis, The Hague, Netherlands

Leiden University, Leiden, Netherlands

M. Mastrogiacomo
Economic Policy Department, De Nederlandsche Bank, Amsterdam, Netherlands

VU University of Amsterdam, Amsterdam, Netherlands

J. de Haan, J. Parlevliet (eds.), *Structural Reforms*,
https://doi.org/10.1007/978-3-319-74400-1_11

In this chapter, we exploit a very large administrative dataset on Dutch households, the Arbeidsmarktpanel (Labour Market Panel) of Statistics Netherlands (2012), to estimate the behavioural responses to changes in financial incentives. Specifically, the size of the dataset allows us to estimate the preferences and corresponding labour supply elasticities for a large number of subgroups on the Dutch labour market. In the estimations we use a discrete choice model for labour supply (Aaberge et al., 1995; Van Soest, 1995; Keane and Moffitt, 1998; Aaberge et al., 1999; Brewer et al., 2006; Bargain et al., 2014).[2] We subsequently use the estimated preferences in a behavioural microsimulation model, and simulate the labour supply effects of a large number of potential reforms that feature prominently in the policy debate. We also simulate the effects of the reform package of the Tax Plan 2016, which was discussed extensively in Dutch parliament.

To preview our results, we uncover large heterogeneity in the labour supply elasticities of different demographic groups and decision margins. We find that childless singles and men in couples hardly respond to changes in financial incentives, whereas single parents and women in couples with young children are quite responsive. We further find that most of the response is in the number of persons employed, not in the response in hours worked per week per employed, and that cross-elasticities for women in couples are non-negligible. These findings have the following implications for tax-benefit reforms. Reductions in the marginal tax rate, via e.g. a decrease in the tax bracket rates, hardly affect labour supply. Reductions in income support for low-income households are relatively effective in stimulating labour supply, but increase income inequality. However, higher in-work benefits for low-income workers are also relatively effective, and do not increase income inequality. Furthermore, the most effective instruments are tax credits and (child care) subsidies for single parents and secondary earners with young children. These groups are the most responsive to changes in financial incentives. The Tax Plan 2016 stimulates labour supply in persons and in hours. Indeed, the Tax Plan 2016 contains a number of policy changes that are relatively effective in stimulating labour supply, like the increase in the in-work tax credit for low-income workers, the in-work tax credit for single parents and secondary earners with a young child and an increase in child care subsidies.

The outline of the chapter is as follows. Section 11.2 gives some context on the Dutch labour market and gives a brief description of the Dutch tax-benefit system in 2015, which will serve as the baseline for our policy simulations. Section 11.3 describes the structural discrete-choice model and the empirical methodology. Section 11.4 discusses the data used in the empirical analysis, and Sect. 11.5

---

[2]Discrete choice models have become popular in labour supply analysis because they greatly simplify the analysis of (joint) labour supply decisions when there are kinks and non-convexities in the budget set (due to e.g. the tax-benefit system).

presents the empirical results in terms of labour supply elasticities. Section 11.6 presents simulations results for a large number of tax-benefit reforms, including the reform package of the Tax Plan 2016. Section 11.7 discusses our findings and concludes.

11.2 The Dutch Labour Market and Tax-Benefit System

Over the past decades, the Netherlands has witnessed a number of relevant demographic changes.[3] The share of couples with children has declined and the share of couples without children has increased. Furthermore, the overall share of couples has been declining, while the share of singles and single parents is now much higher than a few decades ago. Hence, studying the behavioural responses by singles and single parents has become more important over time. The participation rate of women has increased spectacularly. In the mid 1970s, the participation rate of Dutch women was one of the lowest in Europe, whereas by now it is one of the highest. The participation rate of men was and remains high by international standards. This has important implications for labour supply elasticities, as cross-country studies (Bargain et al., 2014) and studies that look at labour supply elasticities over time (Blau and Kahn, 2007) suggest that labour supply elasticities are much lower when the participation rate is higher.[4] In terms of hours worked per week, however, Dutch women still work much less than their European counterparts (about 10 h per week less on average), and so do Dutch men (about 5 h per week on average). So there appears to be still a lot of potential on the intensive margin of labour supply. Below, we consider whether this is the case.

Turning to the tax-benefit system, like most OECD countries, the Netherlands has a progressive income tax system.[5] Labour income is taxed individually and marginal income tax rates increase with income. Table 11.1 gives an overview of the most relevant elements of the Dutch income tax system in 2015 for the current study. The lowest marginal rate in 2015 is 36.5% payable over a taxable income of up to 19,822 euro. For incomes ranging from 19,822 to 57,585 euro, a marginal tax rate of 42% applies. The highest marginal tax rate is 52%.

The tax system contains many tax credits, tax deductions and means-tested benefits, that make it rather complex.[6] Tax credits reduce the total amount of income tax people need to pay. Over the past decade, all instruments described in Table 11.1

[3]De Boer and Jongen (2017) give an overview of changes in the shares of the different household types, and the changes in the participation rates and hours worked per week by household type.

[4]Indeed, as younger women more often participate in the labour market, their behaviour becomes more similar to that of men within the same cohort. Our recent data show indeed much lower labour supply elasticities for women, relative to those estimated in studies based on older data.

[5]For the overview of the tax-benefit system we draw on CPB (2015).

[6]We exclude tax deductions from the analysis, since these could not be observed in our dataset.

Table 11.1 The Dutch income tax system 2015

	Income range	Tax rate	Maximum amount in euro
Income taxes	0–19,822	36.5%	7235
	19,822–33,589	42.0%	13,017
	33,589–57,585	42.0%	23,095
	> 57,585	52.0%	
General tax credit	0–19,822		2203
	19,822–56,935		2203 − 2.32% × (taxable income − 19,822)
	> 56,935		1342
EITC all workers	0–9010		1.8% × labour income
	9010–19,463		163 + 19.7% × (labour income − 9010)
	19,463–49,770		2220
	49,770–100,670		2220 − 4.0% × (labour income − 49,770)
	> 100,670		184
EITC working parents	0–4857		0
	4857–32,832		1033 + 4.0% × (labour income − 4857)
	>32,832		2152
Childcare subsidy			90.7% costs first child
			93.3% costs subsequent children
Income dependent child benefit	Income < 19,463		1 child: 1032
			2 children: 1823
			3 children: 2006
			Subsequent child(ren): 106 extra
			Single parents bonus: 3050
	Income > 19,463		Max. amount − 6.75% × (taxable income − 19,463)
Rent subsidy	Income < 21,950		Single-person household : 4079
	Income < 29,800		Multi-person household: 3759
Health care benefit	0–19,500		Singles: 936
	0–19,500		Couples: 1788
Welfare benefits			Singles: 11,530
			Couples: 16,471

Source: CPB (2015)

have been subject to reform. The general tax credit (*Algemene Heffingskorting* in Dutch) is now income dependent. The maximum amount is 2203 euro in 2015, and is phased out at 2.32% to a minimum of 1342 euro. All tax-paying individuals in the Netherlands are entitled to the general tax credit. Then there are a number of tax credits for workers. There is an earned income tax credit (EITC) for all workers (*Arbeidskorting* in Dutch). Over the first 9010 euro, the EITC increases with income, with a phase-in rate of 1.8%. The subsequent phase-in rate is higher: 19.7% over the income between 9010 and 19,463 euro (which is approximately the full-time minimum wage in 2015). The maximum amount of the EITC for all workers is 2,220 euro. This amount remains constant for incomes between 19,463 and 49,770 euro. The general EITC is phased out for higher incomes, at a rate of 4%, until the minimum amount of 184 euro is reached. For secondary earners and single parents with a youngest child up to 12 years of age there is a specific income-dependent EITC (*Inkomensafhankelijke Combinatiekorting* in Dutch). Working single parents and secondary earners receive a base amount of 1033 euro if their personal labour income exceeds the minimum income level of 4857 euro. This targeted EITC rises with income, with a phase-in rate of 4% up to a maximum of 2152 euro.

Next to tax credits, working parents with young children also qualify for child-care subsidies, which are also income-dependent. The subsidy makes a distinction between the first child and any subsequent children.[7] The maximum subsidy rate in 2015 is 90.7% for the first child, and the minimum subsidy rate is 18%. The parental contribution rate increases with income. The maximum subsidy rate for a second child is higher, 93.3%, and the phase-out of the subsidy is less steep than for the first child. The minimum subsidy rate for the second child is 58.2%.

The tax-benefit system also contains several income-dependent benefits that provide income support to low-income households bearing certain costs. These benefits depend negatively on the level of taxable household income, increasing effective marginal (and participation) tax rates (CPB, 2015). Parents can apply for income-dependent child benefits (*Kindgebonden Budget* in Dutch) for the costs related to their children up to 18 years of age. Households receive an annual amount per child. Households with one child receive a maximum amount of 1032 euro, and households with two children receive a maximum amount of 1823 euro. Single parents receive an additional amount of 3050 euro. This benefit is phased out at a rate of 6.75%. Next, the rent subsidy is an income-dependent benefit that compensates low-income households for rent costs. It depends on household income, household composition and the rent level. The maximum amount in 2015 is 4079 euro for single-person households and 3759 for multi-person households. Finally, the health care benefit is an income-dependent benefit for health care costs. In the Netherlands, standard healthcare insurance is compulsory: adults pay an insurance premium, and their children under the age of 18 are included in the insurance policy for free. The benefit level depends on household income but is independent of actual health care

[7]The first child is the child with the highest number of hours formal childcare.

expenditures. In 2015, the maximum health care benefit is 936 euro for singles and 1788 euro for couples. This benefit is phased out at a rate of 13.4%. Higher income households are not entitled to health care benefits.

Finally, Table 11.1 also gives the level of welfare benefits, distinguishing between singles and couples. Welfare benefits are minimum benefit payments, at the household level, for households without other means of income to guarantee a minimum standard of living. The welfare benefit is higher for couples (16,471 euro) than for singles (11,530 euro).

11.3 Structural Model

We use structural models to estimate the labour supply elasticities of different groups on the Dutch labour market. Households are assumed to maximize a unitary utility function subject to a budget constraint and a time constraint. We use a flexible specification for preferences: a translog utility function, also used in e.g. Van Soest (1995). The choice of hours of work is the result of a coordinated decision of the two adult household members m and f. Define y as household income and h_m and h_f as the number of hours worked by the respective partners. We also explicitly model the use of formal childcare for households with young children, where c denotes the number of childcare hours per week. The most elaborate specification is then as follows:

$$
\begin{aligned}
U^d(\nu) &= \nu'\mathbf{A}\nu + \mathbf{b}'\nu + \mathbf{d}'\mathbf{1}[\mu > 0], \\
\nu &= (\log(y), \log(1 - h_m/T), \log(1 - h_f/T), \log(c)), \\
\mu &= (h_m, h_f, c), \qquad (11.1)
\end{aligned}
$$

where we use the weekly time endowment T to transform the number of working hours into leisure.[8] The vector v consists of the logarithms of disposable household income (y), leisure of the man $(1 - h_m/T)$, leisure of the woman $(1 - h_f/T)$ and hours of formal childcare (c). The matrix $\mathbf{A}$ is the symmetric matrix of quadratic coefficients, and the vector $\mathbf{b}$ contains the coefficients corresponding to vector v. The vector $\mathbf{d}$ captures fixed costs of work for men and women. These are fixed costs related to working, which are expected to be negative terms for options where the respective person is working. As shown by e.g. Van Soest (1995), fixed costs are necessary to reproduce the low share of individuals that work only few hours per week. Of course, there are sound economic arguments to include them. Fixed costs of work represent disutility from work such as travelling costs, search costs or market frictions. They also play a crucial role in the distinction between the

[8]We use total number of hours per week, e.g. 168, as the weekly time endowment. Different values for T hardly affected the results.

extensive (participation) and intensive (hours per week) response to changes in financial incentives. We do not include them in income or leisure, but simply include a dummy in utility metric, as in Van Soest (1995). Similarly, we also include fixed costs of using formal childcare.

We allow for preference variation through observed individual and household characteristics $\mathbf{x}_2$, $\mathbf{x}_3$ and $\mathbf{x}_4$ in parameters b_2, b_3 and b_4:

$$b_2 = \mathbf{x}'_2\boldsymbol{\beta}_2, \quad b_3 = \mathbf{x}'_3\boldsymbol{\beta}_3, \quad b_4 = \mathbf{x}'_4\boldsymbol{\beta}_4, \tag{11.2}$$

which are the linear utility terms in leisure of the male, leisure of the female, and hours of formal child care, respectively. The same variation is also allowed for the fixed costs parameters **d**.

Next to the deterministic part of household utility $U^d(\mathbf{v})$ defined above, utility also contains an individual and option specific random utility term ε_j, necessary to reproduce heterogeneous choices for otherwise similar individuals as observed in the data:

$$U(\nu_j) = U^d(\nu_j) + \varepsilon_j. \tag{11.3}$$

ε_j is assumed to be identically and independently distributed across individuals and options, according to an Extreme Value Type-I distribution: This results in a convenient multinomial logit specification for the probabilities for observing individuals in particular options (McFadden, 1978).

Households choose their preferred combination of hours of work and childcare from a finite set of alternatives $j \in \{1, \ldots, J\}$. We experimented with a number of discretizations, an interval of 8 h (a normal working day in the Netherlands) running from 0 to 40 h gave a good fit to the data and worked well in the estimations. For singles without young children, we then have 6 discrete options, and for couples without young children we have $6 \times 6 = 36$ discrete options. The discrete choice set becomes larger for households who potentially use formal childcare. Specifically, we have $6 \times 4 = 24$ alternatives for lone parents with young children, and $6 \times 6 \times 4 = 144$ alternatives for couples with a young children.

Disposable income in each discrete option is calculated as:

$$y = w_m h_m + w_f h_f - T(w_m, h_m, w_f, h_f; q) - TC(p_c, c; q) + S(p_c, c, y_t; q), \tag{11.4}$$

where w_m and w_f represent the gross hourly wage for the man and the woman. For households with young children, who potentially use childcare, we also take the costs of childcare $TC(.)$ and the childcare subsidy S into account. Here, the vector q denotes individual and household characteristics, $TC(.)$ is the total cost of formal childcare, with p_c denoting the price per hour of formal childcare, and $S(.)$ is the childcare subsidy, which depends on the hourly price of formal childcare, hours of formal childcare, taxable income y_t and the age distribution of the children.

For all household types we also estimated models where we allow for the possibility that families which are observationally equivalent might have different tastes for work and formal childcare, using the so-called latent classes approach (Train, 2008). We assume that there is a finite number K of latent household classes (or types), with households having homogeneous preferences within each class but heterogeneous preferences across classes. In practice, this means that we estimate a finite mixture model with K parametrizations of the utility function, corresponding to K distinct subsets of our data. All the preference parameters therefore become class-specific, which is equivalent to the assumption that they are drawn from a mass-point distribution (Heckman and Singer, 1984). The full set of parameters to be estimated is then:

$$\theta = (\theta_1, \ldots, \theta_K) = (\mathbf{A}_1, \mathbf{b}_1, \mathbf{d}_1, \ldots, \mathbf{A}_K, \mathbf{b}_K, \mathbf{d}_K). \tag{11.5}$$

Since the classes are by definition unobservable, we cannot determine whether a given household belongs to a specific class or not. Instead, we have to construct household-level probabilities of class membership $P_i(class = k)$, which reflect how likely it is that household i has the preferences corresponding to class k, conditional on the household's choices and other observable characteristics. These probabilities are then used as individual weights for a set of class-specific multinomial logit models with separate parameter vectors θ_k.

The resulting log-likelihood function of the finite mixture model has the following form:

$$\mathscr{L} = \sum_{i=1}^{I} \frac{1}{R} \cdot \sum_{r=1}^{R} \log \left(\sum_{k=1}^{K} P_i(class = k) \cdot \sum_{j=1}^{J} \left(\frac{\exp\left(U_{ij}^s(v_r, \theta_k)\right)}{\sum_{j'=1}^{J} \exp\left(U_{ij'}^s(v_r, \theta_k)\right)} \cdot D_{ij} \right) \right). \tag{11.6}$$

For workers we use observed gross wages, while for non-workers we simulate gross wages by using a Heckman selection model. Similarly, we use observed hourly prices for users of formal childcare and we simulate these prices for non-users of childcare. Jongen et al. (2014) provide a detailed description of the empirical specification and the estimation results for the Heckman selection models for gross hourly wages and prices of childcare. We account for wage heterogeneity and price heterogeneity by taking R draws from the estimated wage and price distribution.[9] Consequently, there is no analytical solution for the likelihood function and we need to integrate over these distributions. The approach we follow is to maximize a simulated likelihood. We draw R wages, compute the likelihood, and average it out over the R draws. D_{ij} is an indicator function which takes the value 1 for the observed choice, and zero otherwise.

For part of the household types the latent classes models work well, in particular for couples with a youngest child 0–3 and 4–11 years of age. However, for some household types the latent classes models produce implausible results, in particular

[9]The number of draws in our specification with latent classes is 10, and it is kept relatively low to limit the computational complexity of the model.

for single parents, with a large share having negative marginal utility of income in the observed choices. For the other household types, the labour supply responses using the latent class models are very similar to the 'homogeneous' model (with only 1 class). Based on these results we decided to use the latent classes models for couples with a youngest child which is 0–3 or 4–11 years of age, and the homogeneous specification for all other groups.

11.4 Data

To estimate the preferences of the different household types we use the Labour Market Panel (in Dutch: *Arbeidsmarktpanel*) of Statistics Netherlands (2012). The backbone of the Labour Market Panel are the annual observations of the Labour Force Survey (in Dutch: *Enquete Beroepsbevolking*) for the period 1999–2009, which contains the education level of adult members of the household. Statistics Netherlands supplements this data set with three additional data sources. First, administrative data from municipalities for the period 1999–2009 (in Dutch: *Gemeentelijke Basisadministratie*) that contains information on individual and household characteristics like age, ethnicity, ages of the children and area of residence. Second, administrative data from the Social Statistical Panel for the period 1999–2009 (in Dutch: *Sociaal Statistisch Bestand*) on hours worked and gross income. Third, administrative data on formal childcare from the Formal Childcare Database of the Tax Office for the period 2006–2009 (in Dutch: *Wet Kinderopvangtoeslag*). With respect to formal childcare, a distinction is made between daycare (children 0–3 years of age) and out-of-school care (children 4–11 years of age).

We estimate a structural model for the simultaneous choice of labour supply and, if applicable, the use of formal childcare.[10] Because data on childcare in our data set is available from 2006 onwards, we restrict the sample to the period 2006–2009. Furthermore, formal childcare subsidies are available to parents up to the point where the child goes to secondary school. Therefore, we only allow households with a youngest child of 0–11 years of age to choose formal childcare. Before the age of 4, children can go to daycare, whereas older children can go to out-of-school care. For households without children, or with a youngest child of 12 years of age or older, the childcare terms in the utility function drop out. We exclude households with missing information on individual or household characteristics. Furthermore, to limit the computational burden, we take a 15% sample of the full data set for couples and for childless singles. For single parents we use the full sample.

[10]Unfortunately, informal childcare is not in our administrative dataset. However, De Boer et al. (2015) show that including informal childcare, calculated as the overlap in working hours of parents minus the hours of formal childcare, does not affect the results.

Individuals who adjust their labour supply in our model are employed, on welfare benefits or without any income resources. We do not model and effectively ignore the labour supply of the following types of individuals: students and retired, disabled or self-employed persons. Below we will refer to these individuals as having 'inflexible' labour supply. We do not include these individuals because we do not have reliable information on their hours worked, or because we are unable to determine their budget constraint. We also drop individuals with unemployment benefits, implicitly assuming that they are constrained in their labour supply choice. Furthermore, we also drop same sex households. Finally, we drop individuals under 18 years of age, and individuals over 63 years of age.

For the empirical analysis, we distinguish between '1-flex households' and '2-flex households'. Couples are '2-flex households' when both partners are able to adjust their labour supply, and '1-flex households' if only one partner has a flexible labour supply. However, we account for the 'inflexible' partner income when calculating the budget constraint of the 'flexible' partner. In the estimations we distinguish 15 household types: childless singles (1), single parents with a youngest child aged 0–3, 4–11, 12–17 or 18 years of age or older (2–5), adult children living with their parent(s) (6), couples without children with both partner flexible (7), couples without children where only the man is able to adjust his labour supply (8), couples without children where only the woman is able to adjust her labour supply (9), couples where both partners are flexible and with a youngest child aged 0–3, 4–11, 12–17 or 18 years of age or older (10–13), couples with children where only the man can adjust his labour supply (14), and couples with children where only the woman can adjust her labour supply (15).

We use the tax-benefit model MIMOSI (Koot et al., 2016) to calculate disposable income for each of the alternatives. MIMOSI is an advanced tax-benefit calculator employed by CPB to determine the redistributional and budgetary effects of reform proposals for the tax-benefit system. MIMOSI calculates the budget constraints very accurately, taking into account taxes, premiums and a large number of group-specific, income-independent and income-dependent subsidies and tax credits. Disposable income is defined as gross income after taxes, employees' premiums, the nominal health care fee, expenditures on formal childcare and inclusive of childcare subsidies. Disposable income in the utility function, in the estimations and simulations, is in 2006 prices.

11.5 Empirical Results

In this section we present the labour supply elasticities for all the subgroups. The estimated preferences, fit of the hours distribution and annual gross wage distributions can be found in Jongen et al. (2014). Discrete choice models do not have an analytical solution for the labour supply elasticity. This has to be simulated. We simulate these elasticities by increasing gross hourly wages by 10%. We present the total elasticity (the percentage change in total hours worked over the percentage change in the gross wage rate), and the decomposition of this total elasticity into the extensive margin elasticity (the percentage change in the participation rate over the percentage change in the gross wage rate) and the intensive margin (the percentage change in hours worked by the employed over the percentage change in the gross wage rate).

Figure 11.1 gives the simulated labour supply elasticities for couples in which both partners can choose whether or not to work and for how many days per week. We estimate this for several subgroups, where subgroups are defined by the age of the youngest child, including a category for flexible couples without children. We find small, positive labour suppy elasticities for men, see panel (a). The labour supply elasticities are much higher for women, both on the extensive margin and on the intensive margin, see panel (b). Furthermore, the labour supply elasticities for women in couples are particularly high when the youngest child is 0–3 years of age (pre primary school age) or 4–11 years of age (primary school age). Figure 11.2 gives the so-called cross elasticities for these couples, i.e. the percentage change in total hours worked by one partner over the percentage change in the gross wage rate of the other partner. Panel (a) shows that cross elasticities are negative but close to zero for men. For women however, the cross elasticities are non-negligible.

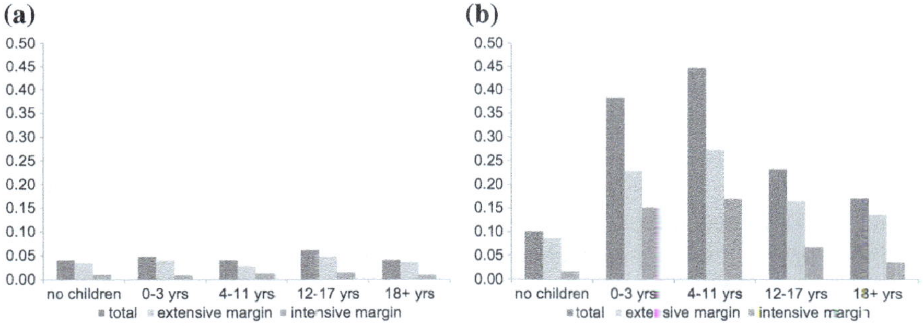

Fig. 11.1 Households with two flexible persons. (**a**) Men. (**b**) Women

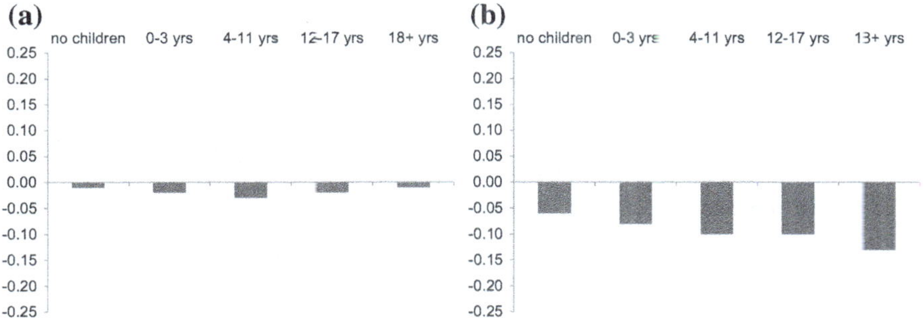

Fig. 11.2 Cross elasticities in households with two flexible persons. (**a**) Men. (**b**) Women

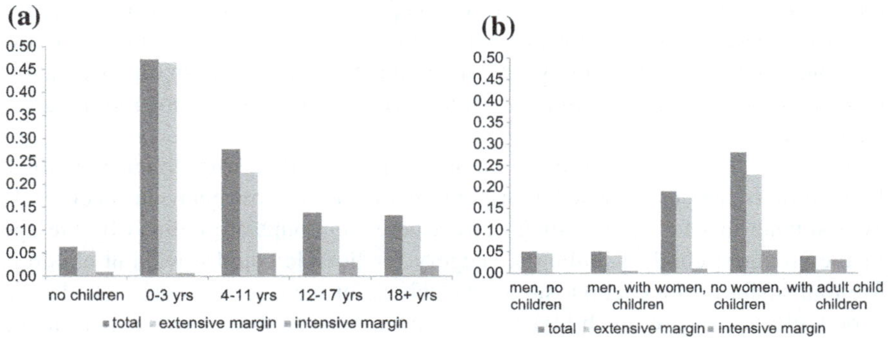

Fig. 11.3 Households with one flexible person, and adult children. (**a**) Singles and single parents. (**b**) Individuals with an inflexible partner, and adult children living at home

Figure 11.3 panel (a) shows that the labour supply elasticity is relatively low for singles without children. The labour supply elasticity is much higher for single parents with young children. The labour supply elasticity of single parents whose youngest child is no longer in primary school is much lower, though still higher than for singles without children. Also note that the differences across single parents are primarily driven by differences in the extensive margin elasticity. The intensive margin response for single parents is quite small.[11]

Figure 11.3 panel (b) gives the labour supply elasticities for men and women in couples where one of the partners labour supply is inflexible (because this person is e.g. disabled or retired). For these groups we pool couples with children of all ages. Most men with an inflexible partner work, and typically also fulltime (see Jongen et al., 2014). Hence, there is little upward potential in terms of total hours worked, and they have a relatively low labour supply elasticity. Women have more upward potential in total hours worked, both in terms of the participation rate and in terms of hours worked per employed. Women with an inflexible partner have a higher labour supply elasticity, in particular on the extensive margin. Panel (b) also gives the labour supply elasticity for adult children living at the home of their parents. They have a very high participation rate (when they are not disabled, etc.), resulting in a very low labour supply elasticity.

A more detailed discussion on the empirical results can be found in Jongen et al. (2014). Here, we also present a comparison of predictions by the structural model with the findings from three recent quasi-experimental studies. More specifically, we use the estimated structural model to simulate a number of key reforms implemented in the past and compare the simulated treatment effects with quasi-experimental studies on the same reforms. In particular, we compare the simulated treatment effects of the 2005–2009 reform of childcare subsidies and in-work benefits for

[11]Their budget constraint plays an important role here, where working only a few days per week often does not generate net income higher than net income out of work.

households with young children with the estimated treatment effects presented in Bettendorf et al. (2015). Furthermore, we compare the simulated treatment effects of the 2002 reform of the in-work benefit for single parents with the estimated treatment effects presented in Bettendorf et al. (2014). Finally, we compare the simulated intensive margin (hours worked per employed person) elasticities of the structural model with the estimated intensive margin elasticities presented in Bosch and van der Klaauw (2012) and Bosch and Jongen (2013), who use the 2001 tax reform that substantially reduced marginal tax rates. We find that the simulated treatment effects of these past reforms in the structural model are in line with the estimated treatment effects in the quasi-experimental studies.

11.6 Policy Simulations

Next, we use the estimated structural models to simulate counterfactual policy reforms, using the 2015 tax-benefit system as the base. We present results for: (1) changes in the tax bracket rates, (2) changes in targeted income support for low-income households, (3) changes in policies targeted at the extensive margin, (4) changes in policies targeted at working parents with young children and (5) the reform package of the Tax Plan 2016.

11.6.1 Changes in Tax Bracket Rates

Table 11.2 gives the simulation results for changes in the tax bracket rates, and the group averages in the base for comparison.[12] Specifically, we consider the effects of decreasing income tax rate in the first, second, third and fourth (open) income tax bracket so that tax receipts decrease by 1.5 billion euro.[13] To keep the table to a manageable size, we report aggregate results for the following groups:

- 'Men in couples young. child 0–17' and 'Women in couples young. child 0–17' are respectively men and women in couples with a youngest child 0–17 years of age, and both partners can choose all hours options.
- 'Men in other couples' and 'Women in other couples' are respectively men and women in couples without children, in couples with a youngest child 18 years of age or older, and in couples with a partner whose labour supply is 'fixed'.

[12]The results are for individuals whose labour supply is determined within the model only, so excluding the 'fixed' labour supply by partners in couples that are e.g. disabled, self-employed, etc.

[13]Due to the smaller tax base in the higher brackets than the lower brackets, the percentage point decrease in the tax rate in the higher brackets is larger than in the lower brackets. Specifically, the decrease in the tax rate is respectively: 0.8, 2.1, 3.4 and 5.2 percentage points.

Table 11.2 Changes in tax bracket rates

Simulation	Base	(1) First bracket	(2) Second bracket	(3) Third bracket	(4) Fourth bracket
Change in bracket rate		−0.8	−2.1	−3.4	−5.2
Ex ante impulse (in billion)		1.5	1.5	1.5	1.5
Percentage changes					
Gini coefficient[a]		−0.22	0.30	0.87	1.33
Hours worked per week	27.5	−0.02	0.09	0.07	0.02
– Men in couples young. child 0–17	35.2	−0.09	0.04	0.10	0.07
– Women in couples young. child 0–17	17.8	0.12	0.17	−0.03	−0.10
– Men in other couples	34.6	−0.03	0.06	0.11	0.05
– Women in other couples	20.5	−0.01	0.06	0.01	−0.02
– Single parents young. child 0–17	20.8	−0.06	0.24	0.17	0.05
– Singles	30.3	−0.01	0.10	0.07	0.01
Participation rate	0.82	0.00	0.04	0.00	−0.02
– Men in couples young. child 0–17	0.93	−0.05	0.05	0.03	−0.02
– Women in couples young. child 0–17	0.77	0.11	−0.02	−0.16	−0.12
– Men in other couples	0.91	−0.02	0.05	0.07	0.03
– Women in other couples	0.71	0.02	0.01	−0.04	−0.04
– Single parents young. child 0–17	0.68	−0.04	0.16	0.07	0.01
– Singles	0.85	−0.02	0.05	0.03	0.01
Effective labour units per hour		−0.01	−0.02	0.03	0.03

[a]Gini coefficient of disposable household income, using equivalence scales. The Gini coefficient is calculated over the full Dutch adult population with gross income above 66% of the annual minimum wage

- 'Single parents youngest child 0–17' are single parents with a youngest 0–17 years of age.
- 'Singles' consists of singles without children, single parents with a youngest child 18 years of age or older, and adult children living with their parents.

For these groups we report the effects on hours worked per week and on the participation rate. We also report the effect on average 'effective labour units per hour', which is calculated as the change in labour costs minus the change in hours worked. The latter captures a composition effect on labour productivity. When workers with low labour costs work less hours and workers with high labour costs work more hours, effective labour units per hour will increase.

Column (1) gives the results for the decrease in the tax rate in the first bracket. Overall, we find hardly any effect of changing the tax rate in the first bracket on hours worked, the participation rate and effective labour units per hour. However, this is the net result of some groups that decrease their labour supply, and some that increase their labour supply. For men in couples, the first bracket is typically inframarginal (not the relevant *marginal* tax rate), and changing the first bracket rate only generates an income effect. They reduce their labour supply. Women in couples with dependent children raise their labour supply. They typically have lower income and lowering the tax rate in the first tax bracket has both an income and a substitution effect. The substitution effect dominates and they increase their labour supply. For women in other couples and singles, the effect on labour supply is close to zero. Single parents show a negative response to the increase in the tax rate in the first tax bracket. A lower first bracket rate increases welfare benefits and as a result single parents reduce their labour supply. Income inequality, as measured by the Gini-coefficient, falls.

Column (2) gives the effect of lowering the tax rate in the second bracket. The effect on overall labour supply in hours is positive, but the effect on labour supply in persons is close to zero, and the effect on effective labour units per hour is slightly negative. For many workers, the second tax bracket is the relevant marginal rate, and their substitution effect dominates their income effect. The same is true for singles. The effect on hours worked by single parents is now also positive, as the lower second tax bracket rate does not increase welfare benefits. Note that the participation rate of women in couples with a child 0–17 years of age decreases. Here the cross effect of higher income for males in these couples plays an important role. This 'income effect' stimulates some women in these couples to leave the labour market, an 'added worker effect' (Lundberg, 1985). Income inequality rises somewhat in this simulation.

Column (3) gives the effects of the decrease in the third tax bracket rate. The increase in overall labour supply in hours is somewhat smaller than in column (2), because the labour supply of women in couples with children falls. Indeed, although for part of these women the third tax bracket is the relevant marginal tax bracket, their own income effect and the income effect from higher income of the male dominates. However, in contrast to column (2), effective labour units per hour increases somewhat. More productive workers increase their hours worked, whereas less productive workers reduce their hours worked.

Finally, column (4) gives the effects of the decrease in the fourth tax bracket. Lowering the fourth tax bracket has only a small positive effect on overall hours worked and the effect on labour supply in persons is even negative (due to the added worker effect). However, effective labour units per hour again increases under in this simulation, due to the composition effect. This simulation generates the largest increase in income inequality.

Overall, changes in marginal tax rates generate rather small effects on the participation rate and hours worked. Indeed, marginal tax rates affect mostly the intensive margin, which is rather unresponsive, and cross-effects in couples also limit the overall effect. Chapter 4 by in 't Veld et al. presents larger labour supply responses from changes in general taxation. However in Chapter 4 the overall labour supply elasticity is calibrated to be 0.3–0.4. This elasticity is relatively high compared to our estimates, especially for men, and ignores the presence of cross-effects in couples. We should note though that we only model changes in labour participation and hours worked. We do not model changes in e.g. human capital accumulation and retirement. Accounting for these additional changes may result in a larger overall response of effective labour supply to tax changes.

11.6.2 Changes in Income Support for Low-Income Households

More pronounced are the effects of changes in income support targeted at low-income households. Indeed, these policies implicitly target the more responsive extensive margin, because they provide more subsidies to households where one or more individuals do not work. Table 11.3 gives the simulation results of three cuts in income support for low-income households.

Column (1) gives the effects of a decrease in the subsidy for low-income households with young children (*Kindgebonden Budget* in Dutch), of 500 million euro in total.[14] This causes a relatively large increase in labour supply in hours and in persons. In this reform, the income effect and the substitution effect work in the same direction. Furthermore, this stimulates secondary earners and single parents to work (more), which is a relatively elastic group.[15] However, this reform also reduces effective labour units per hour somewhat, and leads to a substantial rise in income inequality.[16]

In column (2) we simulate a reduction in the rent subsidy for low-income households (*Huurtoeslag* in Dutch), again for a total amount of 500 million euro.[17] This also has a relatively strong effect on labour participation, in persons and in hours. However, the effect is less pronounced than in column (1) because it does not solely target the elastic group of households with young children.

Finally, column (3) gives the results for a reduction in the health care subsidy for low-income households (*Zorgtoeslag* in Dutch), again for a total amount of 500 million euro.[18] This reform also stimulates labour participation, but the effect is less pronounced than in columns (1) and (2). The health care subsidy is phased out rather gradually, and as a result benefits a large part of the income distribution. Because this subsidy is less targeted at the lowest incomes, reducing it has a more moderate effect on labour supply.

11.6.3 Changes in Policies Targeted at the Extensive Margin

Next, we consider policy reforms that explicitly target the extensive margin: changes in welfare benefits and changes in the general in-work tax credit (*Arbeidskorting* in Dutch).

---

[14] We decrease the maximum amount for all families by 45%, and keep the phase out rate fixed at 6.75%.

[15] Note that there is also a small effect on men and women in other couples, these are the men and women in couples with a partner whose labour supply is fixed, but have a dependent child.

[16] Note that the budgetary impulse in this simulation is only a third of the tax bracket simulations.

[17] We reduce the rent benefit by 18%, but keep the phase-out range the same.

[18] We decrease the maximum amount of the benefit by 14%, and keep the phase out rate at 13.4%.

Table 11.3 Changes in income support for low-income households

Simulation	(1) Income-dependent child subsidy[a]	(2) Income-dependent rent subsidy[b]	(3) Income-dependent health care subsidy[c]
Ex ante impulse (in billion euro)	−0.5	−0.5	−0.5
Percentage changes			
Gini coefficient[d]	0.44	0.67	0.46
Hours worked per week	0.25	0.17	0.12
– Men in couples young. child 0–17	0.48	0.20	0.14
– Women in couples young. child 0–17	0.86	0.15	0.19
– Men in other couples	0.04	0.07	0.10
– Women in other couples	0.17	0.08	0.16
– Single parents young. child 0–17	0.76	0.72	0.20
– Singles	0.00	0.22	0.08
Participation rate	0.22	0.15	0.11
– Men in couples young. child 0–17	0.42	0.19	0.13
– Women in couples young. child 0–17	0.63	0.14	0.16
– Men in other couples	0.04	0.06	0.09
– Women in other couples	0.14	0.07	0.14
– Single parents young. child 0–17	0.59	0.53	0.14
– Singles	0.00	0.18	0.05
Effective labour units per hour	−0.04	−0.04	−0.02

[a] A decrease in the income dependent child benefit (*Kindgebonden Budget*), an income dependent subsidy for parents with a youngest child up to 18 years of age. The subsidy is phased-out from 19,463 euro at a rate of 6.75%. We decrease the subsidy by 45%, and keep the phase-out rate the same. Hence, we extend the phase-out range of the subsidy

[b] A decrease in the income dependent rent subsidy (*Huurtoeslag*), an income dependent subsidy that compensates lower income households for rent costs. It depends on household income, household composition and the rent level. The maximum amount in 2015 is 4079 euro for single-person households and 3759 euro for multi-person households. We lower the rent benefit by 18% but keep the phase-out range the same

[c] A decrease in the income dependent health care subsidy (*Zorgtoeslag*), an income dependent subsidy that compensates lower income households for the compulsory health care insurance. In 2015, the maximum health care benefit is 936 euro for singles and 1788 euro for couples. This benefit is phased out from 19,463 euro at a rate of 13.4% in 2015. We lower the health care benefit by 14% but keep the phase-out range the same

[d] Gini coefficient of disposable household income, using equivalence scales. The Gini coefficient is calculated over the full Dutch adult population with gross income above 66% of the annual minimum wage

Table 11.4 Changes in policies targeted at the extensive margin

Simulation	(1) Welfare benefits[a]	(2) In-work tax credit, across-the-board[b]	(3) In-work tax credit, targeted at low incomes[c]
Ex ante impulse (in billion euro)	−0.5	1.5	1.5
Percentage changes			
Gini coefficient[d]	0.78	0.10	−0.35
Hours worked per week	0.66	0.13	0.17
– Men in couples young. child 0–17	0.67	0.03	−0.04
– Women in couples young. child 0–17	0.54	0.33	0.61
– Men in other couples	0.47	0.10	0.02
– Women in other couples	0.62	0.15	0.23
– Single parents young. child 0–17	2.54	0.33	0.53
– Singles	0.67	0.14	0.20
Participation rate	0.62	0.13	0.22
– Men in couples young. child 0–17	0.67	0.09	0.13
– Women in couples young. child 0–17	0.49	0.20	0.50
– Men in other couples	0.43	0.11	0.07
– Women in other couples	0.57	0.14	0.27
– Single parents young. child 0–17	2.38	0.32	0.60
– Singles	0.60	0.09	0.15
Effective labour units per hour	−0.12	−0.05	−0.10

[a]Reduction in welfare benefits by 14%

[b]An increase in the (maximum) general in-work tax credit (*Arbeidskorting*) of 245 euro, by increasing the phase-in rate from 19.7 to 22.0%

[c]An increase in the (maximum) general in-work tax credit (*Arbeidskorting*) of 441 euro, by increasing the phase-in rate from 19.7 to 23.9%. The higher in-work tax credit is phased out from 34,000 euro onwards at 4%. The phase-out rate is the same as in the current system, but the new phase-out starts at an income of 34,000 euro instead of 49,770 euro in the current system. The level of the general in-work tax credit for incomes above 49,770 euro remains the same as in the current system

[d]Gini coefficient of disposable household income, using equivalence scales. The Gini coefficient is calculated over the full Dutch adult population with gross income above 66% of the annual minimum wage

In the first simulation, column (1) of Table 11.4, we lower welfare benefits by 14% for a total amount of 500 million euro. This leads to a substantial increase in overall labour supply in hours and persons. The response is particularly large for single parents, 32% of single parents are on welfare benefits in the base, and they are also particularly responsive to financial incentives. The effect on effective labour units per hour is negative, as the productivity of the additional workers is below average. Also, lowering welfare benefits leads to a substantial rise in income inequality.

In the second and third simulation we use the 'carrot' rather than the 'stick', and increase the general in-work tax credit, for all workers, for a total amount of 1.5 billion euro.[19] In column (2), we increase the maximum level of the tax credit by 245 euro, such that the maximum tax credit (2465 euro) is reached at the same income of 19,463 euro. The effects are much smaller than in the first simulation, despite the larger budgetary impulse, because the share of employed individuals is much larger than the share of individuals on welfare benefits. This makes the increase in disposable income per working person much smaller than the reduction in disposable income of non-working individuals in the welfare benefits simulation (in absolute terms). Also, this reform is less targeted at the responsive group of single parents. Still, labour supply in hours and persons increases for all groups, and the effects are larger than for the reductions in the tax bracket rates. There is some decrease in effective labour units per hour and a slight increase in income inequality.

In column (3) we target the in-work tax credit more strongly at low income individuals by raising the maximum tax credit even further (to 2661 euro). In order to keep the budgetary impulse identical to the second scenario, we lower the start of the phase out of the tax credit to an income of 34,000 euro. This leads to a larger effect on total hours worked because the tax credit is more targeted at the extensive margin. The higher tax credit now increases labour supply more for women in couples, singles and single parents, than in the second simulation. By contrast, men in couples with dependent children slightly lower their labour supply. Some men, with a high income, now receive a lower tax credit due to the earlier phase out of the tax credit. Effective labour units per hour decreases more in column (3) than in column (2). However, reform (3) decreases rather than increases income inequality.

11.6.4 Changes in Policies Targeted at Working Parents with Children

Table 11.5 gives the results for policies targeted at working parents with children. This group is of particular interest because there are many policies targeted specifically at this group, and because mothers with young children appear to be particularly responsive to changes in financial incentives. We consider simulations with a budgetary impulse of 500 million euro, because these policies target only a subgroup of the working age population (and therefore the budgetary base is relatively small).

[19]In 2015, the general in-work tax credit rises up to an income of 19,463 euro (close to the minimum wage), where the maximum credit is 2220 euro. The tax credit is phased-out with 4% over an income of 49,770 euro and 100,670 euro.

Table 11.5 Changes in policies for working parents with children

Simulation	(1) credit[a] credit[a]	(2) Additional combination credit[b]	(3) Income dependent combination credit[c]	(4) Childcare subsidies[d]
Ex ante impulse (in billion euro)	0.5	0.5	0.5	0.5
Percentage changes				
Gini coefficient[e]	−0.11	−0.10	−0.01	0.01
Hours worked per week	0.05	0.11	0.18	0.11
– Men in couples young. child 0–17	0.03	0.02	0.02	0.04
– Women in couples young. child 0–17	0.25	0.72	1.25	0.92
– Men in other couples	0.01	0.00	0.00	0.00
– Women in other couples	0.03	0.05	0.06	0.00
– Single parents young. child 0–17	0.39	0.76	1.10	0.12
– Singles	0.00	0.00	0.00	0.00
Participation rate	0.10	0.19	0.16	0.08
– Men in couples young. child 0–17	0.09	0.10	0.10	0.05
– Women in couples young. child 0–17	0.39	0.91	0.66	0.47
– Men in other couples	0.01	0.00	0.00	0.00
– Women in other couples	0.04	0.07	0.06	0.00
– Single parents young. child 0–17	0.40	0.77	0.99	0.10
– Singles	0.00	0.00	0.00	0.00
Effective labour units per hour	−0.02	−0.04	−0.05	−0.02
Hours formal childcare	0.95	1.66	2.12	8.76

[a]The combination credit (*Combinatiekorting*) is a flat tax credit for working parents, with gross income above 4857 euro, with a youngest child up to 12 years of age. We set the credit at 270 euro per person

[b]The additional combination credit (*Aanvullende Combinatiekorting*) is a flat tax credit for working secondary earners and working single parents, with gross income above 4857 euro, with a youngest child up to 12 years of age. We set the credit at 600 euro per person

[c]The income dependent combination credit (*Inkomensafhankelijke Combinatiekorting*) is a tax credit for working secondary earners and working single parents with a youngest child up to 12 years of age. The tax credit is income dependent, we increase the phase-in rate from 4 to 8%. The phase-in range runs from 4857 euro to 32,832 euro, at which the maximum credit increases by 1109 euro. The tax credit is not phased out

[d]An increase in childcare subsidies (*Kinderopvangtoeslag*). Families only qualify for childcare subsidies when both parents work. The change in childcare subsidies is set in such a way that there is a proportional decline in the parental contribution rate. Because higher incomes have a higher parental contribution rate, this benefits more the parents with a higher income

[e]Gini coefficient of disposable household income, using equivalence scales. The Gini coefficient is calculated over the full Dutch adult population with gross income above 66% of the annual minimum wage

First, in column (1), we simulate the reintroduction of an in-work tax credit for working parents with a youngest child up to 12 years of age (*Combinatiekorting* in Dutch).[20,21] This has a positive effect on labour supply. However, the effect on labour supply is limited because a large part goes to primary earners in couples, mostly men, who are rather unresponsive to financial incentives.

Next, in column (2), we increase the in-work tax credit for secondary earners and single parents with a youngest child up to 12 years of age (*Aanvullende Combinatiekorting* in Dutch).[22] Primary earners do not receive this tax-credit. Therefore, the increase in labour supply is much larger, because it targets the responsive groups of secondary earners and single parents (typically women) with young children. These groups are rather responsive to changes in financial incentives.

The reform in column (3) is even more effective in terms of labour supply. In this simulation we increase the income dependent part of the income dependent tax credit for secondary earners and single parents with a youngest child up to 12 years of age (*Inkomensafhankelijke Combinatiekorting* in Dutch).[23] The number of hours worked increases more than in column (2). The reform in column (3) not only makes working more attractive, but also encourages secondary earners and single parents to work more days per week.

Finally, we consider the effect of increasing childcare subsidies in column (4). We consider a proportional decrease (of 38%) across incomes in the parental fee that results after deducting the subsidy from the full hourly price. This reform not only targets secondary earners and single parents with a youngest child up to 12 years of age, but also primary earners with children. Again, there is a substantial increase in hours worked. However, the effects on labour supply in hours and persons are smaller than in column (3). Indeed, the childcare reform reduces the effective hourly child care price for parents. This leads to a large increase in the use of formal childcare, see the last row in the table, which leads to substantial additional budgetary costs (which are included in the 500 million euro of the impulse). This makes this reform less effective per additional euro spent than the increase in the income dependent tax credit for working parents with a young child.

---

[20]This tax credit was replaced by an income-dependent tax credit which we consider below.

[21]We reintroduce a tax credit of 270 euro for individuals earning at least 4,857 euro in the targeted group.

[22]We reintroduce a tax credit of 600 euro for individuals earning at least 4,857 euro in the targeted group.

[23]We increase the phase-in rate of 4 percentage points and increase the maximum credit by 1109 euro.

Table 11.6 Reform package of the Tax Plan 2016

Simulation	Tax Plan 2016[a]
Ex-ante impulse (in billion euro)	5.0
	Percentage changes
Gini coefficient	0.30
Hours worked per week	0.47
– Men in couples youngest child 0–17	−0.01
– Women in couples youngest child 0–17	2.27
– Men in other couples	0.03
– Women in other couples	0.53
– Single parents youngest child 0–17	1.08
– Singles	0.45
Participation rate	0.56
– Men in couples youngest child 0–17	0.27
– Women in couples youngest child 0–17	1.59
– Men in other couples	0.12
– Women in other couples	0.68
– Single parents youngest child 0–17	1.17
– Singles	0.38
Effective labour units per hour	−0.18

[a]See the main text for a detailed description of all the elements of the Tax Plan 2016

11.6.5 Tax Plan 2016

Finally, Table 11.6 gives the simulation results of the Tax Plan 2016 of the Dutch government, debated extensively in Dutch parliament. The Tax Plan 2016 reduces income taxation by 5 billion euros. The main goal of this reform was to create more employment (Ministry of Finance, 2015a,b). We first discuss the elements of The Tax Plan 2016, and subsequently discuss the simulation results.

The Tax Plan 2016 consists of the following elements:

- An increase in the in-work tax credit, targeted at low-income workers (+2.5 billion euros).[24]
- A reduction in the second and third tax bracket rate of 2.1 percentage points (+2.7 billion euros).
- An increase in the start of the fourth tax bracket by 8000 euros (+0.9 billion euros).

[24]Here, the maximum level of the in-work tax credit is increased with 665 euros. The phase-out now starts at an income of 33,000 euros instead of 49,895 euros.

- An increase in the income-dependent combination credit for working parents with a youngest child of up to 12 years of age (+0.25 billion euros).[25]
- An increase in the childcare subsidy so that the parental contribution decreases by 38% (+0.25 billion euros).
- The introduction of a wage cost subsidy for employers (+0.5 billion euros).[26]
- The general tax credit is phased out completely for higher incomes (–2.1 billion euros).[27] This increases the effective marginal tax rate for this group.

The simulation results in Table 11.6 show that this reform increases labour supply in persons and hours worked, by 0.6% and 0.5%, respectively. The increase in labour supply is relatively strong for single parents and women in couples with young children. The Tax Plan 2016 includes a number of reforms that are relatively effective in stimulating labour supply, such as the targeted in-work tax credit for workers with a relatively low income, the income-dependent combination credit and childcare subsidies. The reform however also reduces effective labour units per hour and increases income inequality to some extent.

11.7 Discussion and Conclusion

In this chapter we show how the behavioural responses to changes in financial incentives can be estimated and used in the analysis of tax-benefit reforms, using structural models of labour supply. A very large administrative dataset allows us to uncover the behavioural responses for a large number of subgroups on the Dutch labour market. We find large differences in the responses to financial incentives. On the one hand, singles and men in couples are rather unresponsive to changes in financial incentives. On the other hand, single parents are women in couples with young children are relatively responsive. We also find that most of the response is in the participation rate (the extensive margin), the response in hours worked per week per employed (the intensive margin) is much smaller. We further find cross effects for women in couples that are non-negligible; when the income of the husband increases, the women work less hours.

---

[25]The maximum amount of this credit increases by 500 euros, by increasing the phase-in rate from 4.0% to 5.8%.

[26]Employers receive a subsidy of 2000 euros (for a full-time position) for employees with an hourly wage below 110% of the minimum wage. For employees with an hourly wage of between 110% and 120% of the minimum wage, the maximum subsidy is 1000 euros. For employees working part-time, the wage cost subsidy is lowered proportionally. We do not explicitly model the employer side. In the simulation we assume that the wage cost subsidy is fully shifted onto workers, consistent with findings in e.g. Melguizo and Gonzalez-Paramo (2013). This seems particularly likely in a small open economy such as that of the Netherlands, where capital is close to infinitely elastic to labour costs and labour is much less elastic to net wages.

[27]The phase-out rate increases from 3.32% to 4.80%.

These findings have important implications for tax-benefit reforms. Reductions in tax bracket rates are relatively ineffective in stimulating labour supply, because intensive margin responses are relatively small. Furthermore, for reductions in the third and fourth tax bracket, the cross-effect on women's labour supply in couples also mitigates the effect on hours worked. Reductions in income support for low-income households are relatively effective in stimulating labour supply, because they target the more elastic extensive margin. However, the downside is an increase in income inequality. On the other hand, increasing in-work benefits for low-income workers is also relatively effective, and can reduce rather than increase income inequality. The most effective in terms of labour supply are tax credits and (child care) subsidies for single parents and secondary earners with young children, as these groups are the most responsive to changes in financial incentives. We also present simulation results for the Tax Plan 2016. The Tax Plan 2016 stimulates labour supply in persons and in hours, and contains a number of policy changes that are relatively effective, such as an increase in the in-work tax credit for low-income workers, an increase in the in-work tax credit for single parents and secondary earners with a young child and child care subsidies.

We conclude by indicating a number of limitations of the analysis. People are assumed to be free in their choice of whether or not to participate, and how many hours to work. In an extension we estimated a so-called double-hurdle model (Cragg, 1971) for involuntary unemployment. The policy simulation results are very similar to the base model (De Boer, 2015) as very few people in the data are classified as involuntary unemployed.[28] Furthermore, we focus on the labour supply responses to changes in the tax-benefit system, whereas other studies look at a broader range of behavioural responses, by studying the elasticity of taxable income (Saez et al., 2012b). Jongen and Stoel (2013) find that the elasticity of taxable labour income for the average worker is not that different from the labour supply elasticity. But for high-income workers the labour supply elasticity is much lower than the elasticity of taxable income, in line with other studies (Saez et al., 2012b). Therefore, to determine the budgetary consequences of an increase in the top tax rate, we need to consider other behavioural responses next to the labour supply response. We further ignore general equilibrium effects on prices and wages, but this may not be a bad approximation for the long run in a small open economy like the Netherlands (Aaberge and Colombino, 2014). We also ignore the life cycle, accounting for life-cycle effects can be important for the analysis of tax-benefit reform (e.g. Imai and Keane, 2004; Keane, 2011; Blundell et al., 2016). This would be an interesting direction for future research, but requires data on consumption. Finally, recent work by Chetty et al. (2009) shows that informational frictions can play an important role in the behavioural responses to financial incentives. This too seems an interesting direction for future research.

[28]Note that we use data from before the Great Recession, when unemployment was relatively low in the Netherlands.

References

Aaberge R, Colombino U (2014) Labour supply models. In: O'Donoghue C (ed) Handbook of microsimulation modelling. Emerald, Bingley, pp 167–222

Aaberge R, Dagsvik J, Strom S (1995) Labor supply responses and welfare effects of tax reforms. Scand J Econ 97(4):635–659

Aaberge R, Colombino U, Strom S (1999) Labour supply in Italy: an empirical analysis of joint household decisions, with taxes and quantity constraints. Appl Econ 14(4):403–422

Bargain O, Orsini K, Peichl A (2014) Comparing labor supply elasticities in Europe and the United States: new results. J Hum Resour 49(3):723–838

Bettendorf L, Folmer K, Jongen E (2014) The dog that did not bark: the EITC for single mothers in the Netherlands. J Public Econ 119:49–60

Bettendorf L, Jongen E, Muller P (2015) Childcare subsidies and labour supply - evidence from a large Dutch reform. Labour Econ 36:112–123

Blau D, Kahn L (2007) Changes in the labor supply behavior of married women: 1980–2000. J Labor Econ 25(3):393–438

Blundell R, Costa-Dias M, Meghir C, Shaw J (2016) Female labour supply, human capital and welfare reform. Econometrica 84(5):1705–1763

Bosch N, Jongen E (2013) Intensive margin responses when workers are free the choose: evidence from a Dutch tax reform. Paper presented at EALE 2013

Bosch N, van der Klaauw B (2012) Analyzing female labor supply - evidence from a Dutch tax reform. Labour Econ 19:271–280

Brewer M, Duncan A, Shephard A, Suarez M (2006) Did the working families' tax credit work? The impact of in-work support on labour supply in Great Britain. Labour Econ 13:699–720

Chetty R (2009) Is the taxable income elasticity sufficient to calculate deadweight loss? The implications of evasion and avoidance. Am Econ J Econ Pol 1(2):31–52

Chetty R, Looney A, Kroft K (2009) Salience and taxation: theory and evidence. Am Econ Rev 99(4):1145–1177

CPB (2015) Kansrijk Arbeidsmarktbeleid. CPB Netherlands Bureau for Economic Policy Analysis, The Hague

Cragg J (1971) Some statistical models for limited dependent variables with applications to the demand for durable goods. Econometrica 39:829–844

De Boer HW (2015) A structural analysis of labour supply and involuntary unemployment in the Netherlands. CPB Discussion Paper 312, The Hague

De Boer H, Jongen E (2017) The best of both worlds - analysing tax-benefit reforms using structural models and natural experiments. mimeo, CPB, The Hague

De Boer HW, Jongen E, Kabatek J (2015) The effectiveness of fiscal stimuli for working parents. IZA Discussion Paper 9298, Bonn

Heckman J, Singer B (1984) A method for minimizing the impact of distributional assumptions in econometric models for duration data. Econometrica 52:271–320

Imai S, Keane M (2004) Intertemporal labor supply and human capital accumulation. Int Econ Rev 45(2):601–641

Jongen E, Stoel M (2013) Estimating the elasticity of taxable labour income in the Netherlands. CPB Background Document, The Hague

Jongen E, De Boer H, Dekker P (2014) MICSIM: a behavioural microsimulation model for the analysis of tax-benefit reform in the Netherlands. CPB Background Document, The Hague

Keane M (2011) Labor supply and taxes: a survey. J Econ Lit 49(4):961–1075

Keane M, Moffitt R (1998) A structural model of multiple welfare program participation and labor supply. Int Econ Rev 39(3):553–589

Koot P, Vlekke M, Berkhout E, Euwals R (2016) MIMOSI: microsimulatiemodel voor belastingen, sociale zekerheid, loonkosten en koopkracht. CPB Background Document, The Hague

Lundberg S (1985) The added worker effect. J Labor Econ 3(1):11–37

Mastrogiacomo M, Bosch N, Gielen M, Jongen E (2017) Heterogeneity in labour supply responses: evidence from a major tax reform. Oxf Bull Econ Stat 79:769–796

McFadden D (1978) Modeling the choice of residential location. In: Karlqvist A, Lundqvist L, Snickars F, Weibull J (eds) Spatial interaction theory and planning models. North-Holland, Amsterdam, pp 75–96

Melguizo A, Gonzalez-Paramo J (2013) Who bears labour taxes and social contributions? A meta-analysis approach. SERIEs 4:247–271

Ministry of Finance (2015a) 4e nota van wijziging belastingplan. Ministry of Finance, The Hague

Ministry of Finance (2015b) Belastingherziening. Ministry of Finance, The Hague

Mirrlees J (1971) An exploration in the theory of optimum income taxation. Rev Econ Stud 38(2):175–208

Saez E, Slemrod J, Giertz S (2012a) The elasticity of taxable income with respect to marginal tax rates: a critical review. J Econ Lit 50(1):3–50

Saez E, Slemrod J, Giertz S (2012b) The elasticity of taxable income with respect to marginal tax rates: a critical review. J. Econ Lit 50(1):3–50

Statistics Netherlands (2012) Documentatierapport Arbeidsmarktpanel 1999-2009V1. Statistics Netherlands, Leidschenveen, http://www.cbs.nl/NR/rdonlyres/672F45FE-2BA8-41D7-81EA-37D2B40FBF1D/0/arbeidsmarktpanelmicrodata.pdf

Train K (2008) EM algorithms for nonparametric estimation of mixing distributions. J Choice Modell 1:40–69

Van Soest A (1995) Structural models of family labor supply: a discrete choice approach. J Hum Resour 30(1):63–88

Chapter 12
CPB and the Assessment of Structural Reforms

Laura van Geest and Daniel van Vuuren

12.1 Introduction

CPB Netherlands Bureau for Economic Policy Analysis provides the official economic forecasts on which budgetary policy is based. In addition, it produces policy relevant economic research which is academically up to standard. In fulfilling these tasks, CPB is unique in the world and has attracted attention of policy makers in Europe, particularly for its contribution to evidence-based policy. One of the unique features of CPB is its independent status. The idea of (more) independent economic forecasts is embodied in the Independent Fiscal Institutes (IFIs), which have been established in the Eurozone in the aftermath of the 2012 crisis, in line with EU regulation. The notion that independent assessments can lead towards more competitive economies has led to the Council Recommendation on the establishment of National Productivity Boards (2016), in line with the Five Presidents' Report (2015).

The Dutch experience may provide some inspiration for the establishment of new institutes. We give an overview of CPB's history and describe its mission and daily practice. Specifically in view of the Recommendation on National Productivity

The authors thank Peter van den Berg, Frank den Butter, Massimo Giuliodori, Edwin van de Haar, Johannes Hers, Egbert Jongen, Wim Suyker, and Bas ter Weel for useful comments on an earlier draft of this paper.

L. van Geest (✉)
CPB Netherlands Bureau for Policy Analysis, The Hague, The Netherlands
e-mail: L.B.J.van.Geest@cpb.nl

D. van Vuuren
CPB Netherlands Bureau for Policy Analysis, The Hague, The Netherlands

Tilburg University, Tilburg, The Netherlands

J. de Haan, J. Parlevliet (eds.), *Structural Reforms*,
https://doi.org/10.1007/978-3-319-74400-1_12

Boards, we present some case studies in the area of labour market policies. Finally, we confront our experiences with the legislation present and envisaged at the EU level.

12.2 A Bird's Eye View of CPB

This section presents a brief history of CPB and derives some important lessons. In particular, some lessons can be drawn from CPB's inception, its relation with politics, its legal mandate, its position within society, and the kind of analyses it provides.

12.2.1 Never Waste a Good Crisis

In the case of CPB, its inception fits the stylized fact that crises can provide impetus to novel approaches in policy. CPB started in 1945 (although it was formally established only in 1947). The Netherlands and its economy had experienced major destruction during World War II. Moreover, the war was proceeded by a deep economic recession in the nineteen thirties. There was thus a clear need to get up to speed with effective and efficient policies to rebuild the Netherlands.

12.2.2 Water and Oil Don't Mix

It also fits the stylized fact that fragmented political systems favour neutral, third parties or referees. Even after the war, Dutch politics remained 'pillarized' or fragmented. Dutch election results inevitably led to coalition governments, as no single party was ever able to muster a majority in parliament. Under those circumstances, an independent institute is more attractive than an institute that might just speak his master's voice. Unbiased forecasts provided by institutions under a political umbrella are highly unusual. In the Netherlands, independent forecasts and analysis provide a common denominator for the political debate between parties. The non-partisan role of the CPB led to a clear division of labour between analysis and modelling on the one hand, and policy choices and judgment on the other hand. CPB focuses on positive analysis, i.e., the state of the economy (forecasts) and effective policy instruments for a broad range of topics. Rather than discussing or advising on the desirability of certain policy goals, CPB concentrates on the trade-offs between these goals. Policy advice is the purview of the Social Economic Council, in which social partners as well as civil society, academia, the central bank and CPB are represented.

12.2.3 *With a Little Help from My Friends*

In terms of legal mandate and positioning, CPB started off as a typical Dutch (informal) organization. The formal mandate of CPB was quite vague. The law established CPB and required it to contribute to the Central Economic Plan (CEP). Even though CPB still publishes a CEP every year, the document has little to do with formal economic planning. It rather presents one of the four forecasts that CPB publishes every year. While organizationally CPB is part of the Ministry of Economic Affairs, it operates independently. It was only in 2012 that this tradition was formalized through secondary legislation, which explicitly states that CPB cannot receive instructions from politicians or civil servants and determines its own work program. In 2013, the government legally formalized the role of CPB as independent forecaster for the budgetary process, in response to the requirements of the Fiscal Compact and the Two Pack. However, in line with the existing view on the proper division of labour between forecasting and policy analysis on the one hand, and policy decisions on the other, the Dutch government allocated the normative part of the mandate of an Independent Fiscal Institute to the Council of State. The Council of State has a strong reputation in the area of independent policy advice, while close cooperation on the basis of a clear division of labour between these two bodies prevents double work and bureaucracy. In 2017, the CPB was designated as the National Productivity Board.

CPB receives a budget from the Ministry of Economic Affairs, but this budget can be supplemented from other official sources up to a maximum of 20%. Presently, CPB employs around 115 full time equivalent staff. The Director is a civil servant appointed for a non-renewable 7-year period by the Council of Ministers. The Director decides on the annual work program of CPB.

While the focus of CPB remained broadly unchanged, political developments, new technologies, new economic insights and novel policy questions all left their mark on the work of CPB over the decades.

12.2.4 *Rome Was Not Built in a Day*

Initially, CPB had some difficulty to find its voice, as most political parties and employers' organizations had little sympathy for 'the planning of the economy' (Passenier 1994). As member of the Social and Economic Council, CPB gradually found a way to contribute to the decentralized Dutch polder model of decision-making. While the polder model seems to be on the wane, CPB kept its influential position. The practice to analyse election platforms, since 1986, seems a case in point.

12.2.5 Panta Rhei

While CPB's focus remained the same, policy issues and the associated analytical approaches changed over time (Table 12.1). A loosely defined mandate enabled this type of adaptation. Practically, paper and pencil gave way to punched carts and personal computers, allowing for more complex models. Theoretically, existing Keynesian models were complemented with supply side models and short- and medium-term forecasts with long-term projections, also in the form of scenario studies. The macro-economic focus was complemented by micro-economic research on competition and regulatory issues. Cost benefit analyses of individual projects have been undertaken next to studies for the economy at large. Evaluations and micro-econometric research have been added to the portfolio of activities as well. Politically, topics changed over time as well, from rebuilding the Netherlands and the establishment of the welfare state, to lessening labour shortages and later battling high unemployment.

Table 12.1 Major events in the evolution of CPB

1945	Start of CPB with Tinbergen as its first director
1946	Central government budget based on CPB's estimates of the national economy. CPB starts to provide a regular macroeconomic perspective on Dutch public finance. The pre-war ideas of social planning gradually evolve into forecasts and analyses of objectives and tools
1950	Start of Social and Economic Council
1953	First CPB-macro model for analysing and forecasting the Dutch economy
1961	In September each year, simultaneously with the Government Budget, a Macro Economic Outlook on the Dutch economy is published, including estimates of Dutch public finance
1971	First advisory group on fiscal policy; CPB is one of the participants
1976	Supply side included in macro-model (clay-clay vintage-production function), which substantially changed policy recommendations
1986	First analysis of the economic consequences of the election platforms of political parties
1992	First applied general equilibrium model for the labour market (MIMIC)
1992	First long-term scenario analysis stressing the role of institutions (Scanning the future)
1993	Start of first major study on economic institutions: a comparison of economic institutions in Germany and the Netherlands
1994	Cost-benefit analysis of railway freight track to Germany (Betuwelijn)
1998	First analysis of sustainable public finance (generational accounts)
2000	National guidelines by CPB on cost-benefit analysis
2012	Secondary legislation confirming Independence CPB
2013	CPB (positive analysis) and Council of State (normative analysis) IFI for the Netherlands
2017	CPB National Productivity Board for the Netherlands

Source: update of Bos and Teulings (2012)

12.2.6 Bottom Up Is Best

CPB is a typical Dutch animal, established just after a major crisis, tailored to the Dutch political arena. While the CPB experience can provide useful pointers, it is naïve to think it can be effectively implemented in a completely different political biosphere. Institutes like CPB can only play a role if the public at large is convinced of evidence-based policy. Commitment is not achieved through force but through persuasion, tailored to local circumstances.

12.3 CPB's Mission: From Theory to Practice

CPB aims to provide independent, impartial economic analysis that is policy relevant and academically up to standard. How did CPB become and, more importantly, remain a widely trusted source of policy relevant economic analysis, a dependable 'Google translate' between research and policy?

CPB's first director was Jan Tinbergen, front-runner in quantitative economics, who received the Nobel prize in economics in 1969. He was well known and respected, but also modest in outlook. A vocal advocate of a clear division of labour between independent data collection (Statistics Netherlands), independent policy analysis (CPB) and consensus building policy advice (SER), proponent of the delineation between policy instruments and policy goals and well known for his thesis that you cannot have more policy goals than independent instruments. CPB still benefits from its impressive first front man, underscoring that newly established institutes can benefit from prudent early appointments.

CPB strives for neutrality and is perceived as independent and non-partisan. A poll among the public at large shows that 91% of the respondents recognize CPB's name, with 60% knowing what CPB stands for; 58% of the respondents consider CPB to be objective, while 12% regards CPB either left or right leaning (Ipsos 2015).

However, the drive towards neutrality is not straightforward and CPB is not beyond public debate. Firstly, economics is just one of the social sciences and it has taken a hit after the 2008 crisis. Economics as a discipline has a certain perspective on policy issues. Psychologists, lawyers or philosophers might focus on different issues, other instruments and look differently at concepts like trade-offs and the welfare function. Furthermore, economists are more inclined to use figures than scientists from other disciplines, as figures are believed to speak louder than words. Where relevant, CPB enters collaboration with other disciplines, but finding a proper balance remains a challenge.

Secondly, the economics profession is a broad church. There are diverging views and models, both normative and positive. While think tanks often tend to opt for one school of thought or the other, CPB strives for a neutral stance. CPB focuses on empirical work and models and approaches, based on the research issue at hand. This will satisfy most, but certainly not all.

Thirdly, CPB operates in a political and public environment. Maintaining a non-partisan profile requires a clear strategy on the type of work to be undertaken and how to communicate about it. Even then it is not always successful, because parties sometimes confuse the message and the messenger. Most importantly, CPB does not give judgments. It sticks to the presentation of facts and analyses, showing trade-offs between various policy goals, refraining from choices. It is our firm conviction that facts speak louder than words. The allocation of the normative part of the IFI mandate to a different body than CPB should be seen against this background. CPB's prudent approach means that some questions may remain unanswered in order to avoid a descent into speculation. And when presenting results, the uncertainties should be acknowledged, e.g. through fan charts in forecasts and scenario analyses. As a non-partisan body, we provide bespoke analyses to all parties in parliament (on occasion confidentially), including opposition parties. In general, requests are honoured provided adequate knowledge, time and personnel are available. This also underscores our non-partisan profile.

Becoming a trusted source of economic analysis requires high-quality work. Academic standards are the norm and they are maintained through various means. High-quality staff is a key factor and hiring is within the sole purview of the Director, ensuring a meritocratic personnel policy. CPB staff does research themselves, not only relying on available work done by others. This ensures maintenance of adequate analytical skills and sound judgment in the use of academic research done by others. Over time, CPB bolstered academic standards through a stronger focus on publications in academic journals and more interaction with academia. Research is now aimed at publication in a peer reviewed CPB series (CPB Discussion Papers), in international peer reviewed journals, as well as presentation at international seminars. CPB also expanded its network with Dutch economists through its circle of Academic Partners (professors accredited at universities). Some CPB staff members hold part-time positions at universities.

Policy relevance is safeguarded through frequent contacts with departments and other relevant policy makers. This feeds in both to the choice of topics to be analysed and proper institutional detail in the policy options discussed. Civil servants and other policy makers are consulted on the Work Program, while CPB can undertake research that is specifically funded by departments as well. Membership of the Social and Economic Council and several advisory committees within the government provides another channel of information and feedback. Research results are discussed in seminars with civil servants present. Publication of CPB Policy Briefs enhances the chance that research results will be used in policy-making. These short, non-technical papers on policy issues are specifically tailored to policy makers.

A final backstop to ensure non-partisan quality work is public external reviews. CPB's independent position does not mean that it is not accountable. CPB has a monitoring committee which commissions external reviews of both the policy relevance and the academic quality of the output on a regular basis. In the 2016 edition, the Review Committee employed the protocol that is the standard in Dutch academia. It is also the first review that does not focus on just one aspect of CPB (policy relevance or academic standards), but that takes a look at the overall picture.

12.4 CPB Products and Their Role in Policy Making

Short and medium-term forecasting are the bread and butter of CPB. Four times a year CPB produces short-term forecasts for the Dutch economy, varying from growth, inflation and unemployment to the income distribution and public finances. These forecasts feed into the debate about the annual budget, with the CEP, published in March, serving as a starting point for the discussions on the expenditure side, and the MEV, published in September, as the finalization of the negotiations. In the run up to elections, CPB produces a medium-term forecast covering the full term in office of the new government. All these projections are made, using a standard macro econometric model (Saffier-II).[1] Research into academically popular models like DSGE and BVAR did not yield a good alternative for this purpose, which requires a combination of projections, policy simulations and storytelling. CPB also produces the monthly World Trade Monitor, an empirical tool to follow actual developments in world trade and global industrial production. The World Trade Monitor is followed by forecasters across the world. At the specific request of Parliament, CPB also produces an annual Financial Risk Report. In the aftermath of the financial crisis, a clear need was felt to follow financial market developments more closely.

CPB regularly publishes long-term studies. Every 4 years, CPB analyses the sustainability of Dutch public finances (ageing studies). These projections are made using an Overlapping Generations Model (GAMMA). The issue of sustainable fiscal policy plays a major role in the Dutch political debate. Also other sustainability issues have become important in political manifestos and the election debates. Other long-term studies take the form of scenario analyses. On a regular basis, CPB presents a study with scenarios for welfare, prosperity and the quality of the living environment.[2] This study provides the basic parameters for cost benefit analyses, which are mandatory for all large public investment projects. Other long-term scenario studies have been undertaken on a more ad hoc basis.

CPB aims to improve the efficiency and effectiveness of Dutch policy-making through evaluations. CPB undertakes ex ante cost benefit analyses of major investment projects (e.g. Business District Amsterdam, Afsluitdijk, Joint Strike Fighter) and provides the (binding) rules guiding such analyses. Examples of ex

[1]And a series of satellite models, such as a micro simulation model for purchasing power, labour costs, social security and income taxation (MIMOSI).

[2]In collaboration the Netherlands Environmental Assessment Agency (PBL).

post evaluations of major policy reforms are the reorganization of social assistance and various education policies.

Institutional detail is essential to bridge the gap between academic research and the real world. CPB covers institutional issues in a number of areas, varying from the pension sector and financial institutions to health care. The results are widely used—from the Social and Economic Council to the government and parliament. Section 12.5 discusses some CPB studies in the field of labour market policies, illustrating how policy-related research may help improving growth prospects and competitiveness.

Finally, CPB plays a supporting role in the election process and the formation of a new government. CPB provides the medium-term economic scenario and the sustainability analyses before political parties start to draw up their manifestos.[3] Since 1986, CPB offers any party with representation in the lower chamber of parliament the opportunity to have its program assessed. Parties are not required to partake, but almost all have done so, in line with expectations of the media and other political parties. Parties provide CPB with a financial translation of their manifesto (the measures are reported meticulously, so as to enable consistency checks with the manifesto itself by the media and other parties). This set of measures is then reviewed in various ways. First, an ex-ante budgetary test is applied, a kind of reality check: are the proposed measures feasible? Is the costing realistic? Second, a simulation is run, assuming that the party in question has the absolute majority in parliament, using the models mentioned before and more. This provides insights in the effects during the governing period of the next government on economic indicators (such as growth, inflation, unemployment, income distribution, budget) and on the long-term effects on labour supply and sustainable public finances. The results are published in a book entitled Charted Choices a couple of weeks before the election. This exercise sanitizes the debate, because it ensures a level of specificity in the proposals and prevents blatantly false statements.

The assessment of election manifestos has broadened over time. Originally, three parties took part, but in 2017 eleven party programs were assessed. The scope of analysis increased over time and the level of detail rose. The frequency of elections increased, making the available lead-time for the exercise more condense. To cope with this pressure cooker challenge, a series Promising Policies has been started, which is produced during non-election times.[4] The series aims to provide an overview of policy options over a wide political spectrum in a number of policy areas, each with its pros and cons.

Once elections have taken place and a government is formed, CPB analyses the coalition agreement in a comparable manner.

---

[3]In the run up to Budget Day, political parties (generally opposition parties) have the opportunity to have their counter budget assessed by the CPB.

[4]The series is a co-production with the PBL and SCP (Netherlands Institute for Social Research).

12.5 Case Studies

CPB contributes to the policy debate in different ways. This section illustrates CPB's role in four labour market reforms: the participation law aimed at creating employment for low-productive workers, fiscal labour market policy in general, the fiscal treatment of self-employment, and the state pension age. CPB is sometimes agenda setting, presenting an economic problem with sensible ways to address it. At other times its role is more passive, leaving the initiative to politicians and policymakers, in which case CPB typically gives an indication about the effects of different reforms. CPB may also act as a kind of referee. For instance, when different parties negotiate about a new policy and the goal is to reach a certain budget cut, CPB may assess whether the proposal will actually achieve this goal. Some practical examples will be given in the following subsections, with an overview table in the concluding subsection.

12.5.1 Participation Law

The 'Participation Law' is in effect since 1 January 2015. This law aims to improve the position of low-productive workers, and at the same time cut government expenses on social insurance. Before the enactment of the new law, expenses on the disability scheme for starters on the labour market (Wajong) were rising at a fast pace. A second reason for social insurance reform was that the Dutch public employment scheme (Wsw) was among the most expensive in the world. At the same time, the decentralization of social assistance to municipalities was considered a success. Thus, the main ingredients of the new law were to decentralize a large part of Wajong and Wsw to municipalities and simultaneously try to improve chances for low-productive workers to get a normally paid job. In particular, labour of low-skilled workers was made cheaper for employers by introducing wage subsidies.

Discussion about social insurance for low-productive workers started about a decade before the introduction of the Participation Law. In 2007, CPB drew attention to the rapidly rising number of 'Wajong'-benefit recipients.[5] The number of recipients then equalled about 150,000 (Fig. 12.1). By 2014, it had risen to 250,000, which is 2.5% of the total population between the ages of 20 and 65. In 2010, a commission reported on different options for reforming both the Wajong and the public employment scheme Wsw.[6] The Wsw ('Social workplaces') was not

[5]See Suijker (2007). By the end of 2006 the cabinet had already asked the Social and Economic Council (SER) for an advice on the Wajong. But CPB's publication on the matter gave the problem broader attention.

[6]See Werkgroep brede heroverwegingen (2010). The goal of this commission was to find ways to cut budget expenditures after the start of the economic crisis in 2008. Apart from Wajong and Wsw, many other policy options were studied in different reports.

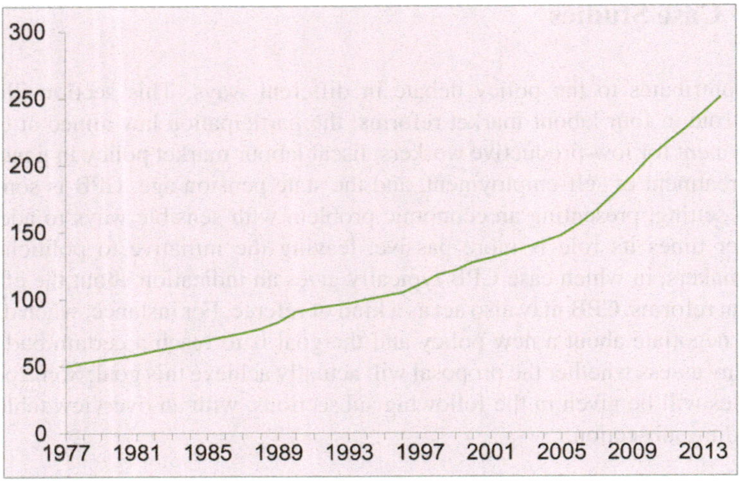

Fig. 12.1 Number of Wajong-benefit recipients (×1000). Source: UWV

considered successful, being one of the most expensive public employment schemes in the western world, while virtually none of the participants could use their public job as a stepping stone towards a normally-paid job.

In 2004, the then-state secretary of Social Affairs Mark Rutte decentralized social assistance to municipalities. Municipalities became responsible for the administration of social assistance and the re-integration into a normally paid job of its recipients. The decentralization involved an important financial incentive for municipalities to contain their social assistance rolls. Municipalities receive a fixed budget to cover the social assistance costs. If they spend less municipalities may keep the money but if they spend more they will have to cover the additional costs from other sources. An early estimation by CPB concludes that the expenditures on social assistance have been lowered by about 6% as a result of this decentralization (Van Es 2010; Van Es and van Vuuren 2010).

In 2011, CPB published a discussion paper on the Wajong in combination with social assistance (SA), which was followed by a Policy Brief (Roelofs and van Vuuren 2011; Van Vuuren et al. 2011). In these publications, CPB argued that the use of Wajong was for an important part a result of the decentralized SA budgets. Municipalities had an incentive to redirect SA-recipients towards the centrally financed Wajong-scheme, which at that time was a close substitute for many SA recipients. According to CPB estimates, nearly half of the Wajong enrolment in 2006 and 2007 was related to the decentralization of SA. The policy advice was therefore to put (the substitutable part of) Wajong and SA in the same hand, namely that of municipalities. This advice boosted the debate on Wajong and Wsw and helped the government to reform the system.

12.5.2 Fiscal Labour Market Policy

In CPB's assessment of fiscal labour market policies, the focus is usually on structural employment effects, budgetary effects, and the effects on purchasing power.[7] Overview publications with univariate policy changes are produced on a regular basis. In this way, policy makers are continuously made aware of the effects of 'standard' fiscal measures, such as lowering the tax rate in a specific tax bracket or increasing the Earned Income Tax Credit (see CPB 2015b). In addition to these regular publications, specific analyses are done at the request of political parties and departments. For instance, plans for a flat tax or a basic income reform have been assessed by CPB (see Jongen et al. 2015).

The effects of fiscal labour market policies are usually assessed using the micro-simulation model 'MICSIM' (see Jongen et al. 2014). This model is evidence-based, i.e. largely based on empirical analyses of Dutch data. For instance, labour supply elasticities for men and women were estimated (see also Chap. 11) and are now part of the MICSIM model. A recent finding is that labour supply elasticities of women are still substantially higher than for men—especially on the extensive margin, i.e. the decision to either participate in the labour market or not (Fig. 12.2). But the difference between men and women is substantially smaller than in earlier years (see Evers et al. 2008). The MICSIM model provides an integrated model, i.e. the impact of policy changes on main indicators (structural employment, income inequality, and productivity) result from the same framework.

Table 12.2 shows some policy simulations with MICSIM.[8] In terms of structural employment, it turns out that lower health care allowances or child allowances generate positive effects. These reductions lead to a lower implicit marginal tax rate for lower-income households, encouraging these relatively elastic households to increase their labour supply. The downside is, however, that poverty among low-income households increases. A higher Earned Income Tax Credit (EITC) for the lowest incomes is also beneficial for structural employment, but in this case the 'price' is paid by the government budget and not so much by lower income households. Lowering income tax rates is—given the budgetary impulse—less successful in terms of its impact on structural employment.

12.5.3 The Fiscal Treatment of Self-Employment

Self-employment in the Netherlands has been growing at a fast pace. Since 2003, the number of self-employed workers has grown by more than 50%, towards about 1 million individuals, whereas the number of employed workers remained more or

[7]Also, effects on productivity are sometimes reported, see e.g. CPB (2015b).

[8]These examples are drawn from CPB (2015b).

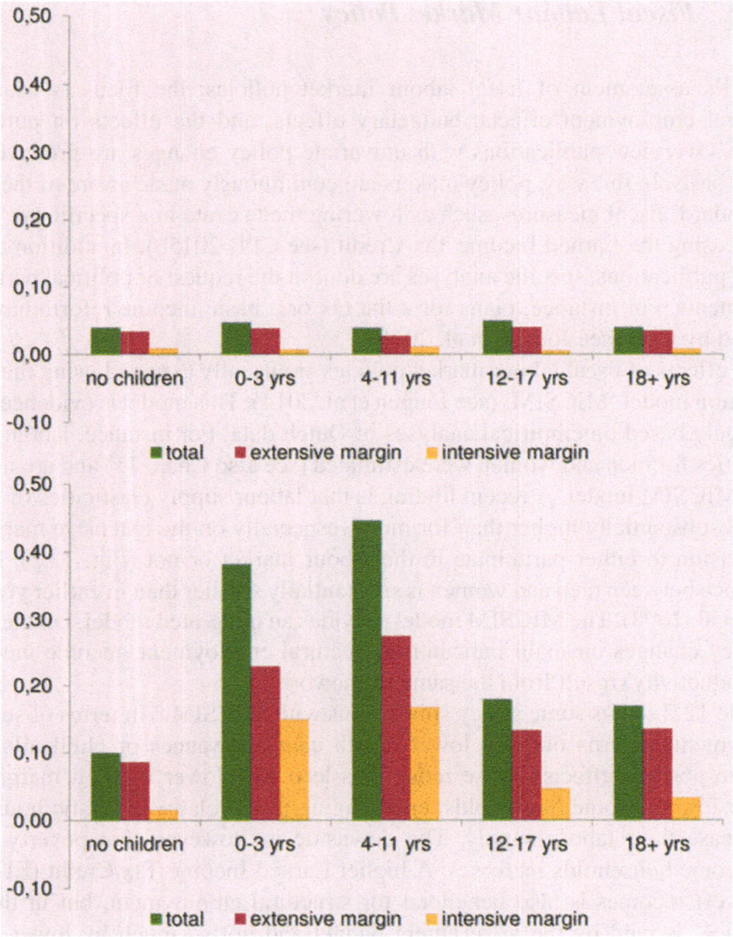

Fig. 12.2 Labour supply elasticities of men (left) and women (right) in couples

less constant (Fig. 12.3). This development has raised concerns about institutional factors encouraging self-employment and discouraging wage employment. The hypothesis that institutional factors have driven the growth in self-employment seems to be confirmed by a decomposition analysis, which finds that less than half of this growth can be explained by socio-demographic and macro-economic determinants (Van Es and van Vuuren 2011). Therefore, more than half of the growth is likely related to institutions and/or social norms.

The precise effect of fiscal incentives on the growth of self-employment has not been quantified yet, but a look at the difference in tax rates between self-employed and employees shows that this might be an obvious explanation (Fig. 12.4). The marginal tax rate is typically 15–25% points lower for self-employed than for

Table 12.2 MICSIM-simulations: some examples

	Budgetary effect (billion euros)	Employment (% change)	Productivity (% change)	Gini-coefficient (% change)	Remarks
Lower health care allowance (zorgtoeslag)	+1.5	+0.4	−0.1	+1.4	Negative disposable income effects for low-income households
Lower child allowance (kindgebonden budget)	+0.5	+0.3	0.0	+0.5	Negative disposable income effects for low-income households with young children
EITC for lowest incomes	−1.5	+0.2	−0.1	−0.3	Positive disposable income effects for low-income households
Lower income taxes	−1.5	[0.0, +0.1][a]	0.0	[−1.0, −0.3][a]	Positive disposable income effects[a]

[a]The exact size of the effect depends on the tax bracket. Disposable income effects are positive for low-income households if the tax rate in the lowest tax bracket is lowered, etc.

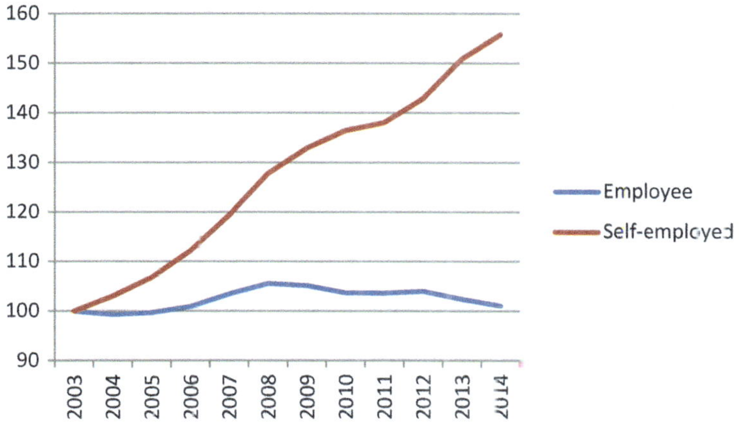

Fig. 12.3 Self-employment grows; wage employment does not (2003 = 100)

employees, and the average tax rate is typically about 20% points lower. The tax incentive is likely one of the explanatory factors for the growth of self-employment.

In 2012, CPB published a critical assessment about the fiscal stimulation of self-employment (Van Vuuren 2012). Some possible arguments in favour of fiscal

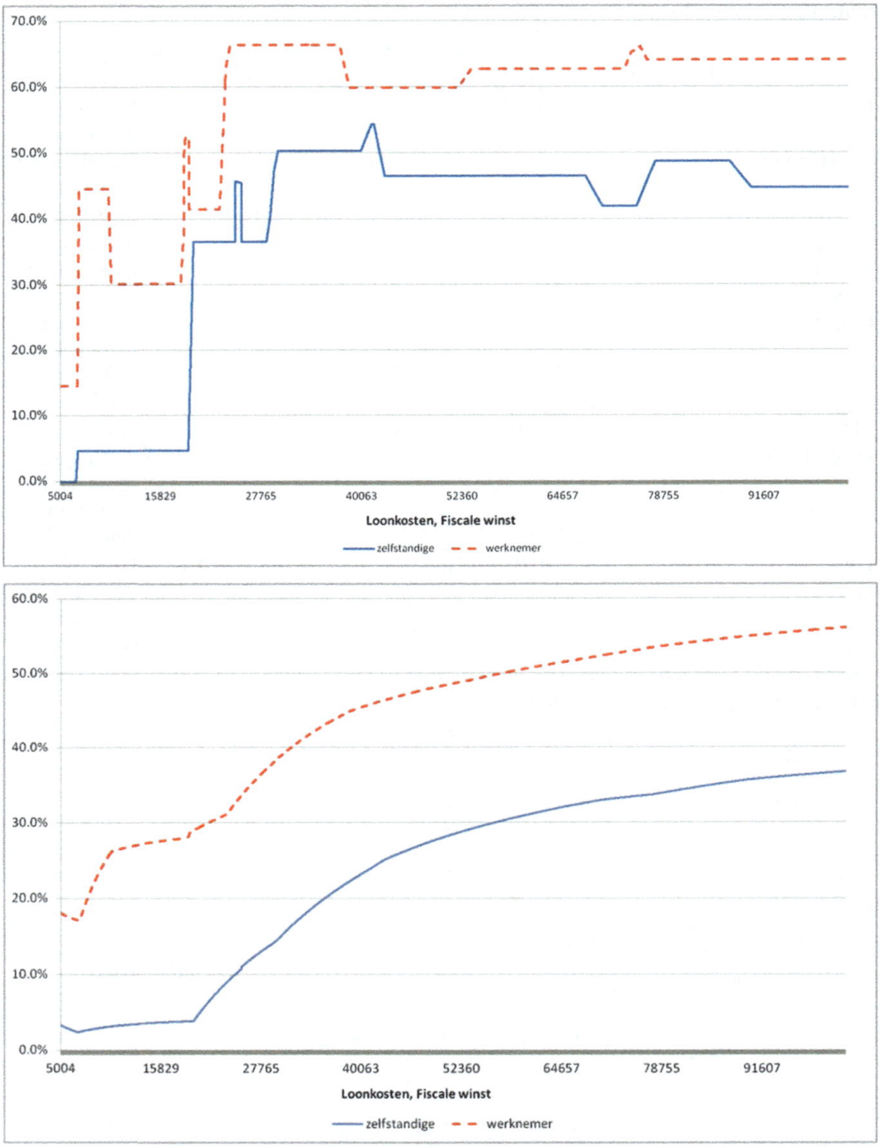

Fig. 12.4 Effective marginal tax rate (left) and average tax rate (right) for employees (dashed line) are higher than for self-employed

stimulation were considered, such as employment growth and the stimulation of innovation, but mostly rejected. Consequently, the government coalition agreement 'Bruggen Slaan' in 2012 included measures to lower the fiscal stimulation of self-employment, in particular the so-called 'Zelfstandigenaftrek'. However, due to a lack of political support, no policy measures in line with CPB's assessment have been taken so far.

In 2014, the cabinet installed a commission to study the phenomenon of self-employment and develop policy options on how it could be dealt with. The report was published in 2015, with policy options in line with CPB's earlier assessments.[9] The government has, however, decided not to take action yet, and leave further policies to the next government (Asscher and Kamp 2015).

12.5.4 *Raising State Pension Age*

In 1997 and 2000, CPB drew attention to the effect of ageing on the sustainability of government finances (CPB 1997; Van Ewijk et al. 2000). As a result of the ageing population, government expenditures would rise more than tax revenues. This would result in a gap in the government budget. Expenditure reduction and/or increasing tax revenues would be necessary in order to avoid this gap. A way to achieve this was to stimulate labour force participation, in particular by reducing social security expenditures. Raising the state pension age would obviously fit into this policy, as it would both reduce state pension expenditures and increase tax revenues as a result of higher labour force participation.

In 2009, the government planned to increase the entitlement age for the state pension 'AOW'. Government expenditures on AOW were close to 5% of GDP at that time, and according to CPB projections would rise to 6% in 2020 and 8% in 2040. However, the trade unions did not accept the government plans and the government gave them room to formulate an alternative policy within 6 months in the context of the Social and Economic Council (SER). Apart from the unions, the SER consists of representatives of employer organizations and experts (including CPB) appointed by the government. The government imposed a restriction on the alternative policy, namely that it should structurally improve the government budget by 0.7% GDP. This figure was computed by CPB as the budgetary effect that would result from increasing retirement age from 65 to 67 (CPB 2009a).

During these 6 months, many alternative policies were studied and CPB had to assess the long-term budgetary impact of each one of them. For instance, increasing the retirement age in combination with a flexible pension age was studied, as were separate arrangements for workers in 'physically demanding jobs' and older unemployed workers. However, the SER negotiations failed, and by the end of 2009 the government announced that the retirement age would be stepwise raised by 2 years. CPB again provided quantitative input for these proposals (CPB 2009b, 2010).

[9]See IBO Zelfstandigen zonder personeel (2015). CPB (2015a) brought out a report for the commission at its request.

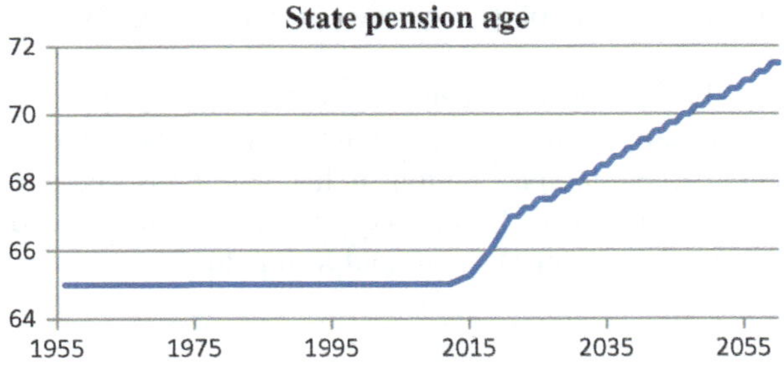

Fig. 12.5 The path for increasing the state pension age, starting in 2015. Notes: the increases after 2021 are based on current estimations of future life expectancy developments. The steps may turn out different in the future in case actual life expectancy developments deviate from these expectations

The new government accelerated these steps in 2012, and on top the retirement age was structurally tied to the 'residual life expectancy'. This has resulted in a stepwise path for the AOW age as shown in Fig. 12.5. The automatic link between the retirement age and residual life expectancy has importantly improved the sustainability gap and made long-term government finances more robust (Smid et al. 2014).

12.5.5 Conclusion

CPB has played five different roles in the four cases discussed in this chapter. Table 12.3 summarizes these roles.

CPB has played—and continues to play in some cases—an agenda-setting role. Examples are the Wajong, the fiscal treatment of self-employment, and the legal retirement age. The issues were known before CPB published about it, but became more important in the policy debate when CPB provided in-depth analyses and figures. Attention for the state pension age was generated indirectly, by publishing reports about the long-term sustainability of government finances. These reports made clear that increasing the state pension age would be one of the most obvious measures to counter the long-term budgetary deficit due to aging. With Wajong and the state pension age, actions in the form of new legislation have been taken already. The fiscal treatment of self-employment has seen little action yet, but will likely be addressed by the next government. With the analysis of fiscal labour market policies, CPB's role is more demand-driven. Outcomes of standard fiscal policies have been published every once in a while.

CPB plays a more structural role in the analysis of fiscal labour market policies. Some fiscal measures are 'standard', like adjusting tariffs in the income tax, and their effects have regularly been published. In this case, CPB's agenda-setting role is smaller, although there can be an indirect effect. For instance, intensifying child-

Table 12.3 CPB's different roles in the four cases discussed

	1. Participation law	2. Fiscal labour market policies	3. Fiscal treatment of self-employment	4. State pension age
Agenda setting	Yes	Sometimes	Yes	Indirectly
Permanent source of information		Yes		
Act as referee during negotiations				Yes
Assist departments in quantifying effects	Yes	Yes	Not yet	Yes
Assist politicians in quantifying effects	Yes	Yes		

care subsidies became less popular after CPB's assessment that they would have a much smaller effect on the labour participation of women than previously thought (Jongen 2010).

CPB has acted as a referee when the pension age reform was discussed among social partners. The government had imposed the restriction that the reform should improve the government budget in the long term by 0.7% of GDP. During the negotiation process between the social partners, CPB assessed whether this goal would be achieved. (And in most proposals, it wasn't.)

Finally, CPB has assisted both ministries and political parties with quantifying the effects of proposals. Before the approval of the Participation Law, several other proposals have been assessed by CPB. In the context of reforming the tax system, CPB has calculated the effects of different variants. It is quite common that CPB either quantifies the effects of policy proposals or checks the quantifications made by the ministries themselves. Requests from politicians, e.g. members of parliament, take place regularly. For instance, in the case of the participation law, CPB was asked to inform the Dutch parliament about the effects (CPB 2012).

12.6 EU Policy Initiatives and the Dutch Experience: Some Pointers

Some initiatives in the aftermath of the Eurozone crisis seem to echo the Dutch experience with CPB. Arguments favouring independent policy-making have been widely accepted in the monetary policy arena, but its application in other areas has traditionally been less straightforward. Choices in labour and product market regulation reflect political preferences, and 'no taxation without representation' is considered a starting point of democracy. The move towards Independent Fiscal Institutes, the decision to establish a European Fiscal Board and the recent Recommendation to establish National Productivity Boards can be seen as experiments in this direction.

The Fiscal Compact and Two Pack require countries to have an Independent Fiscal Institute that (1) endorses or produces the macro-economic and budgetary forecasts in the national budget, and (2) assesses whether the correction mechanism for significant deviations need to be activated or alternatively factors have occurred which may allow for temporary deviations. As such, the Two Pack mixes positive and normative elements; monitoring of indicators needs to be supplemented with judgement of any discrepancies. In the Five Presidents' report the creation of a European Fiscal Board (EBF) was suggested and recently the European Commission decided to establish one (albeit with a somewhat different mandate). According to the Commission's decision, the EBF will (1) evaluate the implementation of the EU fiscal framework (with room for suggestions for the future evolution of the Union fiscal framework), (2) advise on the fiscal stance for the euro area as a whole and (3) cooperate with national fiscal councils. Recently, the Council adopted a recommendation to establish National Productivity Boards (NPBs) with as tasks (1) diagnosis and monitoring of productivity and competitiveness developments and its drivers, (2) independent analysis of policy challenges in this area and, where relevant, assessment of policy options. The NPB should engage with other NPBs with the aim of exchange views etc., as well as the Commission.

With the Dutch experience in mind, the following lessons come to the fore. First: water and oil don't not mix. A division of labour between those producing the facts and analyses and those who decide on policy is a good thing. It enhances a level-headed debate on policy goals and options. This is not to say that producing forecast and analyses is straightforward and value-free per se, but the temptation to doctor the figures is taken out of the equation.

Second: never waste a good crisis. CPB was established in 1945, just after WWII and a deep financial crisis in the 1930s. When things are difficult, the desire for evidence-based policy to solve issues effectively and efficiently may be strongest. The introduction of IFIs during the Great Recession and the recommendation for NPBs reflect this as well.

Third: with a little help from my friends. IFIs or NPBs do not need to start out on their own, from scratch. Existing institutes can become responsible for these tasks. There is nothing wrong with borrowing credibility from existing institutes, like a National Audit Office or a central bank.

Fourth: Rome was not built in a day. In 2015, CPB turned 70. It took time to establish a reputation as a dependable source of economic forecasts and analyses. The portfolio has been expanded gradually. The institute has started modestly and built on its successes.

Fifth: facts speak louder than opinions. The fiscal framework unfortunately requires IFIs to come up with judgments. The mix of positive and normative analysis increases the risk of political appointees. It also makes it easier for politicians to ignore the facts, arguing that they are just personal opinions. An option here is to divide the tasks over two institutes, like the Netherlands has done, or alternatively present the facts and the opinions in separate documents. The IFI regulation cannot be easily adapted. Fortunately, the normative bit was eliminated in the final NPB recommendation.

Sixth: bottom up is best. The strive towards evidence-based policy will work best if institutions are perceived as locally owned, geared towards local issues and problems, and able to provide bespoke solutions. This argues against tasks that might be perceived as policing on behalf of the European Union, such as presently incorporated in the IFI, but fortunately skipped in the NPBs mandate.

Seventh: panta rhei. Competitiveness is a multi-faceted and ever changing concept. This argues against fixating on a simple score board and favours a broad mandate so that the study of the economy and relevant policies can change over time. The case studies in this paper have underscored this point.

Finally: practice what you preach. At the EU level, economic forecasts that feed into SGP procedures are not the product of an independent or autonomous body. Moreover, the EU does not possess an independent body to analyse and evaluate Commission policy or to commission economic research. The Commission's decision on the European Fiscal Board seems a missed opportunity.

References

Asscher L, Kamp H (2015) Aanbieding kabinetsreactie IBO ZZP, letter to the Dutch parliament on behalf of the cabinet, ministries of Social Affairs and Economic Affairs

Bos F, Teulings C (2012) The Dutch CPB: what can be learned from the world's oldest fiscal watchdog? VOX EU

Council (2016) Council Recommendation of 20.9.2016 on the establishment of National Productivity Boards (2016/C 349/01)

CPB (1997) Centraal Economisch Plan 1997

CPB (2009a) Houdbaarheidseffect verhoging AOW-leeftijd. CPB Notitie

CPB (2009b) Houdbaarheidseffect voorstel verhoging AOW-leeftijd. CPB Notitie

CPB (2010) Analyse voorstel verhoging AOW-leeftijd. CPB Notitie

CPB (2012) Notitie voor rondetafelgesprek Tweede Kamer over de Wet Werken naar Vermogen (WWNV). CPB Notitie

CPB (2015a) Position paper t.b.v. 'IBO zelfstandigen zonder personeel'. CPB Notitie

CPB (2015b) Kansrijk Arbeidsmarktbeleid. Serie Kansrijk Beleid CPB/PBL/SCP

Evers M, de Mooij R, van Vuuren D (2008) The wage elasticity of labour supply: a synthesis of empirical estimates. De Economist 156:25–43

Five Presidents' Report (2015) Plans to strengthen Economic and Monetary Union as of 1 July 2015

IBO Zelfstandigen zonder personeel (2015) Eindrapport IBO Zelfstandigen zonder personeel

Ipsos (2015) Bekendheid- en reputatieonderzoek Centraal Planbureau (CPB)

Jongen E (2010) Child care subsidies revisited. CPB Document 200

Jongen E, de Boer H, Dekker P (2014) MICSIM: a behavioural microsimulation model for the analysis of tax-benefit reform in the Netherlands. CPB Background Document

Jongen E, de Boer H, Dekker P (2015) De effectiviteit van fiscaal participatiebeleid. CPB Policy Brief, 2015/02

Passenier J (1994) Van planning naar scanning, Een halve eeuw Planbureau in Nederland, Wolters-Noordhoff

Roelofs G, van Vuuren D (2011) The decentralization of social assistance and the rise of disability insurance enrolment. CPB Discussion Paper 185

Smid B, ter Rele H, Boeters S, Draper N, Nibbelink A, Wouterse B (2014) Minder zorg om vergrijzing. CPB Book 12

Suijker F (2007) Verdubbeling van de instroom in de Wajong: oorzaken en beleidsopties. CPB Document 156

van Es F (2010) Invloed WWB op gebruik bijstand. CPB Document 209

van Es F, van Vuuren D (2010) Minder uitkeringen door decentralisering bijstand. Economisch Statistische Berichten 91:408–410

van Es F, van Vuuren D (2011) A decomposition of the growth in self-employment. Appl Econ Lett 18:1665–1669

van Ewijk C, Kuipers B, ter Rele H (2000). Ageing in the Netherlands. CPB Special Publication 25

van Vuuren D (2012) De fiscale behandeling van zelfstandigen: een kritische blik. CPB Policy Brief 2012/2

van Vuuren D, van Es F, Roelofs G (2011) Van bijstand naar Wajong. CPB Policy Brief 2011/9

Werkgroep brede heroverwegingen (2010) Op afstand van de arbeidsmarkt. Rapport 9 uit de brede heroverwegingen

The manufacturer's authorised representative in the EU is Springer Nature Customer Service Centre GmbH, Europaplatz 3, 69115 Heidelberg, Germany. If you have any concerns regarding our products, please contact ProductSafety@springernature.com

Printed and bound by CPI Group (UK) Ltd, Croydon, CR0 4YY
30/09/2026
02225658-0008